Intellectual Property, Human Rights and Development

Intellectual Property, Human Rights and Development

The Role of NGOs and Social Movements

Duncan Matthews

Reader in Intellectual Property Law, Centre for Commercial Law Studies, Queen Mary, University of London, UK

Edward Elgar
Cheltenham, UK • Northampton, MA, USA

Published by
Edward Elgar Publishing Limited
The Lypiatts
15 Lansdown Road
Cheltenham
Glos GL50 2JA
UK

Edward Elgar Publishing, Inc.
William Pratt House
9 Dewey Court
Northampton
Massachusetts 01060
USA

A catalogue record for this book
is available from the British Library

Library of Congress Control Number: 2010934009

ISBN 978 1 84720 785 2 (cased)

Typeset by Servis Filmsetting Ltd, Stockport, Cheshire
Printed and bound by MPG Books Group, UK

Contents

Acknowledgements

The idea for the book first came when I visited Scotland with my father in June 2004. We were staying at the Steam Packet Inn in a small fishing village called the Isle of Whithorn in Wigtownshire. This is the part of Scotland where my father was born and brought up and there is something about the tranquillity of the place that clears the mind and encourages clarity of thought.

With time to spare, I reflected on a book I had completed two years earlier entitled *Globalising Intellectual Property: the TRIPS Agreement*. It struck me that the book I had written about the role that multinational companies had played in creating a new international regime for intellectual property rights deserved a companion volume, outlining the extent and influence of non-governmental organizations (NGOs) that had subsequently highlighted concerns about the relationship between intellectual property, human rights and development.

Coincidentally, the Economic and Social Research Council (ESRC) had just placed a newspaper advertisement, calling for research proposals to be funded within its Non-Governmental Public Action (NGPA) Programme.* I saw the newspaper advert and decided to apply for funding. Charles Clift, Graham Dutfield, Susan Sell and Sandy Thomas all provided invaluable encouragement and advice as I put the research proposal together. Subsequently, I was fortunate enough to receive a grant from the ESRC (grant RES-155-25-0038) and set about making plans to undertake the research I had envisaged while staying at the Steam Packet Inn. Jude Howell was then appointed by the ESRC as the NGPA Programme Director and proved to be outstanding in her support and encouragement for many years to come.

My academic department, the Centre for Commercial Law Studies at

---

* The research was funded by public money administered by the Economic and Social Research Council (ESRC). The ESRC receives most of its funding through the United Kingdom (UK) Government's Office of Science and Innovation. The ESRC generously funded the research as part of a larger Non-Governmental Public Action (NGPA) programme. The NGPA programme focused on non-governmental action by and on behalf of disadvantaged people, the impact of non-governmental public action in reducing poverty and exclusion, and on social transformation from an international comparative and multi-disciplinary perspective.

Queen Mary, University of London, was kind enough to match the ESRC funding with a period of research leave. The next step was to appoint Viviana Munoz-Tellez as a full-time research assistant. She proved to be an incredibly hard working, loyal, knowledgeable and intelligent assistant and her contribution to the research was simply outstanding.

Once the project got underway, the research itself involved a great deal of travel to places I had little or no experience of visiting. I am particularly indebted to Tenu Avafia for sharing his contacts and advice in South Africa, to André de Mello e Souza and Barbara Rosenberg for providing such valuable introductions in Brazil and to Dwijen Rangnekar for recommending excellent contacts in India. Fabio Pereira and Ana Carolina Cagnoni Ribeiro, two of my best Brazilian LLM students at Queen Mary, also provided excellent research assistance.

I am very grateful to the following organizations for granting permission to reproduce extracts from official documents in this book: the Food and Agriculture Organization of the United Nations for granting permission to reproduce Article 9 of the International Treaty on Plant Genetic Resources for Food and Agriculture (ITPGRFA); the South African Government for granting permission to reproduce from its website (www. gov.za) Section 15C of the Medicines and Related Substances Control Act 101 of 1965 (as amended by the Medicines and Related Substances Control Amendment Act of 1997), Articles 27, 28, 32.1 and 195.1 of the Constitution of the Republic of South Africa 1996 and Section 8 of the South African Competition Act; the United Nations for granting permission to reproduce Articles 25 and 27 of the Universal Declaration of Human Rights, Articles 11, 12 and 15(1) of the UN International Covenant on Economic, Social and Cultural Rights (ICESCR) and Paragraphs 5, 6 and 8 of the Statement of the UN Committee on Economic, Social and Cultural Rights of 2001; and the WTO for granting permission to reproduce Articles 2.1, 6, 7, 27, 29, 30, 31, 63, 65.4 and 70.8 of the TRIPS Agreement and Article 19 of the Doha Ministerial Declaration of 2001.

Malcolm Langely, librarian at the IP Archive at Queen Mary, provided invaluable support while the Wellcome Library on Euston Road in London was a wonderful resource and a perfect place to write up the research. Peter Drahos, Chris May, Susan Sell, Ken Shadlen, Uma Suthersanen and Geoff Tansey provided outstanding support and encouragement during the toughest days of writing. I am also grateful for the enthusiasm of Luke Adams and Tim Williams at Edward Elgar, without whom this book would not have been possible. My mother never ceased to ask me when the book would be finished and was always a great support. Finally, I would like to thank my wife, Louise, who is smart and astute enough to know that when this book appeared in print all the effort would have been worthwhile.

Duncan Matthews
Hackney, London
July 2010

Abbreviations

3D	Trade - Human Rights - Equitable Economy
A2K	Access to Knowledge
ABC	Abacavir
ABIA	*Associação Brasileira Interdisciplinar de AIDS* (Brazilian Interdisciplinary AIDS Association)
ABS	Access and Benefit Sharing
ACTA	Anti-Counterfeiting Trade Agreement
ACTSA	Action for Southern Africa
AFSC	American Friends Service Committee
AIDS	Acquired Immune Deficiency Syndrome
ALP	AIDS Law Project
AMTC	Affordable Medicines and Treatment Campaign
ANVISA	*Agência Nacional de Vigilância Sanitária* (National Health Surveillance Agency)
ARV	Anti-retroviral
AZT	Azidothymidine/Zidovudine
BI	Boehringer Ingelheim
BIPRI	*Bureaux Internationaux Reunis pour la Protection de la Propriete Intellectuelle* (the United International Bureau for the Protection of Intellectual Property)
CALS	Centre for Applied Legal Studies
CAMEX	*Câmara de Comércio Exterior* (Chamber of Foreign Trade)
CBDC	Community Biodiversity Development and Conservation Programme
CBD	Convention on Biological Diversity
CBD-COP	Convention on Biological Diversity – Conference of the Parties
CDIP	Committee on Development and Intellectual Property
CDSCO	Central Drugs Standard Control Organization
CEO	Chief Executive Officer
CEPPWAWU	Chemical, Energy, Paper, Printing, Wood and Allied Workers Union

CESCR	Committee on Economic, Social and Cultural Rights
CGEN	*Conselho de Gestão do Patrimônio Genético* (Council for the Administration of Genetic Resources)
CGIAR	Consultative Group on International Agricultural Research
CGRFA	Commission on Genetic Resources for Food and Agriculture
CIEL	Center for International Environmental Law
CIPIH	Commission on Intellectual Property Rights, Innovation and Public Health
CoFAB	Convention of Farmers and Breeders
COSATU	Congress of South African Trade Unions
CPAA	Cancer Patients Aid Association
CPTech	Consumer Project on Technology
CSIR	Council for Scientific and Industrial Research
CSO	Civil Society Organization
CTE	Committee on Trade and Environment
DFID	Department for International Development
DNA	Deoxyribonucleic acid
DNDi	Drugs for Neglected Diseases Initiative
DNP+	Delhi Network of Positive People
DSB	Dispute Settlement Body
EFF	Electronic Frontier Foundation
EMBRAPA	*Empresa Brasileira de Pesquisa Agropecuária* (Brazilian Agricultural Research Corporation)
EMRs	Exclusive Marketing Rights
ESRC	Economic and Social Research Council
ETC	Action Group on Erosion, Technology and Concentration
EU	European Union
FAO	Food and Agriculture Organization of the United Nations
Farmasa	*Laboratório Americano de Farmacoterapia* (American Pharmacotherapy Laboratory, incorporated by Hypermarcas S.A. in 2008)
FASE	*Federação de Órgãos para Assistência Social e Educacional* (Federation of Organs of Social and Educational Assistance)
FDA	Food and Drug Administration

FDI	Foreign Direct Investment
FENAFAR	*Federação Nacional dos Farmacêuticos* (National Federation of Pharmacists)
FGV	Fundação Getúlio Vargas (Getúlio Vargas Foundation)
FIOCRUZ	*Fundação Oswaldo Cruz* (Oswaldo Cruz Foundation)
FTA	Free Trade Agreement
FTAA	Free Trade Area for the Americas
FURP	*Fundação para o Remédio Popular* (Popular Medicines Foundation)
GAPA	*Grupo de Apoio à Prevenção à AIDS* (AIDS Prevention Support Group)
GARPP	Generic Antiretroviral Procurement Project
GATT	General Agreement on Tariffs and Trade
GCAIPA	Global Coalition against the Indian Patent Amendment
GESTOS	Gestos Pernambuco
GI	Geographical Indications
GIPI	*Grupo Interministerial de Propriedade Intelectual* (Inter-Ministerial Group on Intellectual Property)
GIV	*Grupo de Incentivo à Vida* (Group of Incentive for Life)
GPA	Global Plan of Action on Plant Genetic Resources for Food and Agriculture
GPV	*Grupo pela VIDDA* (Group for Life)
GRAIN	Genetic Resources Action International
Grupo pela VIDDA	*Grupo pela Valorização, Integridade e Dignidade do Doente de AIDS* (Group for Life, which is also an acronym for the Valorization, Integrity and Dignity of the AIDS Patient)
GSK	GlaxoSmithKline
GTA	*Grupo de Trabalhos Amazônicos* (Amazonian Working Group)
GTPI	*Grupo de Trabalho sobre Propriedade Intelectual* (Working Group on Intellectual Property)
HAART	Highly Active Antiretroviral Therapy
HAI	Health Action International
Health GAP	Health Global Access Project
HIV	Human Immunodeficiency Virus
IATP	Institute for Agriculture and Trade Policy
IBASE	*Instituto Brasileiro de Análises Sociais e*

	Econômicas (Brazilian Institute of Social and Economic Analyses)
ICESCR	International Covenant on Economic, Social and Cultural Rights
ICTSD	International Centre for Trade and Sustainable Development
IDCID	Instituto de Direito do Comércio Internacional e Desenvolvimento (International Trade Law and Development Institute)
IDEC	*Instituto Brasileiro de Defesa do Consumidor* (Brazilian Consumer Protection Institute)
IFPMA	International Federation of Pharmaceutical Manufacturers & Associations
IGC	Intergovernmental Committee on Genetic Resources, Traditional Knowledge and Folklore
IIMs	Inter-sessional Intergovernmental Meetings
ILO	International Labour Organization
IMCA	*Instituto Mayor Campesino*
INESC	*Instituto de Estudos Socioeconômicos* (Social Economic Studies Institute)
INP+	Indian Network of Positive Persons
INPI	*Instituto Nacional da Propriedade Industrial* (National Institute of Industrial Property)
Intervozes	*Intervozes – Coletivo Brasil de Comunicação Social* (Brazilian Aggregation for Social Communication)
IP	Intellectual Property
IPC	International NGO/CSO Planning Committee for Food Sovereignty
IP Watch	Intellectual Property Watch
ISA	*Instituto Sócioambiental* (Socio-Environmental Institute)
ISF	International Seed Federation
ITDG	Intermediate Technology Development Group
ITPGRFA	International Treaty on Plant Genetic Resources for Food and Agriculture
IUCN	International Union for Conservation of Nature
JAMA	Journal of the American Medical Association
JPO	Japanese Patent Office
JSA	Jan Swasthya Abhiyan
KEI	Knowledge Ecology International
KRRS	Karnataka State Farmers' Association

LDC	Least-developed country
LRC	Legal Resources Centre
MAB	Man and Biosphere Programme
MMV	Medicines for Malaria Venture
MNP+	Manipur Network of Positive People
MoU	Memorandum of Understanding
MSF	Mèdecins Sans Frontiéres
MTCT	Mother to Child Transmission
NEDLAC	National Economic Development and Labour Council
NEHAWU	National Education, Health and Allied Workers Union
NGF	National Gene Fund
NGO	Non-governmental organization
NGPA	Non-governmental public action
NHRC	National Human Rights Commission
OHIM	Office for the Harmonization of the Internal Market: the Trade Marks and Designs Registration Office of the European Union
Oxfam	Oxford Committee for Famine Relief
PACS	*Instituto de Políticas Alternativas para o Cone Sul* (Institute for Alternative Policies to the South Region)
PAIA	Promotion of Access to Information Act (South Africa)
PATAM	Pan-African Treatment and Access Movement
PBRs	Plant Breeders' Rights
PCDA	Provisional Committee on the Development Agenda
PCIPD	Permanent Committee on Cooperation for Development Related to Intellectual Property
PCT	Patent Cooperation Treaty
PhRMA	Pharmaceutical Research and Manufacturers of America
PMA	Pharmaceutical Manufacturers Association of South Africa
QUNO	Quaker United Nations Office
R&D	Research and Development
RAFI	Rural Advancement Foundation International
RDS	Revised Drug Strategy
REBRIP	*Rede Brasileira pela Integração dos Povos* (Brazilian Network for the Integration of the Peoples)

RFSTE	Research Foundation for Science, Technology and Ecology
RNP+	Brazilian Network of People Living with HIV/AIDS
SASI	South African San Institute
SCP	Standing Committee on the Law of Patents
SIDA	Swedish International Development Cooperation Agency
SPLT	Substantive Patent Law Treaty
SSNC	Swedish Society for Nature Conservation
STD	Sexually Transmitted Disease
SUDS	*Serviços Unificados e Descentralizados de Saúde* (Unified and Decentralized Health Services)
SUS	*Sistema Único de Saúde* (Unique Health System)
TAC	Treatment Action Campaign
TACD	Trans-Atlantic Consumer Dialogue
TAN	TRIPS Action Network
TNNP+	Tamil Nadu Network of Positive People
TRALAC	Trade Law Centre for Southern Africa
TRIPS	Agreement on Trade-Related Aspects of Intellectual Property Rights
TWN	Third World Network
UDF	United Democratic Front
UK	United Kingdom
UN	United Nations
UNAIDS	Joint United Nations Programme on HIV/AIDS
UNCTAD	United Nations Conference on Trade and Development
UNDP	United Nations Development Programme
UNESCO	United Nations Education, Scientific and Cultural Organization
UNGASS	United Nations General Assembly Special Session on HIV/AIDS
UNCHR	United Nations Commission on Human Rights
UN-NGLS	United Nations Non-Governmental Liaison Service
UPD	Union for the Public Domain
UPOV	Union pour la Protection des Obtentions Végétales (International Union for the Protection of New Varieties of Plants)
US	United States of America
USAID	United States Agency for International Development

USP	Universidade de São Paulo (São Paulo University)
USPTO	United States Patent and Trademark Office
USPTO MPEP	Manual of Patent Examining Procedure of US Patent and Trade Mark Office
USTR	United States Trade Representative
VCT	Voluntary Counselling and Testing
WHA	World Health Assembly
WHO	World Health Organization
WIMSA	Working Group of Indigenous Minorities in Southern Africa
WIPO	World Intellectual Property Organization
WTO	World Trade Organization

1. The interface between intellectual property, human rights and development

INTRODUCTION

Only a few years ago, the notion that intellectual property rights promote development remained largely uncontested.[1] International policy-making and norm-setting in the field of intellectual property focused almost entirely on ensuring that national intellectual property regimes provided strong protection for rights holders, with the presumption that benefits would then accrue for developing countries.

When the World Trade Organization (WTO) Agreement on Trade-Related Aspects of Intellectual Property Rights (the TRIPS Agreement) was being negotiated between 1986 and 1994, it was argued that these benefits would include increased foreign direct investment (FDI), higher levels of technology transfer or licensing leading to the transfer of know-how and expertise that would contribute to local economic growth and higher levels of domestic innovation. However, there was relatively little substantive debate about the potential for adverse effects to result from higher standards of intellectual property rights protection and enforcement in the developing world (Matthews 2002, p. 108).

In fact, during the TRIPS negotiations themselves, the paucity of the information about the likely impact of intellectual property rights on developing countries was exacerbated by the fact that many developing countries experienced information deficiencies and lacked the technical expertise to evaluate effectively the costs and benefits of higher standards of intellectual property protection and enforcement for their territories. With only about ten developing countries actually sending intellectual property experts to the TRIPS negotiations, the lack of considered debate on this issue is hardly surprising (Matthews 2002, p. 44). In contrast to developed country delegations that had access to the highest levels of advice from industry and rights holder groups, in the majority of cases developing country delegations to TRIPS negotiations were from national trade ministries or directorates, in some instances augmented by officials from the national patent offices, but even in these cases the patent office officials were career civil servants who were not necessarily aware of the wider societal impact of intellectual property rights on developing countries. In the absence of the necessary expertise, developing countries simply did not have the knowledge necessary to negotiate effectively on the detailed content of the text of the TRIPS Agreement (Matthews 2002, p. 44).

The situation was complicated further by the fact that, while industry and rights holder groups were advising developed country delegations when the TRIPS Agreement was being negotiated (Matthews 2002, p. 44), public interest non-governmental organizations (NGOs) were generally absent from the debate. The General Agreement on Tariffs and Trade (GATT) Secretariat, for instance, reportedly received no complaints about the TRIPS Agreement from consumer groups (Sell 2002, p. 14), prompting Braithwaite and Drahos to conclude that the consumer movement had been largely 'reactive and ineffectual' in this area (Braithwaite and Drahos 2000, p. 202).

However, it was during the subsequent implementation phase of the TRIPS Agreement that the debate on the impact of intellectual property rights on developing countries came sharply into focus. It was during this implementation phase that NGOs began to play a much more significant role. Activists began working with developing country governments that had not fully grasped the scope and depth of the rights obligations enshrined in the TRIPS Agreement when they signed up to these commitments in 1994 (Gervais 2007, p. 20). NGOs also helped to ensure that there is greater awareness of the possible adverse impacts of intellectual property rights and the potential for alternative proposals that take greater account of development orientated objectives. As a result, intellectual property rights are now seen as hugely political issues rather than as purely technical matters (Chon 2010, p. 5).

So the increased engagement of NGOs began to contribute to new levels of debate and understanding about the interface between intellectual property and development. This has served to shift attention away from an unquestioned assumption of the benefits of intellectual property rights, instead giving greater emphasis to public policy objectives that concern sections of society other than industry and rights holder groups.

In particular, NGOs have highlighted the fact that, while intellectual property rights can stimulate innovation, investment in research and development (R&D) and diffusion of knowledge, intellectual property rights can also hinder development if a balance between rewarding innovators and safeguarding the public domain for a wider public good is not achieved.

This relatively recent NGO engagement in the seemingly complex and technical field of international intellectual property rights has been driven by the fact that intellectual property has become part of the wider debate about global justice and equity, trade rules and economic development strategies. Indications of the negative consequences of an unbalanced intellectual property regime, particularly in relation to public health, sustainable agriculture and the protection of biodiversity, have characterized the debate.

Within this wider context, many NGOs came to view the current international intellectual property regime as potentially damaging for developing countries. Particularly through their work on the ground in developing countries, NGOs began to identify evidence that intellectual property rights were having unintended and adverse implications for development. This message began to be heard consistently from NGOs that derived their perspective from different fields of expertise, whether consumer protection, sustainable development, environmental protection, public health, agriculture, technology, or education. Although starting from different backgrounds, many of these NGOs then began to participate more prominently in the initiatives being undertaken in multilateral institutions and in national contexts to monitor and influence intellectual property-related policy-making and norm-setting activities, bringing new evidence-based arguments and new perspectives that had previously been underutilized in international intellectual property debates.

PURPOSE OF THE BOOK

This book describes how coalitions of NGOs have reshaped the debate about the impact of international intellectual property rights on developing countries. It sets out the findings of research to identify detailed patterns of NGO activity relating to intellectual property policy-making and norm-setting in five multilateral institutions: the World Trade Organization (WTO); the World Intellectual Property Organization (WIPO); the World Health Organization (WHO); the Convention on Biological Diversity – Conference of the Parties (CBD-COP); and the Food and Agriculture Organization of the United Nations (FAO).

In addition, only a relatively small amount has been written so far on NGO engagement with intellectual property rights issues and this has tended to focus the role of international NGOs and their relationships with developing country delegations to some or all of these multilateral institutions. As a result, questions remain about the extent that NGOs from developing countries, together with broader social movements, indigenous peoples and local communities in developing countries, have been able to contribute to these debates and engage with intellectual property policy issues at the national, sub-national, regional and local level. To redress the balance, this book sets out evidence of the role played by these types of groups in developing countries, examining the extent and significance of relations between international NGOs and groups in the Global South, and reflecting on the potential of developing country actors to play a greater role in the intellectual property-related policy-making and norm-setting activities of multilateral institutions in the future.

RATIONALE FOR THE BOOK

The research for this book was funded by a generous grant from the United Kingdom (UK) Economic and Social Research Council (ESRC).[2] It began as a response to the UK Commission on Intellectual Property Rights, which was set up in May 2001 as part of the UK Government's commitment in the Second White Paper on International Development, *Eliminating World Poverty: Making Globalisation Work for the Poor* (2000). The Commission was given the task of considering whether and how intellectual property rights could play a role in helping to meet targets identified in the United Nations' *Millennium Development Goals* in relation to the reduction of world poverty and hunger, the improvement of health and education, and ensuring environmental sustainability.

When the Commission on Intellectual Property Rights published its final report *Integrating Intellectual Property Rights and Development Policy* in September 2002, a key finding was the extent and influence of NGO activity in relation to intellectual property rights. Specifically, the Commission reported that NGOs had made, and could continue to make in the future, a positive contribution to the promotion of the concerns of developing countries about the impact of intellectual property rights. This book takes the statement of the Commission on Intellectual Property Rights as its starting point.

COMMISSION ON INTELLECTUAL PROPERTY RIGHTS (2002, p. 165)

We have been struck by the recent extent and influence of NGOs' activity in IP. We believe that NGOs have made and can continue to make in the future, a positive contribution to the promotion of the concerns of developing countries.

The Commission's report went on to suggest that the role of NGOs had been particularly notable in relation to two sets of issues: first, public health and access to medicines; and, second, agriculture, genetic resources and traditional knowledge.

COMMISSION ON INTELLECTUAL PROPERTY RIGHTS (2002, p. 165)

Campaigns to raise awareness by development and health NGOs were important factors in supporting developing countries in the negotiations of the Ministerial Declaration at Doha. In the fields of agriculture, genetic resources and traditional knowledge, certain NGO groups play an important role in highlighting and analysing issues of concern to developing countries.

This book focuses on the two sets of issues identified by the Commission on Intellectual Property Rights, looking first at the role of NGOs in relation to public health and access to medicine (Chapter 2) and, second, in relation to agriculture, genetic resources and traditional knowledge (Chapter 3). The book sets itself the task of seeking to ascertain whether the statements of the Commission on Intellectual Property Rights hold up to closer scrutiny and, if so, how and why NGOs have been able to make this positive contribution to the promotion of the concerns of developing countries in the way that it describes.

COALITION-BUILDING

One theory that has been used to explain how and why NGOs have been able to play a significant role in intellectual property-related policy-making and norm-setting activities is that coalition-building has occurred. The suggestion is that coalition-building makes a strategic difference and occurs because it is an efficient strategy for NGOs seeking to articulate concerns about the impact of international intellectual property regimes on developing countries.

In this context, my previous book *Globalising Intellectual Property Rights: the TRIPS Agreement*, concluded that coalitions of NGOs and local groups in developing countries were highlighting the negative effect of intellectual property rights on vulnerable sectors of society in a way

that was simply not evident when the TRIPS Agreement was being negotiated (Matthews 2002, p. 131). The book also advocated that developing countries, as net importers of intellectual property, should occupy a
negotiating stance as consumers, not producers, of intellectual property
and form global alliances with NGOs, consumers, health care representatives and providers of educational facilities worldwide to devise a coherent and reasoned argument for improved access/lower prices relating to
technology protected by intellectual property rights (Matthews 2002,
p. 135).

Drahos (with Braithwaite 2002, p. 208; hereafter Drahos 2002) has also
argued that coalitions matter, suggesting that coalitions between NGOs
and developing countries may provide a counterweight to the traditionally close relationship between industry groups and developed countries
when international intellectual property rights are being negotiated in
multilateral institutions, with the prospect being for the standstill and
selected rollback on TRIPS provisions. For Drahos (2002, p. 209) a broad
NGO coalition in the Global North, combined with unified developing
country opposition, might be a formidable force against further ratcheting
up of intellectual property standards, leading to standstill and rollback of
intellectual property standards in the interests of reducing distortions and
increasing competition in the world economy.

These coalitions between developing countries and NGOs may not be
as weak as they seem (Drahos 2002, p. 208) because they will be able to
draw on the expertise of 'counter-experts' (Dutfield 2003a, p. 211), who in
many cases will come either from legal practice and/or academia. These
counter-experts will be useful to the coalitions because neither developing countries nor NGOs will be able to afford technical experts on every
important issue (Drahos 2002, p. 209).

For developing countries and NGOs to be effective in relation to international intellectual property rights policy-making and norm-setting
activities, Drahos (2002, p. 209) suggests that members of a coalition will
need to trust one another. Once a relationship of trust has been established, the expectation is that coalitions will nominate a member of the
group to take responsibility and show leadership on a particular issue
relating to the impact of international intellectual property rights on
developing countries (Drahos 2002, p. 209).

Odell and Sell (2006, p. 86) have offered a variant of the coalition-
building scenario, whereby the potential of an intra-state developing country coalition could seek to influence international intellectual
property-related policy-making and norm-setting activities, this model
stressing the significance of intergovernmental coalition-building rather
than the role of NGOs.

More recently, Drahos (2007, p. 35) has refined his earlier statement that coalitions matter by distinguishing between coalitions and networks, the former consisting of governments that coordinate and the latter consisting of nodal actors (whether state or non-state). Stating the distinction in this way, Drahos argues that coalitions in negotiations emphasize enrolling governments while networks look more widely at enrolling 'nodal' actors, such as NGOs, that can help the cause since networks may have much greater information gathering powers than a coalition of governments and may have more technical expertise to deploy in the analysis of problems and positions (Drahos 2008, p. 36).

Using the foregoing coalition-building discourse as a conceptual approach, this book presents evidence on the extent of recent NGO activity in relation to the intellectual property-related policy-making and norm-setting activities of multilateral institutions. It identifies what strategies NGOs have used, the significance of relations between NGOs and developing countries and the specific nature of coalitions that have emerged. The book examines whether coalitions matter in strategic terms, whether they are likely to be of a temporal or a permanent nature, whether they are issue-specific or cut across a range of interests, whether leadership and trust are prerequisites for the success of a coalition and why, and to what extent, NGOs call upon experts to provide technical inputs.

Finally, the book acknowledges that if coalitions do exist, they do not operate in a vacuum, so pre-existing institutions can help to focus coalition activity and even facilitate their mobilization. In this way coalitions may experience institutional pull, that is to say institutions can become focal points for bringing together new coalitions. Given this, the book assesses the appropriateness of current institutional arrangements for NGO participation in the policy-making and norm-setting activities of multilateral institutions relating to intellectual property rights, and considers whether new mechanisms are required to enhance the engagement of NGOs with multilateral institutions. Debates are currently underway in the WTO, the WHO, the CBD-COP, the FAO and the WIPO on how best to engage with the NGO community and these will be reviewed and evaluated in the final chapter of the book.

FRAMING STRATEGIES

As a corollary to coalition-building scenarios, a great deal of attention has been paid to the extent that coalitions will increase their gains if they 'frame' or 'reframe' intellectual property-related issues by using the emotive language of human rights to underpin substantive arguments.

Odell and Sell (2006, p. 87), for instance, suggest that in much the same way as powerful transnational firms and their governments had framed intellectual property protection as a trade issue during TRIPS negotiations, using the emotive language of 'piracy' and 'theft' to describe alleged violations of intellectual property rights in developing countries, critics of TRIPS have attempted subsequently to reframe the debate as a public health issue, arguing that strong intellectual property protection could be detrimental to access to medicines (and hence an infringement of human rights).

Reflecting on the negotiating history of the TRIPS Agreement, Braithwaite and Drahos (2000, pp. 571–6) even argue that had the property-theft-piracy frame of industry and developed country governments been contested at the time of the negotiations, the TRIPS Agreement might not have taken the final form it did and may have been more sympathetic to the development-orientated concerns of the developing world.

Used in this way, framing becomes a tactic utilized by rights-holders and developed country governments to demonstrate that intellectual property rights should be upheld because it is wrong to steal or, alternatively, to demonstrate that intellectual property rights should be applied in a manner that takes account of the need to avoid preventable deaths (Odell and Sell 2006, p. 88). However, these subjective frames of reference imply different policy responses and the more a coalition does to win this subjective contest and establish the dominant frame, the greater that coalition's negotiated gain, the framing strategy increasing the coalition's credibility (Odell and Sell 2006, p. 89).

For Lang (2007, p. 147), the diffusion of human rights language into the work of NGOs must be accompanied by a degree of elaboration if it is to provide meaningful guidance to trade policy-makers (see, for example, Abbott 2005, p. 294). Seen in this way, re-framing the debate on the impact of intellectual property rights for development in terms of human rights performs a number of potentially important functions, but does not provide substantial policy guidance, is not a source of new policy ideas, and does not provide a means of choosing between competing ideas. Instead Lang argues that, to the extent that the human rights movement can mobilize actors and groups presently marginalized and provide effective tools to augment their political influence, framing the issue as one of human rights may help NGOs to achieve real change. In this way, human rights add legitimacy, new constituencies and (to a certain extent) further resources to those groups pressuring for change (Lang 2007, p. 147).

Similarly, Deere (2008, p. 169) has described how framing has been deployed as a strategic tool to influence international discourse on intellectual property issues and the outcomes of international negotiations. For Deere NGOs, international organisations and academics work to reframe intellectual property debates to better facilitate discussion of their public interest priorities (Deere 2008, p. 172). By deploying the language of 'biopiracy', for instance, they draw attention to the misappropriation of traditional and indigenous knowledge related to genetic resources (Deere 2008, p. 174).

Kapczynski (2008, p. 804) also highlights the role of 'frame mobilization' in instigating, promoting, and legitimating collective action, creating areas of overlapping agreement within the coalition and establishing a language of common disagreement between itself and opposing groups. For Kapczynski (2008, p. 883), this explains how actors interpret their interests, build alliances, and persuade others to support their cause.

Reflecting back on the TRIPS negotiations, Drahos (2008, pp. 269–70) has suggested that, in retrospect, drawing on public health and human rights expertise, trade negotiators interested in opposing United States (US) and European Union (EU) pharmaceutical hegemony during the TRIPS negotiations should have built a counter-frame around the principles of timely access to medicines, equity in access, and the cost-effectiveness of medicines. However, Drahos has also cautioned against viewing framing as a master mechanism and has argued that it needs the support of other strategies if it is to bring genuine structural gains in intellectual property regimes (Drahos 2008, p. 272).

Taking into account framing strategies alongside the coalition-building approach in this way, this book examines how human rights have permeated the debate about the impact of intellectual property rights on developing countries. The book then pursues this theme further than earlier analyses have done by highlighting the extent that human rights law (as opposed to human rights rhetoric) has been used as a practical tool by NGOs initiating litigation on intellectual property-related issues in national courts, often with significant results. In addition, Chapter 7 speculates further on the role that international human rights law can inform the debate about intellectual property rights and development in the future.

RESEARCH APPROACH

The research for this book involved over 60 interviews with representatives of international and developing country public interest NGOs, broader social movements, indigenous peoples and local communities in developing countries, together with representatives of developing country governments and the secretariats of intellectual property-related multilateral institutions, augmented by further interviews with representatives from academia, industry associations and rights holder groups. The interviews were conducted face-to-face in Switzerland, South Africa, Brazil, India and the UK.

A list of the individuals interviewed, together with their institutional affiliations, is set out in the Appendix. Interviews were conducted using a structured questionnaire. Interviewees were asked to respond on the understanding that their comments would be reported on a non-attributable basis to elicit as full and frank a response as possible. The research findings presented in this book therefore reflect general trends, common themes and characterizations rather than the views of particular individuals or organizations. As such, the views expressed in this book do not necessarily reflect the opinion of any individuals or organisations that have assisted with the research and any errors remain the author's own.

IMPACT OF THE BOOK

This book is intended to inform the debate about the extent and influence of non-governmental public action and to recommend how NGOs can best play a positive role in shaping future intellectual property policy initiatives. For academic scholars, the book offers a contribution to the on-going discourse on coalition-building scenarios, framing strategies, and the role of NGOs in relation to the impact of intellectual property rights on developing countries. For NGO activists, the book offers a framework within which future strategic decisions can be taken on intellectual property-related issues. This involves identifying recent practice in NGO methods and activities and evaluating what degree of input has been made thus far in terms of intellectual property issues discussed in the context of multilateral institutions.

In particular, identifying current practice is intended to be of value to NGOs in developing countries that, while fast establishing a profile in relation to the impact of intellectual property rights on public health, farmers' rights, biodiversity and the rights of indigenous peoples, are often perceived as lacking the experience of their international NGO counterparts. The book is intended to provide an indication of the significance of inputs from NGOs, identifying instances where these NGOs have worked previously with developing countries and ascertaining whether these relationships have been significant in relation to intellectual property issues during negotiations at the multilateral level.

METHODOLOGICAL ISSUES

NGOs are not a homogeneous group. An important distinction must be made at the outset between public interest NGOs, industry associations, rights holder groups, professional associations made up of intellectual property lawyers and other related professions, and the academic community. All are types of non-governmental organizations.

Furthermore, there is no uniform definition for NGO accreditation to multilateral institutions. As will be discussed later in this book, the definition of accredited NGOs has been subject to much discussion, for instance at meetings of the WIPO Provisional Committee on the Development Agenda (PCDA) and at the Eighth Meeting of the Convention on Biological Diversity – Conference of the Parties (CBD-COP 8). At present, in the WTO and the WIPO context, the definition of NGOs extends to both public action and industry NGOs, while the CBD-COP has different categories of accreditation for NGOs, industry, academics and indigenous peoples.

This book is concerned primarily with public action NGOs. The term is used in this book to denote only this category. The primary reason for this restricted use of the term can be found in the ESRC Non-Governmental Public Action (NGPA) Programme, under which the research for this book was funded. The terms of reference for the NGPA Programme refer explicitly to research on non-governmental public action by, and on behalf, of disadvantaged people and on studying the impact of non-governmental public action in reducing poverty and exclusion. This delineation appeared to the author to be a good tool to set the parameters for this book. In this respect, although a small number of representatives of industry associations, rights holder groups and the academic community were interviewed for the book, these interviews were undertaken primarily in order to ascertain how public action NGOs were perceived by these other actors following intellectual property-related debates and, conversely, how industry associations, rights holder groups and academics interact with public action NGOs in the context of multilateral institutions and the intellectual property rights issues discussed therein.

Complexities also arise in terms of the traditional distinction between international and developing country NGOs. Broadly speaking, international NGOs are considered to be those with an international reach and that are formally established in developed countries, with their head offices and primary sources of funding found there. However, the distinction is not clear-cut. ActionAid, for example, is an international NGO but now has its head office located in Johannesburg, South Africa. ActionAid cannot, however, be considered a developing country NGO, particularly because of the global reach of its activities and its funding, much of which is derived from donors in the United Kingdom. Indeed, there are also a number of large NGOs, such as ActionAid, the Oxford Committee for Famine Relief (Oxfam) and Mèdecins Sans Frontiéres (MSF), that have branches and associate organizations or individuals in numerous countries, including developing countries, and that have long histories of action in the developing world, which again blurs the distinction between the international and developing country NGOs.

There are also NGOs that are historically considered developing country actors that work at an international level, such as Third World Network (TWN), as well as NGOs that work almost exclusively at a national level in developing countries, such as Treatment Action Campaign (TAC) in South Africa or the Instituto de Direito do Comércio Internacional e Desenvolvimento (IDCID – International Trade Law and Development Institute) in Brazil that have received significant funding from donors in developed countries. This is particularly the case when funding comes from large charitable bodies in the United States such as the Ford Foundation or the MacArthur Foundation, so the question arises as to whether these organizations can properly be described as Southern NGOs.

In many respects, therefore, although the relationship between international and developing country NGOs will be investigated further in this book, a key distinction is also the extent that NGOs are either international in focus, with a profile when international property issues are discussed and negotiated in multilateral forums, or national in focus and operating exclusively in the developing country context.

In addition to the role played by formally-structured international and developing country NGOs, wider societal involvement is also crucial in terms of efforts to shape and change intellectual property rules. Non-governmental public action on intellectual property-related issues occurs not only through the activities of formally constituted public interest NGOs, but also through the work of broader social movements such as farmers' groups and indigenous peoples in the Global South. Accordingly, three chapters of this book look specifically at developing countries where not only formally constituted NGOs but also farmers' groups, indigenous peoples and local communities have engaged with intellectual property issues in sophisticated and often important ways.

The developing countries examined in detail in the book are those where the non-governmental public action response to intellectual property rights happened early in the process of NGO engagement with the impact on public health and access to medicines, and on agriculture, genetic resources and traditional knowledge: namely South Africa (Chapter 4), Brazil (Chapter 5) and India (Chapter 6). Evidence of NGO and wider social movement engagement with the relationship between intellectual property rights and development will be presented in these country-specific chapters on the assumption that NGOs and social movements in other developing and least-developed countries may well be experiencing similar challenges in terms of how best to respond to the unintended consequences of intellectual property rights. Lessons may be learnt, therefore, from the previous experiences of South African, Brazilian and Indian NGOs.

There are also other organizations that are not NGOs at all but which have emerged as important actors to support the work of NGOs and developing country delegates when intellectual property issues are discussed and negotiated in multilateral institutions. Intellectual Property Watch (IP-Watch), for instance, undertakes good journalistic work, while the South Centre is an intergovernmental organization that interfaces with both developing countries and NGOs. The contribution that these organizations have made to the debate on the impact of international intellectual property rules on developing countries should not be underestimated, as will become apparent from the significant number of references to these organizations in the endnotes of later chapters of this book.

SELECTION OF CASE STUDIES

As explained above, the selection of case studies for this book was informed by the UK Commission on Intellectual Property Rights report, which suggested that the role of NGOs had been particularly notable in relation, first, to public health and access to medicines and, second, agriculture, genetic resources and traditional knowledge. Given the cross-cutting nature of the two case studies, which relate to intellectual property policy-making and norm-setting in a number of multilateral institutions, this book looks at the impact that NGOs have had in relation to the WTO, the WHO, the CBD-COP, the FAO and the WIPO.

The policy issues involved are at times discussed simultaneously in different multilateral institutions, making it extremely difficult to evaluate the specific impact that NGOs have had, a problem exacerbated by the fact that multilateral institutions are intergovernmental in nature, so the primary focus of intellectual property-related policy-making and norm-setting in these institutions is on member states rather than NGOs. Despite this, we will see that the book has been able to identify particular trends and generically applicable policy messages that are prevalent in relation to NGO engagement with multilateral institutions and the members of those institutions. These trends are set out in subsequent chapters of the book.

Focusing on two case studies also raises questions about how far the findings of the project can be considered as having wider applicability in the context of other intellectual property issues, the Access to Knowledge (A2K) movement being one notable example. It is important to acknowledge, therefore, that further work is needed by others to consider the implications of the findings of this book for other areas of intellectual property-related policy-making and norm-setting activity. This book is intended to be just one contribution to that wider debate.

One further aspect of NGO engagement with intellectual property issues that came to the fore early in the research for this book was the WIPO Development Agenda. Although the Development Agenda process occurred subsequent to the UK Commission on Intellectual Property Rights from which this book takes its starting point, the development-orientated debates that occurred in the WIPO were raised by many of the respondents interviewed for this book and, given the fact that the WIPO Development Agenda relates to and intertwines with the issues addressed in the two primary case studies, NGO engagement with the WIPO Development Agenda is examined further in Chapter 8 of the book. The book will reflect on the role that NGOs have played in the WIPO Development Agenda process, particularly by supporting developing countries in their negotiations to strengthen the development perspective of intellectual property-related issues, and will suggest how the engagement of NGOs can enrich the debate in the future.

Above all, however, the book is an analysis of the role of NGOs and broader social movements in highlighting the interface between intellectual property and development, often by adopting human rights perspectives to bring concerns sharply into focus. It will reflect on what has been done thus far and what the impact is likely to be in the future.

NOTES

1. Intellectual property rights include patents, copyright and related rights, trade marks, design rights, plant breeders' rights and trade secrets. The term intellectual property (IP) refers to the specific legal rights that authors, inventors and other rights holders may hold and exercise. Intellectual property rights are granted by governments and operate in the territory within which they are granted.
2. ESRC Research Grant RES-155-25-0038: *NGOs, Intellectual Property Rights and Multilateral Institutions.*

2. Public health and access to medicines

INTRODUCTION

Nowhere has the role played by NGOs in the debate about intellectual property rights been more profound than in relation to public and health access to medicines. These are critical issues in developing countries where many pharmaceutical products that could save or extend lives have been unavailable, inaccessible, or unaffordable to those who need them most. There is a pressing need for measures to ensure access to existing pharmaceutical products and to provide appropriate incentives for the development of new medicines that effectively address the global disease burden.

This chapter outlines the ways in which NGOs have raised concerns that intellectual property rights (and patents in particular) can have a significant and adverse effect on public health and access to medicines. It explains how NGOs defined their goals and sought to achieve particular policy outcomes by employing a range of strategies, including coalition-building and framing, to get their message across. It also shows how NGOs provided support for developing country delegations to multilateral institutions, particularly the WTO TRIPS Council and the WHO, to assist delegates in their capacity to negotiate and to utilize in-built flexibilities in the TRIPS Agreement in order to ameliorate the impact of higher standards of intellectual property protection and enforcement in the developing country context.

THE TRIPS AGREEMENT

When the WTO TRIPS Agreement was concluded at the end of the Uruguay Round of GATT multilateral trade negotiations in 1994, the unbalanced negotiating process was characterized by the disproportionate influence of the global, patent-reliant, R&D-based pharmaceutical industry. Developing countries were under intense pressure to conclude a package deal of various multilateral agreements and often had little expertise in negotiating complex intellectual property provisions (Matthews 2002, p. 44).

At that time, developing countries did not fully appreciate how the TRIPS Agreement's provisions on patent protection for pharmaceutical products would impact on public health and access to medicines (Matthews 2002, p. 44) and it was only when the obligations of developing countries to implement the TRIPS Agreement came under closer scrutiny that concerns about the impact on public health and access to medicines came to the fore.

Initial concerns focused on the obligations in Article 27.1 of the TRIPS Agreement that require WTO Members to grant patents for pharmaceutical products. Patented medicines cost much more than the equivalent, unpatented, 'generic' versions and the TRIPS Agreement limited the extent that developing countries could produce, import and export cheaper generic versions of medicines.

Prior to the TRIPS Agreement, the main international instrument for patent protection was the Paris Convention for the Protection of Industrial Property of 1883.[1] The Paris Convention did not set out any criteria on the patentability of an invention but, rather, left it to countries contracting to the Paris Convention to determine what constituted a patentable invention within their territory. Some countries regarded the public policy decision not to grant patent protection to pharmaceutical products as necessary to promote access to drugs at competitive prices and more than 50 countries (including Brazil and India) deliberately excluded pharmaceutical products from patent protection on this basis (UNCTAD-ICTSD 2005, p. 353). Other countries, particularly in the developed world, nonetheless criticized this policy as jeopardizing innovation and unfairly depriving inventors of the benefits generated by their contributions (Correa 2000, p. 11).

Article 27.1 of the TRIPS Agreement changed the international patent regime by establishing criteria that were absent from the Paris Convention, obliging WTO Members to make patents available for any inventions, including both product and processes, regardless of the field of technology, provided that they meet the patentability criteria of being new, involving an inventive step and being capable of industrial application.[2]

Because Article 27.1 of the TRIPS Agreement prohibits distinctions relating to the field of technology, the varying policy approaches that had been taken previously on whether or not to grant patent protection for pharmaceutical products have been eliminated. All WTO Members were required, at the end of the appropriate transitional periods, to provide patent protection for pharmaceutical products. With the prospect that higher prices would result from the patenting of pharmaceutical products in developing countries, attention began to focus on the flexibilities contained in the TRIPS Agreement and on how these could be used.

ARTICLE 27.1 OF THE TRIPS AGREEMENT: PATENTABLE SUBJECT MATTER

Subject to the provisions of paragraphs 2 and 3, patents shall be available for any inventions, whether products or processes, in all fields of technology, provided that they are new, involve an inventive step and are capable of industrial application.* Subject to paragraph 4 of Article 65, paragraph 8 of Article 70 and paragraph 3 of this Article, patents shall be available and patent rights enjoyable without discrimination as to the place of invention, the field of technology and whether products are imported or locally produced.

*[Footnote: For the purposes of this Article, the terms 'inventive step' and 'capable of industrial application' may be deemed by a Member to be synonymous with the terms 'non-obvious' and 'useful' respectively.]

TRIPS FLEXIBILITIES

The TRIPS Agreement contained in-built flexibilities that can be used to address public health concerns. The potential significance of these flexibilities was highlighted by the United Nations Commission on Human Rights (UNCHR), which called on member countries to consider taking full advantage of TRIPS flexibilities in order to ensure access to medicines needed to fight diseases such as HIV/AIDS.[3]

TRIPS flexibilities that can be used to address public health concerns include:

- Objectives and principles;
- Transitional periods for implementation of TRIPS;
- Exhaustion of rights;
- Exceptions to patent rights;
- Compulsory licences.

Objectives and Principles

The objectives of the protection and enforcement of intellectual property rights are set out in Article 7 of the TRIPS Agreement. Article 7 emphasizes that intellectual property rights are not an end in themselves but are intended to achieve a balance among social welfare interests, including interests in the transfer of technology, and the interests of producers (see also UNCTAD-ICTSD 2005, p. 132).

ARTICLE 7 OF THE TRIPS AGREEMENT: OBJECTIVES

The protection and enforcement of intellectual property rights should contribute to the promotion of technological innovation and to the transfer and dissemination of technology, to the mutual advantage of producers and users of technological knowledge and in a manner conducive to social and economic welfare, and to a balance of rights and obligations.

The wording of Article 7 is of particular importance because many developing countries are largely users of technologies produced abroad.[4] As the World Bank (2008, p. 146) has acknowledged, for many developing countries there is a tension between the adverse impact of patents on access to medicines, with higher prices for pharmaceutical products, while on the one hand patents also improve the prospects for increased technological diffusion. This will occur if foreign partners are more willing to undertake FDI and enter into licensing agreements because regimes of patent protection and enforcement are in place.

Like Article 7, Article 8 of the TRIPS Agreement is a statement of interpretive principles.

ARTICLE 8 OF THE TRIPS AGREEMENT: PRINCIPLES

1. Members may, in formulating or amending their laws and regulations, adopt measures necessary to protect public health and nutrition, and to promote the public interest in sectors of vital importance to their socio-economic and technological development, provided that such measures are consistent with the provisions of this Agreement.
2. Appropriate measures, provided that they are consistent with the provisions of this Agreement, may be needed to prevent the abuse of intellectual property rights by rights holders or the resort to practices which unreasonably restrain trade or adversely affect the international transfer of technology.

Article 8.1 is of particular significance for policies adopted by developing countries that are designed to ensure access to medicines since it allows WTO Members discretion to adopt internal measures considered necessary to protect public health and nutrition, and to promote public interest in sectors of vital importance to their socio-economic and technological development.

Transitional Periods for Implementation of TRIPS

The transitional periods initially delayed the obligation under the TRIPS Agreement to grant patents for pharmaceutical products in all WTO Member countries. Article 65.4 of the TRIPS Agreement allowed developing country WTO Members that did not grant patents for pharmaceutical products at the time TRIPS entered into force (1 January 1996) a transitional period, ending on 1 January 2005, before they were required to do so.[5]

ARTICLE 65.4 OF THE TRIPS AGREEMENT: TRANSITIONAL ARRANGEMENTS

To the extent that a developing country Member is obliged by this Agreement to extend product patent protection to areas of technology not so protectable in its territory on the general date of application of this Agreement for that Member, as defined in paragraph 2, it may delay the application of the provisions on product patents of Section 5 of Part II to such areas of technology for an additional period of five years.

Article 66.1 of the TRIPS Agreement granted longer transitional periods to least-developed country (LDC) WTO Members. Unlike developing country transitional arrangements, LDCs were not limited to the granting of patent for pharmaceutical products but were of more general application in relation to TRIPS obligations as a whole.[6] LDCs were given until 1 January 2005 to apply virtually all TRIPS provisions although, subsequently, the deadline by which least-developed countries must grant patents for pharmaceutical products was extended until 1 January 2016.[7]

Exhaustion of Rights

Under Article 6 of the TRIPS Agreement, WTO Members are free to determine how they approach exhaustion of rights. This means that developing countries can adopt in their national regimes an international exhaustion principle to permit parallel importation. Parallel importation refers to instances where products produced under protection of a patent (or trade mark or copyright) in one market are subsequently exported to a second market and placed on that market without the authorization of the local owner of the patent. The practical effect is that a patented product becomes available locally from multiple sources, in doing so enhancing market competition between sources of the same products which tends to drive down prices (Matthews and Munoz-Tellez 2007, p. 1429).

ARTICLE 6 OF THE TRIPS AGREEMENT: EXHAUSTION

For the purposes of dispute settlement under this Agreement, subject to the provisions of Articles 3 and 4 nothing in this Agreement shall be used to address the issue of the exhaustion of intellectual property rights.

The key public health implication is that, if parallel importation is permitted by a WTO Member, patented pharmaceutical products could become available in that country from multiple sources. Parallel importing would allow purchasers of pharmaceutical products to bypass official or authorized local suppliers or licensees and obtain products directly from overseas suppliers. This would be particularly useful when the prices of pharmaceutical products are high domestically compared to the prices in other countries (Matthews and Munoz-Tellez 2007, p. 1432).

The United States has opposed parallel importation of pharmaceutical products. At the Council for TRIPS Special Session of 21 June 2001, for instance, the US delegation stated:

> In our view, advocates of parallel importation overlook the fact that permitting such imports discourages patent owners from pricing their products differently in different markets based upon the level of economic development because of the likelihood that, for example, products sold for low prices in a poor country will be bought up by middle men and sent to the wealthiest country markets and sold at higher prices, for the benefit primarily of the middle men. The lack of parallel importation can also have significant health and safety implications. Our law enforcement and regulatory agencies, especially FDA, have commented on how very difficult it is for them to keep counterfeit and unapproved drugs out of our country even with strong parallel import protection provided in the United States. Advocating parallel imports, therefore, could work to the

disadvantage of the very people on behalf of whom the advocates purport to be speaking.

However, if parallel imports are properly regulated in both exporting and importing countries, differential pricing agreements can still function without displacing products marketed locally by patent holders and local licensed dealers. Furthermore, concerns about potential negative effects, such as the quality or authenticity of pharmaceutical products resulting from parallel importation, can be dealt with through adequate monitoring and regulation, rather than through trade restrictions.

Exceptions to Patent Rights

Article 30 of the TRIPS Agreement provides a further public health-related flexibility with possible exceptions to rights conferred by a patent including research and experimentation, prior use, early working, and the export of medicines to non-producing countries.

ARTICLE 30 OF THE TRIPS AGREEMENT: EXCEPTIONS TO RIGHTS CONFERRED

Members may provide limited exceptions to the exclusive rights conferred by a patent, provided that such exceptions do not unreasonably conflict with a normal exploitation of the patent and do not unreasonably prejudice the legitimate interests of the patent owner, taking account of the legitimate interests of third parties.

There have been suggestions that Article 30 could provide a mechanism for producing countries to export medicines to non-producing developing countries, without having to use compulsory licensing measures as mandated under Article 31 of TRIPS that are discussed below.

However, according to the *EC-Canada* WTO Dispute Settlement Panel, any measure justified by Article 30 of TRIPS (including, presumably, the export of medicines to non-producing countries) must meet three cumulative conditions, which must all be satisfied for the exception to fall within the scope of Article 30. First, the exception must be of a limited nature;[8] second, it may not unreasonably conflict with a normal exploitation of the patent; and, third, it may not unreasonably prejudice the legitimate interests of the patent holder, taking into account the legitimate interests of third parties.[9]

In *EC-Canada* the Panel, making general reference to the goals and limitations set out in Articles 7 and 8.1 of the TRIPS Agreement and the negotiating history of the TRIPS Agreement,[10] adopted a strict textual approach to the meaning of Article 30, stressing the limited nature of the exception.[11] In particular, the Panel pointed out that the language of Article 30 mirrors the language of Article 13 of the TRIPS Agreement, which in turn derives its wording from Article 9.2 of the Berne Convention for the Protection of Literary and Artistic Works[12] and provides an exception to copyrights for fair-use.[13] The implication was that, although dealing with a different category of intellectual property rights, Article 30 offers similar exceptions for the granting of compulsory licensing on health grounds. Section 55.2(2) of the Canadian Patent Act, authorizing the manufacture and storage of patented pharmaceuticals by a third party without authorization of the patentee with the intention of placing the patented products on the market upon expiration of the relevant patent (the 'stockpiling' provision), therefore did not constitute a 'limited exception' to patent rights under Article 30.

Following the Panel decision in *Canada – Patent Protection*, there are doubts as to whether a compulsory licence to manufacture and supply generic drugs to another WTO Member could be justified under Article 30. It would be unlikely to meet the requirement of not conflicting with the normal exploitation of the patent, since compulsory licensing could be described as being diametrically opposed to the subject-matter of the patent, which is to reward the inventor for his creative efforts.

Compulsory Licences

A compulsory licence is an authorization granted by a Government to a party other than the holder of a patent on an invention to use that invention without the consent of the patent holder (UNCTAD-ICTSD 2005, p. 461).

Article 31 of the TRIPS Agreement contains flexibilities that allow for the grant of a compulsory licence by a competent national authority in order to permit that national authority or a third party to manufacture a patented product without the authorization of the right holder, in doing so creating a mechanism under which generic medicines can be made available at a lower cost than the equivalent patented products (Matthews 2004, p. 76).

Grounds for the issuance of compulsory licences under Article 31

TRIPS are set out in very broad terms, allowing developing countries wide discretion over their use as a means of ensuring access to medicines (Baker 2004, p. 23). Article 31 sets out the procedures that governments are expected to follow when they grant a compulsory licence. Provided the procedures specified in Article 31 are fulfilled, governments have freedom to determine the grounds upon which compulsory licences can be granted. Under Article 31 of the TRIPS Agreement a compulsory licence can thus be granted by a government to allow a third party to produce a generic version of a patented pharmaceutical product without the authorization of

---

ARTICLE 31 OF THE TRIPS AGREEMENT: OTHER USE WITHOUT AUTHORIZATION OF THE RIGHT HOLDER

Where the law of a Member allows for other use of the subject matter of a patent without the authorization of the right holder, including use by the government or third parties authorized by the government, the following provisions shall be respected:

(a)   authorization of such use shall be considered on its individual merits;

(b)   such use may only be permitted if, prior to such use, the proposed user has made efforts to obtain authorization from the right holder on reasonable commercial terms and conditions and that such efforts have not been successful within a reasonable period of time. This requirement may be waived by a Member in the case of a national emergency or other circumstances of extreme urgency or in cases of public non-commercial use. In situations of national emergency or other circumstances of extreme urgency, the right holder shall, nevertheless, be notified as soon as reasonably practicable. In the case of public non-commercial use, where the government or contractor, without making a patent search, knows or has demonstrable grounds to know that a valid patent is or will be used by or for the government, the right holder shall be informed promptly;

(c)   the scope and duration of such use shall be limited to the purpose for which it was authorized, and in the case of semiconductor technology shall only be for public non-commercial use or to remedy a practice determined after judicial or administrative process to be anti-competitive;

(d)   such use shall be non-exclusive;

(e)   such use shall be non-assignable, except with that part of the enterprise or goodwill which enjoys such use;

(f)   any such use shall be authorized predominantly for the supply of the domestic market of the Member authorizing such use;

(g)   authorization for such use shall be liable, subject to adequate protection of the legitimate interests of the persons so authorized, to be terminated if and when the circumstances which led to it cease to exist and are unlikely to recur. The competent authority shall have the authority to review, upon motivated request, the continued existence of these circumstances;

(h)   the right holder shall be paid adequate remuneration in the circumstances of each case, taking into account the economic value of the authorization;

(i)   the legal validity of any decision relating to the authorization of such use shall be subject to judicial review or other independent review by a distinct higher authority in that Member;

(j)   any decision relating to the remuneration provided in respect of such use shall be subject to judicial review or other independent review by a distinct higher authority in that Member;

(k)   Members are not obliged to apply the conditions set forth in subparagraphs (b) and (f) where such use is permitted to remedy a practice determined after judicial or administrative process to be anti-competitive. The need to correct anti-competitive practices may be taken into account in determining the amount of remuneration in such cases. Competent authorities shall have the authority to refuse termination of authorization if and when the conditions which led to such authorization are likely to recur;

(l)   where such use is authorized to permit the exploitation of a patent ('the second patent') which cannot be exploited without infringing another patent ('the first patent'), the following additional conditions shall apply:

> (i)   the invention claimed in the second patent shall involve an important technical advance of considerable economic significance in relation to the invention claimed in the first patent;
>
> (ii)   the owner of the first patent shall be entitled to a cross-licence on reasonable terms to use the invention claimed in the second patent; and

> (iii)   the use authorized in respect of the first patent shall
>   be non-assignable except with the assignment of the
>   second patent.

the patent holder, in so doing allowing low-price generic pharmaceuticals to be produced locally (Matthews 2004, p. 77).

However, developing countries have faced a number of problems in utilizing available TRIPS flexibilities to protect public health and to promote access to medicines, with particular attention focused on the ability of developing countries to utilize flexibilities contained in Article 31 of the TRIPS Agreement concerning compulsory licensing.

Problems in Utilizing TRIPS Flexibilities

One of the main problems for developing countries attempting to utilize TRIPS flexibilities is that, although the provisions on compulsory licensing permit generic drug companies to manufacture a patented product without the authorization of the right holder, in doing so it creates a mechanism for cheap generic medicines to be made available at a lower cost than the equivalent patented products. Article 31(f) TRIPS also requires that medicines produced under compulsory licence conditions should be predominantly for the supply of the domestic market of the WTO Member authorizing such use. This constitutes a major problem for WTO Members with insufficient or no manufacturing capacities in the pharmaceutical sector, these countries being unable to make effective use of compulsory licensing under the TRIPS Agreement (Matthews 2004, p. 78).

The use of compulsory licensing provisions and other TRIPS flexibilities is also problematic because the procedural requirements for implementing the appropriate national legal provisions are complex and burdensome, particularly for developing and least-developed countries that lack the necessary technical and legal expertise and administrative capacity (Matthews 2005, p. 423).

In addition, bilateral and regional free trade agreements (FTAs) often include measures, commonly referred to as 'TRIPS-plus' provisions, that can undermine the ability of developing countries to utilize TRIPS flexibilities, given that TRIPS-plus FTAs often exceed the obligations under the TRIPS Agreement itself (see also Musungu et al. 2004, p. 30; Matthews 2005, p. 425, Mercurio 2006, p. 224).

As these constraints on the utilization of TRIPS flexibilities and the wider implications of the TRIPS Agreement for public health and access to medicines in developing countries became more widely understood, international NGOs began to support developing countries in their efforts to negotiate solutions to the problems that respond to the concerns on the impact of higher prices for patented medicines and the constraints on utilizing the flexibilities contained in the TRIPS Agreement.

ORIGINS OF NGO ENGAGEMENT

This process of NGO engagement with the scope and effectiveness of in-built TRIPS flexibilities began soon after the TRIPS Agreement came into force in 1995, with public health activists and NGOs voicing concerns that higher standards of patent protection would lead to increased drug prices, with greater reliance on more expensive, patented, drugs and reduced access to the cheaper, generic, drugs that had previously been freely available in countries that did not grant patent protection to pharmaceutical products prior to the entry into force of the TRIPS Agreement.

The significance of access to patented pharmaceutical products was also brought sharply into focus in 1996, when medical experts learned that Acquired Immune Deficiency Syndrome (AIDS) could be suppressed by the use of triple-drug combination therapy, known has Highly Active Antiretroviral Therapy (HAART). In countries where patients had access to HAART regimes, AIDS deaths fell sharply, while in countries without access to HAART regimes, people living with AIDS were dying in large numbers (Love 2006, p. 1).

Public interest NGOs such as Consumer Project on Technology (CPTech) and Health Action International (HAI) were amongst the first to make explicit the link between patents and access to medicines (Sell 2002, p. 15; Matthews 2004, p. 84).

CPTech (which now operates under its new name, Knowledge Ecology International – KEI) was a US-based NGO focusing on information technologies, intellectual property and research and development. It was founded by American consumer activist Ralph Nader and headed by James Love. CPTech had been challenging US policy on the high cost of pharmaceutical products since 1994.[14] One of their strategies has been to reveal the government's (and taxpayers') contribution to the development of drugs and, in October 1995, Nader and Love wrote to then United States Trade Representative (USTR) Mickey Kantor, indicating that there were many different, legitimate views about health care, and that the USTR had been too narrowly focused on protecting the interests of US-based international pharmaceutical companies (Sell 2003, p. 147). Their major concern was drug pricing. It seemed odd that taxpayer-funded drugs had become the very lucrative private property of global pharmaceutical firms. In 1995 and 1996, Nader and Love began to post their information, correspondence, and position papers on their internet newsletter *Pharm-policy* (Sell 2003, p. 147).

Health Action International (HAI) was set up as a global network of health, development, consumer and other public interest groups, working towards a world in which all people, especially the poor and marginalized, are able to exercise their human right to health. It has over 200 members including consumer groups, public interest NGOs, health care providers, academics, media and individuals in more than 70 countries, with a global coordinating office in Amsterdam.

On 4 October 1996, when HAI hosted a meeting in Bielefeld, Germany, on the TRIPS Agreement and public health,[15] this was the first time that a large group of health activists and intellectual property experts had come together to discuss the impact of TRIPS on access to medicines. With participants including Dr. Kumariah Balasubramaniam, from the HAI Regional Office for Asia and the Pacific, Ellen 't Hoen of MSF, and James Love of CPTech, the meeting brought together a number of people who would form the core of the early access to medicines campaign (Sell 2003, p. 148).

The Bielefeld meeting connected MSF and CPTech with a larger network of public health advocates and was the first serious manifestation of the global NGO network that was to become so active on intellectual property rights, public health and access to medicines (Love 2006, p. 1). It identified the targets of the access to medicines campaign that still resonate through the international NGO community more than ten years later, and paved the way for other NGOs to join the burgeoning coalition.

As a result of the Bielefeld meeting, public interest NGOs began to coordinate their statements, articulating arguments to the extent that the TRIPS Agreement could have negative impacts on public health and access to medicines.[16] The coordination of NGO activism in the access to medicines campaign in the mid-1990s also benefited from the global spread of the internet. The increased speed of global communication that the internet facilitated meant that NGOs could coordinate their responses (and even contemplate pro-active initiatives) in a way previously unheard of.

Working initially at the national level in developing countries, in 1997 CPTech and HAI made contact with Latin American generic drug companies, whom they met through Fabiana Jorge, representing the Argentina domestic pharmaceutical companies (Love 2006, p. 3). CPTech and HAI then participated in discussions on the Free Trade Area for the Americas (FTAA) meetings on intellectual property in Belo Horizonte, Brazil, and a subsequent meeting in Costa Rica in 1998. At these meetings, CPTech and HAI called for a trade paradigm that put public health first, by allowing for greater flexibility in intellectual property rules in order to protect consumer interests, and which introduced national obligations to support medical R&D as an alternative to minimum levels of protection of intellectual property rights (Love 2006, p. 3).

Also in 1997, government officials from the Republic of South Africa approached CPTech and another US-based NGO, Essential Action, asking for assistance in dealing with bilateral trade pressures from the US. The context in which these pressures emerged was a Gore/Mbeki Bi-national Commission, set up to manage the relationship between the new post-apartheid South African government and the United States. US Vice-President Al Gore urged the South African government to abandon two legislative proposals designed to facilitate access to medicines. The first proposal was intended to facilitate parallel trade pharmaceutical products, while the second initiative was designed to permit pharmacists to substitute generic products for brand name drugs, when the pharmaceutical products concerned were off patent, a practice which was widely implemented in the United States (Love 2006, p. 3).

Ralph Nader, James Love of CPTech and Robert Weissman of Essential Action wrote to US Vice-President Al Gore, asking that the US reverse its policy toward South Africa on these issues.[17] Gore never responded directly to these letters, a factor which influenced Ralph Nader's decision to run against Gore for president in 2000 (Love 2006, p. 4). After this initial contact with the South African government, from 1997 onwards, CPTech maintained a close working relationship with the staff of Jacob Zuma, then the South African Health Minister and made key technical submissions from CPTech on controversial proposed amendments to the South African Medicines Act.[18]

World Health Organization Resolution on a Revised Drug Strategy

The first international success achieved by NGOs working in support of developing and least-developed countries on issues related to access to medicines came with the adoption of a Revised Drug Strategy (RDS) at the 52nd session of the World Health Assembly (WHA) in May 1999.

This initiative originated on 27 January 1998 when the World Health Organization's Executive Board (EB) proposed a new resolution on an RDS for consideration at the May 1998 World Health Assembly. The resolution, introduced at the EB by Dr. Timothy Stamps, the Zimbabwean Minister of Health, had in fact been drafted with Bas van der Heide, then the Coordinator of the NGO HAI-Europe (Sell 2003, p. 147; Love 2006, p. 4). It urged WHO Member States: 'to ensure that public health rather than commercial interests have primacy in pharmaceutical and health policies and to review their options under the TRIPS Agreement to safeguard access to essential drugs' and requested the Director-General 'to assist Member States to analyse the pharmaceutical and public health implications of agreements overseen by the WTO and to develop appropriate policies and regulatory measures'.

The US and European WHO Member States were strongly opposed to any reference in the RDS to the impact of trade agreements on access to and prices of medicines and the EB approved the resolution only because the United States was not on the rotating Executive Board that year (Sell 2003, p. 147).

By October 1998, WHO Member States had reached a compromise on the RDS, endorsing the public health concerns in what developing country and NGO activists reportedly felt was a 'complete victory' (Sell 2003, p. 149; Love 2006, p. 5). In particular the RDS noted that 'there are trade issues which require a public health perspective' and 'recognizing that the Agreement on Trade-Related Aspects of Intellectual Property Rights (TRIPS) provides scope for the protection of public health [and] taking note of concerns of many Member States about the impact of relevant international agreements, including trade agreements, on local manufacturing capacity and on access to and prices of pharmaceuticals in developing and least developed countries . . . urges Member States: (1) to reaffirm their commitment to developing, implementing and monitoring national drug policies and to taking all necessary concrete measures in order to ensure equitable access to essential drugs; (2) to ensure that public health interests are paramount in pharmaceutical and health policies; (3) to explore and review their options under relevant international agreements, including trade agreements, to safeguard access to essential drugs'.[19]

In December 1998 CPTech, HAI, and MSF met in Paris to formulate a strategy to move forward on the RDS. They took a decision to organize a meeting in Geneva on compulsory licensing and the TRIPS Agreement. A three-day meeting was subsequently held in March 1999, two months before the WHA meeting when the RDS would be considered. The meeting portrayed the expected adoption of the RDS as a referendum in support of compulsory licensing, with two days of private workshops and planning events organized by public health NGOs, and included talks by intellectual property experts such as Carlos Correa. The meeting was seen as the launching of a global campaign to promote compulsory licensing on pharmaceutical products, a lobbyist for the multinational drug company Merck later describing the meeting as a 'boot camp' for the NGO activists (Love 2006, p. 7).

In May 1999, as expected, the WHA formally endorsed the RDS resolution (Sell 2003, p. 149; Love 2006, p. 8), with Member States asked to reaffirm their commitment to develop, implement and monitor national drug policies and take all necessary concrete measures to ensure equitable access to essential drugs; ensure that public health interests are paramount in pharmaceutical and health policies, and explore and review their options under relevant international agreements, including trade agreements, to safeguard access to essential drugs.

The RDS gave a new mandate to the WHO to ensure improved access to essential medicines and to assist countries in their efforts to safeguard public health while implementing trade agreements.[20] It also added momentum to the global campaign on access to medicines.

The MSF Access to Medicines Campaign

The momentum and size of the global campaign on access to medicines had increased further when MSF stepped up its involvement. MSF had been participating in the policy debate on access to medicines since the summer of 1998 when Bernard Pécoul of MSF, who would later build a talented and creative cross-disciplinary team within MSF working on the access to medicines campaign, approached CPTech and HAI, seeking to begin a deeper collaboration on issues concerning access to medicine (Love 2006, p. 5; Sell 2002, p. 19).

In the September of 1999, on the day it was announced that MSF had won the 1999 Nobel Peace Prize, the MSF Campaign for Access to Essential Medicines was launched (Mayne 2002, p. 246).[21] MSF announced it would use the prize money from the Nobel Peace Prize to fund its Campaign for Access to Essential Medicines, and called for a treaty on R&D for neglected diseases (Love 2006, p. 9).[22]

The decision of MSF to join the global access to medicines campaign was crucial. MSF commanded respect, given its strong reputation for providing humanitarian medical assistance and, in addition, MSF was able to bring its considerable financial and organizational resources to the campaign.[23]

The MSF Campaign for Access to Essential Medicines was led by Bernard Pécoul, trade lawyer Ellen 't Hoen, former pharmaceutical industry marketing executive Daniel Berman and James Orbinski, President of MSF (Orbinski 2008, p. 354).

Beyond the fine rhetoric of speeches, the MSF Campaign for Access to

Essential Medicines took pragmatic action to provoke change (Orbinski 2008, p. 356). MSF already had enormous credibility, with over 30 years' experience of working on the ground to provide emergency aid. MSF also pooled its enormous purchasing power to drive down generic drug prices. At the same time, MSF researched the difference in prices between the patented and generic anti-retroviral drugs (ARVs)[24] and other HIV (Human Immunodeficiency Virus) and AIDS drugs in various countries. In June 2000, for instance, MSF published its HIV/AIDS pricing report comparing institutional prices of 10 essential drugs for HIV/AIDS in 8 countries and examined the effect on prices of generic availability and patent status (Pérez-Casas 2000). MSF also encouraged developing governments to utilize TRIPS flexibilities on compulsory licensing and parallel importation to access cheaper medicines for their citizens (Orbinski 2008, p. 358).

Crucial to MSF's strategy in the Campaign for Access to Essential Medicines was the setting up of a working group of intellectual property experts. Most were academics, such as Frederick Abbott and Carlos Correa, together with James Love of CPTech and Sisule Musungu of the South Centre. Unlike the medics who undertook most of MSF's core activities in developing countries, the working group was important because, for MSF, it marked a move into treatment, to allow people to live healthier and longer lives and to continue to contribute to their families and society. MSF expanded its approach to encompass preventing transmission from mother to child, preventing and treating opportunistic infections, and small-scale anti-retroviral programmes. It recognized that treatment is a key component for strengthening preventive efforts.[25]

The Amsterdam Statement

In late 1999, in the run-up to the WTO Seattle Ministerial Meeting, NGOs then made explicit concerns about the impact of the TRIPS Agreement on access to medicines in the WTO context.

The groundwork for this was done on 25–26 November 1999 when CPTech, HAI and MSF jointly organized a conference on *Increasing Access to Essential Drugs in a Globalised Economy Working Towards Solutions* (see also Sell 2003, p. 152). The meeting was attended by over 350 participants from 50 developing and developed countries, from both the private and public sectors, including representatives of UNDP, the WHO, the WTO, representatives of the European Commission and the Dutch and Thai governments, and public interest NGOs and the Pharmaceutical Research and Manufacturers of America (PhRMA). CPTech, HAI and MSF were in search of alternatives to the trade practices that were perceived to impede access to medicines in the developing world (Orbinski 2008, p. 357).

The meeting resulted in the Amsterdam Statement, in which CPTech, HAI and MSF called for the WTO to create a Standing Working Group on Access to Medicines to work within the WTO to consider the impact of trade policies on people in developing and least-developed countries, and provide a public health framework for the interpretation of key features of WTO agreements. The WHO and other relevant international organizations were encouraged to play an active role to support the activities of the WTO working group. It was proposed that the working group on access to medicines would examine a number of important issues in the implementation of the existing TRIPS Agreement, such as compulsory licensing, allowing exceptions to patent rights, and avoiding overly restrictive and anti-competitive interpretations of the TRIPS Agreement. The Statement also called for new and innovative approaches to stimulating research in essential medicines, including increased public and donor funding of health care research, requirements that companies reinvest a percentage of pharmaceutical sales into R&D, and the development of a 'Neglected Disease Act' that could be used to stimulate private investment for communicable disease vaccines and medicines.[26] The Amsterdam Statement is still considered to be the best summary of the issues.[27]

The Statement was underpinned by a consensus at the meeting that the market had failed both to provide equitably priced medicines and to ensure research and development of infectious disease, this lack of affordable medicines and R&D for neglected diseases causing avoidable human suffering. Ultimately, the Amsterdam Statement has been credited with guiding the subsequent work of NGOs and other advocates on the impact of the TRIPS Agreement on public health access to medicines ('t Hoen 2002, p. 35, cited in Sell 2003, p. 152, Drezner 2005, p. 15 and de Mello e Souza 2005, p. 141).

The most dramatic moment at the Amsterdam meeting came with the unexpected and moving declaration by co-founder of South African NGO the Treatment Action Campaign (TAC), Zackie Achmat, who is HIV positive, that he would forego taking anti-retroviral medicines until everyone in South Africa had access (Love 2006, p. 9). With the WTO Ministerial meeting in Seattle only weeks away, the Amsterdam meeting closed with James Orbinski of MSF publicly insisting that the WTO fulfil its responsibility to ensure that 'trade is not a barrier to health' (Orbinski 2008, p. 357).

During the Seattle WTO Ministerial meeting, held from 30 November to 3 December 1999, MSF reiterated calls for a WTO working group to be established on access to medicines and Bernard Pécoul of MSF even went to lobby for health exceptions to trade rules. With the Seattle trade talks heading towards collapse because of disputes on textiles and agriculture, and protestors surrounding the building, his appeal fell on deaf ears (Orbinski 2008, p. 357).

Although NGOs could not participate in the inter-governmental negotiations that took place in Seattle, through the Amsterdam Statement they were able to provide inputs and influence the negotiating process. Although the multilateral trade negotiations in Seattle ultimately failed, NGOs had helped to place access to medicines on the international trade agenda.[28]

The Oxfam 'Cut the Cost' Campaign

WHO World Health Assembly adoption of the RDS also marked the start of Oxfam's involvement with the access to medicines campaign (Mayne 2002, p. 246). Then, in February 2001, Oxfam International launched its 'Cut the Cost' campaign joining forces with other NGOs. Oxfam promoted civic activism and other NGOs involved in the wider access to medicines campaign welcomed Oxfam on board (Sell 2002, p. 155).

Oxfam's decision to launch its own campaign was influenced by its overseas development and emergency work, which had made it acutely aware of the health crisis facing developing countries, in particular in Africa (Mayne 2002, p. 245). By the time Oxfam joined the wider NGO campaign, the issue of patents and medicine was already rising rapidly up the public policy agenda (Mayne 2002, p. 244) and other public interest NGOs were already working on access to medicines issues. Yet while CPTech, HAI and MSF brought technical knowledge, what Oxfam brought to the wider campaign was its unique experience as a well-respected NGO, with significant resources and a well-drilled media machine for mobilizing public and press attention.

Oxfam's 'Cut the Cost' campaign focused on influencing the policy and practice of developed country governments and companies and involved building alliances with other campaign groups, developing country governments, sympathetic individuals in government and opinion-formers, medical and health professionals, and socially responsible scientists. It also raised questions about the broader development-costs of TRIPS (Mayne 2002, p. 248).

Part of Oxfam's campaign involved highlighting the pricing and patenting strategies of research-based pharmaceutical companies. In February 2001 Oxfam released a detailed report on GlaxoSmithKline (GSK) that received widespread press coverage (see also Mayne 2002, p. 251). The report recommended that GSK develop a clearer policy setting out how it would maximize affordable access to medicines in the developing world, and called for changes in the company's pricing and patent policy, increase transparency on which drugs the company intended to make available in which markets, disclose financial information about the amount dedicated to research on tropical diseases, and provide more information about the company's key lobbying positions (Oxfam 2001a, pp. 34–5). Publication of the report had an immediate impact when, shortly afterwards, socially responsible investment teams of five city investment houses hosted a closed meeting with GSK and Oxfam to discuss the report and their concerns that it could damage the company's reputation and consequently its long-term share price (de Mello e Souza 2005, p. 140).

Oxfam subsequently produced a second report in July 2001 on the pricing and patenting practices of a research-based pharmaceutical company, this time Pfizer (Oxfam 2001b), which was seen as one of the companies that had pushed hardest for the TRIPS Agreement in the first place (Mayne 2002, p. 252).

The Quaker United Nations Office

From 2001 onwards, the Quaker United Nations Office (QUNO) in Geneva played a very different, but equally important, role in the access to medicines campaign. QUNO has been active in Geneva since 1923 and has a long-standing role providing quiet, off-the-record space for delegates to meet, talk to each other and interact with experts on particular trade topics and, as will be seen in the next chapter, from 1998 onwards QUNO played an important role supporting developing country delegates in their capacity to negotiate on intellectual property issues relating to agriculture and genetic resources.

When the debate on the TRIPS Agreement, public health and access to medicines gained momentum, government delegations and other Quaker organizations asked QUNO to pick up this issue alongside its highly regarded work on the agriculture and genetic resources (Plaisier and Wijmenga 2004, p. 86). QUNO's objective was to strengthen the capacity and understanding of WTO developing country governments, to obtain greater equity and justice in the TRIPS negotiating process (Plaisier and Wijmenga 2004, p. 85), so it developed a policy of bringing together delegates and academic experts – including Carlos Correa, Frederick Abbott, Jerome Reichman and Keith Maskus – to meet in the off-the-record, supportive environment of Quaker House in Geneva (see also Sell 2003, p. 158).

Throughout the summer of 2001, QUNO provided a venue for these academic legal and economic experts, and intellectual property experts working in-house for other NGOs, to meet with developing country delegates. QUNO also distributed clearly written and concise briefing papers, prepared by the intellectual property experts, and developing country delegations made use of these proposals (Odell and Sell 2006, p. 101).

Third World Network

Third World Network (TWN), an international network of NGOs and individuals based in developing countries, meanwhile added legitimacy to the access to medicines campaign.[29] The Seattle WTO Ministerial Meeting in late 1999 marked the point at which TWN became involved with the access to medicines campaign. TWN was already looking at WTO negotiating processes more generally, and was focused on articulating the concerns of grassroots communities at the international level and on bringing expertise to international policy-making by supporting developing country delegates and improving their capacity to negotiate on a broad range of trade issues. Access to medicines fitted well with these broader activities.

While HAI, CPTech, MSF and Oxfam were able to provide technical knowledge and raise public awareness, TWN was able to bring to the access to medicines campaign good relationships with trade negotiators and a detailed understanding of how multilateral negotiating processes worked.[30] TWN was then able to acquire expertise on intellectual property issues by consulting with outside academic experts, particularly Frederick Abbott and Carlos Correa.

TWN opened an office in Geneva in 2001 and this is seen as having helped tremendously in terms of building relationships of trust with developing country delegates to the WTO. In the context of access to medicines issues, given that TWN organizations and activists are based in developing countries, it added legitimacy to their relations with delegates and their contribution to the wider campaign, addressing concerns that the access to medicines campaign was simply the preserve of a small group of international NGOs based in wealthy, developed country nations who were holding ownership over intellectual property policy issues that were primarily affecting the poor and disadvantaged in developing countries and who were claiming to speak for and on behalf of developing countries. With TWN as an integral part of the access to medicines campaign, it was clear that developing country NGOs were also articulating concerns about the TRIPS Agreement and public health.[31]

International Centre for Trade and Sustainable Development

The International Centre for Trade and Sustainable Development (ICTSD) added a further dimension to the international NGO coalition that took shape in support of the access to medicines campaign. ICTSD undertakes policy-oriented research to inform and promote dialogue. It disseminates its work to try to build consensus linking in with the work of QUNO, for example, which focuses instead on providing the conditions for consensus building, and the ICTSD mission statement makes explicit the goal of empowering stakeholders in trade policy through information, networking, dialogue, targeted research and capacity building.

The idea for ICTSD grew out of a proposal, in October 1995, by 12 environmental NGOs to create an international resource centre to advance the understanding of links between trade and sustainable development.[32] Subsequently, in September 1996, ICTSD was formed by five founding members: the Consumer Unity and Trust Society (India), Fundacion Futuro Latinamericano (Ecuador), the International Institute for Sustainable Development (Canada), the Swiss Coalition of Development Organizations (Switzerland) and the World Conservation Union (Switzerland).

Since 2001, ICTSD has collaborated in a Joint Project on Intellectual Property Rights and Sustainable Development with the United Nations Conference on Trade and Development (UNCTAD) and has also benefited from significant financial support from the UK Department for International Development (DFID), the Swedish International Development Cooperation Agency (SIDA) and the Rockefeller Foundation. The ICTSD-UNCTAD Project has been particularly successful in building capacity amongst developing country representatives to multilateral institutions, improving their understanding of the development implications of intellectual property rights and facilitating informed participation in ongoing multilateral, regional and bilateral negotiations as well as assisting national authorities in the implementation and adoption of progressive policies on intellectual property rights.

THE FIRST TRIPS COUNCIL DISCUSSION ON PATENTS AND ACCESS TO MEDICINES

As the public mood began to shift, emboldened by NGO campaigns and public condemnation over the South African court case (see Chapter 4), the US complaint to the WTO against Brazil (see Chapter 5) and the US complaint to the WTO against India (see Chapter 6), developing countries proposed in April 2001 that the WTO hold a special session on patents and access to medicines, to discuss the impact of patents on medicines and to clarify the existing flexibilities in TRIPS (Mayne 2002, p. 253). The first TRIPS Council discussion on intellectual property and access to medicines took place on 20 June 2001, developing countries present-ing strong statements expressing their concerns about the public-health impact of TRIPS,[33] backed up by a joint NGO statement issued the previ-ous day by MSF, Oxfam and TWN, calling on the TRIPS Council to take action on the public health crisis.[34] The NGO statement carried particular weight for the international community given that it bore the signatures not only of MSF and Oxfam, with their longstanding reputations for undertaking humanitarian work, but also because it was endorsed by a network of developing country NGOs and grassroots activists under the umbrella of TWN, articulating the concerns of civil society in developing countries.

COALITION-BUILDING: THE DOHA DECLARATION ON THE TRIPS AGREEMENT AND PUBLIC HEALTH

The real success of international NGOs working as a functioning coali-tion on access to medicines issues came with the adoption of the WTO Doha Declaration on the TRIPS Agreement and Public Health in November 2001 (see also Drahos 2007, p. 11).[35] In the run-up to the Doha Declaration, HAI, CPTech, MSF, Oxfam and TWN formed the core group of international NGOs that worked well together on a day-to-day basis. They also worked closely with ICTSD, which in June 2001 hosted an informal roundtable on TRIPS, biological resources and public health for the African negotiators based in Geneva (Odell and Sell, 2006, p. 99), QUNO provided a forum for legal scholars including Carlos Correa, Frederick Abbott, Jerome Reichman and Peter Drahos to meet with and advise developing country delegates (de Mello e Souza 2005, p. 256), while the intergovernmental organization the South Centre, which has an explicit mandate to support developing country delegates in multi-lateral negotiations, produced valuable briefing papers and events for delegates in Geneva. According to Bernard Pécoul, the arrogance of the research-based pharmaceutical industry at that time also helped to give the campaign a moral validity.[36]

The resulting Declaration reaffirmed the flexibilities and safeguards contained in the TRIPS Agreement to protect public health and clarified how these could be used. The Declaration, which affirmed that 'the TRIPS Agreement should be interpreted and implemented in a manner support-ive of WTO Members' right to protect public health and, in particular, to promote access to medicines', and reaffirmed 'the right of WTO Members to use, to the full, the provisions in the TRIPS Agreement, which provide flexibility for this purpose' (Matthews 2004, p. 82; Sell 2003, p. 160), was a major victory for the coalition of developing countries and NGOs (Drahos 2007, p. 12).

The Doha Declaration did not, however, provide a solution for countries without manufacturing capacity in the pharmaceutical sector that wanted to make use of the compulsory licensing provisions of the TRIPS Agreement. Instead, Paragraph 6 of the Doha Declaration on the TRIPS Agreement and Public Health called on the TRIPS Council to find an expeditious solution to the problem which could ultimately be incorporated as a permanent amendment to the TRIPS Agreement (Matthews 2004, p. 82).

In the run-up to the Doha Declaration international NGOs coordinated their activities effectively, working well together and forging links with developing countries on the access to medicines issue in the run up to the 2001 Doha Declaration on the TRIPS Agreement and Public Health. This indicates that coalition-building is a realistic strategy for NGOs and developing countries to counter-balance the influence of industry and developed countries during negotiations taking place on intellectual property issues in multilateral institutions (see also Drahos 2002, p. 208).

NGOs combined strong public campaigning messages and actions based on powerful human illustrations that help generate public outrage and high media coverage, using TV, radio and print to get their message across. Global and cross-sectoral alliances of NGOs began to develop, built on strong national campaigns (Mayne 2002, p. 257). The growth of the internet also allowed NGOs to network and exchange information and ideas almost instantaneously in a way that had hitherto not been possible.

And while international NGOs helped ease the pressure on developing country negotiators from developed countries and global pharmaceutical interests, a crucial role was also played by NGOs working collaboratively in developing countries and by broader social movements working together at a grassroots level. As Chapters 4, 5 and 6 of this book will demonstrate, national coalitions of NGOs played an important role by highlighting the plight of people living with HIV/AIDS in South Africa, Brazil and India (and elsewhere in countries such as Thailand) and by pressuring their national governments to implement TRIPS-compliant legislation in such a way as to make full use of the flexibilities available to protect public health and ensure access to medicines.[37]

To this extent, the Doha Declaration on the TRIPS Agreement and Public Health was important as a political success and raised awareness of the fact that developing countries can act legitimately to protect public health. However, it is impossible to attribute particular outcomes solely to the inputs of international NGOs. In reality, the Doha Declaration on the TRIPS Agreement and Public Health came about as the result of a number of factors including 9/11, the Anthrax attacks in the United States, public disquiet about the HIV/AIDS pandemic, all interfacing with the complex world of multilateral negotiations.

The Limits of Coalition-building: The 30 August 2003 WTO Decision

In any event, the coalition on access to medicines in the run-up to the Doha Ministerial Conference in November 2001 proved to be short-lived. After the Doha Declaration on the TRIPS Agreement and Public Health had been agreed, some international NGOs that have been involved previously with public health and access to medicines issues began to prioritize other trade issues and focused less systematically on TRIPS issues, with the result that the momentum generated by NGO engagement with access to medicines issues was not maintained. Oxfam, for instance, focused less on access to medicines issues after Doha, incorporating its 'Cut the Cost' campaign into the broader 'Make Trade Fair' agenda and to some extent moved on to prioritizing other concerns.

Nonetheless, unlike the original TRIPS negotiations, developing countries began to be much more involved in the negotiating process prompted by Paragraph 6 of the Doha Declaration, supported by NGOs (Matthews 2006, p. 84). Paragraph 6 of the Declaration on TRIPS and Public Health recognized that WTO Members with insufficient or no manufacturing capacities in the pharmaceutical sector could face difficulties in making effective use of compulsory licensing under the TRIPS Agreement, and instructed the Council for TRIPS to find 'an expeditious solution' to the problem. During the subsequent two-year period of negotiations to find this expeditious solution, NGOs provided developing country negotiators with crucial technical expertise, support and advice, as well as engaging in raising public awareness through campaigns and undertaking advocacy work to pressurize developed country governments to adopt a more progressive stance on patents, public health and access to medicines.

Newer NGOs such as Trade - Human Rights - Equitable Economy (3D) also began to emerge,[38] and a core group of international NGOs that remained focused on the technical detail of what an amendment to the TRIPS Agreement should look like continued to provide support and inputs to developing countries. They articulated concerns that the Paragraph 6 solution was likely to be more restrictive, more burdensome and more problematic than alterative approaches that were available (see also Jawara and Kwa 2003, p. 254).

Yet, it proved impossible to keep the broader NGO coalition intact after the Doha Declaration on the TRIPS Agreement and Public Health given the specialist nature of the negotiations by then underway in the TRIPS Council.[39]

Over the next two years, international NGOs and academic experts continued to support developing countries, particularly the African Group, in the articulation of proposals on implementing Paragraph 6 of the Doha Declaration.[40] However, the increasingly technical nature of the proposals being formulated and differences in the viewpoints of NGOs and developing countries on what could be achieved altered the dynamics of the access to medicines campaign.

In 2002, a joint letter to the WTO TRIPS Council from NGOs CPTech, Essential Action, MSF, Oxfam International, Health Gap Coalition and the Third World Network advocated the use of Article 30 instead of Article 31 of the TRIPS Agreement to ensure access to medicines in developing countries. The letter argued that Article 30 was the most direct, administratively simple and least contentious approach in that an activity falling within an Article 30 exception is not an infringement of the patent and did not need permission from the patent holder. Nor did an Article 30 exception require notice to be given to the patent holder or compensation to the patent holder arranged, as under the Article 31 compulsory licensing provisions.[41] Similarly, submissions to the TRIPS Council by both the EC[42] and Brazil, on behalf of a group of developing countries,[43] endorsed a broad interpretation of Article 30 that would permit its use to meet the public health needs of developing countries that do not have the capacity to manufacture medicines locally.

But while international NGOs recommended an approach based on Article 30 of the TRIPS Agreement, the African Group of developing countries opted instead to support a solution based on a temporary waiver of Article 31(f) of the TRIPS Agreement.

As explained earlier in this chapter, there were doubts about whether Article 30 TRIPS could in fact be used as a limited exception for the exportation of medicines to non-producing developing countries. This is because there has been strong opposition from the United States and the research-based pharmaceutical industry. The *EC-Canada* WTO Dispute Settlement Panel had also created uncertainties by stressing the limited nature of exceptions to exclusive rights conferred by a patent under Article 30.[44] Due to uncertainties surrounding Article 30, the African Group instead opted for an Article 31 solution, based on compulsory licensing provisions, for the exportation of medicines to non-producing developing or LDC WTO Members.

On 30 August 2003, WTO Members accordingly agreed on a temporary waiver to the TRIPS Agreement to allow the export and import of medicines under compulsory licences.[45] The Paragraph 6 process thus culminated in the 30 August Decision, which set out a mechanism to allow countries with insufficient or no pharmaceutical manufacturing capacity to import generic versions of essential medicines from a foreign generic producer (Matthews 2004, p. 95). However, the 30 August Decision involved only a temporary waiver and a permanent solution was not reached until 6 December 2005 when the agreement was made permanent (Matthews 2006, p. 91). The 6 December 2005 agreement was criticized by NGOs, in particular MSF, which expressed alarm that the decision to amend the TRIPS Agreement was based on a mechanism that had failed to prove that it could improve access to medicines (Matthews 2006, p. 115).

The waiver was to terminate when a final amendment to the TRIPS Agreement, incorporating the new solution, was achieved. NGOs were dissatisfied with the outcome. Procedures for utilizing the temporary waiver were considered burdensome and unworkable in practice (Matthews 2006, p. 115),[46] and there were also differences of opinion amongst developing countries about the best way to proceed on both the timing and substantive content that the permanent amendment should take.

On 6 December 2005, after a long negotiating process, WTO Members reached agreement to make permanent the 30 August 2003 temporary waiver of Article 31(f) of the TRIPS Agreement.[47] However, international NGOs had been advising developing countries to reject the deal.[48] They criticized the agreement on grounds that agreement had been hastily reached under duress, with developing country negotiators bullied and pressured by the big pharmaceutical companies and the EU.[49] MSF, for instance, pointed out that delaying the amendment would have been a preferable strategy as it would have left open the door for testing the temporary waiver and, if necessary, improving the mechanism before a permanent solution was enshrined in an amendment to the TRIPS Agreement.[50]

So, the limits of what can be achieved by coalitions are demonstrated clearly by the fact that, ultimately, international NGOs were dissatisfied with the 6 December 2005 agreement to amend the TRIPS Agreement. International NGOs and developing countries had good relationships in the context of public health and access to medicines but these relationships were not without their tensions. Ultimately, developing countries went their own way, agreeing to the amendment of Article 31 of the TRIPS Agreement against the advice of international NGOs which did not see this as a workable solution and advocated instead greater use of Article 30 of TRIPS. On this evidence, coalitions can be seen as temporary and issue-specific.

Subsequently, although good relations remain in place between NGOs and developing countries, with the possible exception of the WIPO Development Agenda (which will be discussed in Chapter 7 of this book) nothing as tightly knit and focused as the access to medicine coalition has existed since. In part this is because NGOs and developing countries may well have agendas that do not necessarily coincide.

International NGOs initially worked well together and with developing countries until the issues became increasingly technical and the rhetoric derived from framing the issue and language of human rights was no longer sufficient to hold the broader coalition together.

Ultimately, therefore, an important lesson to be learnt from NGO engagement with intellectual property rights and access to medicines is that any NGO agenda, even if well coordinated, using the media and with public support, does not necessarily go forward unless there are long-term commitments on the part of NGOs to remain involved with the issue and that there are developing countries that are willing to take the issue up, act as champions and articulate policy positions during intergovernmental negotiations.

Two further issues should be borne in mind. First, the impact of international NGOs in relation to public health and access to medicines may be difficult to replicate in the context of other issues, such as agriculture, genetic resources and traditional knowledge. The extent to which the access to medicines campaign represents a 'repeat play game' that could be replicated for agriculture, genetic resources and traditional knowledge is discussed in detail in Chapter 3.

Second, developing country NGOs provided, and continue to provide, important inputs into the work of international NGOs in the access to medicines campaign. The significance of this contribution to the campaign by developing country NGOs in South Africa, Brazil, India and also, although beyond the scope of this book, in Thailand, should not be underestimated and will be discussed at greater length in Chapters 4, 5 and 6.

THE IMPACT OF NGO ENGAGEMENT WITH PUBLIC HEALTH AND ACCESS TO MEDICINES

Coalition-building was an important factor in the success of the access to medicines campaign (Odell and Sell 2006, p. 86). Developing countries working in coalition with international NGOs were able to raise public awareness of their problems and reframe the existing debate on intellectual property protection in a manner more favourable to their interests in the light of the HIV/AIDS pandemic (Odell and Sell 2006, p. 106). The coalition was neither dogmatic nor ideological, but a practical and highly flexible, decentralized network that allowed international NGOs to bring different skills and different strengths to the coalition while retaining the flexibility to join and leave the campaign when appropriate.

International NGOs were able to generate cognitive change by challenging previously accepted ideas on the relationship between pharmaceutical patents and public health (de Mello e Souza 2005, p. 24). Part of the NGO strategy to achieve this involved presenting evidence-based arguments of how ARV treatment could improve public health in developing countries and how the high cost of patented drugs had become a barrier to the provision of such treatment in the developing world. MSF and Oxfam, well-respected for their humanitarian work in crisis zones, were able to demonstrate how and why access to medicines was being hindered by intellectual property rights.

In January 1999, for instance, an article in the Journal of the American Medical Association (JAMA) entitled *Access to Essential Medicines in Poor Countries: A Lost Battle?* written by Bernard Pécoul and other MSF activists, drew on the experiences of MSF doctors in the field, made the case that patents can be a barrier to access to medicines, and crystallized concerns about the impact of the patent provisions of the TRIPS Agreement on access to medicines (Pécoul et al. 1999, p. 361).

In addition to using evidence-based arguments to put pressure on politicians in developed countries, NGOs played an important role in Geneva providing developing country negotiators with technical expertise on complex intellectual property issues that improved their capacity to negotiate (see also Drezner 2005, p. 15). They achieved this despite the fact that, in contrast to other multilateral institutions working on intellectual property-related issues, there are no arrangements for NGO accreditation as observers to the WTO TRIPS Council. The relatively closed nature of the WTO policy-making process has led to concerns that public confidence in the fairness and authoritativeness of WTO decisions is undermined (see, for instance, Dunoff 1998, p. 433). However, in practice, NGOs played a subtle yet important role on access to medicines by providing technical inputs to eliminate some of the information asymmetries that had previously been seen during the original TRIPS negotiating process (Matthews 2002, p. 44; de Mello e Souza 2005, p. 25).

Alongside the presentation of evidence-based arguments and the provision of technical expertise, NGOs played a crucial role in framing access to medicines as a human rights issue, making explicit the link between the protection of pharmaceutical patents with key principled ideas and rhetoric of human rights discourse (see also de Mello e Souza 2005, p. 25).

The public, the media and politicians in both the developed and the developing countries were able to engage in a relatively straightforward way with the notion that the provision of ARVs to treat people living with

HIV/AIDS in the developing world was being hindered by the TRIPS Agreement. This contributed to the ability of NGOs to make the link between the HIV/AIDS crisis and intellectual property rights, an issue that had resonance in both the developed and the developing world (see also de Mello e Souza 2005, p. 28).

That resonance was articulated through the framing of the issue so that intellectual property began to be seen not only or primarily as a trade issue, but also as one relevant to health and human rights (de Mello e Souza 2005, p. 10), rooted in the dignity of the other in relation to the self (Orbinski 2008, p. 373).

By framing the TRIPS Agreement in terms of health and human rights, activists were able to resort to accountability politics, gaining moral leverage to pressure governments and international organizations previously committed to upholding such rights (de Mello e Souza 2005, p. 159; Schultz and Walker 2006, p. 8).

In many respects, the reframing strategies of NGOs in the access to medicines campaign mimicked and acted as a counterweight to the framing that corporate activists had employed to such great effect when linking intellectual property to trade in the run-up to the TRIPS Agreement (Matthews 2002, p. 21; de Mello e Souza 2005, p. 25). In the run-up to the TRIPS Agreement corporate interests had portrayed intellectual property not only as a critical public policy tool for encouraging disclosure of inventions and encouraging investment in R&D, but also as an inalienable private property right. Corporate interests had also equated copying with 'piracy' and 'theft', even when this practice was entirely legal (Sell and May 2001, p. 485; Watal 2001, p. 2, quoted in de Mello e Souza 2005, p. 8).

By replicating the strategies adopted by corporate interests in negotiation of the TRIPS Agreement, the reframing strategies of NGOs weakened the public sense of legitimacy about the achievements of the TRIPS Agreement, especially in the HIV/AIDS context (Sell 2003, p. 182). While, in the 1980s, TRIPS advocates had framed it as an alternative to tolerating piracy of private property, the access to medicines campaign compared TRIPS to a different reference point – saving the lives of poor people suffering from HIV/AIDS (Odell and Sell 2006, p. 93).

The framing strategy also facilitated contestation, with the traditional model of patents as a driver for new drug development challenged by reframing the debate using the language of 'human rights' and 'the right to health' as a threat to public health and access to medicines and, through the mobilization of moral outrage, helped to generate a widespread sense that the TRIPS Agreement in its current form could not be justified (Lang 2007, p. 147).

Yet, the shortcomings of a framing strategy in the access to medicines campaign are readily apparent. The delivery pipeline of the media drives an innate tendency on the part of NGOs to reduce complex ideas to their binary function.[51] Slogans of 'human rights' and 'the right to life' become the default mode if complex ideas are pushed through narrow media bandwidth in which immediacy and accessibility of newsworthy stories outweigh the realities of complex legal concepts that demand long-term attention and long-term solutions on the part of NGOs, their funders and the international policy community.

In the case of the access to medicines campaign, the reductionism of complex legal ideas reframed as human rights rhetoric secured short-term gains by temporarily attracting media attention and mobilizing public opinion. But once the immediacy of human rights rhetoric hit home, the access to medicines reframing strategy reached the limits of its effectiveness, with the inevitable consequence that the broader access to medicines coalition dissipated. Larger NGOs that were working more generally on trade agendas moved on to other issues not least because they were under pressure to identify new campaigning issues to guard against media fatigue, and media and public attention shifted to new ground. This left a smaller core of NGOs including CPTech, MSF, TWN and QUNO (along with the intergovernmental organization the South Centre) to carry on the more difficult, specialist, technical work of supporting developing countries in their capacity to negotiate a permanent solution to the access to medicines problem via an amendment to the text of the TRIPS Agreement.

The fact that HIV/AIDS does not discriminate between the rich and poor in developed or developing countries also helps to mobilize people. In the case of other diseases that disproportionately affect the poorest sectors of society in developing countries, it is much more difficult to mobilize people around a particular policy approach.

Using human rights as a frame of reference, NGOs were able to raise awareness that access to medicines was a trade issue, mobilizing the press in developed countries and bringing the issue to the attention of the public as a means of pressurizing politicians in these countries (Drezner 2005, p. 15). In part this task was made easier by developed country guilt about the post-colonial legacy, particularly in sub-Saharan Africa.

In the US, HIV/AIDS activist groups such as ACT-UP Philadelphia and the Health Global Access Project (Health GAP) played an important role raising public awareness and putting pressure on the US government to change its trade and public health policy. This process began in the summer of 1999, when US HIV/AIDS activists undertook a highly publicized campaign to disrupt the Gore presidential campaign (Love 2006, p. 9). ACT-UP Philadelphia and Health GAP also put pressure on President Clinton to issue an Executive Order in May 2000 which stated that the USA would no longer threaten sanctions against sub-Saharan African countries if they were using TRIPS safeguards to gain access to HIV/AIDS medicines (Mayne 2002, p. 245).

The public awareness generated by NGOs influenced a number of events. These included the pharmaceutical company climb-down over South Africa and the US decision to drop its trade dispute with Brazil. This widened the political space for poor countries to implement pro-public health patent policies; the pharmaceutical giants further cut the price of some vital patented medicines in some poorer countries; and a global health fund for drug purchases was set up in 2002 (Mayne 2002, p. 245).[52]

By raising awareness about the link between access to medicines and intellectual property rights issues to an extent hitherto not acknowledged, NGOs created pressure on governments in both the developed and developing world that counterbalanced the role played by industry, opening up the debate on intellectual property rights and development policy. This helped facilitate a more open discussion on the impact of the TRIPS Agreement on public health and access to medicines.

While some of the work of international NGOs involved mobilizing the media and public opinion in developed countries, other inputs were of a more technical nature in terms of providing support and expertise to developing country delegates in Geneva and developing country officials in the national governments back in their capitals.

CPTech, ICTSD and TWN were particularly active in providing technical inputs on the complex issues of intellectual property law involved and helped developing country delegates to understand and negotiate on these issues. James Love of CPTech, for instance, played a pivotal role with his knowledge of drug development costs, intellectual property law and trade agreements, and technology transfer issues (Mayne 2002, p. 246).

When a small group of developing country negotiators were brought together by QUNO at Quaker House in Geneva to undertake the drafting work for the Doha Declaration on the TRIPS Agreement and Public Health, academic experts brought in by the NGOs to advise developing countries added to this technical support, as did Sisule Musungu of the South Centre.

The work of TWN was also very important. In part this was because TWN works directly with developing country delegates and is very close to them but, importantly, TWN is also active at a national level within developing countries, not just in Geneva, and provides direct support through technical assistance to officials within developing country governments in national capitals.

TWN had particularly strong links with the African Group in the WTO.

This was important because the African Group is not normally part of this type of coalition and, ultimately, collaboration between India, Brazil and the African Group was the critical factor in the adoption of the Doha Declaration on the TRIPS Agreement and Public Health in 2001.

NEGLECTED DISEASES

In addition to the contribution that international NGOs made to the process leading to the Doha Declaration on the TRIPS Agreement and Public Health, these groups have also played a role in deliberation on the development of alternatives to an incentive system for research and development (R&D) based on patent protection for pharmaceutical products in order to improve R&D into neglected diseases. These are preventable diseases that disproportionately affect the poor and where the incentive for investment in R&D is lacking.

One strategy utilized by NGOs in this respect is to present arguments to counter the previously unchallenged claim that patent protection was necessary to fund R&D for new drugs (Drezner 2005, p. 15). Activists working on neglected diseases have not historically been as well organized as NGOs campaigning on access to medicines for people living with HIV/AIDS, not least because neglected diseases predominantly affect the poor living in developing countries. Nevertheless, the challenges of neglected diseases have more recently gained greater attention with examples of alternative models of new drug development in the form of proposals for a global R&D Treaty and the activities of two more recently formed NGOs: the Drugs for Neglected Diseases Initiative (DNDi), which began its existence as an MSF initiative (Orbinski 2008, p. 369),[53] and the Medicines for Malaria Venture (MMV).[54]

CONCLUSION

Multiple factors accounted for the relative success of short and medium term outcomes to the access to medicines campaign. Strong internal coordination helped sustain the NGO coalition with developing countries but, after the Doha Declaration on the TRIPS Agreement and Public Health, differing priorities and pressure felt by developing countries to conclude the agreement reached in the 6 December 2005 Decision to amend the TRIPS Agreement, led to fragmentation of the coalition.

Nevertheless, at least in the run-up to the Doha Declaration on the TRIPS Agreement and Public Health, the relatively successful interaction between NGOs and developing countries can be attributed to a variety of factors. In particular, NGOs brought a combination of skills to the access to medicines campaign that included expertise in media and public mobilization (Oxfam), technical and legal expertise (CPTech, ICTSD), a permanent presence in Geneva where the negotiations were taking place (CPTech, ICTSD, MSF, Oxfam, TWN, QUNO), a reputation for working on the ground during crises in developing countries (Oxfam, MSF) and a history for bringing delegates together in a supportive environment where they could meet and discuss issues of concern with academic experts (QUNO, ICTSD), and close relations with developing country delegates.

NOTES

1. The full text version of the Paris Convention for the Protection of Industrial Property is available at: http://www.wipo.int/treaties/en/ip/paris/trtdocs_wo020.html.
2. Article 27.1 of the TRIPS Agreement also includes a footnote to make clear that the terms 'inventive step' and 'capable of industrial application' are to be deemed synonymous with the terms 'non-obvious' and 'useful'. This is to take into account, in particular, the provisions of United States patent law which refer to the latter terms when determining the patentability of inventions.
3. See *ICTSD Bridges Weekly Trade News Digest*, 9(13) 20 April 2005, available at: http://www.ictsd.com/weekly/05-04-20/inbrief.htm#1.
4. Although TRIPS covers trade marks and copyrights as well as patents, Article 7 of TRIPS only refers to 'technological' knowledge which is generally understood to refer only to patented technology.
5. Under Article 70.8 of the TRIPS Agreement, the transitional arrangements under Article 65.4 were conditional on developing country WTO Members allowing the filing of patent applications (the so-called 'mailbox' provisions) and, under Article 70.9 of the TRIPS Agreement, on conferring an exclusive marketing right to the mailbox patent applicant for a maximum period of 5 years.
6. There are currently 49 least-developed countries (LDCs) on the UN list, 32 of which to date have become WTO members. A list of WTO members that are LDCs is available at: http://www.wto.org/english/thewto_e/whatis_e/tif_e/org7_e.htm.
7. Decision on the Extension of the Transitional Period Under Article 66.1 of the TRIPS Agreement for Least-Developed Country Members for Certain Obgliations with Respect to Pharmaceutcal Products, adopted by the TRIPS Council on 27 June 2002, IP/C/25, 1 July 2002.
8. For criticism of the Panel's failure to consider properly the meaning of the word 'limited' see Robert Howse, 'The Canadian Generic Medicines Panel: A Dangerous Precedent in Dangerous Times', 3(4) *Journal of World Intellectual Property* 493 (2000), at 498.
9. WTO Panel Report, *Canada – Patent Protection of Pharmaceutical Products (Canada – Patent Protection)*, WT/DS114/R, adopted 17 March 2000, para. 7.20. See also Dara Williams, 'Developing TRIPS Jurisprudence: The First Six Years and Beyond' 4(2) *Journal of World Intellectual Property* 177 (2001), at 186.
10. WTO Panel Report, *Canada – Patent Protection*, para. 7.29.
11. WTO Panel Report, *Canada – Patent Protection*, para. 7.31.
12. The full text of the Berne Convention for the Protection of Literary and Artistic Works is available at: http://www.wipo.int/treaties/en/ip/berne/trtdocs_wo001.html.
13. WTO Panel Report, *Canada – Patent Protection*, para. 7.71.

14. On 5 October 2006 James Love, Sakiko Fukuda-Parr and Manon Reece received a MacArthur Award for Creative and Effective Institutions on behalf of CPTech in recognition of the NGO's work over the previous 16 years and to support the creation of a new corporate entity, Knowledge Ecology International (KEI). CPTech's earlier work has been continued and expanded by KEI. See: http://www.keionline.org/.

15. *Health Action International Report Examines Impact of Trade Agreements on Consumers' Access to Drugs.* Available at: http://www.haiweb.org/pubs/gatt-pub.html.

16. *New HAI report on* WTO, posted on e-drug listserver by Lisa Hayes, HAI-Europe, 28 April 1997. Available at: http://www.essentialdrugs.org/edrug/archive/199704/msg00076.php.

17. 19 July 1997, letter from Ralph Nader, James Love and Robert Weissman to Vice President Gore regarding US policy toward South African pharmaceutical policies. Available at: http://www.cptech.org/pharm/goreonsa.html.

18. On 5 February 1999, the US Department of State issued a report to Congress, titled 'US Government Efforts to Negotiate the Repeal, Termination or Withdrawal of Article 15(c) of the South African Medicines and Related Substances Act of 1965.' The report, which CPTech obtained and distributed to AIDS activists, outlined in considerable detail the pressures the Clinton Administration had put on South Africa to modify its Medicine Act. See US Department of State report: *US Government efforts to negotiate the repeal, termination or withdrawal of Article 15(c) of the South African Medicines and Related Substances Act of 1965.* Available at: http://www.cptech.org/ip/health/sa/stdept-feb51999.html.

19. World Health Organization, Executive Board, 103rd Session, 25 November 1998, EB103/4, Revised Drug Strategy, Report by the Chairman of the ad hoc working group. Available at: http://www.cptech.org/ip/health/who/rds-report.html.

20. *Health Assembly Adopts New Health Strategy*, South-North Development Monitor (SUNS), 24 May 1999. Available at: http://www.twnside.org.sg/title/assembly-cn.htm. See also *Joint NGO Release on WHA Revised Drug Strategy*, HAI, MSF, CPTech, 24 May 1999. Available at: http://lists.essential.org/pharm-policy/msg00095.html.

21. See MSF Access to Essential Medicines Campaign website: http://www.accessmed-msf.org.

22. Although there is no generally accepted definition of neglected diseases they are generally considered those diseases for which there is an insufficient market or political status to drive adequate private sector and public sector R&D. Examples of neglected diseases may fall into this category, like human African trypanosomiasis, buruli ulcer, Chagas disease, dengue fever, filariasis, guinea worm, leishmaniasis, leprosy, malaria, onchocerciasis, rabies, schistosomiasis and tuberculosis. Source: Medicus Mundi Schweiz. Available at: http://www.medicusmundi.ch/mms/services/bulletin/bulletin200401/kap01/08burri.html.

23. James Love, CPTech, interview with the author, 22 November 2005.

24. ARVs retard the development of AIDS and during treatment provide a better quality of life to carriers of the virus. They also act to reduce viral load and help to strengthen the immune system.

25. Ellen 't Hoen, MSF, interview with the author, 22 November 2005.

26. *Amsterdam Statement to WTO Member States on Access to Medicine.* Available at: http://www.cptech.org/ip/health/amsterdamstatement.html (visited 6 April 2009).

27. Ellen 't Hoen, MSF, interview with the author, 22 November 2005.

28. *Major US Policy Change Opens Door for Poor Countries To Produce Affordable Drugs*, MSF, HAI, CPTech Press Release, 2 December 1999. Available at: http://www.cptech.org/ip/health/seattle.html.

29. With offices in Malaysia, Africa and Uruguay, TWN has a long record of engagement with intellectual property issues relating to agriculture, genetic resources and traditional knowledge, which will be discussed in Chapter 3.

30. Cecilia Oh, formerly TWN, interview with the author, 8 February 2006.

31. Another developing country NGO that has been active on multilateral trade issues

more generally is Focus on the Global South. However, Focus on the Global South has not been active specifically on issues relating to intellectual property, public health and access to medicines.

32.   *ICTSD History*. Available at: http://www.ictsd.org/about/index.htm.
33.   *Developing Country Group's Paper for the special session on intellectual property and access to medicines*, submission by the Africa Group, Barbados, Bolivia, Brazil, Dominican Republic, Ecuador, Honduras, India, Indonesia, Jamaica, Pakistan, Paraguay, Philippines, Peru, Sri Lanka, Thailand and Venezuela to the TRIPS Council, 20 June 2001, IP/C/W/296, advance copy received 19 June 2001. Available at: http:// www.wto.org/english/tratop_e/TRIPs_e/paper_develop_w296_e.htm.
34.   Chakravarthi Raghavan, *NGOs Demand 'Pro-Public Health' Interpretation of TRIPS*, TWN, 19 June 2001. Available at: http://twnside.org.sg/title/pro.htm.
35.   *Declaration on the TRIPS Agreement and Public Health*, Doha WTO Ministerial Declaration 2001, WT/MIN(01)/DEC/2, 20 November 2001. Available at: http://www. wto.org/english/thewto_e/minist_e/min01_e/mindecl_trips_e.htm.
36.   Bernard Pécoul, DNDi, interview with the author, 10 May 2006.
37.   Thailand is another example of a developing country with a highly organized and active NGO community working on access to medicines and intellectual property issues although not the primary focus of this book.
38.   3D has sought to make explicit the link between human rights, intellectual property and access to medicines by bringing clarity to the often misleading use of human rights language and to provide developing country delegates with the knowledge to use human rights principles as a tool for facilitating a development approach to intellectual property. As such, 3D is essentially a capacity-building NGO, ensuring that human rights groups, intellectual property NGOs and developing country delegates work together to achieve a more equitable outcome to trade policy.
39.   Cecilia Oh, formerly TWN, interview with the author, 8 February 2006.
40.   See, for instance, *Conference Report – Implementation of the Doha Declaration on the TRIPS Agreement and Public Health: Technical Assistance – How to Get it Right*, Geneva, 28 March 2002. MSF, CPTech, Oxfam, HAI. Available at: http://www. haiweb.org/campaign/access/ReportPostDoha.pdf.
41.   The full text of the joint letter from CPTech, Essential Action, MSF, Oxfam International, Health GAP Coalition, and the Third World Network to the WTO TRIPS Council of 28 January 2002 is available at: http://www.cptech.org/ip/health/ art30exports.html.
42.   *Concept Paper Relating to Paragraph 6 of the Ministerial Declaration on the TRIPS Agreement and Public Health*, Communication from the European Communities and their Member States to the TRIPS Council, IP/C/W/339, para. 24.
43.   *Paragraph 6 of the Ministerial Declaration on the TRIPS Agreement and Public Health*, Communication received from the Permanent Mission of Bolivia, Brazil, Cuba, China, the Dominican Republic, Ecuador, India, Indonesia, Pakistan, Peru, Sri Lanka, Thailand and Venezuela, IP/C/W/355.
44.   WTO Panel Report, *Canada – Patent Protection*.
45.   *Implementation of Paragraph 6 of the Doha Declaration on the TRIPS Agreement and Public Health*, Decision of the WTO General Council of 30 August 2003, WT/L/54, 1 September 2003. Available at: http://www.wto.org/english/tratop_e/trips_e/implem_ para6_e.htm.
46.   See, for example, *Joint NGO Statement on TRIPS and Public Health WTO Deal on Medicines: A 'Gift' Bound In Red Tape*, 10 September 2003. Available at: http://www. cptech.org/ip/wto/p6/ngos09102003.html. See also, *WTO Members Should Reject Bad Deal on Medicines*, Wim De Ceukelaire, People's Health Movement. Available at: http://www.phmovement.org/cms/en/node/70.
47.   *Amendment to the TRIPS Agreement*, General Council of the WTO Decision of 6 December 2005, WT/L/641, 8 December 2005. Available at: http://www.wto.org/ english/tratop_e/trips_e/wtl641_e.htm.

48. *WTO members should reject bad deal on medicines*, Joint statement by NGOs on TRIPS and Public Health, 3 December 2005. Available at: http://www.cptech.org/ip/wto/p6/ngos12032005.html.

49. *Statement of CPTech on TRIPS Amendment*, James Love, CPTech, 6 December 2005. Available at: http://www.cptech.org/ip/wto/p6/cptech12062005.html.

50. *Amendment to WTO TRIPS Agreement Makes Access to Affordable Medicines Even More Bleak*, MSF Press Release, 6 December 2005. Available at: http://doctorswithout-borders.org/press/release.cfm?id=1640&cat=press-release.

51. With apologies to Brian Eno, who inspired this paragraph with an intervention during *Conversation Piece: Brian Eno and Jon Hassell*, part of the Ether Festival 2009 at the South Bank Centre, London, 9 April 2009.

52. The Global Fund to Fight AIDS, Tuberculosis and Malaria. See: http://www.theglobalfund.org/en/about/.

53. DNDi is a not-for-profit organization with a small staff in Geneva and two liaison offices abroad: one in Brazil and one in Kenya. It seeks to target neglected diseases and to develop new treatments for these diseases.

54. MMV is a not-for-profit public-private partnership that works on research and development of anti-malarial drugs. MMV's main objective is to bring together public and private sector partners, namely from academic institutions and industry, and to provide managerial and logistical support for the discovery, development and delivery of affordable new medicines to treat and prevent malaria. *MMV: Curing Malaria Together*. Available at: http://www.mmv.org/rubrique.php3?id_rubrique=15.

3. Agriculture, genetic resources and traditional knowledge

INTRODUCTION

The development of intellectual property-related assets derived from agriculture, genetic resources and traditional knowledge has made an enormous contribution to the improvement of human livelihoods and to the technological advancements of society. In agriculture, for example, the exploitation of genetic resources has led to improved crop varieties and, ultimately, contributed to greater food security. The appropriation of genetic resources has created the prospect of valuable tradable assets given the potential for their commercial use that could benefit the economies of many developing countries rich in biodiversity. Potentially, it could also benefit the indigenous peoples and local communities who developed uses for genetic resources in the first place as part of their traditional knowledge.

However, the nature and terms under which genetic resources can be accessed have changed dramatically in recent years. The free flow and trade of genetic resources has been replaced by a wide range of national and international legal instruments that seek to regulate access, control and use of genetic biodiversity and to protect traditional knowledge. Of particular concern has been the trend to extend intellectual property rights (patents and plant breeders' rights) to plant genetic resources.

The link between intellectual property rights and biodiversity arises from the fact that in many instances bio-prospectors engaged in the systematic search for, and development of, new sources of chemical compounds, genes, micro-organisms and other valuable biological products are granted patents or plant breeders' rights without any acknowledgement of the contribution of countries of origin or of indigenous peoples and local communities (Watal 2001, p. 171).

The concern is therefore that, if access is not managed appropriately at the international level, exploitation of agriculture, genetic resources and traditional knowledge may be nothing more than misappropriation (also known as 'biopiracy'). In recent years, a number of high profile cases of biopiracy or the granting of invalid patents based on genetic material derived from the traditional knowledge of indigenous peoples and local communities have heightened anxieties about the unequal exploitation of such resources.

In fact, many developing countries and NGOs have even argued that the current operation of the international intellectual property system is not only failing to prevent biopiracy, but is actually encouraging it. They have raised concerns about the exploitation of genetic resources through measures which permit the granting of patents or plant breeders' rights with relative ease without recognizing or rewarding the contribution of the holders of traditional knowledge in that process. In support of their arguments, they point to cases in developed countries where excessively broad patents or low thresholds for establishing patentability criteria of novelty and inventive step have led to the granting of patents over inventions derived from genetic resources, and where no monetary transfer then flows back to the indigenous peoples and local communities which provided information about the potential use of those genetic resources through their traditional knowledge. They argue that the current international intellectual property system has failed to provide for benefit sharing. They are pressing to introduce mechanisms into the international intellectual property system to address these issues.

The relationship between intellectual property rights and agriculture, genetic resources and traditional knowledge involves a complex set of inter-relationships between different multilateral institutions with different mandates and responsibilities (see also Stannard et al. 2004, p. 398). This complexity has had profound implications for the strategies and approaches of NGOs seeking to interface with the policy-making and norm-setting activities at stake and to engage with intellectual property implications of issues as diverse as the regulation of biological and genetic material and biodiversity control, and access, use and exchange of genetic material. The sheer range of issues and multiple institutional forums involved have created problems for NGOs with scare resources seeking to engage with intellectual property-related issues in these areas.

International instruments that contain intellectual property-related provisions that concern agriculture, genetic resources and traditional knowledge have been (and are being) negotiated under the auspices of the WTO, the Union pour la Protection des Obtentions Végétales (UPOV – the International Union for the Protection of New Varieties of Plants), the FAO, the CBD-COP, and the WIPO.

This means that multiple forums address overlapping sets of issues, with deliberations often tending to cover the same ground (see also Stannard et al. 2004, p. 399). The picture is rendered even more complicated by the fact that different national government ministries (for example agriculture, trade, industry, environment) tend to lead policy negotiations in different multilateral institutions, thus contributing to a relative absence of coherence even within national governments in an already complex policy environment.

Certainly, some of the multilateral institutions addressing intellectual property-related issues on agriculture, genetic resources and traditional knowledge have cooperated with each other. The FAO and the CBD secretariats, for instance, regularly cooperate on issues of common interest in agriculture (Correa 2001, p. 20). Yet the degree of cooperation between institutions has been hindered by the fact that the role and mandate of each organization differs significantly. While the WTO deals with international trade (including trade-related intellectual property rights through the TRIPS Agreement), UPOV administers common rules for the recognition and protection of plant variety rights, the CBD and FAO have a thematic focus on issues relating to genetic resources (as applied to agriculture in the case of FAO) and the WIPO is a specialized UN organization that promotes the protection of intellectual property (see also Correa 2001, p. 20).

Several international agreements emanating from these multilateral institutions contain intellectual property-related provisions on agriculture, genetic resources and traditional knowledge. These international agreements are the TRIPS Agreement, the UPOV International Convention for the Protection of New Varieties of Plants, the FAO International Undertaking on Plant Genetic Resources and the subsequent FAO International Treaty on Plant Genetic Resources for Food and Agriculture (ITPGRFA), and the CBD.

The fact that these international agreements all concern intellectual property-related issues in some way, sometimes overlapping with their coverage of the issues, complicates implementation and allows for different interpretations of the various obligations contained therein. Related work on benefit sharing is also being carried out by a number of multilateral institutions, particularly the WTO and FAO, CBD-COP and the WIPO Intergovernmental Committee on Genetic Resources, Traditional Knowledge and Folklore (IGC).

With the support of NGOs, developing countries have increasingly become aware of, and have engaged with, these parallel processes and begun to actively promote the need to create coherence between the various international agreements to ensure that the interests of people living in developing countries are appropriately addressed by the international agreements negotiated in each multilateral institution.

THE TRIPS AGREEMENT

As we saw in the last chapter, Article 27.1 of the TRIPS Agreement required WTO Members to provide patents for 'all inventions, whether products or processes, in all fields of technology'. However, Article 27.3(b) of the TRIPS Agreement allows Members to exclude from patentability plants and animals and essentially biological processes (but micro-organisms, and non-biological and microbiological processes have to be eligible for patenting). It also requires Members to provide for the protection of new plant varieties either by using patents or an effective *sui generis* (of its own kind) system, or a combination of the two. In this way, the TRIPS Agreement allows intellectual property rights to be extended to agriculture and genetic resources.

ARTICLE 27.3(b) OF THE TRIPS AGREEMENT: PATENTABLE SUBJECT MATTER

Members may also exclude from patentability:

. . .

plants and animals other than micro-organisms, and essentially biological processes for the production of plants or animals other than non-biological and microbiological processes. However, Members shall provide for the protection of plant varieties either by patents or by an effective *sui generis* system or by any combination thereof. The provisions of this subparagraph shall be reviewed four years after the date of entry into force of the WTO Agreement.

Prior to the TRIPS Agreement, many developing countries excluded from patentability materials found in nature, even if isolated from nature in a scientific laboratory. These countries included Argentina, Brazil, and the Andean Community countries (Bolivia, Colombia, Ecuador and Peru) (Tansey 1999, p. 8).

At the time the TRIPS Agreement was negotiated, the US and the EU favoured different approaches to the patenting of such inventions, the US allowing 'anything under the sun made by man' to be patentable and the EU facing strong internal resistance on the patenting of living organisms from some of its own Member States (Watal 2001, p. 131; Matthews 2002,

p. 58). These differences in approach explain the flexibilities contained in Article 27.3(b) and the commitment to a review, which began in 1999 and is still on-going.[1]

UPOV

Although Article 27.3(b) of the TRIPS Agreement does not specify how WTO Members should comply with the obligation to provide for the protection of plant varieties, one possible *sui generis* system of protection is the UPOV system of Plant Breeders' Rights (PBRs). These were developed as an alternative to patents because plant breeders found it difficult or impossible to meet two of the fundamental requirements for the granting of patents, namely inventiveness and a written description of how to make and use the invention (Tansey 1999, p. 8). UPOV adopted the first version of its Convention in 1961 and it has since been revised three times: in 1972, 1978 and 1991. The criteria for protection under the UPOV Convention are that plant varieties must be new,[2] distinct,[3] uniform[4] and stable.[5]

Critics of the UPOV Convention have argued that it promotes commercially bred plant varieties geared to industrialized agriculture systems in which farmers have to pay royalties on the seeds that they purchase from the holders of PBRs. There has also been concern that the replacement of locally adapted seeds with genetically uniform modern varieties will lead to genetic erosion. This is because PBRs are only available for varieties that are genetically uniform so the UPOV Convention discourages the use of genetically diverse and locally adapted seeds (Tansey 1999, p. 10).

A further concern has been that any WTO Member wishing to meet its obligations under Article 27.3(b) of the TRIPS Agreement by providing a *sui generis* system of protection of plant varieties by joining UPOV can only sign the 1991 version of the Convention. This has been seen as problematic because although the 1978 text of the UPOV Convention gave a greater degree of flexibility (Watal 2001, p. 146) by allowing farmers to reuse the seed they had purchased for the following year's sowing under certain conditions, the 1991 version does not contain the so-called 'farmers' privilege' to use freely seeds gathered from their harvest as further planting material (see also Sell 2003, p. 143). Instead, in such cases, farmers must obtain the authorization of the breeder before doing so.[6]

THE FOOD AND AGRICULTURE ORGANIZATION

The FAO began to engage with intellectual property-related issues in 1983 with the adoption of the International Undertaking on Plant Genetic Resources (hereafter 'the Undertaking'), which was the first comprehensive international agreement on plant genetic resources for food and agriculture.[7] It was adopted by the FAO Conference in 1983 by Resolution 8/83 as an instrument to promote international harmony in matters regarding access to plant genetic resources for food and agriculture.[8]

Countries adhering to the Undertaking agreed to a common interpretation of the treaty because many found that the relationship between intellectual property and genetic resources, in particular PBRs, was problematic. The Undertaking therefore reflected a delicate balance between the developed countries' need for access to plant genetic resources for food and agriculture, and the desire of developing countries for a more equitable sharing of benefits (Stannard et al. 2004, p. 406).

One hundred and thirteen countries have adhered to the Undertaking, which frames genetic resources as the common heritage of humanity and aims to protect them by seeking to ensure that plant genetic resources of economic and/or social interest, particularly for agriculture, will be explored, preserved, evaluated and made available for plant breeding and scientific purposes.

At the same time, the FAO established what is now called the Commission on Genetic Resources for Food and Agriculture (CGRFA) to monitor the International Undertaking.[9] Resolution 9/83 set up the CGRFA as a forum for governments to address questions related to access and benefit sharing (ABS) on plant genetic resources for food and agriculture.[10] NGOs attend its meetings as observers.[11] The CGRFA uses a multi-stakeholder model with NGOs, academia, industry and farmers' representatives all sitting together in the Commission.

The Undertaking also provided an international framework for the *ex situ* collections of plant genetic resources of the Consultative Group on International Agricultural Research (CGIAR).[12] The CGIAR holds these collections in trust for the international community under agreements signed in 1994 with the FAO. International Research Centres of the CGIAR agree not to seek legal ownership of these materials and recognize the intergovernmental authority of the FAO and the CGRFA in setting relevant policies (Stannard et al. 2004, p. 406).

The International Undertaking was the subject of a series of agreed interpretations, in the form of three FAO Conference resolutions, which are now annexed to it. They were intended to achieve a balance between the products of biotechnology (commercial varieties and breeders' lines) on the one hand, and farmers' varieties and wild material on the other, and between the interests of developed and developing countries, by balancing the rights of breeders (formal innovators) and farmers (informal innovators).

For instance, Resolution 4/89[13] recognized that Plant Breeders' Rights, as provided for by UPOV, were not inconsistent with the Undertaking, and simultaneously recognized farmers' rights defined in Resolution 5/89.[14] In 1991 governments also recognized that ABS was not incompatible with PBRs, which led to the revised 1991 version of the UPOV Convention. The sovereign rights of nations over their genetic resources were recognized in FAO Resolution 3/91,[15] and it was agreed that Farmers' Rights would be implemented through an international fund for plant genetic resources.

Agenda 21 and the Nairobi Final Act

Agenda 21 was adopted at the United Nations Conference on Environment and Development Earth Summit in Rio de Janeiro on 14 June 1992, where 178 governments voted to adopt a programme for sustainable development. Based on concepts derived from dialogues between NGOs and governments from the early 1980s onwards, Agenda 21 called for the strengthening of the FAO Global System on Plant Genetic Resources, and its adjustment in line with the outcome of negotiations on the CBD.[16] In adopting the agreed text of the CBD in May 1992, countries also adopted Resolution 3 of the Nairobi Final Act, which recognized the need to seek solutions to outstanding matters concerning plant genetic resources, in particular: (a) access to *ex situ* collections not addressed by the Convention, and (b) the question of farmers' rights.[17]

The Nairobi Final Act was important because it preserved the role of the CGRFA and avoided the constant risk that agriculture would become absorbed by the CBD process. The Nairobi Final Act ensured that these matters were addressed within FAO's forum.

In 1993, the FAO Conference accordingly adopted Resolution 7/93 for the revision of the Undertaking and requested that the FAO provide a forum for negotiations among governments in the form of regular and extraordinary sessions of the CGRFA,[18] in particular to facilitate: (a) the adaptation of the Undertaking, in harmony with the CBD; (b) consideration of the issue of access on mutually agreed terms to plant genetic resources, including *ex situ* collections not addressed by the CBD; and (c) the realization of Farmers' Rights.

This mandate led to the development of discussions in the CGRFA that focused on the revision of the Undertaking to ensure it was in harmony with CBD,[19] commencing at the First Extraordinary Session of the CGRFA on 7–11 November 1994.[20]

The CGRFA, at its Fifth regular Session in 1993, had requested the preparation of a rolling Global Plan of Action on Plant Genetic Resources for Food and Agriculture (GPA), in order to identify the technical and financial needs for ensuring conservation and promoting sustainable use of plant genetic resources.[21]

The FAO Leipzig Declaration and the International Treaty on Plant Genetic Resources for Food and Agriculture

This was followed, by a pivotal moment in 1996 when, after five years of intense negotiations, 150 countries attending the FAO Leipzig International Technical Conference on Plant Genetic Resources,[22] formally adopted the Leipzig Declaration and the Global Plan of Action on Plant Genetic Resources for Food and Agriculture.[23] The meeting was attended by over 150 NGOs, two thirds of which were from the Global South.[24] They also declared that it was important to complete the revision of the Undertaking.

The entry into force of the CBD, together with the adoption of the GPA, in 1996 moved the discussions toward a new treaty for a binding instrument that would deal with the key ideas underpinning the Undertaking, namely the need for a countervailing balance to PBRs with access to plant genetic resources; the fair and equitable sharing of benefits arising from the use of plant genetic resources for food and agriculture; and the realization of Farmers' Rights. Countries have agreed that the Undertaking should maintain a multilateral system of access and benefit sharing, that meets the specific needs of agriculture.

By 1998 negotiations in the CGRFA were in deadlock, but the appointment of a new Chair in the form of Ambassador Fernando Gerbassi of Venezuela that year was an important turning point because he made clear that the CGRFA had a straightforward mandate and pushed delegates to negotiate a successful outcome.

The negotiations in the CGRFA culminated in the adoption of the International Treaty on Plant Genetic Resources for Food and Agriculture (ITPGRFA) by the FAO Conference on 3 November 2001.[25] The ITPGRFA, which came into force on 29 June 2004, sought to find a balance between the interests of developing and developed countries and between the rights of farmers and plant breeders. To achieve these aims, the ITPGRFA established a multilateral system for providing access to seeds and germplasm and for the sharing of benefits obtained from their

use. Article 9 of the ITPGRFA contains specific provisions on farmers'
rights. Farmers' rights are based on the recognition of the enormous
contribution made by local and indigenous communities and farmers in
all regions of the world, particularly those who are in centres of origin or
crop diversity. Furthermore, farmers' rights cover the conservation and
development of plant genetic resources that constitute the basis of food
and agriculture production throughout the world.[26]

However, whether Article 9 of the ITPGRFA is in fact a positive

ARTICLE 9 OF THE ITPGRFA – FARMERS' RIGHTS

1.   The Contracting Parties recognize the enormous contribution that the local and indigenous communities and farmers of
all regions of the world, particularly those in the centres of origin
and crop diversity, have made and will continue to make for the
conservation and development of plant genetic resources which
constitute the basis of food and agriculture production throughout
the world.

2.   The Contracting Parties agree that the responsibility for real-
izing Farmers' Rights, as they relate to plant genetic resources for
food and agriculture, rests with national governments. In accordance with their needs and priorities, each Contracting Party,
should, as appropriate, and subject to its national legislation, take
measures to protect and promote Farmers' Rights, including:

(a)   protection of traditional knowledge relevant to plant
        genetic resources for food and agriculture;
(b)   the right to equitably participate in sharing benefits
        arising from the utilization of plant genetic resources for
        food and agriculture; and
(c)   the right to participate in making decisions, at the
        national level, on matters related to the conservation
        and sustainable use of plant genetic resources for food
        and agriculture.

3.   Nothing in this Article shall be interpreted to limit any
rights that farmers have to save, use, exchange and sell farm-
saved seed/propagating material, subject to national law and as
appropriate.

breakthrough for farmers in developing countries remains to be seen. Some NGO activists believe it was more harmful than helpful. On the one hand, it is remarkable that the value to the management of the ecosystem by local communities in developing countries has been recognized at all in an international treaty and what makes the ITPGRFA a major achievement is its formal endorsement of farmers' rights through a legally binding instrument at the multilateral level.[27]

On the other hand, while Article 9 of the ITPGRFA appears to acknowledge the farmers' right to save, use, exchange and sell farm-saved seeds, it is generally considered a weak statement because it leaves responsibility to national governments, without the backing of any international mechanism or enforcement procedure, and because it gives insufficient protection for farmers' rights.[28]

Whilst the ITPGRFA acknowledges the farmers' right to save, use, exchange and sell farm-saved seed, responsibility is left to national governments to provide implementing legislation. The potential impact of ITPGRFA is being undermined because Article 27.3(b) of TRIPS obliges WTO Members to provide for patents or establish an effective *sui generis* system. In order to comply with this obligation, many developing countries are choosing UPOV 1991 (which, as we saw above, restricts the farmers' privilege to save, use, exchange and sell farm-saved seeds) as their plant variety protection model, not least because TRIPS-plus Free Trade Agreement (FTA) provisions often require membership of UPOV 1991 (Matthews and Munoz-Tellez 2006, p. 634).[29]

Furthermore Article 9.2 of the ITPGRFA is narrower in scope than Article 8(j) of the CBD, and would not apply, for instance, to knowledge relating to medicinal or industrial uses of plant genetic resources. Under this approach, the issue of protection of traditional knowledge may be circumscribed to knowledge incorporated in farmers' varieties (landraces) and certain associated knowledge (for example specific cultivation practices). The development of a *sui generis* regime for the protection of farmers' varieties becomes, in this context, one of the possible components of farmers' rights (Correa 2001, p. 22).

THE CONVENTION ON BIOLOGICAL DIVERSITY

While the TRIPS Agreement was still being negotiated, the text of the CBD was adopted in May 1992. The CBD includes, in Article 8(j), a provision which has triggered the consideration of the intellectual property implications of traditional knowledge to an extent previously not undertaken (see also Correa 2001, p. 20).[30]

ARTICLE 8(j) OF THE CONVENTION ON BIOLOGICAL DIVERSITY

Each Party shall . . . Subject to its national legislation . . . respect, preserve and maintain knowledge, innovations and practices of indigenous and local communities embodying traditional lifestyles relevant for the conservation and sustainable use of biological diversity and promote their wider application with the approval and involvement of the holders of such knowledge, innovations and practices and encourage the equitable sharing of the benefits arising from the utilization of such knowledge, innovations and practices.

Article 8(j) of the CBD contains two important concepts on the protection and participation of traditional knowledge holders. First, it sets out the principle of prior informed consent. This presupposes active authorization prior to the use or even custody of the resources and/or knowledge. Second, Article 8(j) of the CBD sets out the principle of equitable benefit-sharing, to the effect that any use of traditional knowledge should include remuneration to the holders of that knowledge (see also Mutter 2005, p. 327).

The CBD therefore deals with access to genetic resources and creates an obligation for the fair and equitable sharing of benefits arising out of the utilization of genetic resources on mutually agreed terms and informed consent.

ATTEMPTS TO ACHIEVE COHERENCE BETWEEN THE TRIPS AGREEMENT AND THE CBD

Nowhere is the absence of coherence more prevalent than in the TRIPS Agreement and the CBD, which both address the relationship between genetic resources and intellectual property in different but overlapping ways.

The relationship between Article 27.3(b) of the TRIPS Agreement and the CBD has thus been highly contentious. At its third meeting in November 1996, the governing body of the Convention, the CBD-COP, requested that the CBD Secretariat co-operate with the WTO through the latter institution's Committee on Trade and Environment (CTE) to explore the extent to which there may be linkages between the CBD and

Article 27.3(b) of the TRIPS Agreement (see also Cabrera Medaglia 2009, p. 5).

Subsequently, in April 1998, the fourth meeting of the CBD-COP established an Ad Hoc Open-ended Inter-Sessional Working Group on Article 8(j) to undertake the task of developing a programme of work for the implementation of Article 8(j) and related provisions. The Working Group was also mandated to provide advice on the development of legal and other appropriate forms of protection for subject matter covered by Article 8(j).

In June 1999, the Inter-Sessional Meeting on the Operation of the Convention then explored explicitly the relationship between intellectual property rights, the TRIPS Agreement and the CBD. The meeting recognized the need to ensure mutual supportiveness between the TRIPS Agreement and the CBD and recommended that COP-5 transmit its findings on Article 8(j) to the WTO and the WIPO. It also recommended to the fifth meeting of the CBD-COP to invite the WTO to acknowledge the relevant provisions of the CBD and to take into account the fact that the objectives of the TRIPS Agreement and the CBD are interrelated.

Meanwhile, in 2002, the CBD adopted the voluntary 'Bonn Guidelines on Access to Genetic Resources and Fair and Equitable Sharing of the Benefits Arising out of their Utilization' to serve as inputs when developing and drafting legislative, administrative or policy measures on access and benefit-sharing.[31]

In 2004 the CBD mandated one of its working groups to elaborate and negotiate an international regime on access to genetic resources and benefit-sharing (see also Stannard et al. 2004, p. 408).[32] In terms of the relationship between the CBD working group and other relevant international regimes, paragraph 10 of the Bonn Guidelines states that: 'The guidelines should be applied in a manner that is coherent and mutually supportive of the work of relevant international agreements and institutions'. The Guidelines are without prejudice to the access and benefit-sharing provisions of the FAO ITPGRFA.[33]

At the eighth meeting of the CBD-COP in March 2006 a decision was reached that, regarding the international regime on access and benefit-sharing under negotiation, the Working Group on ABS should complete its work at the earliest possible time before COP-10 in 2010. The CBD-COP further requested the collaboration and contribution of the Working Group on Article 8(j) to the mandate of the ABS Working Group, by providing views on the elaboration and negotiation of an international ABS regime relevant to traditional knowledge. On the development of *sui generis* systems for the protection of traditional knowledge, the CBD-COP urged parties and governments to develop, or recognize, national and local *sui generis* models for the protection of traditional knowledge with the full and effective participation of indigenous and local communities.

To date the CBD-COP negotiations continue, with few substantial outcomes as regards introducing measures to ensure the defensive protection that developing countries seek in order to prevent the misappropriation of genetic resources and traditional knowledge.

The relationship between Article 27.3(b) of the TRIPS Agreement and the CBD has been rendered more problematic by the fact that the CBD Secretariat has not been given permanent observer status at the WTO TRIPS Council. This is largely because the US is a signatory to, but has not yet ratified, the CBD and would therefore have diplomatic difficulties with an explicit link between the CBD and TRIPS Council negotiations. The US has refused to ratify the CBD because of concerns about its intellectual property provisions (Abbott 2008, p. 3).[34]

With the support of NGOs, developing countries and the African Group in particular have been active in the on-going review of Article 27.3(b) of the TRIPS Agreement with the intention of achieving harmonization between Article 27.3(b) of the TRIPS Agreement and Article 8(j) of the CBD in order to protect the rights of indigenous people and local farming communities and to protect and promote biological diversity. Some developing countries have gone so far as to argue that the TRIPS Agreement must be reviewed in the light of the obligations on CBD Contracting States under Article 8(j) (see also Correa 2001, p. 23).[35]

Brazil, however, has been cautious in its approach and has noted the conceptual and operational difficulties in bringing traditional knowledge under the TRIPS Agreement and stated that while it is open to discuss adequate ways of protecting traditional knowledge at the multilateral level, the review of Article 27.3(b) is the appropriate forum to discuss the establishment of *sui generis* protection systems (see also Correa 2001, p. 23).[36]

So, while developing countries' positions generally aim at some recognition and protection of traditional knowledge, considerable hesitation seems to exist about how to deal with the subject, the nature and scope of protection, and the extent to which the issue should be brought under the TRIPS Agreement (Correa 2001, p. 26).

NGOs have supported developing country positions by emphasizing the importance of implementing the CBD and creating coherence between the various international agreements that deal with genetic resources and traditional knowledge. They point, in particular, to the importance for developing countries of harmonizing the TRIPS Agreement with the CBD in order to ensure the sustainable use of biodiversity, prevent misappropriation, and protect traditional knowledge.

In order to create coherence with the CBD, the amendment to the TRIPS Agreement that many developing countries and NGOs envisage would primarily aim to address concerns about biopiracy. In this regard, developing countries, with the support of NGOs, as part of their wider effort to create an international regime, are seeking to amend the TRIPS Agreement in order to introduce internationally binding disclosure requirements in patent applications, including proof of consent and benefit sharing.

In 2001, Paragraph 19 of the Doha Declaration specifically mandated the TRIPS Council with the task of examining the relationship between the TRIPS Agreement and the CBD, the protection of traditional knowledge and folklore, and other new and relevant developments pointed out by WTO Members (see also Cabrera Medaglia 2009, p. 6).[37]

PARAGRAPH 19 OF DOHA WTO MINISTERIAL DECLARATION 2001

We instruct the Council for TRIPS, in pursuing its work programme including under the review of Article 27.3(b), the review of the implementation of the TRIPS Agreement under Article 71.1 and the work foreseen pursuant to paragraph 12 of this declaration, to examine, inter alia, the relationship between the TRIPS Agreement and the Convention on Biological Diversity, the protection of traditional knowledge and folklore, and other relevant new developments raised by members pursuant to Article 71.1. In undertaking this work, the TRIPS Council shall be guided by the objectives and principles set out in Articles 7 and 8 of the TRIPS Agreement and shall take fully into account the development dimension.

The topics raised subsequently in the TRIPS Council's on-going review of Article 27.3(b) have included the following:

- how to apply the existing TRIPS provisions on patenting biotechnological inventions, including the extent that life forms should be patentable;
- the meaning of effective *sui generis* protection for new plant varieties, including the question of allowing farmers to continue to save and exchange seeds that they have harvested;

- how to deal with traditional knowledge, folklore and genetic material, and the rights of communities where these originate, including questions of how to prevent patents from being granted wrongly and whether to support the creation of databases to help patent examiners, to what extent existing intellectual property rights help to protect traditional knowledge and folklore and to what extent a *sui generis* law is desirable, and what is the right forum to develop this subject further;
- how to implement the TRIPS Agreement and the CBD together, and whether the TRIPS Agreement should be amended, in particular whether patent applications should have to disclose the source of the traditional knowledge or genetic material, what kind of approval researchers and inventors might have to obtain before they can use these in their inventions, and possible methods of sharing benefits with local communities when inventors in other countries have rights to inventions based on materials obtained from the locality.

In particular, the discussion in the TRIPS Council has gone into considerable detail on issues relating to whether the TRIPS Agreement should be amended to require disclosure of the source and origin of genetic material or associated traditional knowledge contained in patent applications (see also Cabrera Medaglia 2009, p. 6). The different positions on disclosure of origin can be briefly summarized as follows:

- Disclosure as a TRIPS obligation: A group represented by Brazil and India[38] and including Bolivia, Colombia, Cuba, Dominican Republic, Ecuador, Peru,[39] and Thailand, supported by the African Group[40] and some other developing countries, has advocated amending the TRIPS Agreement so that patent applications are required to disclose the country of origin of the biological resources and traditional knowledge used in the inventions, provide evidence that they have received 'prior informed consent' (a term used in the CBD) and that they can demonstrate evidence of 'fair and equitable' benefit sharing;
- In response, the United States has argued that the CBD's objectives on access to genetic resources, and on benefit sharing, could best be achieved through national legislation and contractual arrangements based on the legislation, which could include commitments on disclosure;[41]
- Disclosure through the WIPO: Switzerland has proposed an amendment to the WIPO's Patent Cooperation Treaty (PCT) so that

domestic law may ask inventors to disclose the source of genetic resources and traditional knowledge when they apply for patents;[42]

- Disclosure outside patent law: the EU's position includes a proposal to examine a requirement that patent applicants disclose the source or origin of genetic material as a subject in itself, with legal consequences of not meeting this requirement lying outside the scope of patent law.[43]

Subsequently, on 26 May 2006, Brazil, India, Pakistan, Peru, Thailand and Tanzania issued a communication to the TRIPS Council proposing an amendment to Article 29 of the TRIPS Agreement.

ARTICLE 29 OF THE TRIPS AGREEMENT: CONDITIONS ON PATENT APPLICANTS

1. Members shall require that an applicant for a patent shall disclose the invention in a manner sufficiently clear and complete for the invention to be carried out by a person skilled in the art and may require the applicant to indicate the best mode for carrying out the invention known to the inventor at the filing date or, where priority is claimed, at the priority date of the application.
2. Members may require an applicant for a patent to provide information concerning the applicant's corresponding foreign applications and grants.

Article 29 of the TRIPS Agreement concerns the disclosure of the invention that must be made by the applicant for a patent. The proposed amendment would see the incorporation of a new Article 29*bis*, which would require the disclosure of the origin of genetic resources and associated traditional knowledge in patent applications along with evidence of prior informed consent for access and fair and equitable benefit-sharing arising from the commercial or other utilization of such resources.[44]

The week before the WTO Mini-Ministerial Conference in June 2008, an unprecedented coalition of developed and developing countries put forward a proposal, often referred to as the 'draft modalities' text on intellectual property issues at the WTO.[45] The text was proposed by a coalition led by Brazil, the EU, India, and Switzerland,[46] and calls for the inclusion of intellectual property issues as part of the horizontal process of the Doha Development Round,[47] advocating that the three controversial intellectual property issues (that is proposals to create a multilateral register for geographical indications (GIs) for wines and spirits; a 'GI extension' proposal to extend to other products the higher level of geographical indications protection now given to wines and spirits; and disclosure of origin) be included in the negotiations as part of the 'single undertaking'.[48]

The coalition that supported the 'draft modalities' included more than two-thirds of WTO Members, but that stance was met with strong opposition from Australia, Canada, Chile, Mexico, New Zealand, South Korea, Taiwan and the US, who had sponsored a competing initiative known as the 'joint proposal'. The 'joint proposal' argued that including intellectual property issues in the horizontal negotiations on modalities in the industrial and agricultural sectors would 'substantially set back efforts to arrive at a viable way forward for the Doha negotiations'.[49]

According to the 'draft modalities', Members would agree – prior to official negotiations on the issue – to amend the TRIPS Agreement such that all patent applications would be required to disclose the origin of 'genetic resources and/or associated traditional knowledge' used in the product in question. Patent applicants would also have to provide proof of prior informed consent and benefit-sharing.

Disclosure of origin has been pushed by developing countries, including India, Brazil and China, which consider a disclosure requirement necessary to prevent the granting of 'bad' patents that use biological resources or traditional knowledge without proper acknowledgement or compensation. Preventing such biopiracy is important for ensuring a supportive relationship between the TRIPS Agreement and the CBD. The CBD, the most important international agreement on biodiversity, recognizes the sovereign rights of states over their natural resources, and requires access to genetic resources to occur only on the basis of mutually agreed terms and the equitable sharing of benefits.[50]

A large coalition of 110 developing and developed countries led by Brazil, India, the EU and Switzerland, were advocating strongly for all on-going intellectual property issues under discussion in the TRIPS Council (including disclosure of origin) to be moved forward in a single undertaking in the Doha Round,[51] but the proposal stalled when other WTO Members contended that intellectual property issues should not be discussed in tandem with the Doha negotiations on liberalizing trade in agriculture and industrial goods (see also Cabrera Medaglia 2009, p. 7).

Movement on the disclosure requirement continues to be delayed by deep divisions among WTO Members as to how to move forward the discussions on this issue. Since 2006 a number of developing countries have called for an amendment to the TRIPS Agreement to include a mandatory requirement for patent applications to disclose the origin of any genetic resources and/or associated traditional knowledge involved in their inventions.

When the TRIPS Council met on 28 October 2008, discussions returned to the issue at the heart of the disclosure of origin deliberations – the need for coherence between the TRIPS Agreement and the CBD.[52] It is in this issue that the fate of any agreement in the future ultimately rests.

COHERENCE BETWEEN THE CBD AND THE FAO AGREEMENTS

While the CBD covers *all* biological diversity issues, the more agriculturally-focused forum of the FAO has dealt with two outstanding issues that the CBD did not address, namely access to *ex situ* collections not acquired in accordance with the CBD and farmers' rights (see also Stannard et al. 2004, p. 407).

From the point of view of many developing countries and NGOs, there is an urgent need for an internationally binding system that prevents farmers' rights being subordinated to those of plant breeders, and that prevents the misappropriation of genetic resources and traditional knowledge. The issues highlighted include: (i) balancing the rights of breeders with the rights of local farmers in developing countries to save, share, sell, and replant seed; and (ii) equitable sharing of benefits between plant breeders and farmers to take account of the latter's contribution to innovations in plant breeding and plant patenting.

Generally, developing countries and NGOs consider the FAO agreements to be in harmony with the CBD. The former cover the specific needs of agriculture, and are considered to hold the middle ground between the CBD that focuses on the protection of biodiversity and the TRIPS Agreement that extends proprietary rights over intangible assets, including plant genetic resources.

THE WIPO INTERGOVERNMENTAL COMMITTEE ON GENETIC RESOURCES, TRADITIONAL KNOWLEDGE AND FOLKLORE

A further process which has impacted on international arrangements for genetic resources is the work of the Intergovernmental Committee (IGC) of the WIPO (see also Stannard et al. 2004, p. 409) which, as mandated by the 2003 WIPO General Assembly, 'will focus, in particular, on a consideration of the international dimension of those questions, without prejudice to the work pursued in other [forums], and . . . no outcome of its work is excluded, including the possible development of an international instrument or instruments'.[53]

Traditional knowledge has long been a concern of WIPO Members, with calls for the protection of traditional knowledge 'folklore' made as early as the WIPO Stockholm Conference of 1967 (Halbert 2006, p. 28). These calls re-emerged in the WIPO due to the focus given to genetic resources and traditional knowledge by the CBD in the 1990s and, in 1998, it created a Global Intellectual Property Issues Division which began to occupy policy space relating to traditional knowledge that had previously largely been the preserve of other multilateral institutions, particularly the CBD (Halbert 2006, p. 28).

The WIPO Global Intellectual Property Issues Division began its work by convening a number of roundtable meetings, the first of which took place on July 1998 and included some 200 representatives of indigenous groups from Africa, the Americas, Asia, Europe, and the South Pacific, together with representatives of WIPO member state governments, inter-governmental organizations and NGOs. The meetings were 'intended as a forum for indigenous peoples to share experiences and aspirations concerning the protection of traditional knowledge, innovations and culture by means of intellectual property'.[54]

In 1998 and 1999, the Global Intellectual Property Issues Division also undertook a two-year project, undertaking fact-finding missions to engage with indigenous groups and local communities in 28 countries to identify intellectual property needs and expectations of traditional knowledge holders (see also Correa 2001, p. 21). The indigenous groups and local communities had a direct input into the design and implementation of the project and, in April 2001, the findings of these missions were published in the report *Intellectual Property Needs Expectations of Traditional Knowledge Holders: Report on Fact-finding Missions on Intellectual Property and Traditional Knowledge (1998–1999)* (WIPO 2001).

The IGC met for the first time on 30 April to 2 May 2001 following a decision of the WIPO General Assembly with a mandate to discuss a range of issues in the field of intellectual property.[55] Since then, the IGC has concentrated on activities related to the protection of traditional knowledge against misappropriation and misuse of traditional knowledge – including disclosure of origin in patent applications – and has not dealt substantively with other issues such as safeguarding and conserving traditional knowledge.[56] The IGC is open to all member states, while inter-governmental organizations and other accredited NGOs may participate as observers.[57]

Initially, however, IGC meetings were attended by only a small number of NGOs representing indigenous and other local communities and, although over 130 NGOs, indigenous and other local communities have now been granted accreditation to the IGC, and no application for accreditation to the IGC has ever been refused, many choose not to attend meetings regularly (CIEL 2007, p. 4). In part this is because few of the accredited groups have the capacity and technical knowledge to contribute substantively to the process by suggesting drafting language or commenting on specific provisions of the text (CIEL 2007, p. 7). In practice this means that the accreditation of indigenous and other local communities adds legitimacy to the IGC process without necessarily leading to effective involvement of those groups.

Over half of the accredited organizations to the IGC are indigenous peoples and local communities, while the other half is comprised of international NGOs dealing with intellectual property and broader environmental and sustainable orientated NGOs such as Genetic Resources Action International (GRAIN), the International Union for Conservation of Nature (IUCN), ICTSD, TWN, and industry and rights-holder groups such as the International Federation of Pharmaceutical Manufacturers & Associations (IFPMA), which represents the global research-based pharmaceutical industry.

Defining traditional knowledge has been a challenge for the IGC, largely due to the fact that such knowledge is complex in nature and because traditional knowledge embraces different meanings for the wide variety of indigenous peoples and local communities who depend on it for their livelihoods. For indigenous peoples and local communities, traditional knowledge constitutes the very foundation of cultural heritage, cultural identity and social integrity. It is closely related to the communities' relationship with their land and natural resources and should not be viewed primarily from a commercial perspective (CIEL 2007, p. 3).

For indigenous peoples and local communities, a holistic approach to the protection of traditional knowledge adopted within the realm of the IGC is mutually supportive of other international systems and processes discussed at the CBD and the FAO. Moreover, these communities have called for a commitment that will ensure that IGC members comply with their obligations under international human rights treaties and conventions, particularly the International Labour Organization (ILO) Convention No. 169, concerning Indigenous and Tribal Peoples in Independent Countries. In this light, indigenous peoples and local communities have also linked their pursuit for the protection of self-determination, cultural heritage, and sovereign rights over the natural resources associated with their traditional knowledge. They have expressed concern about the fact that the draft IGC framework does not explicitly recognize the human rights linkage to their right to protection of their traditional knowledge (CIEL 2007, p. 3).

However, in practice there is a relative absence of accredited indigenous or other local communities and NGOs from IGC meetings that reflects a decision on the part of these groups to vote with their feet, given the perception that the IGC is a member state-driven committee and that the interests of indigenous or other local communities are often not consistent with the positions adopted by their national governments. There is a perception that the intellectual property system has served to enable the taking and use of traditional knowledge by trans-national corporations, with little recourse or remedies available to indigenous and other local communities to prevent misappropriation (CIEL 2007, p. 1) and harness for themselves the commercial opportunities to exploit their traditional knowledge.

The perceived problem of misappropriation and the recognition of the value of traditional knowledge have in turn given rise to two general trends. First, developing countries are increasingly pursuing a mechanism aimed at preventing misappropriation and providing positive obligations for the protection of traditional knowledge (CIEL 2007, p. 1). Second, indigenous and other local communities are increasingly becoming involved in international forums where discussions on intellectual property and traditional knowledge are taking place (CIEL 2007, p. 1). In these forums, indigenous and other local communities have expressed concerns regarding the misappropriation of their knowledge and cultural heritage, as well as lack of recognition by the current intellectual property regime of their collective ownership rights over their intellectual property (CIEL 2007, p. 1).

Several multilateral institutions, including the WIPO and the CBD, are discussing 'appropriate' frameworks for the protection, preservation and promotion of traditional knowledge. Within the WIPO, the IGC is the primary arena in which both developing countries and indigenous peoples have been allocated policy space to seek to achieve their aims regarding the protection of traditional knowledge, genetic resources, traditional cultural expressions, access and benefit sharing, as well as compliance with prior informed consent for access (CIEL 2007, p. 2).

But although the IGC has made significant efforts to enhance the participation of representatives of indigenous and other local communities (CIEL 2007, p. 2), these groups continue to reiterate their concerns and reservations regarding the work of the IGC, noting that 'the Committee's work to-date has been developed without the broad-based participation of indigenous peoples' (CIEL 2007, p. 2).

In addition, the IGC process has often been criticized on grounds that, while it provides a useful forum for discussion, it has effectively marginalized traditional knowledge issues that would be more appropriately fit within the work programmes of the WIPO Standing Committee on Patents and the Standing Committee on Copyright and Related Rights (CIEL 2007, p. 3). From this perspective, the IGC only serves as a discussion forum that sidelines traditional knowledge issues in a forum that will not lead to any substantive outcome (CIEL 2007, p. 11).

Furthermore, while the IGC has produced a wealth of materials that provide background to contextualize the issues, only a few constitute actual working documents (CIEL 2007, p. 4). Certainly, progress at the IGC has been painfully slow. This can be explained largely by the reluctance of developed countries to fully engage with the topic, adopting instead the tactic of repeatedly calling for 'further study' instead of undertaking substantive discussions (CIEL 2007, p. 4). There is also a question mark over how groups accredited to the IGC are able to voice their concerns effectively when policy-making and norm-setting processes in the WIPO ultimately remain inter-governmental.

Despite the accreditation of indigenous peoples and local communities, in practice their substantive participation will continue to be limited by the structure of the IGC, which is member-driven. This is problematic for indigenous peoples and local communities because many have a tense relationship with their governments, often derived from conflicts over land rights, the right of self-determination, and the application and enforcement of customary law (CIEL 2007, p. 12). Similarly, developing country governments are often uncomfortable with the participation of indigenous peoples and local communities in WIPO processes.

For the majority of indigenous peoples and local communities, a comprehensive framework for the protection of traditional knowledge can only be achieved if their right to self-determination, land rights and customary laws are recognized, meaning that the more limited mandate of the IGC is only part of a wider structural problem for these groups in their domestic setting (CIEL 2007, p. 12). In other instances, even where indigenous peoples and local communities have a working relationship with their national governments and form part of national delegations, this has meant that representatives of these groups have not been able to speak beyond the established national positions formulated by government officials, if at all (CIEL 2007, p. 12).

Substantive participation has also been hindered by the failure of the IGC to think sufficiently about how to improve qualitatively the participation of indigenous peoples – instead, the emphasis has been on increasing the quantity of indigenous peoples and local communities, for instance through the creation of a Voluntary Fund.[58]

For local and indigenous communities without access to the Voluntary Fund, the cost of attending the IGC meetings can be prohibitively expensive. Whereas most other committee meetings at the WIPO last for only a week, the IGC usually sits for a minimum of 10 days, requiring significant investment for delegations and representatives travelling to Geneva. In practice, few self-funded organizations are capable of sending a delegation to participate actively for the entire duration of the meeting (CIEL 2007, p. 12).

In addition, immediately before the IGC sessions, half-day panel presentations are organized, chaired by a representative from a local or indigenous community so that the experiences and concerns of holders and custodians of traditional knowledge can be voiced.[59] But there have been concerns that panel discussions themselves further sideline the views of local or indigenous communities if they are not fully considered part of the IGC work programme.[60] There have also been concerns about the complexity of accreditation and the long time lag between applying and being granted accreditation, which can take up to one year (CIEL 2007, p. 11).

In conclusion, the IGC tries to place traditional knowledge within the existing intellectual property rights framework, applying its underlying concepts and justifications. Indigenous peoples and local communities have generally viewed this approach with scepticism, with the intellectual property system itself seen as the enabler of misappropriation (CIEL 2007, p. 7). Despite the IGC's efforts to adopt measures for the protection of traditional knowledge that reflect the needs and expectations of traditional knowledge holders and to involve indigenous peoples and local communities in its policy discussions, the concerns and demands of these communities continue to receive insufficient attention (CIEL 2007, p. 10).

Yet the involvement of developing country NGOs, indigenous peoples and local communities in the IGC process has arguably helped to shift attention away from an overly Geneva-centric view of intellectual property policy-making and norm-setting activities, encouraging a broader perspective of and wider engagement with the implications of intellectual property rights for developing countries.

THE ROLE OF INTERNATIONAL NGOS AS ADVOCATES OF FARMERS' RIGHTS

The role played by international NGOs as advocates of farmers' rights has varied depending on the multilateral institution involved. UPOV restricts the granting of observer status at its meetings to international (not domestic) NGOs with competence in areas of direct relevance to matters governed by the UPOV Convention. Accredited NGOs are also granted observer status only to UPOV Council sessions and not to the Consultative Committee that normally meets in closed sessions restricted to members.[61] The impact of NGOs in UPOV processes has, consequently, remained limited.

The FAO, on the other hand, has a much more open relationship with NGOs. It adopts a broad definition of NGOs, encompassing all not-for-profit actors who are not governmental or intergovernmental. The rules of procedure for NGO engagement with the Governing Body of the ITPGRFA were agreed at the First Session of the Governing Body in Madrid on 12–16 June 2006.[62] They provide for NGOs to be granted observer status at sessions of the Governing Body and, at the invitation of the Chair, may participate in meetings without the right to vote, unless at least one third of the Contracting Parties present at the session object.[63]

Due to the relatively easy access that NGOs have to FAO processes, their role as advocates of farmers' rights,[64] is widely acknowledged as having been important to the negotiation of the ITPGRFA.[65] ActionAid, the Gaia Foundation, RAFI/ETC, ITDG/Practical Action, and the Berne Declaration,[66] amongst others, have made important inputs by providing technical expertise and multiple sources of evidence-based and practical information that has been a valuable support for developing country delegates to the FAO and to the CGRFA in particular.[67] One significant enabling aspect of the ITPGRFA negotiating process that has facilitated the engagement of NGOs has been the openness of the FAO to civil society engagement and the apparent synergy between NGOs and the FAO on what the preferred outcome in the final text of the ITPGRFA should be. The way that NGOs highlighted the issue of farmers' rights and brought technical knowledge and expertise to the policy debate is an example of how NGOs can work positively with multilateral institutions in relation to intellectual property issues.

NGOs have a relatively long history of engagement with policy issues related to agriculture and intellectual property rights. In 1978 Cary Fowler and Pat Mooney founded the Rural Advancement Foundation International (RAFI), which later changed its name to Action Group on Erosion, Technology and Concentration (ETC) as an NGO focusing on the socio-economic impact of new technologies on rural societies.[68] In 1979 Mooney, who later became RAFI's executive director, wrote *Seeds of the Earth*, widely cited as being the first analysis to draw attention to the erosion of the world's agricultural genetic resources. Having made the first link between intellectual property rights and seeds and genetic resource erosion, in 1983 Mooney wrote *The Law of the Seed: Another Development and Plant Genetic Resources* and subsequently played a major role in the formation of the International Undertaking at the CGRFA. This was followed, in 1988, by another publication by Fowler, Lachkovics, Mooney and Shand, entitled *The Laws of Life: Another Development and the New Biotechnologies*, reflecting and updating on the earlier discussions.

RAFI/ETC were, and remain, trusted by a variety of governmental and non-governmental groups in developing countries, both because of their long history of engagement with issues relating to intellectual property rights, agriculture and genetic resources, and by virtue of their tendency to present evidence-based arguments, providing hard data on the situation in developing countries.[69] In fact, so close was the relationship between the FAO and RAFI/ETC that, in 1993, the FAO hired Fowler to help draft the GPA. He then stayed on at the FAO to help organize the Leipzig Conference in 1996, at which the GPA was adopted.

Before that, however, a key moment came at the *Gene Traders* conference in London on 14–15 April 1992, organized by Intermediate Technology Development Group (ITDG, now renamed Practical Action), the New Economics Foundation and a range of UK development NGOs. Intended as preparation for the UN Conference on Environment and Development in Rio de Janeiro, the first day of the *Gene Traders* conference addressed two global issues: the impact of trade and intellectual property right rules on conserving biodiversity and the role of the CBD in designing alternatives for farmer-based strategies. The second day of the *Gene Traders* conference focused on specific experiences of farmer-based organizations from Africa, Asia and Latin America and the role of development agencies in supporting their work. Several working groups were set up to enable all the participants to contribute towards developing future strategies for cooperation.

The *Gene Traders* conference was a significant event because it brought together a broad range of NGO and civil society networks, organizations and individuals from Latin America, Africa, Europe and Asia.[70] Discussions focused on seeds and biotechnology, and on issues related to technology and intellectual property. At the meeting there was general consensus that seed saving was important for conservation and food security. This principle had already been developed by Pat Mooney and others and was then brought to the UK by ITDG. Thereafter, Patrick Mulvany of ITDG became involved with the FAO processes related to International Undertaking and its relationship with the CBD and, in many ways, the International Undertaking was overtaken by the CBD which linked access to genetic resources to ABS.

The Gaia Foundation played an important role as the focal point for NGO meetings, particularly in 1995 when it hosted a meeting at Gaia House in Hampstead, London.[71] The purpose of the meeting was for representatives of 12 NGOs to plan and coordinate their inputs into a number of significant intergovernmental meetings that would take place the following year, including the World Food Summit, the CBD-COP 3, the FAO Leipzig International Technical Conference on Plant Genetic Resources, and the WTO Singapore Ministerial meeting. At the Gaia House meeting, NGOs agreed to allocate tasks amongst themselves to avoid duplication and coordinate their activities with the aim of altering the discourse about agriculture, genetic resources and traditional knowledge in the different forums.

Since the CGRFA was conceived as a body where different stakeholders could discuss and seek solutions to problems related to plant genetic resources for food and agriculture, that forum has been particularly useful as a point of access for NGOs. RAFI/ETC and ITDG/Practical Action have participated regularly in its meetings and have often played an important role in articulating farmers' rights. In particular, both inside and outside meetings of the CGRFA, NGOs have been very involved in advocating farmers' rights and preventing traditional varieties from being subject to intellectual property rights.

Inside meetings, the CGRFA Secretariat, particularly Clive Stannard and Pepe Esquinas Alcazar, used NGO expertise to add momentum to the negotiations, bringing in Pat Mooney of RAFI to assist in the preparation of CGRFA meetings. Meanwhile Patrick Mulvany of ITDG played a crucial role in the final stages of inter-governmental negotiations of the ITPGRFA in 2001, intervening at the Ministerial meeting to unblock negotiations when, at one point, negotiations stalled, reputedly because the then UK Environment Minister, Michael Meacher, did not consider the treaty a good outcome for farmers and perceived it as lacking sufficiently robust farmers' rights. Patrick Mulvany spoke to Meacher and convinced him that it was symbolically important to have the treaty because the alternative would be that farmers' rights would fall off the agenda of the FAO, leaving the CBD-COP as the only multilateral institution likely to discuss farmers' rights and genetic resources in the future.[72] NGO inputs were important, therefore, in ensuring that the FAO remained a negotiating forum for farmers' rights.

The main challenge for NGOs now is how best to assist in translating the objectives of Article 9 of the ITPGRFA into national legislation. Few countries have enacted legislation on farmers' rights. One exception is India where, as will be discussed in Chapter 6, there has been a great deal of involvement by public interest NGOs in the process of enshrining farmers' rights in legislation.

NGOS AND THE FIGHT AGAINST BIOPIRACY

Outside meetings of the CGRFA, NGOs have continually highlighted issues of biopiracy. In 1999, for example, RAFI initiated the challenge against the patent granted to US-based seed company POD-NERS by the USPTO for genetic material derived from the Enola (or 'yellow') bean.[73] RAFI denounced the Enola bean patent as biopiracy and formally requested that the FAO and the CGIAR investigate the patent as a likely violation of their 1994 Trust agreement that obliges them to keep designated crop germoplasm in the public domain and off-limits to intellectual property claims.[74] The Colombia-based CGIAR centre, called the Centro Internacional de Agricultura Tropical (CIAT – International Center for Tropical Agriculture),[75] with support from FAO, filed an official challenge to the Enola bean patent with the USPTO on 20 December 2000. Following re-examination by the USPTO, the patent was eventually revoked on 29 April 2008.[76] For Pat Mooney of RAFI/ETC, however, while the NGO has been successful in the revocation of some individual patents, in general all that has been achieved is a wider recognition that these are important issues.[77]

In Geneva, the Quaker United Nations Office (QUNO) and the Center for International Environmental Law (CIEL) have both played important roles in terms of providing analysis of issues relating to the interface between intellectual property and agriculture, genetic resources and traditional knowledge (see, for example, Correa 2001; GRAIN 2001; Smolders 2005).

Quaker United Nations Office

QUNO launched its TRIPS Programme in 1999. The Programme has its origins in concerns in the early 1990s about the environment and development policy more widely. The British Quaker Peace and Social Witness (QPSW) started the Environmental Intermediaries Programme (EIP) on genetic resources, which tried to help Southern African countries to play an effective role in the negotiations for the revision of the International Undertaking on Plant Genetic Resources in the FAO. By the mid-1990s, it became clear that the TRIPS Agreement would also affect the future of genetic resources and in 1998 it was decided to move the work on genetic resources from the QPSW to QUNO in Geneva. QUNO would focus on the review of Article 27.3(b) of the TRIPS Agreement (Plaisier and Wijmenga 2004, p. 81).

QUNO's involvement in intellectual property issues relating to agriculture, genetic resources and traditional knowledge began in 1998, when the UK Department for International Development (DFID) expressed an interest in funding a discussion paper on the review of Article 27.3(b) of the TRIPS Agreement. With financial assistance from DFID, QUNO published the resulting paper in February 1999 (Tansey 1999). With the aim of contributing to a better informed public debate, the paper was written for policy makers, primarily in developing countries, working on agriculture, environment and trade issues. It outlined the different policy options on intellectual property-related issues over plants, animals, micro-organisms and new plant varieties. The QUNO paper was extremely important in setting out the issues.

In 1999 and 2000, QUNO also organized a series of informal, off-the-record meetings for developing country delegates from missions in Geneva that were to prove invaluable. The meetings aimed at helping strengthen the capacity of developing countries to safeguard the interests of their people and to bring these countries into dialogue with industrialized countries around issues raised by the review of Article 27.3(b) of the TRIPS Agreement (see also Correa 2001, Preface). During these meetings, delegates from developing countries could debate issues and develop confidence to engage with developed countries whose interest they saw as different from their own.

It was during these meetings that QUNO brought academic experts together with developing country delegates to discuss the main options for the Article 27.3(b) review process. In fact, people from all sides of the debate were invited to attend: delegates from developed and developing countries and representatives of the secretariats of multilateral institutions. In this respect, QUNO played a significant role in giving delegates the space to come together.[78]

In this first phase of the QUNO TRIPS Programme, with the exception of the 1999 DFID-funded discussion paper, the activities were funded from the Quakers' own resources. Then, in 2001, it was decided to extend the range of participants and to broaden the range of stakeholders involved. To realize this, a number of donors were approached. The Netherlands government subsequently provided significant funding for QUNO's TRIPS Programme work (Plaisier and Wijmenga 2004, p. 82).

With support from the Directorate General for International Co-operation of the Netherlands Ministry of Foreign Affairs, a further QUNO paper followed in July 2002. This second discussion paper focused more specifically on the question of how biotechnology and minimum standards of intellectual property protection and enforcement would affect food security (Tansey 2002).

Center for International Environmental Law

The work of CIEL on intellectual property issues relating to agriculture, genetic resources and traditional knowledge has been with the objective of providing substantive inputs to enhance developing country delegates' capacity to negotiate. They have sought to do this by organizing dialogues and workshops, bringing in experts to discuss the issues, monitoring negotiations, preparing substantive papers, and making interventions when invited to speak at multilateral institutions such as the WIPO in support of developing country positions.[79]

The TRIPS Action Network

One of the earliest NGO initiatives in response to concerns about the adverse effect of the TRIPS Agreement on development policy occurred in September 2001 when the TRIPS Action Network (TAN) published a groundbreaking report entitled *TRIPS on Trial: The Impact of WTO's Patent Regime on the World's Farmers, the Poor and Developing Countries* (Lewis 2001). TAN was a global coalition of farmers, development, consumer, health and environmental groups including the international NGOs Misereor, ActionAid, the Berne Declaration and the Institute for Agriculture and Trade Policy (IATP). The *TRIPS on Trial* report published by TAN highlighted the negative impact of intellectual property rights on public health and access to medicines and on agriculture, genetic resources and traditional knowledge. It advocated an immediate and substantive review of Article 27.3(b) and a fundamental rethinking of the TRIPS Agreement at the Doha Ministerial Conference.

International NGO/CSO Planning Committee for Food Sovereignty

NGOs from developing countries have found it more difficult to participate regularly in FAO meetings, partly because they lack financial resources to travel to the FAO's headquarters in Rome. In this respect, the International NGO/CSO Planning Committee for Food Sovereignty (IPC) is a useful focal point for developing country NGOs to allow them to make inputs into FAO processes indirectly. The IPC is a global network of some 40 NGOs and civil society organizations (CSOs) concerned with food sovereignty issues and programmes.[80] The origins of the IPC date back to the World Social Forum in 1996, when NGOs organized a parallel NGO Forum on Food Security, launching the concept of food sovereignty and, in 2000, came together to form the IPC. It includes social organizations representing small farmers, fisher folk, indigenous peoples, agricultural workers' trade unions; sub-regional/regional NGOs which act as regional focal points; and NGO networks with particular expertise and a long history of lobbying and action and advocacy on issues related to food sovereignty and agriculture, which act as thematic focal points.

Third World Network

TWN has also been a major player. It identified biodiversity issues as a priority area for their work in the run-up to the Rio Earth Summit in 1991. At that time, few NGOs in the South were engaging with global processes relating to the sustainable use of biological resources and how this could impact on the rights of indigenous peoples, fisher folk and small farmers. TWN played an important role in alerting groups at the national and sub-national level in the South (including indigenous peoples and local communities) that the drafting of the CBD could have profound implications in terms of regulating access to resources and also on indigenous and community rights. TWN linked these groups in the South with NGOs at the multilateral level and also worked with developing country delegations to provide analysis and information that was otherwise lacking from government sources. TWN's research on biopiracy, in particular, was important in helping to shape the early debate on this issue.[81] Since then, TWN has continued to play a role by facilitating an informal network of scientific experts, government officials, NGO representatives and academics on issues related to disclosure of origin, access to genetic resources and ABS regimes relating to the WTO, the WIPO and the CBD negotiating processes.

The Complexity of Negotiating Processes

As was explained at the beginning of this chapter, one readily apparent explanation of why it is extremely difficult to reach international consensus on plant genetic resources policy in multilateral institutions is the complexity of the issues involved. It is also unlikely that the position of the US will change so dramatically as to allow not only a disclosure requirement to be accepted, but also to incorporate a requirement to provide evidence of prior informed consent and benefit sharing in the light of the US refusal to ratify the CBD or ITPGRFA (Abbott 2008, p. 4).

The negotiation processes themselves are also a contributory factor. While the primary forum for international negotiations on plant genetic resources is the CPGRFA, closely interrelated negotiations are taking place concurrently in other multilateral forums, particularly the CBD-COP and the WTO TRIPS Council. In itself, that would not necessarily be a problem if countries were able to demonstrate coherence between different government departments that take the policy lead in different multilateral institutions but, for many developing countries, that coherence is often lacking (Petit et al. 2000, p. 2).

Nevertheless, NGOs have played an important role in raising awareness of biopiracy and identifying the issues to be challenged, particularly in the CBD context, where Southern NGOs, indigenous peoples and local communities have also been able to contribute to a relatively healthy consultation process.[82] Yet, today, the key issue remains how the provisions of the CBD should be implemented and, here, NGOs and other groups are increasingly being required to engage in more technical detail, going beyond sloganeering and campaigning work. In order to engage in this way, NGOs and other non-governmental groups are trying to increase their expertise and, at the same time, continue to mobilize public opinion. Outside the biopiracy context, there has been only limited success, for example in relation to patenting life issues, but here again levels of awareness have been raised.[83]

Developing country NGOs have played an important role in the formulation of policy relating to plant genetic resources. TWN, the African Biodiversity Network, the Community Biodiversity Development and Conservation Programme (CBDC) network and developing country NGOs such as Comutech in Zimbabwe have all contributed enormously. The Gaia Foundation has also played an important role. It held seminars and workshops before negotiating meetings on the draft ITPGRFA to brief delegates, particularly from African countries, about the issues involved. At these meetings, representatives from different NGOs would be on hand to talk to delegates and briefing papers written by Pat Mooney of RAFI/ETC were also considered useful by delegates because they helped to unpack the bureaucratic language of the draft text of the treaty so that delegates could fully understand the real meaning of the provisions and what was at stake. Crucially, although international NGOs such as ETC, GRAIN and ITDG/Practical Action were on hand to support delegates at these events, developing country NGOs were also on hand so that, for example, African NGOs were able to interface directly with African delegates when the ITPGRFA was being negotiated.

Policy Space, TRIPS Council and Disclosure of Origin

Following the 30 August 2005 Decision on the TRIPS Agreement and Access to Medicines, there was a perception that policy space would be created in TRIPS Council that would allow for a similar strategy to be utilized by developing countries, supported by NGOs, on disclosure of origin requirements relating to generic resources and traditional knowledge. This scenario, however, has failed to materialize. Even after the Doha Declaration in November 2001 there was evident civil society fatigue amongst some in the NGO community, this despite the fact that disclosure of origin is considered so important because it relates to the ownership of knowledge.

THE IMPACT OF NGO ENGAGEMENT WITH AGRICULTURE, GENETIC RESOURCES AND TRADITIONAL KNOWLEDGE

As multilateral institutions increased their engagement with intellectual property-related issues on agriculture, genetic resources and traditional knowledge, NGOs moved to support developing country positions by providing ideas and technical expertise unavailable elsewhere.

However, the nature of NGO relationships with developing country delegates on agriculture, genetic resources and traditional knowledge issues differed from public health and access to medicines issues. This was because, in the CBD and FAO processes for instance, government officials tend to be based in the ministries of national capitals rather than based in Geneva, as is the case for the WTO TRIPS Council and the WIPO. This had the effect that, while delegates in Geneva may well not have had the kind of technical capacity or back up from their national capitals that they needed, and may have had close relationships with international NGOs in Geneva that enhanced their capacity to negotiate in WTO and WIPO policy-making and norm-setting processes, developing country delegates to the CBD and FAO were likely to be national government officials based in ministries of environment or agriculture and often had greater technical support and achieved greater policy coherence within the national government processes by virtue of being embedded in the national governmental system.

Despite this, as with public health and access to medicines issues, developing country delegations have proved to be open and receptive to research and analysis prepared by NGOs on agriculture, genetic resources and traditional knowledge when they consider these inputs useful. In this respect, there has been an important shift in the perception of developing country governments, which now view NGOs as being capable of contributing to the policy process rather than merely being critical of national government approaches.

NGOs were also successful because they built strategic international coalitions and framed issues in creative and politically emotive ways to pursue their agendas, developing new terminology that included slogans such as biopiracy, farmers' rights, traditional resource rights, community intellectual rights, disclosure of origin, food security, food sovereignty, genetic pollution and no patents on life.

Yet, while coalition-building was an important factor in the outcome achieved in the Decision on the TRIPS Agreement and Public Health at the Doha WTO Ministerial meeting in 2001, on intellectual property-related issues of agriculture, genetic resources and traditional knowledge alliances were piecemeal and no grand coalition to mirror the access to medicines campaign ever materialized. In part this is because, on agriculture, farmers from developed countries have a very different perspective from farmers from the developing world – and tensions exist between the two groups. It is also because, on genetic resources and traditional knowledge, while links exist between international and developing country NGOs, there are relatively few groups working on these issues, making it extremely difficult to build and sustain effective coalitions.

By framing the issue as one of biopiracy – a term originally used by Pat Mooney of RAFI/ETC – the misappropriation of genetic resources could nevertheless be seen as a new form of Western imperialism in which multinational seed, pharmaceutical and biotechnology companies plunder the biodiversity and traditional knowledge of the developing world (Sell 2003, p. 140). Framed in this way, the unauthorized and uncompensated expropriation of genetic resources and traditional knowledge permits the 'theft' of genetic resources, with the derived products or processes then resold at exorbitant rates to the very people from whom they were stolen in the first place (Sell 2003, p. 140). Pat Mooney of RAFI/ETC also developed the concept of farmers' rights in 1985 as a counterweight to plant breeders' rights, introducing this principle in the FAO deliberations over plant genetic resources in the so-called 'seed wars' of the 1980s (Sell 2003, p. 144).

But while intellectual property policy-making and norm-setting activities relating to intellectual property rights, public health and access to medicines are highly emotive, NGOs working on issues relating to agriculture, genetic resources and traditional knowledge have found it harder to frame their cause in terms of pre-existing notions of human rights as has been employed so successfully in the access to medicines campaign (de Mello e Souza 2005, p. 27).

By way of comparison with the access to medicines campaign, some attempts have been made by NGOs to link farmers' rights to human rights. For example, at the second Governing Body Meeting of the ITPGRFA in Rome, from 29 October to 2 November 2007, to underpin its argument that mechanisms should be developed to link ABS frameworks under the ITPGRFA to those under the CBD, particularly Article 8(j), the CBDC network of NGOs highlighted the relationship between the Universal Declaration on Human Rights of 1948, which declares the right to food and therefore the right to life, and the fact that farmers' rights are crucial to obtaining the right to food and therefore the right to life.[84]

Yet attempts to frame farmers' rights issues as human rights or, for that matter, the human rights implications of access to genetic resources and traditional knowledge, have been nowhere near as pronounced as the linkages that have been made by NGOs between access to medicines and human rights. The harsh reality is that issues relating to agriculture, genetic resources and traditional knowledge do not carry the same resonance, nor have the same level of attention or profile, as access to medicines in the developed world.

While access to medicines is seen as a global social problem, with the public, the media and politicians in affluent developed countries readily able to engage with the concept of access to ARVs to treat people living with HIV/AIDS in the developing world, this resonance has not been possible with agriculture, genetic resources and traditional knowledge, where the direct impact of intellectual property rights is less clear, with no victims readily identifiable and the intellectual property issues involved often seen as complex, distant and moreover primarily a problem for the Global South.

In the case of agriculture, genetic resources and traditional knowledge, the absence of a sudden emergence of a crisis, such as the South African court case involving global pharmaceutical companies (discussed in Chapter 4), with a high profile in developed countries has also hindered the extent to which NGOs have been able to attract media attention, raise public awareness and subsequently put pressure on governments for reform of international intellectual property regimes.

NOTES

1. *TRIPS: Reviews, Article 27.3(b) and related issues: background and the current situation*, WTO. Available at: http://www.wto.org/english/tratop_e/trips_e/art27_3b_background_e.htm.
2. Article 6 of the UPOV Convention 1991: 'The variety shall be deemed to be new if, at the date of filing of the application for a breeder's right, propagating or harvested material of the variety has not been sold or otherwise disposed of to others, by or with the consent of the breeder, for purposes of exploitation of the variety (i) in the territory of the Contracting Party in which the application has been filed earlier than one year before that date and (ii) in a territory other than that of the Contracting Party in which the application has been filed earlier than four years or, in the case of trees or of vines, earlier than six years before the said date.'
3. Article 7 of the UPOV Convention 1991: 'The variety shall be deemed to be distinct if it is clearly distinguishable from any other variety whose existence is a matter of common knowledge at the time of the filing of the application. In particular, the filing of an application for the granting of a breeder's right or for the entering of another variety in an official register of varieties, in any country, shall be deemed to render that other variety a matter of common knowledge from the date of the application, provided that the application leads to the granting of a breeder's right or to the entering of the said other variety in the official register of varieties, as the case may be.'

4. Article 8 of the UPOV Convention 1991: 'The variety shall be deemed to be uniform if, subject to the variation that may be expected from the particular features of its propagation, it is sufficiently uniform in its relevant characteristics.'
5. Article 9 of the UPOV Convention 1991: 'The variety shall be deemed to be stable if its relevant characteristics remain unchanged after repeated propagation or, in the case of a particular cycle of propagation, at the end of each such cycle.'
6. Article 14 of the UPOV Convention 1991: '(1) [*Acts in respect of the propagating material*] *(a)* . . . the following acts in respect of the propagating material of the protected variety shall require the authorization of the breeder: (i) production or reproduction (multiplication) . . .'
7. FAO website: http://www.fao.org/ag/cgrfa/IU.htm#negotiations.
8. *Resolution 8/83, International Undertaking on Plant Genetic Resources, Twenty-Second Session of the FAO Conference – Rome, 1983.* Available at: ftp://ftp.fao.org/ag/cgrfa/Res/C8-83E.pdf.
9. Until 1995 the CGRFA was called the Commission on Plant Genetic Resources. In 1995 the name change took effect and its mandate was expanded to include all components of biodiversity of interest to food and agriculture (Stannard et al. 2004, p. 406).
10. *Resolution 9/83, Establishment of a Commission on Plant Genetic Resources, Twenty-Second Session of the FAO Conference – Rome, 1983.* Available at: ftp://ftp.fao.org/ag/cgrfa/Res/C9-83E.pdf.
11. The CGRFA holds Regular Sessions every two years. In addition, Extraordinary Sessions and Inter-Sessional meetings of the subsidiary bodies of the Commission are held as necessary. FAO Conference Resolution 3/2001 gives the CGRFA the status of the Interim Committee for the International Treaty on Plant Genetic Resources for Food and Agriculture. Source: *Meetings of the CGRFA.* Available at: http://www.fao.org/ag/cgrfa/meetings.htm.
12. The CGIAR is a strategic alliance of members, partners and international agricultural centres that mobilizes science to benefit the poor. See: http://www.cgiar.org/.
13. *Resolution 4/89, Agreed Interpretation of the International Undertaking, Twenty-Fifth Session of the FAO Conference – Rome, 1989.* Available at: ftp://ftp.fao.org/ag/cgrfa/Res/C4-89E.pdf.
14. *Resolution 5/89, Farmers' Rights, Twenty-Fifth Session of the FAO Conference – Rome, 1989.* Available at: ftp://ftp.fao.org/ag/cgrfa/Res/C5-89E.pdf.
15. *Resolution 3/91, Twenty-Sixth Session of the FAO Conference – Rome, 1991.* Available at: ftp://ftp.fao.org/ag/cgrfa/Res/C3-91E.pdf.
16. *Agenda 21: Chapter 14 – Promoting Sustainable Agriculture and Rural Development.* Available at: http://www.un.org/esa/sustdev/documents/agenda21/english/agenda21chapter14.htm.
17. *Resolution 3 of the Nairobi Conference for the Adoption of the Agreed Text of the Convention on Biological Diversity: The Interrelationship Between the Convention on Biological Diversity and the Promotion of Sustainable Development*, 22 May 1992. Available at: ftp://ftp.fao.org/ag/cgrfa/Res/CBD3E.pdf.
18 *Resolution 7/93 Revision of the International Undertaking on Plant Genetic Resources, Twenty-Seventh Session of the FAO Conference – Rome, 1993.* Available at: ftp://ftp.fao.org/ag/cgrfa/Res/C7-93E.pdf.
19. Although the scope of the International Undertaking is limited to plant genetic resources for food and agriculture, this mandate, adopted after careful negotiation, is not limited to the *ex situ* collections not addressed by the CBD. The mandate, context and background for this process are explained in the document *Commission on Plant Genetic Resources. First Extraordinary Session – Rome, 7–11 November 1994. Revision of the International Undertaking: Mandate Context, Background and Proposed Process*, CPGR-Exl/94/3. Available at: ftp://ftp.fao.org/ag/cgrfa/Ex1/E1W3E.pdf.
20. *Report of the First Extraordinary Session of the Commission on Genetic Resources for Food and Agriculture.* Available at: http://www.fao.org/ag/cgrfa/DocsEx1.htm.
21. *Documents of the Fifth Regular Session of the Commission for Genetic Resources for*

Food and Agriculture, 19–23 April 1993. Available at: http://www.fao.org/ag/cgrfa/ Docs5.htm.

22. *Report of the International Technical Conference on Plant Genetic Resources – Leipzig, 17–23 June 1996*. Available at: http://www.fao.org/ag/AGP/AGPS/Pgrfa/pdf/itcrepe. pdf.

23. *Global Plan of Action for the Conservation and Sustainable Utilisation of Plant Genetic Resources for Food and Agriculture and the Leipzig Declaration. Adopted by the International Technical Conference on Plant Genetic Resources, Leipzig, 17–23 June 1996*. Available at: ftp://ftp.fao.org/ag/cgrfa/GS/gpaE.pdf.

24. Patrick Mulvany, Practical Action, interview with the author, 6 June 2006.

25. *International Treaty on Plant Genetic Resources for Food and Agriculture*. Available at: ftp://ftp.fao.org/ag/cgrfa/it/ITPGRe.pdf.

26. *Ibid.*

27. *International Treaty on Plant Genetic Resources for Food and Agriculture* (ITPGRFA). Available at: http://www.fao.org//docrep/007/y5636e/y5636e03.htm.

28. For instance, Francois Meinberg, The Berne Declaration, interview with the author, 6 February 2006, and Patrick Mulvany, Practical Action, interview with the author, 6 June 2006. See also: *The International Treaty on Plant Genetic Resources: A Challenge for Asia*, GRAIN and Kalpavriksh (India), February 2002. Available at: http://www. grain.org/briefings/?id=37.

29. *Resolution 3 of the Nairobi Conference for the Adoption of the Agreed Text of the Convention on Biological Diversity: The Interrelationship Between the Convention on Biological Diversity and the Promotion of Sustainable Development*, 22 May 1992. Available at: ftp://ftp.fao.org/ag/cgrfa/Res/CBD3E.pdf.

30. *The Convention on Biological Diversity*. Available at: http://www.cbd.int/convention/.

31. *Bonn Guidelines on Access to Genetic Resources and Fair and Equitable Sharing of the Benefits Arising out of their Utilization*, CBD-COP 6 Decision VI/24. Available at: http://www.cbd.int/decisions/view.shtml?id=7198.

32. *Terms of Reference for the Ad Hoc Open-Ended Working Group on Access and Benefit-Sharing*, Annex to CBD-COP 7 Decision VII/19. Available at: http://www.cbd.int/decisions/view.shtml?id=7756.

33. *Bonn Guidelines on Access to Genetic Resources and Fair and Equitable Sharing of the Benefits Arising out of their Utilization*, CBD-COP 6 Decision VI/24, paragraph 10. Available at: http://www.cbd.int/decisions/view.shtml?id=7198.

34. The US has also refused to ratify the International Treaty on Plant Genetic Resources for Food and Agriculture (ITPGRFA) for similar reasons.

35. 'Protection of Biodiversity and Traditional Knowledge – The Indian Experience', *WTO Committee on Trade and Environment and Council for Trade-Related Intellectual Property Rights*, WT/CTE/W/156 and IP/C/W/198, 14 July 2000.

36. *Review of Article 27.3(b): Communication from Brazil*. Council for Trade-Related Intellectual Property Rights, IP/C/W/228, 24 November 2000. Available at: http:// docsonline.wto.org/GEN_viewerwindow.asp?http://docsonline.wto.org:80/ DDFDocuments/t/IP/C/W228.doc.

37. Doha WTO Ministerial Declaration adopted 14 November 2001, WT/MIN(01)/DEC/1. Available at: http://www.wto.org/english/thewto_e/minist_e/min01_e/mindecl_e.htm.

38. For submissions to the TRIPS Council on the review of Article 27.3(b) of the TRIPS Agreement, and the relationship between the TRIPS Agreement and the CBD and the protection of traditional knowledge see, for example, IP/C/W/356, IP/C/W/403, IP/C/W/420, IP/C/W/429, IP/C/W/438, IP/C/W/442, IP/C/W/443. Available at: http:// www.wto.org/english/tratop_e/TRIPs_e/art27_3b_e.htm.

39. For submissions to the TRIPS Council by Peru on the relationship between the TRIPS Agreement and the CBD and the protection of traditional knowledge see, for example, IP/C/W/441 and IP/C/W/447. Available at: http://www.wto.org/english/tratop_e/ TRIPs_e/art27_3b_e.htm.

40. For submissions to the TRIPS Council by the African Group on taking forward the

review of Article 27.3(b) of the TRIPS Agreement see, for example, IP/C/W/404. Available at: http://www.wto.org/english/tratop_e/TRIPs_e/art27_3b_e.htm..

41.   For submissions to the TRIPS Council by the US on Article 27.3(b), the relationship between the TRIPS Agreement and the CBD, and the protection of traditional knowledge and folklore see, for example, IP/C/W/434 and IP/C/W/434. Available at: http://www.wto.org/english/tratop_e/TRIPs_e/art27_3b_e.htm..

42.   For submissions to the TRIPS Council by Switzerland on the relationship between the TRIPS Agreement and the CBD see, for example, IP/C/W/400, IP/C/W/423, IP/C/W/433, IP/C/W/446. Available at: http://www.wto.org/english/tratop_e/TRIPs_e/art27_3b_e.htm.

43.   For submissions to the TRIPS Council by the EU on the review of Article 27.3(b) of the TRIPS Agreement, the relationship between the TRIPS Agreement and the CBD and the protection of traditional knowledge and folklore see, for example: IP/C/W/383. Available at: http://www.wto.org/english/tratop_e/TRIPs_e/art27_3b_e.htm.

44.   'Doha Work Programme – The Outstanding Implementation Issue on the Relationship between the TRIPS Agreement and the Convention on Biological Diversity', Communication from Brazil, India, Pakistan, Peru, Thailand and Tanzania, *WTO General Council Trade Negotiations Committee*, WT/GC/W/564 & TN/C/W/41, 31 May 2006.

45.   *North-South Coalition Sets Out 'Draft Modalities' on TRIPS*, International Centre for Trade and Sustainable Development, 23 July 2008. Available at: http://ictsd.net/i/p/13903/.

46.   Previously, the EU and Switzerland were sympathetic to the concept of disclosure, but not necessarily through a TRIPS amendment.

47.   The 'horizontal process' means giving sufficient reassurance that all the other negotiating issues are advancing as they should, bringing together the key elements to reach convergence on modalities. See: WTO News Item *Lamy signals start of 'horizontal process' in negotiations*, 17 April 2008.

48.   Three controversial intellectual property issues were: (i) the disclosure of the source of genetic information in patent applications; (ii) the extension of geographical indications (GIs) to all goods; and (iii) the establishment of a multilateral register for GIs for wines and spirits.

49.   *Way Forward on IP Issues at the WTO Still Unclear*, Bridges Weekly Trade Digest, Volume 13, Number 22, 17 June 2009. Available at: http://ictsd.net/i/news/bridgesweekly/49064/.

50.   'Issues Related to the Extension of the Protection of Geographical Indications Provided for in Article 23 of the TRIPS Agreement to Products other than Wines and Spirits and those Related to the Relationship between the TRIPS Agreement and the Convention on Biological Diversity', Report by the Director-General, *General Council Trade Negotiations Committee*, WT/GC/W/591 &TN/C/W/50, 9 June 2008.

51.   'Draft Modalities for TRIPS Related Issues', Communication from Albania, Brazil, China, Colombia, Ecuador, the European Communities, Iceland, India, Indonesia, the Kyrgyz Republic, Liechtenstein, the Former Yugoslav Republic of Macedonia, Pakistan, Peru, Sri Lanka, Switzerland, Thailand, Turkey, the ACP Group and the African Group, *WTO Trade Negotiations Committee*, TN/C/W/52, 19 July 2008.

52.   'TRIPS Council Discusses Biodiversity, Health, Reviews China's Implementation', *WTO News Item*, 28 October 2008. Available at: http://www.wto.org/english/news_e/news08_e/trips_28oct08_e.htm.

53.   In April 2002 the sixth meeting of the CBD-COP invited the WIPO to prepare a technical study on methods within the patent system for requiring disclosure relevant to genetic resources and traditional knowledge, and to report its findings to the seventh meeting of the COP (Decision VI/24C, paragraph 4). Following this request, a draft Study was prepared by the WIPO, based on responses to a questionnaire circulated to the Member States of the WIPO (see WIPO/GRTKF/IC/Q.3 and WIPO/GRTKF/IC/5/10).

In September 2003 the Thirtieth Session of the WIPO General Assembly approved the transmission of the WIPO Technical Study on Disclosure Requirements Concerning Genetic Resources and Traditional Knowledge (see WO/GA/30/8, paragraph 97). The seventh meeting of the COP considered and accepted the Technical Study (see UNEP/CBD/COP/7/INF/17).

The seventh meeting of the COP then invited the WIPO 'to examine, and where appropriate address, taking into account the need to ensure that this work is supportive of and does not run counter to the objectives of the CBD, issues regarding the interrelation of access to genetic resources and disclosure requirements in intellectual property rights applications, including, *inter alia*: a) Options for model provisions on proposed disclosure requirements; b) Practical options for intellectual property rights application procedures with regard to the triggers of disclosure requirements; c) Options for incentive measures for applicants; d) Identification of the implications for the functioning of disclosure requirements in various WIPO-administered treaties; e) Intellectual property-related issues raised by a proposed international certificate of origin/source/legal provenance; and regularly provide reports to the CBD on its work, in particular on actions or steps proposed to address the above issues, in order for the CBD to provide additional information to WIPO for its consideration in the spirit of mutual supportiveness.' (Decision VII/19E, paragraph 8).

54. *WIPO Hosts A Roundtable On Intellectual Property and Indigenous Peoples*, WIPO Update 98/30, Geneva, 6 August 1998. Available at: http://www.wipo.int/edocs/prdocs/en/1998/wipo_upd_1998_30.html.

55. 'Matters Concerning Intellectual Property, Genetic Resources, Traditional Knowledge and Folklore', WIPO General Assembly, Twenty-Sixth (12th Extraordinary) Session, Geneva, 25 September–3 October 2000, WO/GA/26/6, 25 August 2000, paragraphs 13 and 14. Available at: http://www.wipo.int/edocs/mdocs/govbody/en/wo_ga_26/wo_ga_26_6.pdf.

56. The draft objectives and principle of the IGC are set out in: *Intergovernmental Committee on Intellectual Property and Genetic Resources, Traditional Knowledge and Folklore, Tenth Session – The Protection of Traditional Knowledge: Draft Objectives and Principles*, Geneva, 30 November–8 December 2006, WIPO/GRTKF/IC/10/5, 2 October 2006. Available at: http://www.wipo.int/edocs/mdocs/tk/en/wipo_grtkf_ic_10/wipo_grtkf_ic_10_5.pdf.

57. *WIPO Member States Agree to Fast-Track Work on Traditional Knowledge*, WIPO Press Release PR/2003/362, Geneva, 29 September 2003. Available at: http://www.wipo.int/edocs/prdocs/en/2003/wipo_pr_2003_362.html.

58. *Intergovernmental Committee on Intellectual Property and Genetic Resources, Traditional Knowledge and Folklore, Seventh Session – Participation of Indigenous and Local Communities*, Geneva, 1–5 November 2004, WIPO/GRTKF/IC/7/12, 15 July 2004. Available at: http://www.wipo.int/edocs/mdocs/tk/en/wipo_grtkf_ic_7/wipo_grtkf_ic_7_12.pdf.

59. *Intergovernmental Committee on Intellectual Property and Genetic Resources, Traditional Knowledge and Folklore, Seventh Session - Report*, Geneva, 1–5 November 2004, WIPO/GRTKF/IC/7/15, 10 June 2005, paragraph 63(iv). Available at: http://www.wipo.int/edocs/mdocs/tk/en/wipo_grtkf_ic_7/wipo_grtkf_ic_7_15.pdf.

60. *Ibid.*, paragraph 37.

61. *Rules Governing the Granting of Observer Status to States, Intergovernmental Organisations and International Non-Governmental Organisations in UPOV Bodies and Access to UPOV Documents*, adopted by the Council, 27 October 2005, C/39/13. Available at: http://www.upov.int/en/about/members/pdf/Rules_Observer_Status_e.pdf.

62. FAO, *First Session of the Governing Body of the International Treaty on Plant Genetic Resources for Food and Agriculture*, Madrid, 12–16 June 2006, IT/GB-1/06/report. Available at: ftp://ftp.fao.org/ag/cgrfa/gb1/gb1repe.pdf.

63. *Ibid.* Annex D, Rule V.II: Observers, paragraph 7.2: 'The Secretary shall notify any other body or agency, whether governmental or non-governmental, qualified in the fields relating to the subject-matter of the Treaty, which has informed the Secretary of its wish to be represented as an observer, of the sessions of the Governing Body at least twelve weeks before the opening of the session. Such observers may, upon invitation of the Chairperson, participate without the right to vote in sessions of the Governing Body on matters of direct concern to the body or agency they represent unless at least one third of the Contracting Parties present at the session object.'

64. United Nations Non-Governmental Liaison Service (UN-NGLS) *NGLS Handbook FAO: Food and Agriculture Organisation of the United Nations.* Available at: http://www.un-ngls.org/orf/documents/publications.en/ngls.handbook/4fao.htm.

65. See, for instance, David Cooper of the FAO's Seed and Plant Genetic Resources Service, quoted in *Finding Common Ground on Protecting Genetic Resources,* World Summit News, 10–13 June 2002. Available at: http://www.fao.org/WorldFoodSummit/English/newsroom/news/6980-en.html.

66. The Berne Declaration is a Swiss NGO with 19,000 members that engages in research, public education and advocacy work. The Berne Declaration is completely independent and derives most of its revenues from membership fees and donations. Source: The Berne Declaration website. Available at: http://www.evb.ch.en/p474.html.

67. United Nations Non-Governmental Liaison Service (UN-NGLS) *NGLS Handbook FAO: Food and Agriculture Organisation of the United Nations.* Available at: http://www.un-ngls.org/orf/documents/publications.en/ngls.handbook/4fao.htm.

68. *The Right Livelihood Award – Roll of Honour.* Available at: http://www.rightlivelihood.org/recip/fowler.htm.

69. Pat Mooney, ETC, interview with the author, 19 May 2006.

70. Koos Neefjes (1992), *Gene Traders: Security or Profits in Food Production? Proceedings of an International Conference The Gene Traders: Security or Profit in Food Production?,* London: Intermediate Technology Development Group/New Economics Foundation.

71. 'Gaia Theory', the idea that the Earth is a living entity, was formulated by James Lovelock in the 1960s and 1970s. The stimulus for creating a Gaia Foundation then came in the early 1980s when Liz Hosken, Edward Posey and a group of ecological pioneers from developing countries, including Prof. Wangari Maathai (Kenya) and José Lutzenberger (Brazil) put into practice their common vision of demonstrating how human development and wellbeing are derived from the health and understanding of the living planet (Gaia), by establishing a network of associates, advisors and partner organizations. Gaia works at all levels, from the grassroots with peasant farmers and indigenous communities, through to the regional and international level with policy-makers and governments. Source: *GAIA Foundation – About Us.* Available at: http://www.gaiafoundation.org/about/about.php.

72. Patrick Mulvany, Practical Action, interview with the author, 6 June 2006.

73. US Patent No. 5,894,079. The abstract of the patent reads as follows: 'This invention relates to a new field bean variety that produces distinctly colored yellow seed which remain relatively unchanged by season. The invention also relates to a method for producing a field bean plant by crossing a first parent field bean plant with a second parent field bean plant, wherein the first and/or second field bean plant is the field bean plant of the present invention.'

74. *Enola Bean Patent Challenged: International Center for Tropical Agriculture (CIAT) Upholds FAO Trust Agreement and UN Biodiversity Convention by Challenging US Patent on Mexico's Yellow Bean,* RAFI News Release, 5 January 2001. Available at: http://www.etcgroup.org/en/materials/publications.html?id=286.

75. The CGIAR network includes the International Center for Tropical Agriculture (CIAT), based in Cali, California. CIAT's gene bank holds more than 27,000 samples of *Phaseolus* (dry bean) seeds, among other crop species. See: http://www.ciat.cgiar.org/.

76. *Hollow Victory: Enola Bean Patent Smashed At Last (Maybe),* ETC Group News

Release, 29 April 2008. Available at: http://www.etcgroup.org/en/materials/publications.html?pub_id=683.

77. Pat Mooney, ETC, interview with the author, 19 May 2006.
78. Geoff Tansey, interview with the author, 15 November 2005.
79. Julia Oliva, CIEL, interview with the author, 22 November 2005.
80. *The International Planning Committee for Food Sovereignty: Food Sovereignty – A Right for All.* Available at: http://www.foodsovereignty.org/downloads/Template%20 IPC%20colours.doc.
81. Chee Yoke Ling, TWN, interview with the author, 28 April 2006.
82. Chee Yoke Ling, TWN, interview with the author, 28 April 2006.
83. Rachel Wynberg, Biowatch, interview with the author, 7 December 2005.
84. Statement of the CBDC Network on the occasion of the 2nd Governing Body Meeting of the International Treaty on Plant Genetic Resources for Food and Agriculture, 29 October–2 November 2007, Rome, Italy.

4. South Africa

INTRODUCTION

In 1994 South Africa emerged from the traumatic period of apartheid (separateness) that had been in force since 1948. Under apartheid, the rights of the majority non-white inhabitants had been curtailed and minority white rule maintained on racial grounds. Following the end of apartheid, events in South Africa proved crucial in highlighting the complex relationship between intellectual property rights and development. South African NGOs played a particularly significant role in this process in two respects.

First, NGOs campaigned to improve access to anti-retroviral drugs (ARVs) for people living with HIV/AIDS in South Africa. The activities of NGOs, based on a strategy of building coalitions, framing the issue in terms of human rights, and utilizing litigation strategies developed during the apartheid era, have had an immense impact on the debate about the relationship between intellectual property rights and public health and access to medicines. This impact has been felt not only in South Africa but also internationally, highlighting to the world's media, governments and public how and why intellectual property rights can become a barrier to access to medicines for disadvantaged people living in developing countries.

Second, South African NGOs intervened with significant effect to address the relationship between intellectual property rights and genetic resources and traditional knowledge. They did so by negotiating an agreement on the sharing of benefits derived from the commercial use of the succulent *Hoodia gordonii*. The beneficial properties of *Hoodia gordonii* as an appetite suppressant have been known to the indigenous San peoples of the Kalahari in Southern Africa for centuries and constitute an important part of their traditional knowledge.

Following the granting of a patent on an appetite suppressant derived of an extract of the *Hoodia gordonii* succulent to a South African research institute, human rights lawyers intervened and negotiated on behalf of the San people of South Africa an access and benefit sharing (ABS) agreement. These lawyers had been active in support of disadvantaged people in South Africa since the days of the anti-apartheid struggle but they were not intellectual property specialists. Initially the agreement they negotiated was hailed as a step forward in the recognition of the collective rights of indigenous communities as holders of biodiversity-related traditional knowledge by providing a model of what could be done not only in South Africa but also throughout the developing world. Subsequently, however, the deal has been criticized on a number of levels that will be discussed in the second half of this chapter.

At the outset it should be acknowledged that the recent history of anti-apartheid struggle affected profoundly how South Africa has developed a culture of social activism in relation to intellectual property-related issues and how NGOs have embraced and utilized principles of human rights in articulating their concerns. The end of the apartheid regime also had a short-term negative effect on the NGO movement. It led to many talented and experienced former activists who were trusted for their commitment to the struggle leaving the activist movement to take up positions in the South African government. However, initial expectations that having former anti-apartheid activists in government would create a better, fairer system and inform the policy-making process were tempered by a realization that former activists appointed to government are often reluctant to appear disloyal by speaking out against government policy.

This meant, for instance, that NGOs confronting government with arguments that it was failing people living with HIV/AIDS by refusing to make available patented ARVs faced difficulties because they were dealing with government officials they had been working alongside during the anti-apartheid struggle and who had then taken up a different view of how post-apartheid South Africa should address the pandemic.

On the other hand, those activists who remained in the NGO community post-apartheid in South Africa, and new activists who joined them subsequently, became increasingly adept at addressing issues relating to intellectual property rights in an extremely sophisticated way. In this respect, the South African experience is ahead of most other sub-Saharan African countries, where NGOs have been slower to acquire the specialist knowledge on intellectual property rights that would enable them to engage effectively with issues such as public health and access to medicines, or agriculture, genetic resources and traditional knowledge.

ACCESS TO ANTI-RETROVIRAL DRUGS FOR PEOPLE LIVING WITH HIV/AIDS

HIV/AIDS in South Africa

AIDS is the leading cause of mortality in the country. In 2001, approximately 200 000 people were dying of AIDS or AIDS-related illness each year (Boulle and Avafia 2005, p. 14) and by 2008 there were an estimated 5.7 million adults living with HIV/AIDS in South Africa, about 18 per cent of all people between the ages of 15 and 49 (UNAIDS 2008).

The wider socio-economic costs of HIV/AIDS for South Africa have also had catastrophic implications. HIV/AIDS leads to a loss of household income due to illness or death of a household member and time spent on caring. In economic terms, it is the poor who are the worst affected by HIV/AIDS since in situations of minimal income these additional costs cannot be absorbed easily by the family, resulting in increasing poverty and deteriorating food security (Boulle and Avafia 2005, p. 14). It is often women who bear the increased responsibilities of caring for ill household members and for orphaned children, in addition to their other domestic and economic responsibilities (SIDA 2001).

The socio-economic costs of HIV/AIDS are exacerbated by AIDS denialism, social stigmatization, fear of violence and other social realities such as exclusion. The tragic case of Gugu Dlamini, a 36-year-old South African woman, sums up the extent of these problems. After disclosing that she was HIV positive, Gugu Dlamini was beaten to death in December 1998 outside a shebeen in KwaManchinza, an informal settlement near KwaMashu, a town in eastern KwaZulu-Natal province where an estimated 20 to 30 per cent of the population were at that time living with HIV or AIDS.[1]

The murder of Dlamini, who was survived by her 13-year-old daughter, galvanized many community leaders and organizations at the grassroots level to begin an information campaign about HIV/AIDS. The resulting campaign, called the KwaMashu Aids Action Forum, aimed to educate the local population about how AIDS is transmitted, how to prevent transmission and what to do once the disease has been contracted.[2]

Despite the horrendous loss of human life and the socio-economic costs of HIV/AIDS for South Africa, the government's response to the HIV/AIDS crisis was initially controversially slow. South African President Thabo Mbeki, for instance, questioned whether AIDS was caused by HIV and said that it was not certain that ARV drugs were safe and effective. He denied knowing anyone who had died of AIDS, despite so many South Africans succumbing to the virus. This institutional AIDS denialism had terrible implications for the provision of ARVs for people living with HIV/AIDS in South Africa.[3]

The Treatment Action Campaign

The catalyst for NGO activism to challenge the government's inaction came on 10 December 1998 – Human Rights Day. That day a group of about 15 people protested on the steps of St George's Cathedral in Cape Town, demanding ARVs for people living with HIV/AIDS (Boulle and Avafia 2005, p. 15). By the end of the day a new NGO, the Treatment Action Campaign (TAC) had been created and over 1000 people had signed up as supporters.

TAC's formation was grounded in on a distinctly post-apartheid period of South Africa's history when human rights issues were particularly to the fore and, by linking the right to health to human rights principles, TAC shared historical continuities with the late 1980s' and early 1990s' anti-apartheid and gay rights activism. The objectives of TAC were set out in clause 4 of its constitution. These included campaigning for equitable access to affordable treatment for all people with HIV/AIDS and challenging, by means of litigation, lobbying, advocacy, and all forms of legitimate social mobilization, any barrier or obstacle that limits access to treatment for HIV/AIDS (see also Fourie 2006, p. 130).[4]

To achieve these objectives, TAC's campaigns framed access to ARVs for people living with HIV/AIDS as a human right (Boulle and Avafia 2005, p. 23; Halbert 2005, p. 108; Mbali, 2005, p. 2) using to great effect the language and principles of human rights enshrined in the South African Constitution to do so.

Grassroots activism is at the heart of TAC's activities. TAC's membership has grown to approximately 10 000 individual volunteers organized within 220 branches nationwide. At the end of each year, many of these members attend the TAC Annual Congress and hold the national leadership to account – the members are reportedly fierce and demanding of the TAC leadership. Throughout the year, TAC volunteers also attend branch meetings, organize events, participate in campaigns and mobilize others in their communities. TAC therefore draws its legitimacy to speak for and on behalf of people living with HIV/AIDS in South Africa directly from the strength of the grassroots activism of the organization. It is also able to mobilize activists to demonstrate publicly in support of its campaigns.

Another important aspect of TAC's strategy has been building coalitions both domestically and internationally (see also Friedman and Mottair 2004, p. 20; Siplon 2002, p. 119). Domestically, TAC has aligned itself with the Congress of South African Trade Unions (COSATU), which is the largest labour union federation in South Africa with approximately two million members. TAC's relationship with COSATU has been very important to both organizations and is a good example of how partners with at times fairly divergent views can continue to find areas of common concern (Boulle and Avafia 2005, p. 40).

TAC has also developed a very close partnership with the AIDS Law Project (ALP), which has undertaken legal work on TAC's behalf, as will be discussed later in this chapter. In addition, TAC has worked closely with the AIDS Consortium, the Children's Rights Centre, the National Coalition for Gay and Lesbian Equality, the National Education, Health and Allied Workers Union (NEHAWU) and a number of religious groups, including the South African Council of Churches.

Internationally, TAC has developed a good profile and the extent of its international activities and collaborations has been impressive (Boulle and Avafia 2005, p. 34). The main focus has been on building a coalition of activists on the African continent via the Pan-African Treatment and Access Movement (PATAM), which was set up in June 2002. Passing on TAC's experience by building a coalition of activists under the umbrella of PATAM has been a key priority (Friedman and Mottair 2004, p. 21) and TAC has helped to coordinate the work of PATAM, with the result that there is an ever growing sharing of information on treatment-related issues via PATAM email list server. Learning from the experience of TAC has proved invaluable to other access-to-treatment organizations building their technical expertise on HIV/AIDS-related issues elsewhere on the African continent (Boulle and Avafia 2005, p. 41).

TAC has also built coalitions outside Africa with international NGOs. For the most part, international NGOs regard TAC highly and partnerships have been worthwhile. Its partnership with MSF, for example, has been important in helping TAC to develop as an organization. In some instances, MSF has also provided a direct service to TAC members, for example by bringing ARVs into South Africa and providing direct support to TAC by training its staff.

TAC has been financed by donations from individuals and organizations including the Australian Foundation of AIDS Organizations, MSF, Oxfam, the European Coalition of Positive People and the South African Development Fund/Arca Foundation. It does not accept money from drug companies or the South African government. But, by its own admission, TAC has been too reliant on a small pool of international donors, and has attempted to diversify its funding base to include local corporate and individual donations (Boulle and Avafia 2005, p. 36).

TAC's strategy of utilizing the human rights principles enshrined in South Africa's constitution (see also de Waal 2006, p. 36) and framing issues in the language of human rights and constitutional obligations (Fourie 2006, p. 163) is consistent with the personal experiences of Zackie Achmat, its chairperson. Achmat was active in the United Democratic Front (UDF) during the later apartheid years in South Africa and used non-violent methods of political activism that included strikes and demonstrations. While never ceding the legitimacy of the apartheid government, UDF activists used the law to challenge every aspect of racist and arbitrary rule (de Waal 2006, p. 36). Informed by experience, TAC has developed its human rights approach from an initial framing of the issues to litigation based on human rights principles enshrined in the South African Constitution, working closely with lawyers based in the Law and Treatment Access Unit of the ALP to achieve its objectives.

AIDS Law Project

The ALP is a human rights organization that seeks to influence, develop and use the law to address human rights implications of HIV/AIDS in South Africa, regionally and internationally.[5] As with TAC, the ALP's human rights approach grew out of the experiences of the anti-apartheid struggle. Mark Heywood, project head of the ALP, for example, was involved in the anti-apartheid movement for a decade and was also a member of the UDF. Originally based at the University of Witwatersrand in Johannesburg, the ALP believes that the progressive realization of a set of human rights principles is fundamental to achieving sustainable progress in tackling the HIV/AIDS pandemic. It uses a variety of legal approaches to put these human rights principles into practice in order to protect, promote and advance the rights of people living with HIV/AIDS, and to change the socio-economic and other conditions that lead to the spread of HIV/AIDS and its disproportionate impact on the poor (AIDS Law Project 2007, p. 4).

The ALP believes that empowering vulnerable people living with or affected by HIV/AIDS with knowledge of the law and human rights is effective and sustainable in tackling the epidemic. To this end, it works in partnership with TAC to educate and train people about law, human rights and how they can use the legal framework (AIDS Law Project 2007, p. 4), as evidenced by the cases outlined below.

The High Court Challenge to the South African Medicines and Related Substances Control Amendment Act 1997

On 1 March 2001, 39 global pharmaceutical companies, represented by the Pharmaceutical Manufacturers Association (PMA) of South Africa, brought an action before the High Court of South Africa (Transvaal

Provincial Division).[6] The action concerned Section 10 of the South African Medicines and Related Substances Control Amendment Act 1997, which added Section 15C to the 1965 Medicines and Related Substances Control Act and gave the Health Minister significant powers to issue compulsory licences and allow parallel imports of patented pharmaceutical products in order to increase availability and lower the cost of medicines (see also Orbinski 2008, p. 355).

SECTION 15C OF THE MEDICINES AND RELATED SUBSTANCES CONTROL ACT 101 OF 1965 (AS AMENDED BY THE MEDICINES AND RELATED SUBSTANCES CONTROL AMENDMENT ACT 90 OF 1997): MEASURES TO ENSURE SUPPLY OF MORE AFFORDABLE MEDICINES

The Minister may prescribe conditions for the supply of more affordable medicines in certain circumstances so as to protect the health of the public, and in particular may –

(a) notwithstanding anything to the contrary contained in the Patents Act, 1978 (Act 57 of 1978), determine that the rights with regard to any medicine under a patent granted in the Republic shall not extend to acts in respect of such medicine which has been put onto the market by the owner of the medicine, or with his or her consent;

(b) prescribe the conditions on which any medicine which is identical in composition, meets the same quality standard and is intended to have the same proprietary name as that of another medicine already registered in the Republic, but which is imported by a person other than the person who is the holder of the registration certificate of the medicine already registered and which originates from any site of manufacture of the original manufacturer as approved by the council in the prescribed manner, may be imported;

(c) prescribe the registration procedure for, as well as the use of, the medicine referred to in paragraph (b).

What the South African legislation appeared to lack were the detailed provisions required by Article 31 of the TRIPS Agreement, particularly the requirement that compulsory licences be granted only on a non-exclusive and non-assignable basis, with the possibility of judicial review and with adequate remuneration for the right holder (Matthews 2004, p. 79). The complaint of the PMA was that the compatibility of the South African compulsory licensing provisions with Article 31 of the TRIPS Agreement was difficult to ascertain conclusively since the provisions of the South African Amendment Act were so ambiguous. The case also attracted particular attention because access to patented ARV drugs for the treatment of HIV/AIDS, such as AZT (Zidovudine), was constrained by the prohibitively high price of those medicines in South Africa.

While preparations for the High Court case were underway, the Thirteenth International AIDS Conference took place in Durban, South Africa, on 9–14 July 2000, marking the first time the event had been held in a developing country. The Conference was opened by South African President Thabo Mbeki, who argued that extreme poverty rather than AIDS was the leading killer in sub-Saharan Africa. Juxtaposed against this view was a speech by South African High Court Justice Edwin Cameron who had been open about his HIV-positive status for some time and argued that such complacency was comparable to supporting a system as wrong as Nazi Germany or apartheid South Africa (Siplon 2002, p. 111).

By bringing the HIV/AIDS crisis in South Africa so sharply into focus, the Conference provided the stimulus to consolidate opposition to the lawsuit in a concerted way, building an international NGO and grassroots coalition in opposition to the PMA complaint. The conference radically shifted attitudes to the relationship between intellectual property rights and access to medicines in developing countries and strengthened the global NGO coalition on the access to medicines campaign (Cameron and Berger 2005, p. 356).

At the opening of the High Court case TAC obtained permission to intervene in the proceedings as *amicus curiae*, or a friend of the court. This turned a dry legal contest into a matter about human lives. The global NGO access to medicines campaign also added to the pressure on the PMA to withdraw the lawsuit. International NGOs such as MSF and Oxfam helped ensure the story had a high public profile around the world. Oxfam's campaigning work, for example, received extensive global coverage which helped raise awareness (Mayne 2002, p. 249). Other international NGOs helped by organizing campaigns and lobbying petitions, and writing letters to governments and industry, calling on the pharmaceutical companies to withdraw from the case. Company directors were publicly named and shamed in press briefings. MSF, for instance, presented a petition with 250 000 signatures to the South African PMA. The South African court case, more than any other, was the event that ignited public concern about the impact of intellectual property rights on access to medicines (see also Mayne 2002, p. 249).

In the face of intense media attention and adverse public opinion, the PMA abandoned the High Court action but by then the case had brought the link between intellectual property rights, public health and the access to medicines to the fore in public consciousness, not only in South Africa but also on a global scale. The case had focused global attention on the catastrophic impact of HIV/AIDS in Africa and the problems that patents could cause for public health and access to medicines. It had acted as a trigger for international NGOs and grassroots activists to engage with the debate on the relationship between intellectual property rights and development in a way that had not previously been apparent (see also Halbert 2005, p. 89).

The National Economic Development and Labour Council

After effectively supporting the South African government in the face of global pharmaceutical companies' complaint about Section 15C of the South African Medicines and Related Substances Control Amendment Act, TAC and COSATU then attempted to use the National Economic Development and Labour Council (NEDLAC) as a stakeholder forum in which to put their views across. In particular, they attempted to negotiate with the government a strategic plan to roll out highly active antiretroviral therapy (HAART) and mother to child transmission (MTCT) prevention throughout South Africa.[7] The outcome was initially successful. A plan was agreed that would potentially reduce by nearly 3 million the number of HIV-related deaths between 2002 and 2015, halve the number of children that will otherwise be orphaned by the HIV epidemic by 2015, and produce an average life expectancy in South Africa of approximately 50 years of age as opposed to 40 years in the absence of such interventions (Fourie 2006, p. 165).

However, after the plan had been agreed by NEDLAC, the South African government refused to endorse it. TAC and COSATU responded by starting a national campaign of grassroots action and legal challenges (Fourie 2006, p. 166). In the face of this opposition, in November 2003 the government relented and announced an Operational Plan for HIV and AIDS Care and Treatment for South Africa to roll out HAART and MTCT programmes. Yet implementation of the Operational Plan remained slow (Fourie 2006, p. 166).

Minister of Health & Others v. Treatment Action Campaign & Others

The most effective ARV for the prevention of MTCT is Nevirapine, the patent for which is owned by the German pharmaceutical company Boehringer Ingelheim (BI).[8] In 2001 BI had offered to donate Nevirapine to South Africa at no cost. The South African government had nonetheless declined this offer and refused to adopt a full-scale Nevirapine treatment programme for HIV-infected pregnant women on the grounds that the ARV's efficacy and side-effects had not been adequately studied by the government's pilot programmes. The Ministry of Health also contended that treatment would not prevent infected mothers from transmitting the virus through breast feeding and that it did not have sufficient resources to provide the counselling and monitoring required by treatment programmes (de Mello e Souza 2005, p. 247).

As a result, in July 2002, TAC and its allies brought a legal action before the Pretoria High Court in *Minister of Health & Others v. Treatment Action Campaign & Others*.[9] The complaint concerned the refusal of the South African government to make Nevirapine available in the public health sector and not setting out a timeframe for a national programme to prevent MTCT of HIV.

The applicants (TAC, Dr Haroon Saloojee and the Children's Rights Centre, together with the Institute for Democracy in South Africa, First Amicus Curiae, the Community Law Centre, Second Amicus Curiae, and the Cotlands Baby Sanctuary, Third Amicus Curiae) contended that restrictions on the availability of Nevirapine were unreasonable when measured against the human rights principles of the South African Constitution.

The Constitution commands the state and all its organs to give effect to the rights guaranteed in the Bill of Rights, in particular: Sections 27(1), 27(2) and 28(1).[10]

SECTION 27 OF THE CONSTITUTION OF THE REPUBLIC OF SOUTH AFRICA 1996: HEALTH CARE, FOOD, WATER AND SOCIAL SECURITY

(1) Everyone has the right to have access to–

(a) health care services, including reproductive health care;
(b) sufficient food and water; and
(c) social security, including, if they are unable to support themselves and their dependants, appropriate social assistance.

(2) The state must take reasonable legislative and other measures, within its available resources, to achieve the progressive realisation of each of these rights.
(3) No one may be refused emergency medical treatment.

SECTION 28 OF THE CONSTITUTION OF THE REPUBLIC OF SOUTH AFRICA 1996: CHILDREN

(1) Every child has the right–

> *(a)* to a name and a nationality from birth;
> *(b)* to family care or parental care, or to appropriate alternative care when removed from the family environment;
> *(c)* to basic nutrition, shelter, basic health care services and social services;
> *(d)* to be protected from maltreatment, neglect, abuse or degradation;
> *(e)* to be protected from exploitative labour practices;
> *(f)* not to be required or permitted to perform work or provide services that–
> > (i) are inappropriate for a person of that child's age; or
> > (ii) place at risk the child's well-being, education, physical or mental health or spiritual, moral or social development;
>
> *(g)* not to be detained except as a measure of last resort, in which case, in addition to the rights a child enjoys under sections 12 and 35, the child may be detained only for the shortest appropriate period of time, and has the right to be–
> > (i) kept separately from detained persons over the age of 18 years; and
> > (ii) treated in a manner, and kept in conditions, that take account of the child's age;
>
> *(h)* to have a legal practitioner assigned to the child by the state, and at state expense, in civil proceedings affecting the child, if substantial injustice would otherwise result; and
> *(i)* not to be used directly in armed conflict, and to be protected in times of armed conflict.

(2) A child's best interests are of paramount importance in every matter concerning the child.
(3) In this section 'child' means a person under the age of 18 years.

Finding in favour of the applicants, the South African Constitutional Court held that Sections 27(1) and (2) of the Constitution require the government to devise and implement within its available resources a comprehensive and co-ordinated programme to realize progressively the rights of pregnant women and their newborn children to have access to health services to combat MTCT of HIV. The Court also confirmed that the state is obliged to ensure that children are accorded the protection contemplated by Section 28(1)(c) of the Constitution. The South African government was ordered to remove the restrictions that prevent Nevirapine from being made available for the purpose of reducing the risk of MTCT of HIV without delay.

By seeking recourse to the human rights principles enshrined in the South African Constitution, TAC and its allies had succeeded not only in improving access to Nevirapine but also in creating an alternative moral framework for understanding the relationship between patents, access to medicines and human life.

This changed the discourse not only in South Africa but on patents and access to medicines internationally. The rights of people living with HIV/AIDS to have access to ARVs came to be more widely seen as an inalienable human right distinct from the temporary property right associated with intellectual property. Thus, the debate over the implications of intellectual property rights for development were no longer simply framed in terms of the prevention of piracy and counterfeiting and the benefits of the patent system as a stimulus for innovation, but also about balancing that system with the fundamental human rights to life and to health care.

Hazel Tau and Others v. GlaxoSmithKline and Boehringer Ingelheim

A few months after initiating the Nevirapine case, in September 2002, TAC demonstrated a willingness to broaden its litigation strategy beyond recourse to human rights principles. Competition law was also to be used to challenge global pharmaceutical companies and secure access to ARVs for people living with HIV/AIDS.

The complaint to South Africa's Competition Commission in *Hazel Tau and Others v. GlaxoSmithKline and Boehringer Ingelheim* arose when 11 complainants (joined in February 2003 by a further two new complainants), brought an action against GlaxoSmithKline (GSK) and BI. They alleged that the two companies were acting in violation of competition law by charging excessive prices for their ARV medicines and because of this they were directly responsible for the premature, predictable and avoidable loss of life, including of people living with HIV/AIDS (see also Avafia et al. 2006, p. 37; Berger 2006, p. 197).[11]

GSK marketed and sold several ARVs and fixed-dose combination ARV drugs authorized for use in South Africa. These were: zidovudine

(AZT), branded as Retrovir®; lamivudine, branded as 3TC®; abacavir (ABC), branded as Ziagen®; amprevavir, branded as Preclir®; and AZT/lamivudine, branded as Combivir®, a popular fixed-dose combination that helps to reduce the number of pills or capsules that patients have to take each day. BI distributed one ARV in South Africa: Nevirapine, branded as Viramune®.

Both GSK and BI had granted licences to generic drug company Aspen Pharmacare to manufacture and sell these patented ARVs in return for royalty payments that were in some cases as high as 40 per cent. In the case of GSK, sales by Aspen Pharmacare were also permitted only to the South African public sector.

Five of the 11 complainants were people living with HIV/AIDS: Hazel Tau; Nontsikelelo Patricia Zwedala; Sindiswa Godwana; Issac Mthuthuzeli Skosana; and Matomela Paul Ngubane (a policeman, who died of AIDS-related complications on 16 June 2003 before the case was resolved). A further four of the complainants were healthcare workers with experience of the impact of HIV/AIDS on patients: Sister Susan Roberts; Dr William Nkhangweni Mmbara, Dr Steven Murray Andrews; and Dr Willem Daniel Francois Venter. Two of the complainants represented organized labour: COSATU; and the Chemical, Energy, Paper, Printing, Wood and Allied Workers Union (CEPPWAWU), while the final two of the complainants were organizations working directly in the area of HIV/AIDS: TAC; and the AIDS Consortium.[12]

In addition, organizations including Action for Southern Africa (ACTSA),[13] Oxfam International, MSF, the Canadian HIV/AIDS Legal Network, the Consumer Project on Technology (CPTech) and the Council for Medical Schemes provided support and advice to the complainants.[14] James Love of CPTech, for instance, was asked by the complainants to submit an expert affidavit on R&D costs. In his affidavit, Love used hard data to argue that the actual costs of R&D spent by drug companies in respect of many ARVs cannot be more than a small fraction of the figures claimed by the industry.[15]

Bringing their action under Section 49B(2)(b) of the South African Competition Act, which permits 'any person' to 'submit a complaint against an alleged prohibited practice', the complainants alleged that, contrary to Section 8(a) of the Competition Act, which prohibits dominant firms from charging 'an excessive price'.[16]

An excessive price is defined as a price for a good or service which bears no reasonable relation to the economic value of that good or service and is higher than the economic value. The complainants argued that the prices charged for certain ARV medicines by GSK and BI were directly responsible for the 'premature, predictable and avoidable deaths of people

SECTION 8 OF THE SOUTH AFRICAN COMPETITION ACT: ABUSE OF DOMINANCE PROHIBITED

It is prohibited for a dominant *firm* to–

    (a) charge an *excessive price* to the detriment of consumers;

    (b) refuse to give a competitor access to an *essential facility* when it is economically feasible to do so;

    (c) engage in an *exclusionary act*, other than an act listed in paragraph (d), if the anti-competitive effect of that act outweighs its technological, efficiency or other pro-competitive gain; or

    (d) engage in any of the following *exclusionary acts*, unless the *firm* concerned can show technological, efficiency or other pro-competitive gains which outweigh the anti-competitive effect of its act–

        (i) requiring or inducing a supplier or customer to not deal with a competitor;

        (ii) refusing to supply scarce goods to a competitor when supplying those goods is economically feasible;

        (iii) selling *goods or services* on condition that the buyer purchases separate *goods or services* unrelated to the object of a contract, or forcing a buyer to accept a condition unrelated to the object of a contract;

        (iv) selling *goods or services* below their marginal or average variable cost; or

        (v) buying-up a scarce supply of intermediate goods or resources required by a competitor.

living with HIV/AIDS'[17] and that, even when full allowance was made for the costs of research and development, the prices charged were excessive (Avafia et al. 2006, p. 27). The complainants also argued that the constitutional guarantee of access to health care services was not being upheld.[18]

The complainants alleged that the companies had engaged in excessive pricing of ARVs to the detriment of consumers, as prohibited by section 8(a) of the Competition Act, and that the excessive pricing was directly responsible for the premature, predictable and avoidable deaths of people living with HIV/AIDS, including both children and adults. The focus on excessive pricing was intentional since the complainants believed that, if framed in these terms, it was likely to elicit broad public support without having to challenge the patent system head on, while still focusing on the abuse of exclusive rights in patents (Berger 2006, p. 198).

The litigation was accompanied by a robust and well orchestrated public campaign by the TAC (Boulle and Avafia 2005, p. 25). A publication and numerous press releases, fact sheets and advertisements were produced.[19] Other activities designed to achieve a high profile for the case were legal literacy workshops, at which the technical aspects of the case were explained, and high profile events such as the first South African AIDS Conference held in August 2003, to mobilize the public and raise awareness of the case (Avafia et al. 2006, p. 30).

Settlement negotiations with GSK began on 11 September 2003 although, at that time, BI did not enter into negotiations to find a mutually agreeable solution. Two events then changed the landscape. On 26 September 2003, the TAC Treatment Project, together with another non-profit organization, the Generic Anti-Retroviral Procurement Project, formally requested non-exclusive voluntary licences from BI 'to import generic Nevirapine for use in combination antiretroviral therapy', notifying BI that failing that they would seek compulsory licences in court.[20] The request followed earlier attempts by TAC and MSF South Africa to obtain voluntary licences for Nevirapine in 1999 and 2001 respectively. Nevirapine is used to reduce the risk of mother-to-child HIV transmission and is considered an essential component of triple drug therapy for pregnant women with HIV/AIDS.

On 16 October 2003 the Competition Commission announced that it had decided to refer the complaint to the Competition Tribunal for adjudication. The Commission's investigation had revealed that GSK and BI had contravened the Competition Act of 1988 by refusing to license their patents on ARVs to generic manufacturers in return for a reasonable royalty.[21] More specifically, GSK and BI were found to have abused their dominant positions in their respective ARV markets by engaging in restrictive practices consisting of: first, denying a competitor access to an essential facility; second, excessive pricing; and, third, engaging in an exclusionary act. According to the Commission, GSK and BI were using their exclusive patent rights to deny appropriate licences to other manufacturers, whilst simultaneously keeping their own prices high.

The Commission referred the matter to the Competition Tribunal and asked it to make an order authorizing any person to be able to exploit the patents to market generic medicines or fixed dose combinations that require the patents, on return for the payment of a reasonable royalty. The Commission also recommended a penalty of 10 per cent of the annual turnover of GSK and BI's sale of ARVs in South Africa for each year that they were found to have violated the Act.[22] Based on the evidence gathered during this investigation, the Competition Commission decided to refer the case of *Hazel Tau and Others* to the Competition Tribunal for adjudication.

Then, on 10 December 2003, the Competition Commission announced that it had concluded a settlement agreement with GSK which resulted in the grant of non-exclusive royalty-free voluntary licences and that it was in discussions with BI, also regarding a settlement agreement. At the time the complaint was lodged, both GSK and BI had already granted licences to South African pharmaceutical company Aspen Pharmacare, but the terms and conditions had been found by the Competition Commission to be unacceptable (Berger 2006, p. 199). Under the terms of the settlement agreement with GSK, the company undertook to: extend the voluntary licence granted previously to Aspen Pharmacare in respect of the public sector to include the private sector; grant up to three more voluntary licences on terms no less favourable than those granted to Aspen Pharmacare, based on reasonable criteria which include registration with the Medicines Control Council and the meeting of safety and efficacy obligations; permit the licensees to export the relevant ARV drugs to sub-Saharan African countries; where the licensee did not have the manufacturing capacity in South Africa, GSK would permit the importation of the drugs for distribution in South Africa; permit the licensees to combine the relevant ARV with other antiretroviral medicines; and charge royalties of no more than 5 per cent of the net sales of the relevant ARVs.[23]

GSK and BI subsequently confirmed that they had voluntarily entered into separate agreements with the complainants.[24] The licence to Aspen Pharmacare was amended in accordance with the settlement agreement to extend sales to the private sector, also allowing for exports to all sub-Saharan African countries and a royalty rate of not more than 5 per cent. By the end of 2004, GSK and BI had licensed to five and three generic manufacturers respectively (Avafia et al. 2006, p. 32). This resulted in significantly lower prices and improved sustainability of supply for the pharmaceutical products involved (Berger 2006, p. 199).

GSK and BI had decided to settle out of court rather than face a protracted public hearing. For their part, the complainants chose to abandon a particularly strong case in favour of a relatively speedy resolution in a pragmatic manner that was not to the liking of CPTech. The case thus resulted in the reduction of royalty fees paid by generic companies to brand name pharmaceutical companies from as high as 40 per cent to 5 per cent for ARVs (Boulle and Avafia 2005, p. 25).

It also had the secondary effect of increasing pressure on the South

African government to commit itself to the development and implementation of a public sector ARV treatment programme. In fact, the Operational Plan for Comprehensive HIV and AIDS Care, Management and Treatment for South Africa (hereafter the Operational Plan) was adopted on 19 November 2003, some 20 days before the complainant entered into settlement agreements with both GSK and BI (Avafia et al. 2006, p. 28).[25] The case had shown that competition law could be used to great effect, particularly when developing country governments are either unwilling or unable to act (Berger 2006, p. 199).

The 'Annexure A' Case

The least successful instances of litigation undertaken by TAC have occurred when public support did not occur and where TAC's own membership was not fully engaged with the facts of the case. Using the constitutional right of access to information enshrined in *TAC v. Minister of Health* (the 'Annexure A' case), for example, TAC focused on a legal technicality in an attempt to secure a copy of the government's implementation plan.[26]

The right of access to information is set out in Section 32.1 of the Constitution, which provides that everyone has the right of access to any information held by the state or by another person.

SECTION 32.1 OF THE CONSTITUTION OF THE REPUBLIC OF SOUTH AFRICA, 1996: ACCESS TO INFORMATION

(1) Everyone has the right of access to–

(a) any information held by the state; and
(b) any information that is held by another person and that is required for the exercise or protection of any rights.

(2) National legislation must be enacted to give effect to this right, and may provide for reasonable measures to alleviate the administrative and financial burden on the state.

In addition, Section 195.1 of the Constitution requires that public administration must be governed by the democratic values and principles including, under sub-paragraph (g), the principle that transparency must be fostered by providing the public with timely, accessible and accurate information.

SECTION 195.1 OF THE CONSTITUTION OF THE REPUBLIC OF SOUTH AFRICA, 1996

Basic values and principles governing public administration.

(1) Public administration must be governed by the democratic values and principles enshrined in the Constitution, including the following principles:

> *(a)* A high standard of professional ethics must be promoted and maintained.
> *(b)* Efficient, economic and effective use of resources must be promoted.
> *(c)* Public administration must be development-oriented.
> *(d)* Services must be provided impartially, fairly, equitably and without bias.
> *(e)* People's needs must be responded to, and the public must be encouraged to participate in policy-making.
> *(f)* Public administration must be accountable.
> *(g)* Transparency must be fostered by providing the public with timely, accessible and accurate information.
> *(h)* Good human-resource management and career-development practices, to maximize human potential, must be cultivated.
> *(i)* Public administration must be broadly representative of the South African people, with employment and personnel management practices based on ability, objectivity, fairness, and the need to redress the imbalances of the past to achieve broad representation.

These Constitutional principles were subsequently enshrined in implementing legislation in the form of the Promotion of Access to Information Act, 2 of 2000 (also known as PAIA).

The case arose because when, on 19 November 2003, the South African Cabinet approved the Operational Plan, this committed government to implement a national ARV treatment rollout scheme, hiring an additional

22 000 employees to bolster the ailing public health care sector, providing nutritional programmes for all those living with HIV, improving access to voluntary counselling and testing (VCT), and significantly developing prevention of MTCT services. Despite this, the Operational Plan lacked a formal implementation timetable to ensure targets were met. This resulted in the programme falling well short of its target of 54 000 people on treatment by March 2004 (at which time only 15 000 people were receiving treatment).

The Operational Plan contained various clauses which referred to an additional document known as 'Annexure A' which was believed to contain such an implementation timetable, but was being kept out of the public domain. The Annexure was referred to as two documents with one allegedly containing a schedule of the core-implementation period ('A1') and the second containing a week-by-week schedule of the implementation timeframe ('A2'). Based on the constitutional right to information, TAC approached the Department of Health on 20 February 2004 to demand the release of this information crucial to the success of the Operational Plan. This demand was ignored by the Minister of Health.

TAC then submitted numerous further formal and informal written requests, as well as an internal appeal under the PAIA to obtain access to these documents. After these attempts failed, TAC initiated legal action to clarify the issue of costs by stating that the South African governments' failure to provide the information requested on 2 March 2004 was in contravention of the PAIA, and inconsistent with Sections 32.1 and 195.1(g) of the Constitution. The Minister of Health filed her responding affidavit seven weeks late on 29 September 2004, which stated that any reference to the Annexures in the Operational Plan was a mistake as no such Annexures existed.

The Minister also stated that, while timeframes were discussed and designed (by the Clinton Foundation which was serving as a consultant to the government), they were not adopted by the task team and therefore excluded from the eventual Operational Plan. An 'oversight' had resulted in all references to these documents being erroneously included in the final published document. After TAC became aware of this development, it contacted government lawyers to inform them that the application for the acquisition of these documents would be withdrawn on the condition that the Minister of Health agree to cover the applicant's costs on an attorney and client scale.

The court action was initiated by TAC on the belief that the Annexures existed, and that the Minister's refusal to communicate caused considerable confusion and subsequent expense when she could have simply announced the actual scenario at the time of TAC's initial request almost ten months earlier. That request was ignored by the Minister, at which time TAC filed its replying affidavit seeking an order from the court to compel the respondent to cover these costs. Government argued that such a ruling would be unreasonable as TAC had technically failed in its application, and as such the applicant should in fact field the costs of the respondent. They further argued that the initial request for the release of the Annexures was 'frivolous and vexatious', alleging that, had the documents been acquired, they would serve no real purpose if released into the public domain.

On hearing the above evidence, the Transvaal High Court ruled on 14 December 2004 that constitutional infringements of the right of access to information had taken place. In the light of the Minister of Health's behaviour, punitive costs were awarded in TAC's favour.[27] TAC grassroots activists were not, however, inspired to mobilize in great numbers in support of such an obscure and opaque legal technicality to the extent they had been by previous cases brought by TAC and its allies.

EVALUATION OF TAC'S ACHIEVEMENTS

For some of its members, TAC has become too reliant on litigation. They have suggested that TAC needs instead to pursue other strategies and not to rely on legal action to achieve its objectives. Overall, however, it is well understood by TAC that achieving a court victory or policy gain is not enough on its own. For concrete results to be achieved for its members, court victories must be put into practice through campaigns that target delivery and monitoring of the implementation of policy victories (Boulle and Avafia 2005, p. 26).

In fact, TAC is widely recognized as one of the most successful advocacy campaigns, providing a model of how to combine mobilization, litigation and mass action. The court victories and their subsequent impact on the lives of HIV-positive people are evidence of TAC's effectiveness as an organization. Thanks to TAC's work, South Africans have access to prevention of MTCT, cheaper drugs and a state-funded ARV rollout programme (see also Boulle and Avafia 2005, p. 62). In recognition of their work fighting HIV/AIDS, on 1 December 2003 TAC and its chairperson, Zackie Achmat, were jointly nominated for the Nobel Peace Prize by the American Friends Service Committee (AFSC), a Quaker humanitarian service organization.[28]

However, the tensions between TAC and the South African Minister of Health that resulted in several court cases soured its relationship with government, with the effect that international NGOs often have closer relations with government officials than does TAC itself, the latter seen as antagonistic by government, while international NGOs are considered supportive of the South African government's approach.

These tensions exist despite the fact that, during the apartheid struggle, many TAC members had been loyal ANC supporters. As a result, TAC does not see itself as being in permanent opposition to the South African government. In fact, on many issues TAC has been sympathetic to the ruling ANC. Nonetheless, the South African government is reluctant to engage with TAC or its allies. TAC and the ALP are trying to build bridges with the government, but this has not been achieved at the time of writing and there is certainly lingering animosity as a result of the litigation.

Despite the active resistance to TAC by the Minister of Health and others within the South African leadership, the situation changed dramatically in an 18-month period from January 2006 to June 2007. The AIDS denialism that had emanated previously from the South African government, and from the Ministry of Health in particular, was replaced by a greater focus on the part of the South African government on tackling the HIV/AIDS pandemic (AIDS Law Project 2007, p. 11).

The extent of this change was evidenced by the then South African Deputy President, Phumzile Mlambo-Ngcuka, who told a conference of AIDS activists on 27 October 2006: 'We must take our fight against AIDS to a much higher level . . . We must tighten up so that ARV drugs are more accessible, especially to the poor. Education and prevention of HIV infection must be scaled up. Our people want us to unite on this issue in the best interests of the health and wellbeing of our nation. Working together we can defeat this disease.'[29]

Mark Heywood, director of the ALP commented: 'This is a sea change . . . We're not across the ocean yet, but now the government is sailing in the right direction.'[30] Zackie Achmat of TAC added: 'This is a serious and significant change. The government wants to work with us, not against us.'[31]

By late 2006, about 200 000 people living with HIV/AIDS in South Africa were receiving ARVs from the government programme, making it one of the biggest public programmes in the world, but still reaching only one quarter of the estimated 800 000 people living with HIV in South Africa.

Then, on 1 December 2009 (World AIDS Day), President Jacob Zuma launched a massive campaign to encourage all South Africans to undertake a voluntary test for HIV. He also announced that all children under one year of age will receive ARV treatment if they test positive for HIV, while pregnant women living with HIV would have access to treatment.[32] The conversion of the South African government to the cause of prevention and treatment of HIV/AIDS, following years of AIDS denialism and a reluctance to provide ARVs, appeared complete.

Nonetheless, while there is still much to be done to achieve universal access to ARVs in South Africa, TAC and the ALP are now focusing less on using human rights principles to ensure access and more on implementation and improving accessibility. They are also working to a greater extent on technical assistance and capacity building rather than on the advocacy and litigation strategies that had been to the fore in the past.

Yet perhaps TAC's greatest achievements have been in terms of building coalitions, utilizing human rights principles and raising public awareness of the link between intellectual property rights, public health and access to medicines. These strategies provided the single most important catalyst for NGOs to campaign on access to medicines issues internationally and focused the world's attention on the plight of people living with HIV/AIDS in the developing world.

GENETIC RESOURCES AND TRADITIONAL KNOWLEDGE: THE CASE OF HOODIA GORDONII

The Hoodia gordonii Appetite Suppressant

As we saw in Chapter 3, the complex relationship between intellectual property rights, genetic resources and traditional knowledge has been an issue of contention in a number of multilateral institutions for some time. We saw, in particular, that the CBD and the Bonn Guidelines refer explicitly to the importance of obtaining informed consent from holders of traditional knowledge before the benefits of commercialization of material derived from genetic resources are equitably shared with the original holders of that knowledge. Yet, despite the efforts of multilateral institutions on these issues, it is rare to find practical examples of instances where prior informed consent and ABS agreements have actually been put in place. One rare example of this arose in the case of *Hoodia gordonii* in South Africa.

Although no prior informed consent or access was sought before the commercialization of intellectual property rights associated with *Hoodia gordonii* was undertaken, the benefit agreement subsequently concluded broke new ground in the recognition of the collective rights of indigenous people and set important precedents for future consultation with indigenous people.

Hoodia gordonii is a genus of succulent plants in the Apocynaceae family and is used widely by the indigenous peoples of Southern Africa as an appetite suppressant, thirst quencher and as a cure for ailments such as abdominal cramps, haemorrhoids, tuberculosis, indigestion, hypertension and diabetes. It is a spiny succulent which, in mature plants, can have as many as 50 individual branches and weigh as much as 30kg. Plants can reach a height of 1 metre with flowers having a carrion-like smell (similar to rotten meat) designed to attract fly larvae. Various uses of succulent plants in the Apocynaceae family have been recorded among Anikhwe (Northern Botswana), Hai‖om (northern Namibia), ‡Khomani (north western South Africa), and the !Xun and Khwe (originally from Angola) communities.[33] However, although the genus *Hoodia* is widespread in Southern Africa, herbarium records indicate that *Hoodia gordonii* only occurs in South Africa and Namibia. Indigenous communities living in these regions include the San people and non-San groups such as the Nama, Damara and Topnaar.

The traditional knowledge of indigenous peoples on the use of *Hoodia gordonii* as an appetite suppressant had been passed on to anthropologists and researchers as long ago as the 1930s. Tribal healers had explained how *Hoodia gordonii* had been used by them since time immemorial to reduce their hunger and thirst, at times of hardship and whilst hunting (Chennells 2007, p. 420).

This traditional knowledge provided the crucial lead on *Hoodia gordonii* guiding scientific research by the Council for Scientific and Industrial Research (CSIR), a South African state research institute, to ascertain why the succulent acted as such an effective appetite suppressant.[34] By the early 1990s, scientists working at the CSIR had been able to isolate an active compound (P57) that was responsible for appetite suppression in *Hoodia gordonii* and, in 1996, the CSIR was granted South African patent no. 983170 to P57 derived from this genetic resource.

At the time, no consultation on commercialization of the resource was undertaken with indigenous communities, despite the fact that they had provided the traditional knowledge leading to this patent in the first place. In fact, there was nothing in South African law requiring the prior informed consent of communities before accessing and using their traditional knowledge, nor were there requirements for the sharing of commercial benefits derived from the exploitation of that knowledge.

In August 1998 the rights to further development research, clinical trials and eventual commercial exploitation of the patented P57 were licensed by the CSIR to Phytopharm, a private company based in the UK. Dr Richard Dixey, then the Chief Executive Officer (CEO) of Phytopharm, explained how P57 works: 'There is a part of your brain, the hypothalamus. Within that mid-brain there are nerve cells that sense glucose sugar. When you eat, blood sugar goes up because of the food, these cells start firing and now you are full. What the *Hoodia* seems to contain is a molecule that is about 10000 times as active as glucose. It goes to the mid-brain and actually makes those nerve cells fire as if you were full. But you have not eaten. Nor do you want to.'[35]

Phytopharm in turn sub-licensed the rights to Pfizer Inc. in the US for development and global commercialization for a reported US$ 32 million plus royalties on future sales.[36] At this point, in June 2001 Antony Bennett, a journalist from UK newspaper *The Observer*, telephoned Roger Chennells to ask whether the San peoples knew about the commercialization of intellectual property rights associated with *Hoodia gordonii* or whether they were, in fact, extinct.

The South African San Institute

Roger Chennells, a lawyer and partner in the firm of Chennells Albertyn, had specialized in human rights cases during the apartheid era. In 1996, together with a group of trustees, Chennells used funds from Chennells Albertyn to set up an NGO called the South African San Institute (SASI). The San people are traditionally hunter-gatherers, part of the Khoisan group and are related to the traditionally pastoral Khoikoi. The term 'San' means 'outsider' in the Nama language and was originally intended as a derogatory term because it distinguished the hunter-gatherers from other more pastoral tribes.

SASI was set up to protect the human rights and the heritage rights of the San people and carry out grassroots community development work. Funds were to be devoted to organizational development, capacity building, job creation activities, development of tourism initiatives based on the heritage of the San people.[37]

When *The Observer* newspaper article was published on 17 June 2001, it focused on the role of the !Kung, one of the individual groups of San people, in providing the traditional knowledge on the product that had been derived. The article failed to mention the role of the non-San groups such as the Nama, Damara and Topnaar.[38]

The Working Group of Indigenous Minorities in Southern Africa

The San people number about 100000 in South Africa and had begun to organize themselves with the formation of an NGO called the Working Group of Indigenous Minorities in Southern Africa (WIMSA) in 1996. There were also scattered populations of San in other parts of Southern Africa – 55000 in Botswana, 35000 in Namibia, and a further approximately 8000 in Angola, Zimbabwe and Zambia (Chennells 2007, p. 421). Following publication of *The Observer* newspaper article, the CSIR was immediately contacted by WIMSA, which demanded an explanation and an explicit recognition of the San peoples' rights as a precondition to further talks (Chennells 2007, p. 421).

Until *The Observer* newspaper article in 2001, the San themselves had been oblivious to the fact that their knowledge of *Hoodia gordonii* had commercial application, and that this knowledge had led to research, scientific validation, and the filing of international patents by the CSIR. Moreover, they had been excluded from the lucrative deals being struck to develop P57 (Wynberg 2004, p. 852).

Together with WIMSA, SASI then set about devising a strategy aimed at claiming that the San people held intellectual property rights over the patented P57 derived from *Hoodia gordonii*. *The Observer* newspaper had also contacted a small South African NGO called Biowatch, which played an important role.

Biowatch

Biowatch had been working on issues relating to biodiversity, food security, genetic engineering and social justice since it was set up in 1997 by David Fig and Rachael Wynberg. Biowatch received funding from international donors including Comic Relief, GTZ German Technical Cooperation, HIVOS, Heinrich Boell Stiftung, Interfund, Stichting DOEN, Both Ends, and Third World Network. It used these funds to develop its work upholding people's rights to a safe and healthy environment increasingly aware of the problems associated with privatizing natural resources and with the aggressive commercialization of modern biotechnology. Biowatch's experience had highlighted the importance of network-building as a strategy to increase awareness and strengthen collaboration about issues relating to genetic resources and food security.

Through this work Biowatch had established coalitions with a range of international NGOs including ActionAid, the ETC Group and GRAIN. It had also developed contacts with NGOs in other African countries, particularly in issues related to genetically modified crops and the promotion of sustainable agriculture.[39] In this way, Biowatch was able to mobilize a coalition of NGOs in response to the controversial patenting and commercialization of products derived from the succulent *Hoodia gordonii*. As well as the SASI, WIMSA and Biowatch, the Legal Resources Centre (LRC) provided important legal expertise.

The Legal Resources Centre

The LRC began its work during the apartheid era, providing legal expertise and support to the poor and marginalized in society. Since the ending of apartheid, it had developed a twin identity as a grassroots community-based NGO and also as a public interest law organization. In the second of these roles, litigation is the core activity. In both these capacities, the LRC was already working on land reform and, through this work, became involved in intellectual property rights. Since many of its clients were indigenous communities, it developed expertise on issues such as access and ownership of genetic resources. Henk Smith, the LRC's legal counsel on natural resources, in particular had a long history of working on ABS issues so was well placed to assist in the *Hoodia gordonii* case.

Negotiating a Benefit Sharing Agreement

In 2002, supported by a powerful coalition of South African and international NGOs,[40] WIMSA and SASI approached the CSIR to ask why, prior to the P57 patent application and subsequent negotiations with commercial partners to licence *Hoodia gordonii*, the CSIR had failed to consult with the San people. The NGOs argued that the CSIR should have sought prior informed consent from the San before acquiring and using *Hoodia gordonii* and the traditional knowledge associated with it. They argued that the rights of the San to control and determine the grounds for use of *Hoodia gordonii* had been undermined because they were not consulted or involved in the process of collecting *Hoodia gordonii* plants.

Given that the process of commercializing *Hoodia gordonii* was by this time already underway, WIMSA, SASI and the other NGOs involved decided that the interests of the San people would best be served by not challenging the validity of the patent on grounds that it lacked novelty and inventive step. SASI was asked to initiate negotiations with the CSIR to secure a benefit sharing agreement on the San people's behalf. The benefit sharing agreement envisaged was to be between the CSIR and the South African San Council, a voluntary association established by the ǂKhomani, !Xun and Khwe communities in South Africa.

To its credit, the CSIR agreed to open negotiations leading to a benefit sharing agreement with the San peoples (Chennells 2007, p. 421). Following months of negotiations, including workshops and meetings funded by the CSIR that brought together representatives of the San people, the CSIR government representatives and NGOs (Wynberg 2004, p. 856), on 1 February 2002 an agreement was reached in the form of a Memorandum of Understanding (MoU). The MoU between the CSIR and the South African San Council was considered a significant step forward in that the CSIR recognized the San people as holders of the ancient traditional knowledge that had led to the identification of the novel molecule which formed the basis of the P57 patent (Chennells

2007, p. 421). It also committed the CSIR to negotiating a benefit sharing agreement with the South African San Council in recognition of their collective rights, including arrangements for financial benefits on commercial exploitation of the P57 patent.

The benefit sharing agreement was formally signed on 24 March 2003. Under the terms of the agreement, the San were to set up a San Hoodia Benefit-Sharing Trust that, in the event of the continued success of the clinical trials and commercial release, would receive 1.8 per cent of all milestone payments paid to the CSIR over the subsequent three years and 6 per cent of all royalty payments received by the CSIR from Phytopharm for the duration of the patents as a result of the successful exploitation of products, and this for the duration of the royalty period or for as long as the CSIR received financial benefits from commercial products. The San would also receive 8 per cent of the milestone income received by the CSIR from Phytopharm when certain performance targets were reached during the product development period.

In the event of successful commercialization, these monies would be payable into the San Hoodia Benefit Sharing Trust (Chennells 2007, pp. 422–4; Wynberg 2004, p. 863). The Trust would then use this money to raise the standard of living and well-being of the San peoples of Southern Africa. The Trust's membership would comprise representatives of the three San clans in South Africa, plus representatives of the San clans of Botswana, Namibia and Angola, representatives of the CSIR and WIMSA, a representative of the Department of Culture, Arts, Science and Technology, and a professional lawyer or accountant (Chennells 2007, p. 424).[41]

Initial expectations that the agreement would head to tangible benefits for the San people were extremely high. On the day that the agreement was signed, a San Hoodia Benefit Sharing Agreement Celebration was held at Molopo Lodge in the Kalahari. At the Celebration, Kxao Moses ‡oma, Chairperson of the Board of Trustees of WIMSA, announced that all benefits accruing from the benefit sharing agreement would be used to implement sound and sustainable development projects, provide skills training and education to San, and build institutional capacity among San groups across the region.[42]

Criticisms of the Benefit Sharing Agreement

One problem with the benefit sharing agreement was the relatively low figure of 6 per cent of royalties that would be paid to the San Hoodia Benefit Sharing Trust. It led to accusations that NGOs had encouraged the San to 'sell out' by advising them to accept this figure. Nonetheless, it was hoped by those negotiating on behalf of the San that, if the commercialization of P57 was successful, the money received would be considerable by any standards (Chennells 2007, p. 422).

A further criticism of the benefit sharing agreement was that any income received by the San Hoodia Benefit Sharing Trust would be derived from royalty and milestone payments obtained by the CSIR. No royalties would flow from profits received by Phytopharm and its partners commercializing P57. Moreover, the agreement explicitly protected Pfizer and Phytopharm from any further financial demands by the San people and prevented the San from using their knowledge of *Hoodia gordonii* in any other commercial applications so that they would not be able to independently pursue less lucrative but perhaps more viable commercialization options based on non-patented herbal medicines (as opposed to patented products). They would also be unable to claim any benefits from the dozens of new *Hoodia*-based products that have recently emerged in the market, which blatantly use San traditional knowledge of *Hoodia gordonii* in their promotion (Wynberg 2004, p. 865).

There were also concerns that, even if monies were eventually received by the San Hoodia Benefit Sharing Trust, extremely difficult issues would still need to be addressed in terms of determining how the benefits are spread across geographical boundaries and within communities (Wynberg 2004, p. 876). Indicative of this problem is that although, through WIMSA, the South African San Council was formally mandated to represent the Hai‖om, one of the largest San groups in Namibia and Botswana, the agreement excluded non-San groups, such as the Nama, Damara and Topnaar, who had historically occupied – and still occupy – areas where *Hoodia gordonii* grows, and who had undoubtedly used the plant as a medicinal remedy and as a food and water substitute (Wynberg 2004, p. 863). The Damara, for instance, share ethnographically identified cultural markers and language with the Hai‖om. They also share parallel histories of dispossession and marginalization as well as the imposition of negative identity stereotypes with which these processes are associated. However, Damara people were not represented by WIMSA, even though many of them and some *!haoti* in particular, had experienced the same and continuing marginalizing processes as Hai‖om and others (Sullivan 2001, p. 188).

There were also concerns that the agreement was almost exclusively confined to financial benefits which hinged upon product sales and successful commercialization of *Hoodia gordoniii* (see, for instance, Wynberg 2004, p. 866). Yet commercialization never actually occurred, highlighting the need for a more comprehensive and holistic approach to benefit-sharing that is not exclusively contingent on successful drug development. The CSIR, for instance, purportedly benefited substantially from licensing P57 and was likely to earn significant milestone payments linked to the success of the drug during different stages of the clinical trials (Wynberg 2004, p. 867).

Nonetheless, amongst the San people, the benefit sharing agreement was considered an important empowering tool to enable more informed decisions to be made about their intellectual property and ways to protect it (Wynberg 2004, p. 875). Meanwhile, for the South African government, the case led directly to an increased focus and prominence for biodiversity and its potential value, the inclusion of prior informed consent and benefit-sharing within new biodiversity legislation and proposals to require disclosure of origin prior to the granting of patents. Internationally, the prominence given to the *Hoodia gordonii* benefit sharing agreement was widely considered to have set precedents about the ways in which holders of traditional knowledge should be compensated for this knowledge in the future.

EVALUATION OF NGO'S ACHIEVEMENTS WITH THE HOODIA GORDONII BENEFIT SHARING AGREEMENT

The *Hoodia gordonii* benefit sharing agreement demonstrated how a coalition of South African NGOs, comprising SASI, WIMSA, Biowatch and the LRC could engage with intellectual property-related issues on behalf of disadvantaged sections of society. Biowatch used its links with international NGOs to generate the awareness of the issue and frame the CSIR's P57 patent as 'theft' of the San people's traditional knowledge. While WIMSA mobilized grassroots support from San communities, SASI and the LRC were then able to provide legal expertise to negotiate the best possible deal for the San people.

The case also demonstrated how, post-apartheid, human rights activists in South Africa had begun to engage increasingly with intellectual property-related issues on genetic resources, traditional knowledge and access and benefit sharing agreements. They did so not by framing the issue as a human rights abuse, but by providing the legal advice and technical expertise needed to support the rights of San people to benefits derived from the patenting of their traditional knowledge.

The agreement also set a precedent by embedding the link between patents, traditional knowledge and the rights of indigenous peoples in the public consciousness in a way that had not been done previously (see also Wynberg 2004, p. 860).[43] It demonstrated how NGOs in developing countries could play a decisive role in shaping the debate on the relationship between intellectual property rights and development, providing practical, evidence-based arguments to inform the international debate.

It also reaffirmed the importance of having grassroots, community-based organizations through which the interests of holders of traditional knowledge could be articulated and represented in negotiations. These community-based organizations such as SASI and WIMSA worked in tandem with campaigning NGOs such as Biowatch and legal experts working in the LRC (see also Wynberg 2004, p. 875).

Yet despite the success of NGOs in securing a benefit sharing agreement for the San people, in practice no money was ever paid to the San Hoodia Benefit-Sharing Trust. Pfizer rescinded the clinical development rights to P57 in 2004 without ever manufacturing and selling a single slimming pill containing P57.[44] Phytopharm subsequently granted a licence to Unilever in the hope that they could instead commercialize the product. Unilever had intended to include the *Hoodia gordonii* extract in a liquid form in its range of SlimFast diet drinks. However, on 15 November 2008, following four years of work, Unilever too announced that it had abandoned plans to use P57, saying it was 'unsuitable' for further development with its SlimFast range and dashing hopes for commercialization of P57. Unilever had found that Hoodia extract was bitter in taste, caused nausea and was metabolized too quickly, reducing its efficacy. Unilever's decision led to the resignation of Daryl Rees, who had succeeded Richard Dixey as the CEO of Phytopharm in 2007, and Piers Morgan, its Chief Financial Officer who had joined the company from Ernst and Young.[45] Phytopharm shares fell 42.8 per cent when Unilever's announcement was made. While the P57 patent expires in 2017 in some markets, Phytopharm still hopes that it can find a new commercial partner to incorporate Hoodia extract into a solid dietary food. Unilever had invested £17m in Hoodia plantations in South Africa and also paid Phytopharm's development costs, which were £2.6 million from January to September 2008 alone and which amounted to all but £500 000 of Phytopharm's total income.[46]

So, overall, there were shortcomings in the benefit sharing agreement, non-San people were excluded from the Trust that was set up to distribute the income generated and no money was ever received because of the failure to bring products containing P57 to market. Nonetheless, the lessons learnt appeared to be that NGOs and activists with human rights backgrounds could work effectively together, in coalition with communities at a grassroots level, with legal experts and with international NGOs to achieve outcomes sympathetic to the rights and interests of indigenous people in the developing world on intellectual property-related issues.

NOTES

1. 'HIV positive S. Africa woman murdered', The Associated Press (28 December 1998). Available at: http://www.aegis.com/news/ap/1998/AP981219.html.
2. Aaron Nicodemus,'Africa still stigmatises HIV-positive people: Many HIV-positive people in South Africa fear that revealing their positive status could mean isolation from their communities, or even murder . . .' Mail & Guardian (Johannesburg) (7 May 1999). Available at: http://www.aegis.com/news/dmg/1999/MG990504.html.
3. While other large developing countries like Brazil had begun offering large scale public health treatment programmes as early as the 1990s, the South African Cabinet only announced a national treatment plan in 2003 after years of ever-increasing mortality rates and NGO activism.
4. *Constitution of the Treatment Action Campaign.* Available at: http://www.tac.org.za/ Documents/Constitution/Constitution13Dec04.PDF.
5. Donors to the AIDS Law Project include Atlantic Philanthropies, Ford Foundation, HIVOS, the Kingdom of Belgium, the Royal Netherlands Embassy and the Swedish International Development Agency (SIDA) (AIDS Law Project 2007, p. 8).
6. *The Pharmaceutical Manufacturers' Association of South Africa and Others v. The President of the Republic of South Africa, the Honourable Mr N.R. Mandela, and Others,* The High Court of South Africa (Transvaal Provincial Division), Case no: 4183/98. Available at: http://www.cptech.org/ip/health/sa/pharmasuit.html.
7. NEDLAC is a government forum for South African policy officials to come together with organized business, organized labour and organized community groupings to discuss and try to reach consensus on issues of social and economic policy through 'social dialogue'. NEDLAC's aim is to make economic decision-making more inclusive, to promote the goals of economic growth and social equity. The main government department in the NEDLAC process is the Department of Labour, while the Departments of Trade and Industry, Finance and Public Works are also involved.
8. Nevirapine is a non-nucleoside reverse transcriptase inhibitor for use against mother-to-child transmission of HIV which has been shown to reduce MTCT of HIV in approximately 50 per cent of cases.
9. Constitutional Court of South Africa, *Minister of Health & Others v. Treatment Action Campaign & Others,* Case CCT 8/02, 5 July 2002, 10 BCLR 1033 CC. Available at: http://www.saflii.org/za/cases/ZACC/2002/15.html.
10. Constitution of the Republic of South Africa, 1996. Available at: http://www.info.gov. za/documents/constitution/1996/a108-96.pdf.
11. In June 2003, before the case was resolved, one of the complainants died of AIDS-related complications.
12. The AIDS Consortium, established in 1992 by Justice Edwin Cameron, later a Judge of the South African Supreme Court of Appeal and other HIV/AIDS activists, was originally part of the Centre for Applied Legal Studies (CALS) at the University of Witwatersrand. Its objective was to promote a non-discriminatory response to HIV/ AIDS based on people's basic human rights as enshrined in the South African constitution. The founding document of The AIDS Consortium was the AIDS Charter, which set out the basic human rights of people living with HIV/AIDS. Its objective was to promote a non-discriminatory response to the HIV/AIDS epidemic based on people's basic human rights as enshrined in the Constitution. The AIDS Consortium was established as an independent NGO in Braamfontein at its first AGM in 1998 where 225 members ratified the constitution. In July 2000 the AC registered as a Section 21 company and is a membership-based organization bringing together a network of over 1000 AIDS service organizations (ASOs) and individuals addressing the AIDS pandemic in Southern Africa. The AIDS Consortium website is available at: http://www. aidsconsortium.org.za/index.htm.
13. Based in the UK, Action for Southern Africa (ACTSA) is the successor organization to the Anti-Apartheid Movement. Since 1994 ACTSA has been campaigning with the

people of Southern Africa as they strive to build a better future, working for peace, democracy and development across the region. The ACTSA website is available at: http://www.actsa.org/index.php.

14. The Council for Medical Schemes is a statutory body established by the South African Parliament to provide supervision over medical schemes. The Council for Medical Schemes website is available at: http://www.medicalschemes.com/.

15. *The Price of Life: Hazel Tau and Others vs GlaxoSmithKline and Boehringer Ingelheim*: *a report on the excessive pricing complaint to South Africa's Competition Commission*, page 36. A joint publication by the Law and Treatment Access Unit of the AIDS Law Project and the Treatment Action Campaign, July 2003, page 43. Available at: http:// alp.org.za/modules.php?op=modload&name=News&file=article&sid=222.

16. Competition Act of the Republic of South Africa. Available at: http://www.ictregula-tiontoolkit.org/en/Publication.1595.html.

17. *Ibid.*

18. Section 39 Interpretation of Bill of Rights:

   (1) When interpreting the Bill of Rights, a court, tribunal or forum–
       (a) must promote the values that underlie an open and democratic society based on human dignity, equality and freedom;
       (b) must consider international law; and
       (c) may consider foreign law.
   (2) When interpreting any legislation, and when developing the common law or cus-tomary law, every court, tribunal or forum must promote the spirit, purport and objects of the Bill of Rights.
   (3) The Bill of Rights does not deny the existence of any other rights or freedoms that are recognized or conferred by common law, customary law or legislation, to the extent that they are consistent with the Bill.

19. *The Price of Life – Hazel Tau and Others vs GlaxoSmithKline and Boehringer Ingelheim: a report on the excessive pricing complaint to South Africa's Competition Commission*. A joint publication by the Law and Treatment Access Unit of the AIDS Law Project and the Treatment Action Campaign, July 2003. Available at: http://alp.org.za/modules. php?op=modload&name=News&file=article&sid=222.

20. Generic Antiretroviral Procurement Project (GARPP) and TAC Treatment Project Request Permission to Import Generic Nevirapine, 28 September 2003. Press release available at: http://www.tac.org.za/newsletter/2003/ns28_09_2003. htm#LicenseApplication.

21. 'Competition Commission finds pharmaceutical firms in contravention of the Competition Act', *Competition Commission Press Release*, 16 October 2003.

22. 'Commission Questions Conduct of Anti-retroviral Companies', *Competition News*, December 2003, Edition 14, p. 1. Available at: http://www.compcom.co.za/assets/ Uploads/AttachedFiles/MyDocuments/Dec-03-Newsletter.pdf.

23. *Competition Commission concludes an agreement with pharmaceutical firms.* CPTech, 10 December 2003. Available at: http://www.cptech.org/ip/health/sa/cc12102003.html.

24. A copy of the GSK settlement agreement with the complainants is available at: http://alp.org.za.dedi20a.your-server.co.za/images/upload/Settlement%20agreement% 20with%20GSK--9%20December%202003.pdf. A copy of the BI settlement agree-ment with the complainants is available at: http://alp.org.za.dedi20a.your-server.co.za/ images/upload/Settlement%20agreement%20with%20BI--9%20December%202003. pdf.

25. A copy of the Operational Plan for Comprehensive HIV and AIDS Care, Management and Treatment for South Africa is available at: http://www.info.gov.za/issues/hiv/care-plan.htm.

26. *Treatment Action Campaign (TAC) v. Minister of Health*, Case No: 215991/04, Transvaal High Court (2004).

27. Case summary available at: http://www.tac.org.za/community/node/2103.

28. 'TAC contender for Nobel Peace Prize', *South African Press Association* (7 October 2004). Available at: http://www.aegis.com/news/sapa/2004/SA041001.html.
29. 'South African Government Ends Aids Denial', Andrew Meldrum, *The Guardian*, 28 October 2006, page 21.
30. 'A Dramatic and Welcome Change', *The Good News*, Friday 1 December 2006. Available at: http://www.sagoodnews.co.za/newsletter_archive/a_dramatic_and_welcome_change_3.html.
31. 'South Africa Ends AIDS Denial', *Buzzle.com*, Guardian News and Media, 27 October 2006. Available at: http://www.buzzle.com/articles/114050.html.
32. The text of President Jacob Zuma's speech on World AIDS Day, 1 December 2009, is available at: http://www.info.gov.za/speeches/2009/09120112151001.htm.
33. Information document on trade in *Hoodia gordonii* and other *Hoodia* species available at: http://www.plantzafrica.com/planthij/hoodia.htm.
34. The CSIR is one of the largest research organizations in Africa and accounts for about 10 per cent of the entire African research and development budget.
35. Tom Mangold (2003) 'Sampling the Kalahari cactus diet', *BBC News*. Available at: http://news.bbc.co.uk/1/hi/programmes/correspondent/2947810.stm.
36. 'San Bushmen Sue Pfizer. Hoodia gordonii: Miracle cactus or another fly trap?' Available at: http://www.dolfzine.com/page612.htm.
37. Roger Chennells, SASI, interview with the author, 1 December 2005.
38. *The Observer* (2001), 'In Africa the Hoodia cactus keeps men alive. Now its secret is "stolen" to make us thin', 17 June.
39. Rachel Wynberg, Biowatch, interview with the author, 7 December 2005.
40. International NGOs got in touch to offer moral support – the Berne Declaration was particularly active. Roger Chennells, SASI, interview with the author, 1 December 2005.
41. In August 2004, the San Trust, formally named the San Hoodia Benefit-Sharing Trust, was registered.
42. Kxao Moses ‡oma (2003), 'Celebrating the Fruits of San Traditional Knowledge: the Hoodia plant', speech delivered to the San Hoodia Benefit Sharing Agreement Celebration at Molopo Lodge, South Africa, 24 March.
43. Roger Chennells, SASI, interview with the author, 1 December 2005.
44. CBS News (2004), 'African Plant May Help Fight Fat'. Available at: http://www.cbsnews.com/stories/2004/11/18/60minutes/main656458.shtml.
45. Karen Attwood, 'Phytopharm chief quits business for Buddhism', *The Independent*, 10 January 2007. Available at: http://www.independent.co.uk/news/business/news/phytopharm-chief-quits-business-for-buddhism-431523.html.
46. Andrew Jack and Jenny Wiggins, 'Unilever Drops Plans to Use Slimming Extract', *Financial Times*, 15 November 2008.

5. Brazil

INTRODUCTION

The recent history of democratic struggle in Brazil, which culminated in the end of military rule in 1985, has had significant implications for the culture of social activism on intellectual property-related issues and how NGOs have embraced and utilized principles of human rights in articulating their concerns. When military dictatorship came to an end in Brazil in the 1980s, there followed a profound period of national self-reflection. Public policy objectives were gradually restructured around a new social agenda for the country. This social agenda was underpinned by a new democratic constitution, firmly grounded in human rights principles that should be upheld at all costs to avoid a repeat of abuses experienced during the era of military dictatorship.

These human rights principles have since proved central to government initiatives on a range of issues in Brazil and have been particularly prevalent in campaigns to ensure access to medicines for people living with HIV/AIDS. To a lesser extent, the belief that indigenous peoples and local communities in the Amazon have an inalienable human right to protect the biodiversity over which they are custodians has also informed campaigns to secure the rights of these peoples with regard to their traditional knowledge of uses for genetic resources.

HUMAN RIGHTS AND ACCESS TO MEDICINES

The end of military rule coincided with a new public health imperative as the first cases of HIV/AIDS were reported in Brazil in 1985. This public health crisis led to the emergence of new NGOs representing people living with HIV/AIDS. The new NGOs took advantage of the democratization process that followed military rule to make the case that the healthcare system should take fully into account the welfare needs of the HIV/AIDS community.

The first of many NGOs created solely with the task of representing the interests of people living with HIV/AIDS was *Grupo de Apoio à Prevenção à*

AIDS (GAPA – AIDS Prevention Support Group), founded in São Paulo in 1985. The following year, the *Associação Brasileira Interdisciplinar de AIDS* (ABIA – Brazilian Interdisciplinary AIDS Association) was established in Rio de Janeiro with the aim of linking academics working on HIV/AIDS with the broader grassroots social movement.

The period from 1985 to 1989 then saw a rapid growth in the number of NGOs in Brazil acting for and on behalf of people living with HIV/AIDS. In particular, these NGOs made explicit the link between the provision of ARVs and the fundamental human rights of people living with HIV/AIDS. This link had profound resonance in a Brazilian society still recovering from the painful legacy of 21 years of military rule.

Articulate and well-educated people living within the gay community took the lead in these NGOs, advocating that the government make the provision of ARVs for people living with HIV/AIDS a priority (Smallman 2007, p. 80). Prominent amongst these new NGOs was *Grupo pela VIDDA* (GPV – Group for Life), founded in Rio de Janeiro in May 1989. This was followed, in 1995, by the founding of the Brazilian Network of People Living with HIV/AIDS (RNP+), which today has a membership in excess of 2500 people. In total there are now more than 600 different NGOs working on issues related to HIV/AIDS in Brazil under the umbrella of the State Forum of AIDS NGOs (Távora dos Santos Filho 2000).

These Brazilian NGOs are responsible for a number of significant initiatives that advocate improved access to ARVs. In the early 1990s, for instance, the *Grupo pela VIDDA* (GPV – Group for Life) and GAPA sued the federal and state governments to assure access to medication for HIV/AIDS patients in hospitals by guaranteeing private or public insurance policies (Távora dos Santos Filho 2000).

A key strategy of the NGOs campaigning for improved access to ARVs in Brazil was Article 196 of the 1988 *Constituição da República Federativa do Brasil* (Constitution of the Federal Republic of Brazil) which enshrined the right to health in federal law.

ARTICLE 196, CONSTITUTION OF THE FEDERAL REPUBLIC OF BRAZIL 1988

Health is a right of all and a duty of the State and shall be guaranteed by means of social and economic policies aimed at reducing the risk of illness and other hazards and at the universal and equal access to actions and services for its promotion, protection and recovery.

Using strategies that had worked to such good effect in opposition to the previous military regime, these HIV/AIDS NGOs began to use human rights principles to frame the health policy on the right to health care as a right for all (see also Galvão 2005, p. 112). The right to health enshrined in Article 196 of the Brazilian Constitution quickly became the focus of attention for NGOs representing people living with HIV/AIDS seeking to articulate the universal right of access to ARVs.

Universal Access to ARVs

The universal right to health care in Brazil in Article 196 of the Constitution operates through a system that allows for full therapeutic treatment, including access to pharmaceutical products and which implies the obligation of the State to provide medicines for all who need it (Rosina et al. 2008, p. 169).

Public health care service delivery in Brazil is shared equally by the different levels of government: federal, state, municipal and the national government health system, the latter known as *Serviços Unificados e Descentralizados de Saúde* (SUDS – Unified and Decentralized Health Services). SUDS was later replaced by the *Sistema Único de Saúde* (SUS – Unique Health System), which provides healthcare to approximately 123 million Brazilians (74 per cent of the total population) who cannot afford private health care plans (Cohen and Lybecker 2005, p. 216) and is regulated by Laws 8.080/90 and 8.142/90.

This legislation has transferred most of the responsibility for health care delivery to municipalities and implemented accompanying financial mechanisms for the financial allocation of federal funds to states and municipalities (Smallman 2007, p. 83). While the federal government defines the policies and regulations, grants technical and financial support to the states and municipal governments and provides some service delivery, it is the state and municipal governments that share responsibility for health care delivery (Cohen and Lybecker 2005, p. 211).

Laws 8.080/90 and 8.142/90 also established the three founding principles of the SUS.[1] First, that it should be universal, meaning that no citizen could be excluded from SUS coverage. Second, that it should be characterized by equality of access with no discrimination regarding the public health services and products provided to users. Third, that it should provide full health care coverage, from the most basic to the most complex health care needs.

These three principles of universality, equality and integrated health care define the Brazilian state's promotion of health as a fundamental social right and, although the Brazilian constitution does not mention specifically access to medicines as part of the right to health, it is generally acknowledged that the right to access to medicines is derived from this implementing legislation (see, for instance, Rosina et al. 2008, p. 170). Specifically, Article 6(I)(d) of Law 8.080/90 provides that SUS 'must be responsible for promoting full medical assistance, which includes pharmaceutical assistance'.

In line with this obligation, in 1990 the federal government began free delivery of AZT, one of the first ARVs, to the citizens of Brazil. Initially, the Brazilian federal government purchased AZT from Burroughs Wellcome Company (now GlaxoSmithKline), the multinational pharmaceutical company that had undertaken research and development work and had subsequently been granted patents on the drug.

As the number of people living with HIV/AIDS increased and demands for treatment became more pressing, the federal government struggled to provide free ARV treatment to its citizens. The high prices of patented pharmaceutical products then started to come to the fore. Given the costs associated with purchasing large consignments of these patented pharmaceutical products at the market price, in 1993 the federal government instead began to purchase ARVs manufactured by Brazilian pharmaceutical companies which produced cheaper, equally effective, generic versions of AZT and other patented medicines.

By November 1996, this policy of universal access to ARVs at no cost to patients had become a legislative right for all Brazilian citizens as a result of Federal Law 9.313/96. This guaranteed that the SUS had a federal responsibility to provide ARV treatment to all Brazilian citizens and made it mandatory for the SUS to provide ARV treatment to all citizens living with HIV/AIDS (see also Galvão 2005, p. 112; Rosina et al. 2008, p. 189). As a result, Brazil became one of the few countries in the world with a policy of universal free access to ARV treatment.

By 2008 there were an estimated 730 000 adults living with HIV/AIDS in Brazil, about 0.6 per cent of all people between the ages of 15 and 49 (UNAIDS 2008). ARVs take up a significant portion of public health spending in Brazil and the purchasing of ARVs has consequently become an increasing financial burden for the State (Rosina et al. 2008, p. 182). According to the Ministry of Health, the growth of drug expenditure has outpaced the total growth in health expenditure.[2] In order to guarantee drug purchases, the Ministry of Health has had to re-allocate its budget, thus significantly reducing expenses in other areas of the public healthcare programme.

The impact of the Brazilian ARV programme has been significant. By 2007 the *Programa Nacional de Doenças Sexualmente Transmissíveis e AIDS* (National Sexually Transmitted Disease (STD) and AIDS Programme) was providing free of charge 18 ARVs to over 220 000 people living with HIV/ AIDS in Brazil.[3] It was also providing free medicines to combat opportunistic infections related to HIV/AIDS, that is to say infections which would not usually affect healthy people but can be deadly to persons with weak immune systems caused by HIV/AIDS (Rosina et al. 2008, p. 190).

Life expectancy for people living with HIV/AIDS had increased and there had been a reduction of 80 per cent in the number of cases of hospitalizations of people living with HIV/AIDS, generating a cost saving to the SUS amounting to US$2.3 billion per annum.

Patents, Human Rights and Access to ARVs in Brazil

While 1996 saw the adoption of Federal Law 9.313/96 and marked the beginning of a policy of universal access to ARVs in Brazil, it also marked the point at which awareness grew about the relationship between patents, public health and access to medicines. This occurred with the adoption of Industrial Property Law 9.279/96, which introduced patent protection for an area of technology – pharmaceutical products – not previously patentable in Brazil.

Until 15 May 1997, when Law 9.279/96 came into force, Brazilian pharmaceutical manufacturers were permitted to legally reverse-engineer and manufacture cheaper, generic versions of pharmaceutical products that were subject to patent protection elsewhere in the world. This practice was permitted prior to 1997 under previous legislation, Industrial Property Law 5.772/71 that came into force on 21 December 1971 and, as a result, during the 1970s many private firms, such as Aché, Farmasa, Libbs, Sintofarma and public sector manufacturers, such as *Fundação Oswaldo Cruz* (FIOCRUZ – Oswaldo Cruz Foundation) in Rio de Janeiro and *Fundação para o Remédio Popular* (FURP – Popular Medicines Foundation) in São Paulo, were able to supply generic pharmaceutical products in this way (Cohen and Lybecker 2005, p. 215).

In the pre-TRIPS era, this was permissible under international law because, as we saw in Chapter 2, a developing country Member of the WTO was not required to grant patents to all areas of technology, such as pharmaceuticals. This changed with the provisions of Article 27.1 of the TRIPS Agreement, which required all WTO Members to make available patents in all fields of technology (including pharmaceutical products).

In 1996, only a year after the TRIPS Agreement had come into force, Law 9.279/96 was introduced in Brazil to provide for the protection of pharmaceutical products by patent law in accordance with Article 27.1 of TRIPS (see also Rosina et al. 2008, p. 183). In fact, the legislation was introduced despite concerns that patent protection for pharmaceutical products would increase the financial burden on the SUS, given its obligation to purchase ARVs and provide these drugs free of charge to all citizens living with HIV/AIDS. Controversially, the legislation extending patent protection to pharmaceutical products was even introduced ahead of schedule. As a developing country, Brazil could legitimately have utilized transitional arrangements set out in Article 65.4 of the TRIPS Agreement to delay implementing TRIPS until as late as 1 January 2005.

What is more, Articles 230 and 231 of Law 9.279/96 allowed patent applications to be filed for previously non-patentable subject matter with minimal administrative review, provided that the patent was already granted in another territory. This TRIPS-plus mechanism is commonly known as a method of permitting 'pipeline' patent protection.

From the perspective of public health and access to medicines, two issues arise from Law 9.279/96. The first issue is that it subjected patent requests to a mere formalities check by the national intellectual property office in Brazil, which is called the *Instituto Nacional da Propriedade Industrial* (INPI – National Institute of Industrial Property).[4] The INPI proceeds on the assumption that the pharmaceutical product in question met the requirements of patentability in Brazil because a patent had already been granted elsewhere in the world even though the patent may have been granted in a country with lower patentability standards (Rosina et al. 2008, p. 186).[5] The second issue is that Law 9.279/96 allowed for retrospective patents for medicines already invented and, as a result, pipeline patents granted in Brazil had a strong impact on the public health budgets as they inhibited the production and purchase of generic medicines by the SUS.

Following the introduction of pipeline patent protection for pharmaceutical products, while the SUS could purchase significant quantities of generic ARVs that were invented before 1996,[6] these drugs were all patented in Brazil via the pipeline mechanism that year, dramatically raising the public cost of supplying these drugs in Brazil by US$420 million per year.[7]

Nevertheless, despite coming forward early to demonstrate full compliance with TRIPS obligations, Law 9.279/96 also sought to achieve a balance between the patents accorded to pharmaceutical products and the right to health, in particular, the need to ensure the adequate provision of ARVs to people living with HIV/AIDS in Brazil.

The mechanism used to achieve this balance was compulsory licensing. Law 9.279/96 allowed the government to issue a compulsory licence where a patent holder exercises patent rights in an abusive manner, or by means of an abuse of economic power proven by an administrative or court decision. Other instances were also specified where compulsory licences may be issued, particularly under Articles 68 and 71.

ARTICLE 68 OF THE INDUSTRIAL PROPERTY LAW (1996), BRAZIL, No. 9.279/96[8]

(1) A patent owner shall be subject to the grant of compulsory license of his patent if the rights resulting therefrom are exercised in an abusive manner or if the patent is used in abuse of economic power, as proven by an administrative or judicial decision pursuant to the provision of the law.

The following shall also entail a compulsory license:
1 – Failure to exploit the subject matter of the patent within Brazilian territory by reason of lack of manufacture or insufficient manufacture of the product. . .

Under Article 68, the holder of a patent in Brazil was required to 'work' the subject matter of a patent, either by producing the patented good in the country, or by allowing the patented process to be used in Brazil. If this requirement was not met within three years of the issuance of the patent, the government could issue a compulsory licence allowing others to utilize the patent against the patent holder's wishes. Article 68 also stated that if a patent owner chooses to utilize the patent through importation rather than the local working of the patent, then others besides the patent holder would be allowed to import the patented product or products obtained from the patented process.

ARTICLE 71 OF THE INDUSTRIAL PROPERTY LAW (1996), BRAZIL, No. 9.279/96

In cases of national emergency or public interest, declared in an act of the Federal Authorities, insofar as the patentee or his licensee does not meet such demand, a temporary non-exclusive compulsory license for the exploitation of the patent may be granted, without prejudice to the rights of the respective patentee.

Under Article 71, compulsory licences could also be issued by the federal government in cases of national emergency or public interest (see also Shadlen 2009, p. 48). A Presidential Decree on Compulsory Licensing 3.201/99 was subsequently issued in 1999 to define, in Article 2, what might constitute such situations of national and public interest in which compulsory licences could be issued for patented products.[9]

ARTICLE 2 OF THE PRESIDENTIAL DECREE ON COMPULSORY LICENSING (1999) BRAZIL, No. 3.201/99

(1º§) National emergency is understood to be a condition of impending danger to the public, even if existing only in a part of the national territory. . .

(2º§) There are considered to be within the public interest those facts, among others, related to the public health, nutrition, protection of the environment, as well as those of primordial importance to the technological or social and economic development of this country.

Yet despite these legislative developments, in policy terms the relationship between patents and access to medicines at that time remained a topic largely unknown to NGOs in Brazil, particularly given the legal complexity of the issues involved.[10]

By 2001, however, faced with the challenge of carrying on its HIV/AIDS programme at a considerably higher cost,[11] the Brazilian federal government opted to initiate negotiations with a number of the major pharmaceutical companies designed to reduce the price of ARVs. These negotiations were backed by the threat of compulsory licensing, with the possibility of using in particular the procedures mandated by Articles 68 and 71 of Law 9.279/96.

Using the threat of compulsory licences as a negotiating tool, by 2001 the Brazilian federal government had been able to agree substantial price reductions for ARVs with several pharmaceutical manufacturers, including a 64.8 per cent price reduction for Indinavir, 59 per cent for Efavirenz, 40 per cent for Nelfinavir and 46 per cent for Lopinavir. In addition, a technology transfer agreement was established between Merck and the Ministry of Health's main national laboratory Farmanguinhos (Love 2006, p. 2) to enable local working of some of Merck's patented pharmaceutical products.

Then, on 9 January 2001, the US requested that the WTO Dispute Settlement Body (DSB) establish a panel to resolve its complaint against Brazil in relation to the provisions of Law 9.279/96 that authorize the use of compulsory licences and parallel importation to promote the local working of patents.[12] In what was widely viewed as a reaction to the Brazilian federal government's interference on the production and pricing of highly profitable ARV drugs patented by or exclusively licensed to US-based pharmaceutical multinationals, the US government then began consultation procedures.

The US Complaint to the WTO Dispute Settlement Body

The US complaint focused on Article 68 of the 1996 Brazilian Industrial Property Law 9.279/96. The US complained that Article 68 violated Articles 27.1 and 28.1 of the TRIPS Agreement which set out the principle of non-discrimination in the protection of patent rights and the exclusive rights to be enjoyed by patent holders by discriminating against US owners of Brazilian patents whose products are imported into Brazil but not locally produced and curtailing the rights of these owners to utilize the patents.[13] The US demanded from Brazil written guarantees that it would not issue compulsory licences for products patented or exclusively licensed to US companies. Following the refusal of the Brazilian government to meet these demands, the US requested the opening of a WTO panel against Brazil, on 1 February 2001. The DSB then established a WTO dispute settlement panel to report on this matter on 30 May 2001 (see also de Mello e Souza 2005, p. 201).

For its part, Brazil argued that Article 27.1 should be understood in light of Article 2.1 of the TRIPS Agreement.

ARTICLE 2.1 OF THE TRIPS AGREEMENT: INTELLECTUAL PROPERTY CONVENTIONS

In respect of Parts II, III and IV of this Agreement, Members shall comply with Articles 1 through 12, and Article 19, of the Paris Convention (1967).

Article 2.1 of the TRIPS Agreement explicitly incorporates into the TRIPS Agreement an obligation on WTO Members to comply with the provisions of Article 5(A)(4) of the Paris Convention that relate to local working.

In the light of Article 2.1 of the TRIPS Agreement and Article 5(A)(4) of the Paris Convention, Brazil argued that Article 68 of the 1996 Brazilian Industrial Property Law 9.279/96 was in fact TRIPS compliant. Brazil also insisted that Article 68 did not render the lack of domestic production a

---

ARTICLE 5(A)(4) OF THE PARIS CONVENTION ON THE PROTECTION OF INDUSTRIAL PROPERTY (1967)

A compulsory licence may not be applied for on the ground of failure to work or insufficient working before the expiration of a period of four years from the date of filing of the patent application or three years from the date of the grant of the patent, whichever period expires last; it shall be refused if the patentee justifies his inaction by legitimate reasons. Such a compulsory licence shall be non-exclusive and shall not be transferable, even in the form of the grant of a sub-licence, except with that part of the enterprise or goodwill which exploits such licence.

---

sufficient condition for compulsory licensing, but only applied in cases where there is abuse of patent rights or economic power (de Mello e Souza 2005, p. 201). From a public policy perspective, Brazil felt that Article 68 was essential as a bargaining tool to help the Ministry of Health achieve the most cost-effective price for ARVs when negotiating with multinational drug companies, thereby helping sustain its highly successful HIV/AIDS treatment programme (see also de Mello e Souza 2005, p. 202).

The Response of Brazilian HIV/AIDS NGOs to the US Complaint

For HIV/AIDS NGOs in Brazil, the US complaint was a catalyst that focused attention on the fact that patents can act as a barrier to access to medicines, particularly for people living with HIV/AIDS in developing countries.[14] Brazilian NGOs such as *Grupo de Incentivo à Vida* (GIV – Group of Incentive for Life) and ABIA articulated their opposition to the US complaint by using the language of human rights and the right to health enshrined in Article 196 of the Brazilian Constitution to claim that the complaint by the US to the WTO had the potential to infringe the human rights of people living with HIV/AIDS.

In recognition of the fact that the Brazilian HIV/AIDS programme had been a success and should be protected, HIV/AIDS NGOs in Brazil were quick to support their federal government, and, on 7 March 2001, began to demonstrate against the US outside the US Embassy in São Paulo.

The international NGO community soon also became involved. ActionAid, which was already working in Brazil on issues relating to seeds and transgenics, approached ABIA to offer help and advice on how best to respond to the US complaint. As a result, a workshop was organized on 25 and 26 March 2001, attended by Brazilian HIV/AIDS NGOs, together with a representative from WHO, Eloan Pinheiro from Farmanguinhos, Adriano Campolina from ActionAid, representatives of the Brazilian pharmaceutical industry and *Agência Nacional de Vigilância Sanitária* (ANVISA – the National Health Surveillance Agency), along with activists such as David Hathaway and Gisela Alencar, who had encountered intellectual property issues previously in relation to genetic resources and traditional knowledge, and Nélio Diniz, Senator Marina Silva's assistant.

This was the first time that the relationship between patents and access to medicines had been discussed openly by NGOs in Brazil and the timing of this meeting was significant. Faced with the need to respond to the US complaint against Brazil at the WTO, Brazilian HIV/AIDS NGOs began to act and to collaborate with their international counterparts on the implications of the TRIPS Agreement for public health and access to medicines.

By May 2001, a larger meeting of NGOs had been organized in Recife. This was the first national meeting of all NGOs working on HIV/AIDS in Brazil. Amongst the active NGOs attending were ABIA, GIV and GESTOS (Gesto Pernambuco). In addition, the meeting was attended by representatives from *Instituto Brasileiro de Análises Sociais e Econômicas* (IBASE – Brazilian Institute of Social and Economic Analyses), *Federação de Órgãos para Assistência Social e Educacional* (FASE – Federation of Organs of Social and Educational Assistance), GAPA-BA, the *Instituto de Políticas Alternativas para o Cone Sul* (PACS – Institute for Alternative Policies to the South Region) and INESC, the NGO Forum on HIV from Rio, CEDUS, the *Instituto Brasileiro de Defesa do Consumidor* (IDEC – the Brazilian Consumer Protection Institute), while the international NGOs ActionAid, Oxfam and MSF were also represented at the meeting. With the support and advice of ActionAid, Brazilian HIV/AIDS NGOs then started to articulate their opposition to the US complaint against Brazil in a coherent way, engaging directly with the global debate about the impact of intellectual property rights on people living with HIV/AIDS.

In particular, the May 2001 Recife meeting was the point at which Brazilian NGOs adopted a strategy of coalition building in response to intellectual property-related issues. This occurred with the formation of the *Grupo de Trabalho de Propriedade Intelectual da REBRIP* (GTPI – the Intellectual Property Working Group of REBRIP). REBRIP (*Rede Brasileira pela Integração dos Povos*) is a coalition of NGOs that means the 'Brazilian Network for the Integration of the Peoples' and the setting up of an intellectual property working group allowed the coordination of a coalition of Brazilian NGOs working the impact of intellectual property rights on HIV/AIDS and human rights in Brazil.

The involvement of international NGOs in the May 2001 meeting was also crucial. MSF brought with it a good reputation and an international profile on access to medicines issues in Brazil. MSF also appears to have had particularly good routes of access to government policy channels and within five months of taking up his position, Michel Lotrowska found that he was being invited to government consultations in Brazil as the MSF spokesperson even though Brazilian HIV/AIDS NGOs were not asked to attend. Lotrowska also played an important role in translating postings on the IP-Health list server for the Portuguese speaking NGO community in Brazil to try and minimize the extent that language would become a barrier to understanding the issues for non-English speaking HIV/AIDS activists.[15]

Oxfam participated in the Recife meeting in May 2001 and continued to attend some of the subsequent meetings with Brazilian NGOs after that. Oxfam also played an important role by providing technical inputs to help the HIV/AIDS community in Brazil to be more knowledgeable on patents and access to medicines issues.

International NGOs also made important technical inputs on intellectual property issues to assist their Brazilian counterparts. At the time, HIV/AIDS NGOs in Brazil feared that they were not sufficiently well informed about patents and access to medicines to keep the momentum going without the support of international NGOs. It was here that international NGOs such as Oxfam and MSF were able to help significantly, providing information and links to wider NGO networks working on the access to medicines campaign.

In particular, international NGOs provided crucial technical expertise to counter the US complaint to the WTO. Specifically, academic experts brought in by international NGOs were able to highlight the fact Articles 204 and 209 of Title 35 of the US Patent Code, which specified local manufacturing of publicly-financed patented products and products patented by the US government, were remarkably similar to those that the US had challenged Brazil on at the WTO.[16]

The US countered this by arguing that, whereas the aforementioned articles of its Patent Act referred to contractual terms for publicly-financed projects, Article 68 of Brazil's Law 9.279/96 was a blank requirement applicable to all patented goods, regardless of their origin.

The mobilization of international NGOs therefore helped Brazil to counter the US complaint to the WTO DSB. International NGOs and the academic experts associated with them had provided crucial information on the US Patent Code and had also brought pressure to bear on the US by means of protests with ample media coverage. In fact, the extent of international mobilization was such that Paulo Roberto Teixeira, head of the Brazilian National STD and AIDS Programme at the time, commented that 'we could not have resisted were it not for the support of the global civil society' (quoted in de Mello e Souza 2005, p. 213).

On 25 June 2001 in the face of enormous negative publicity from international and Brazilian NGOs and legal arguments about the similarity between Articles 204 and 209 of Title 35 of the US Patent Code and Article 68 of Brazilian Law 9.279/96, the US withdrew the complaint. It did so after receiving assurances that it would be notified before any products patented by or exclusively licensed to US companies were subject to compulsory licensing in Brazil (de Mello e Souza 2005, p. 203). Brazil and the US also agreed that, before using the disputed provision in Article 68 of Brazilian Law 9.279/96 against a US patent holder, a 'Consultative Mechanism' would be initiated in an attempt to resolve the matter bilaterally (see also Deere 2008, p. 166).[17]

Alongside the technical inputs from academic experts brought on board by international NGOs, Brazilian NGOs were able to provide arguments about how the provision of ARVs to people living with HIV/AIDS would be adversely affected by the continued use of patents for pharmaceutical products in Brazil. Technical assistance between developing country NGOs (so-called 'South-South' technical assistance) was also evident, with Jonathan Berger from the ALP in South Africa also travelling to Brazil to provide technical inputs into the arguments that countered the US complaint.

Timing was crucial in these information sharing activities. The international and Brazilian NGOs needed to get the right information to the right people in the Brazilian government at the right time and this was facilitated by the close relationships between NGOs, both international and Brazilian, and people working within the National STD and AIDS Programme of the Brazilian Ministry of Health, as will be discussed later in this chapter.

Outcome of the US Complaint to the WTO Dispute Settlement Body

With public perception that Brazil's successful HIV/AIDS programme would be undermined by the US complaint to the WTO, and against the backdrop of the recent withdrawal of the South African lawsuit by global pharmaceutical companies in March of that year, the US WTO case against Brazil looked increasingly unsavoury (Sell 2003, p. 158).

In June 2001 the US finally announced that it was officially withdrawing its case against Brazil on the first day of the first United Nations Special Session devoted to a public health issue. The session culminated in 'The Declaration of Commitment' on HIV/AIDS on 27 June 2001. The Declaration framed the issue in terms of access to medicines and human rights to explain why it was of such crucial significance (Sell 2003, p. 158; de Mello e Souza 2005, p. 214).[18]

The US and Brazil subsequently notified the WTO DSB that a mutual agreed understanding had been reached to settle the dispute but, in effect, the US had stepped back from further confrontation on this issue, subject to a bilateral understanding to the effect that, should Brazil seek to issue a compulsory licence on grounds of failure to work the patent locally, it would consult the US before doing so.[19]

The continued existence of the safeguard provisions on compulsory licences in Articles 68 and 71 of Law 9.279/96 in Brazil has been described by the Report of the UN High Commissioner on the impact of the TRIPS Agreement as helpful in improving the implementation of the country's HIV/AIDS treatment programme.[20] Moreover, while no compulsory licence was actually issued under Brazilian Law 9.279/96 until 2007, the provisions were nevertheless instrumental in negotiating lower prices with the owners of patents on pharmaceutical products.[21] The Report of the High Commissioner concluded that: 'on the facts that have been provided by the Government of Brazil, it is possible to say that the Brazilian case demonstrates how the provisions of the TRIPS Agreement can be implemented in ways that respect, protect and fulfil the right to health. Through careful legislative implementation of TRIPS provisions . . . the Brazilian IP law supports the implementation of national health policy aimed at providing essential drugs to those who need them'.[22]

GTPI/REBRIP

Following the withdrawal of the US complaint to the WTO in June 2001, the Intellectual Property Working Group of Brazilian Network for the Integration of the Peoples (GTPI/REBRIP) continued to focus on access to medicines issues. The following month, on 29 and 30 July 2001, a meeting of GTPI/REBRIP took place at which a number of high profile activists participated, including members of the *Instituto Sócioambiental* (ISA – Socio-Environmental Institute) and Jorge Beloqui of GIV, an articulate mathematics professor and passionate AIDS activist, who acted as the most vocal spokesperson for GTPI/REBRIP from then onwards.

After that meeting, links between international and Brazilian NGOs continued to develop with Michel Lotrowska of MSF and Carlos Passarelli of ABIA (later Pedro Chequer's deputy at the National STD and AIDS Programme in the Ministry of Health) working together closely. They used MSF's contacts with international NGOs involved with the access to medicines campaign (including James Love of CPTech) and ABIA's contacts in Brazil. Lotrowska also had good working relationships with Ellen 't Hoen of MSF and Bernard Pécoul of DNDi and trusted their advice on how best to proceed.

By the end of the July 2001 meeting GTPI/REBRIP had defined an action plan. The main activities of GTPI/REBRIP were to involve public action to advocate the use of compulsory licences, inputs to the patent examination process undertaken by the INPI and to patent annulment cases,[23] legal opinions on draft legislation, and petitioning the Brazilian Attorney General on the constitutionality of pipeline patents.[24]

Within this remit, GTPI/REBRIP activities would range from monitoring and obtaining further information, formulating actual proposals to amend national and international legislation, and contributing to policy negotiations. The guiding principle of all these interventions would be the defence of the public interest and, specifically, of minorities.[25] With its strategy in place, GTPI/REBRIP structured its activities around specialists working on three themes: genetic resources, agriculture and access to medicines, all of which were considered to have a public interest perspective.

Initially GTPI/REBRIP's activities were coordinated by the *Instituto de Estudos Socioeconômicos* (INESC). Later, this role was taken over by ABIA, which worked closely with Michel Lotrowska of MSF, and helped to connect it with other organizations working on HIV/AIDS issues. Today, membership of GTPI/REBRIP includes ABIA, Conectas,[26] GAPA, Gestos, GIV, IDEC, IDCID, INESC, Intervozes, MSF, Pela Vida and Oxfam International. Over time, this coalition of NGOs working on intellectual property issues in Brazil has continued to have a significant impact.

In 2005 GTPI/REBRIP developed a strategy of focusing its efforts on securing price reductions for the most used ARV in Brazil, Lopinavir/Ritonavir (sold under the brand name Kaletra) the patent for which was held by the US-based multinational pharmaceutical company Abbott. In an attempt to negotiate a reduced price for the supply of Kaletra, the government commenced talks with Abbott. In this case, also, the negotiations were unsuccessful. As negotiations for reduced drug prices became less and less effective, the government explored a new approach.

Pedro Chequer, head of the National STD and AIDS Programme,[27] invited NGOs to discuss the issue with the Ministry of Health and put them in touch with other groups of people in different government ministries. Chequer wanted to put pressure on other government officials, particularly to highlight to them the problems related to access to ARVs and it suited him to have NGOs involved. Through Chequer, the NGOs involved with the GTPI/REBRIP were able to exert pressure at various points in the Brazilian federal government.

After failed attempts to negotiate a price reduction for Kaletra with Abbott, in June 2005 Brazil's then Minister of Health, Humberto Costa, signed a decree declaring Kaletra to be in the public interest, paving the way for a generic version of the drug to be produced by the Farmanguinhos laboratory of the Oswaldo Cruz Foundation.

However, at the same time that it declared Kaletra to be in the public interest, the Brazilian government also gave Abbott a timeframe in which to offer a lower price for the drug and so avert the compulsory licence from being issued and, in October 2005, an agreement was signed between the Brazilian government and Abbott to supply the drug at a lower price than had previously been available. In return for a lower price, the Brazilian government undertook not to issue a compulsory licence, or engage in other technology transfer or foreign direct investment activities to manufacture the drug locally, and fixing of the stipulated price until the end of 2011, when Kaletra would be close to patent expiry.

Once the agreement was signed GTPI/REBRIP, in conjunction with the Public Prosecution Service, filed a civil public action, seeking judicial review. On first hearing, the case received a negative preliminary decision, on the grounds that issuing a compulsory licence would trigger retaliation by the developed world and possible shortages of the drug, while the very capacity of domestic industry to produce the medicine in Brazil was also called into question. As a result, in order to counter the arguments used in the preliminary decision, the Brazilian federal government, with the support of the international NGO MSF, enlisted domestic and international specialists in 2006 to assess the technical capacity of four Brazilian pharmaceutical firms (two public and two private) to produce antiretroviral medicines. The specialists determined that the Brazilian firms do indeed have the capacity to produce both first-line and second-line antiretroviral drugs.

These results were corroborated by two additional studies conducted simultaneously in Brazil by the Clinton Foundation and the United Nations Development Programme (UNDP). Local firms could therefore fully supply domestic demand for the drug and, until production got up to speed, the medicine could be imported from other countries where the patent holder sells it.

These arguments were employed in the civil public action to influence the ruling. On 1 December 2005 the Brazilian Federal Prosecuting Authority together with GTPI/REBRIP, submitted a public civil action against the Ministry of Health to the Federal Justice with the objective of obtaining a compulsory licence for production of Kaletra. The announcement was made in Brasília at a press conference attended by the State Prosecutor, Peterson Pereira, NGO representatives and members of parliament.[28]

What is particularly notable about the Kaletra case is that, when the Ministry of Health announced that it had reached a deal with Abbott on Kaletra whereby the government would not issue a compulsory licence and in return Abbott would lower the price of Kaletra within five years, on condition that Brazil increase the number of patients using Kaletra, the National STD and AIDS Programme headed by Chequer was excluded from the ministerial decision-making process.[29] The Abbott agreement was seen by the NGOs as an indication of the strength of influence that global pharmaceutical companies had over not only the Ministry of Health but also the finance and trade ministries.[30]

The work of GTPI/REBRIP continued thereafter. On 6 March 2006, it organized a national seminar on 'Intellectual Property: Interfaces and Challenges' to debate the potentially adverse implications of intellectual property rights on access to knowledge, and health and food security.[31] The meeting culminated in the signing of the Leme Charter, which pointed out that participating civil society organizations and individuals form part of a global organized civil society movement which has consistently demonstrated the negative impact of intellectual property rights on poor peoples, on the environment and on biodiversity, and argued that if the current intellectual property is maintained, technologically-dependent countries and their peoples would suffer from having their human rights greatly undermined.

Then, on 28 November 2007, GTPI/REBRIP collaborated with the *Federação Nacional dos Farmacêuticos* (FENAFAR – National Federation of Pharmacists) to present evidence to the General Attorney of the Republic of Brazil, Antônio Fernando Barros e Silva e Souza on the unconstitutionality of the 'pipeline' provisions contained in Articles 230 and 231 of Brazilian Industrial Property Law 9.279/96.[32] The pipeline mechanism, it will be recalled, allows for the filing of patents in technological fields, including pharmaceutical products, not patentable prior to 1996.[33]

More recently, in December 2008, GTPI/REBRIP launched a campaign, coordinated by ABIA, on abuses of the patent system relating to access to medicines, including those used to treat HIV/AIDS. Specifically, the campaign (in the form of a sign-up letter) was motivated by concern that a review of the INPI guidelines of examination for pharmaceutical patents would lead to a relaxation of the way the novelty criteria was applied, leading to the granting of patents for previously known medicines.[34] Also in December 2008 GTPI/REBRIP mobilized against a number of legislative proposals before the House of Deputies of the Brazilian Congress that would restrict the use of TRIPS flexibilities in Brazilian patent law. These legislative measures concern, in particular, a proposal permitting the patenting of substances extracted from living beings, and a proposal to cancel the prior consent mechanism of ANVISA.[35]

EVALUATION OF BRAZILIAN HIV/AIDS NGOS' ACHIEVEMENTS

Using coalition building strategies, Brazilian HIV/AIDS NGOs helped to shape a favourable environment in which demands for universal access to ARVs could be framed as a human right of every Brazilian citizen. The impact of NGOs in securing a universal right of access to ARVs for people living with HIV/AIDS in Brazil should not therefore be underestimated.

Brazilian NGOs and the federal government worked well together on the introduction of programmes on the prevention and treatment of HIV/AIDS work. The Ministry of Health's National STD and AIDS Programme has had close relationships with NGOs dating back to 1999, when MSF helped to draft the text of the 1999 Presidential Decree on Compulsory Licensing, which established rules concerning the granting, *ex officio*, of compulsory licences in cases of national emergency and public interest.[36]

The GTPI/REBRIP had similarly open and frequent discussions with the National STD and AIDS Programme, particularly when the latter was headed by Pedro Chequer. The strength of that relationship was underpinned by the fact that there is a strong tradition of NGO activists (such as Carlos Passarelli of ABIA) moving into the National STD and AIDS Programme of the Ministry of Health, and there are frequent exchanges, close relationships and generally good dialogue between HIV/AIDS NGOs and the National STD and AIDS Programme.

Under the leadership of Pedro Chequer, the National STD and AIDS Programme of the Ministry of Health often adopted policy positions close to those advocated by NGOs. In May 2005, for instance, the National STD and AIDS Programme turned down funding of approximately $40 million from the United States Agency for International Development (USAID) because of a clause in the agreement condemning prostitution. Pedro Chequer made the decision to turn down any further US donations as long as the anti-prostitution pledge requirement was in place, quoted as saying that US demands were 'interference that harms the Brazilian policy regarding diversity, ethical principles and human rights'.[37]

The radical stance of the National STD and AIDS Programme under Pedro Chequer and its close relationships with NGOs were not, however, replicated by the rest of the Brazilian government system. Although NGOs played an important role in helping the Brazilian federal government to respond to the US complaint to the WTO DSB by mobilizing activists to demonstrate outside US Consulates and bringing on board academic experts to provide detailed legal analysis to undermine the US complaint, relations between NGOs and the Brazilian government soured when GTPI/REBRIP brought a civil action against the Ministry of Health, demanding the issuance of a compulsory licence for Kaletra.

HIV/AIDS activists in Brazil interviewed for this book also expressed concerns that, outside of the National STD and AIDS Programme, Ministry of Health officials prefer to talk to international NGOs or legal experts on access to medicines rather than engage in dialogue with Brazilian NGO activists. The conclusion that can be drawn from this is that, as in South Africa, individuals from international NGOs or from foreign universities have greater access to officials when intellectual property policy issues are being discussed by the Brazilian government than do locally-based NGO activists.

Furthermore, even though the National STD and AIDS Programme of the Ministry of Health has historically a strong relationship with NGOs, there has been criticism of this close relationship with government because some in the NGO community feel that it threatens the independence of NGOs. It also has the effect that the way that Brazilian NGOs working on HIV/AIDS issues tend to engage with intellectual property issues at the international level is through the government rather than directly. Brazilian NGOs do not send delegates to meetings convened by multilateral institutions engaged in intellectual property-related norm-setting and policy making activities and instead rely on government officials to make the case on their behalf.

In this way, although the close relationship between Brazilian NGOs and government can have positive effects, the fact that government takes the lead on policy at the international level can also mean that there is a risk that the inputs of Brazilian NGOs are filtered by government, and the controversial aspects edited out, because the NGOs themselves do not have a presence in terms of sending representatives to the multilateral institutions that are working on intellectual property issues.

One consequence of this has been the absence of Brazilian NGO engagement with the broader concerns of intellectual property and development. For instance, despite the leading role played by the federal government of Brazil in the Development Agenda process at the WIPO in Geneva, discussed later in this book in Chapter 8, Brazilian NGOs working on HIV/AIDS domestically that have raised concerns about the relationship between patents and access to medicines were often completely unaware of the government's role in the Development Agenda process when the interviews in Brazil were conducted for this book.

The picture is complicated further by the fact that the National STD and AIDS Programme may well differ from the positions held by officials in other parts of the Ministry of Health on compulsory licences. There is a perception amongst NGO activists interviewed for this book that the Ministry of Development, Industry and Foreign Trade is not interested in consumer problems or the public interest, but instead is more likely to represent the interests of multinational pharmaceutical companies, while the Ministry of Foreign Affairs does not engage with Brazilian NGOs representing people living with HIV/AIDS to a great extent at all.

Ironically, this meant that when the Brazilian Ministry of Foreign Affairs took the lead on the Development Agenda process at the WIPO, as discussed in Chapter 8 of this book, the relatively distant relationship that Ministry officials had with Brazilian NGOs was markedly different to the much closer relationship that Brazilian delegates in Geneva have with international NGOs working on intellectual property issues.

Brazilian NGOs did not participate in preparation of the WIPO Development Agenda proposal and, despite their links with international NGOs, did not have access to the text until after it was presented in Geneva. Similarly, the Ministry of Foreign Affairs presented the joint Brazil-Argentina proposal for a Development Agenda without any evidence of public discussion at the domestic level.

In part this paradox arises because different government agencies in Brazil have different agendas. A further illustration of this point can be seen by the fact that the Ministry of Health led the negotiations with multinational pharmaceutical companies to lower the prices of ARVs, but the Ministry of Agriculture is concerned with intellectual property from a different perspective. Its concern was more that if the US imposes trade sanctions on Brazil then market access for Brazilian agricultural exports could be put in jeopardy. As a result, the Ministry of Agriculture tends to adopt a more cautious approach than the Ministry of Health as regards the issuance of compulsory licences.

Overall, then, there was a perception amongst Brazilian HIV/AIDS NGO activists interviewed for this book that there is a disconnection between global events and the daily reality of people living in Brazil. There is also concern amongst Brazilian NGOs that there is a communication gap between the international NGOs working on patents and access to medicines issues in Geneva and the realities of the people on the streets in Brazil.

Relations between NGOs and the Brazilian government tend to be temporary and issue specific. The strength of the interaction between NGOs and the Ministry of Health has not been replicated on other intellectual property issues, such as traditional knowledge or genetic resources. In the latter case, even though Brazil is the most biodiverse country in the world, there is little evidence of coordinated action by indigenous people, local communities, NGOs and government on issues related to traditional knowledge or genetic resources in the same way as has been evident in terms of the close relations between NGOs and government on the patents and access to medicines issue in Brazil.

It should also be noted that the relationship between NGOs and government on access to medicines issues in Brazil is very different to the situation in South Africa. As we saw in Chapter 4, TAC in South Africa has often been critical of government policies on the provision of ARVs to a far greater extent than has been the case in Brazil. In contrast to South Africa, the STD and AIDS Programme in Brazil has generally been extremely responsive to the NGO community. This has meant that NGOs in Brazil have not had the same conflicts with the Ministry of Health that South African NGOs have experienced with their own government and have not generally had to resort to the same tactics as in South Africa to achieve desired outcomes in relation to patents and access to medicines.

Even so, HIV/AIDS NGOs in Brazil often feel unduly excluded from the negotiations held between government and the pharmaceutical industry. NGOs are not, for instance, invited to participate in the federal government's *Grupo Interministerial de Propriedade Intelectual* (GIPI – Inter-Ministerial Group on Intellectual Property), which is coordinated by the Ministry of Development, Industry and Foreign Trade. GIPI grew out of the Brazilian coordination committee for the Uruguay Round of General Agreement on Tariffs and Trade (GATT) negotiations on intellectual property. In 1995, after the Uruguay Round had ended, the *Câmara de Comércio Exterior* (CAMEX – Chamber of Foreign Trade) decided to continue the GIPI because of the need to maintain a group to coordinate government intellectual property policy.

The GIPI was then formally established as part of CAMEX by a Presidential Decree of 2001 and is composed of: the Ministry of Agriculture, Livestock and Food Supply; the Ministry of Science and Technology; the Ministry of Culture; the Ministry of Development, Industry and Foreign Trade; the Ministry of Foreign Relations; and the Ministry of Health (see also Deere 2008, p. 213). Other government bodies, particularly the INPI and ANVISA, also participate in the GIPI meetings through its thematic subgroups.

However, despite the fact that the GIPI is designed to undertake a holistic evaluation of Brazilian intellectual property policy,[38] in practice the Ministry of Health has been largely marginalized from the policy process with priority given instead to ministries that are primarily responsible for trade issues.

GTPI/REBRIP consequently attempted to bypass the GIPI by establishing contact directly with the Ministry of Development, Industry and Foreign Trade, which is responsible for the INPI, but its efforts were unsuccessful. GTPI/REBRIP then took the decision to change its strategy from one of engagement with the Ministry to one based on a media campaign, highlighting that it felt the government was not inclusive of civil society and drawing attention to its policies on access to medicines. In particular, the campaign highlighted the fact that INPI was granting patents for new formulations of existing drugs.

In the latter case, the GTPI/REBRIP received valuable technical inputs from the Instituto de Direito do Comércio Internacional e Desenvolvimento (IDCID – the International Trade Law and Development Institute), headed by Maristela Basso of the Universidade de São Paulo (USP).[39] A meeting convened by Basso at the University of São Paulo in 2003, for instance, introduced Brazilian NGO activists to legal experts who had technical knowledge of patent law and were able to explain the issues clearly to a non-technical audience.

Although the close working relationship that NGOs have had with the National STD and AIDS Programme has continued over time, the relationship that NGOs have more generally with the Ministry of Health and other ministries in the Brazilian government soured when agreement was reached with Abbott on price reductions for Kaletra.

More generally, the task of explaining the relationship between patents and access to ARVs to the general population in Brazil has, however, not been an easy one for NGOs. In Brazil, unlike South Africa, activists at the grassroots level initially considered the link between patents and access to medicines to be an abstract topic and failed to engage with it. To some extent this perception changed with the US complaint to the DSB in 2001 and, subsequently, GTPI/REBRIP has worked hard to frame the issue in terms of the right to health enshrined in Article 196 of the Brazilian Constitution.

Nevertheless, the difficulty of making intellectual property-related issues clear and immediate for the public at the grassroots level in Brazil, and explaining the link between patents and the availability of ARVs in particular, remains an ongoing task for Brazilian HIV/AIDS NGOs to achieve.

GENETIC RESOURCES AND TRADITIONAL KNOWLEDGE IN THE AMAZON

The term biopiracy refers to the appropriation and monopolization of a traditional population's knowledge of biological resources and diverse uses for local flora and fauna. Through advances in biotechnology and the registering of trade marks and patents related to biological resources, appropriation and monopolization has increased, with international agreements on intellectual property, such as the TRIPS Agreement, raising the possibility for this exploitation further.[40]

The Brazilian Amazon contains some of the most diverse life forms and ecosystems within the largest unspoiled tropical rainforest in the world. Hence, the conservation of its ecological and biological diversity is a key concern of the Brazilian government and the indigenous and other local communities that inhabit it.[41]

The policy approach adopted by the Brazilian government to conserve this biodiversity has been to promote the sustainable development of the region through the production and commercialization of goods derived from the Amazon. It is held that this activity may lead to substantial economic benefits for Brazil and its indigenous communities, provided that the benefits are adequately shared. Furthermore, the sustainable production of derived goods may act as an incentive for improving the management and conservation of biodiversity and help combat deforestation and unsustainable farming practices that have put the Amazon at risk.

One of the difficulties the country has been facing is the lack of a legal framework to protect the natural resources of the Amazon region and domestic capacity to make effective use of its biodiversity, including the range of genetic resources and associated traditional knowledge that, given the development of modern technology, increasingly become sources of potential economic and cultural value.[42] As was discussed in Chapter 3, the CBD recognized the sovereign rights of nations over their genetic resources,[43] and established the principle of access to genetic resources, subject to prior informed consent of the providing country and the sharing in a fair and equitable way of the results of research and development and the benefits arising from the commercial and other utilization of genetic resources upon mutually agreed terms. However, the CBD and the TRIPS Agreement also recognize that the intellectual property rights of the researchers or other stakeholders covering the use of genetic resources in processes should be protected.

Environmental and sustainable development NGOs and indigenous and local communities in Brazil have been at the forefront of the efforts to address issues related to the application of the intellectual property framework under the TRIPS Agreement related to biodiversity and to create public awareness and challenge cases of biopiracy in the Amazon.

NGOs in Brazil have been actively participating in the formulation and implementation of national laws related to genetic resources and traditional knowledge since the early 1990s. Following ratification of the CBD by the Brazilian National Congress in 1994, the then Senator Marina Silva (Brazilian Environment Minister 2003–2008)[44] initiated a law project, presented to the Senate in 1995 and approved in 1998, to implement CBD principles. The law project was not made permanent and deliberations on establishing legislation on genetic resources and traditional knowledge continued to be debated in the intra-Ministry working group *Conselho de Gestão do Patrimônio Genético* (CGEN – Council for the Administration of Genetic Resources) in which NGOs are excluded. This process was paralysed largely due to the divergence of the positions of different ministries. Historically, the Brazilian Environment Ministry has had a good working relationship with NGOs and indigenous and local communities, but is relatively weak vis-à-vis other ministries in the federal government.

The national NGO-led movement against biopiracy in Brazil has grown significantly since 2002, driven by the common objective of seeking the protection of national biodiversity and recognition of traditional knowledge held by Brazilian indigenous and local communities.

An important stimulus in the fight against biopiracy came at the 'Growing Diversity' workshop[45] in Rio Branco, the capital city of the state of Acre in Brazil, held from 9 to 19 May 2002 and organized by the international NGO GRAIN in partnership with the *Grupo de Trabalhos Amazônicos* (GTA – Amazonian Working Group).[46] Over 100 representatives of farmers groups, fisher folk, indigenous people and NGOs from 32 Asian, African and Latin American countries participated in the event. The resulting *Rio Branco Commitment* of 19 May 2002, declared that local communities and indigenous peoples are the custodians of biodiversity, that they have an inalienable human right and responsibility to continue to manage, save, exchange and further develop the biodiversity under their custody, over and above any commercial or other interests. It rejected biopiracy and the patenting of products and knowledge because they go against biological diversity and cultural identity, objecting in particular to the patenting of life forms.[47]

By working in coalition to make clear that they have inalienable human rights over the biodiversity under their custody, the activists responsible for the *Rio Branco Commitment* achieved a great deal. They increased awareness on the central importance of biodiversity in rural livelihood systems, galvanized NGO action and raised awareness about biopiracy amongst activist groups in Brazil and further afield.

The relative success of the *Rio Branco Commitment* can be attributed, in part, to the fact that it was the result of a sustained two-year process that allowed for a regionally-driven 'bottom up' approach involving a broad range of local experiences. It also succeeded in enabling farmers and other people's organizations with NGOs and with scientists aiming to support them. The coordinating role of international NGOs in the form of GRAIN, SSNC, Bread for the World and Centro Internazionale Crocevia was crucial in this coalition building process, but it was the participants themselves, mostly from developing countries, who contributed most in terms of bringing to the meeting their direct and relevant experience in local management of biodiversity, and it was developing countries themselves who benefited most from the process.

Amazonlink

For the NGO Amazonlink, the *Rio Branco Commitment* was crucial in making it more fully aware of the issues involved in biopiracy. It also encouraged Amazonlink to engage with what was perceived to be the misappropriation and monopolization of products derived from biodiversity and traditional knowledge.

Amazonlink was founded in Rio Branco in September 2001 by Michael Schmidlehner, an Austrian national living in Brazil, with the aim of providing small, rural producers in the Amazon with buyers of sustainable products abroad. This raised concerns that intellectual property rights could have negative impacts on the livelihoods of traditional communities and the sustainable development of the Amazon region. As a result of its work supporting and promoting traditional and scientific knowledge and craft objects from the forest peoples, Amazonlink became involved in a number of campaigns adopting the language of 'biopiracy'. It developed strong alliances with farmers and indigenous peoples and with national and international NGOs in the fight against the misappropriation and monopolization of resources and traditional knowledge.[48] Some products that Amazonlink was seeking export markets for were derived from Cupuaçu.

'Cupuaçu is Ours'

Cupuaçu (pronounced *coo poo uh sue*) is a small to medium sized tree, growing to a height of 15 to 20 metres. It is native to the south-east of the state of Pará, Brazil and is found throughout the Amazon region. Cupuaçu (*Theobroma grandiflorum*) is closely related to the cocoa tree (*Theobroma cacao*). The Cupuaçu fruit is known for its creamy, exotic tasting pulp, used throughout Brazil and Peru to make fresh juice, ice cream, yogurts and jam. The fruit ripens in the rainy months from January to April and is considered a culinary delicacy in South American cities where demand outstrips supply.[49]

Given the close relationship to the cocoa tree, in addition to using the pulp of Cupuaçu as a foodstuff, the seeds of the tree are used to manufacture Cupuaçu chocolate, known in Brazil as 'Cupulate', manufactured by local Amazonian communities for generations. In the mid-1980s, it was industrially produced by *Empresa Brasileira de Pesquisa Agropecuária* (EMBRAPA – the Brazilian Agricultural Research Corporation), a leading Brazilian governmental research institute in the agricultural field, and a patent was granted by the INPI in 1990 as patent PI1100074-0 (Rodrigues 2006, p. 101). The advantage of Cupulate is the fact that its taste and smell closely resemble that of chocolate without containing caffeine, thus rendering it a healthier product for potential consumers.

Given the popularity of Cupulate in Japan, on 11 April 1996 Japanese foodstuffs manufacturer Asahi Foods Co. Ltd. applied for registration of 'Cupuaçu' as a trade mark at the Japanese Patent Office (JPO); registration was granted by the JPO on 20 March 1998.[50] Asahi Foods Co. Ltd. also applied for trade mark registration of 'Cupuaçu' in the European Union and the United States and filed patent applications for 'Cupulate' with the JPO,[51] the European Patent Office[52] and in other Patent Cooperation Treaty (PCT)[53] countries (Rodrigues 2006, p. 101).

In December 2002, in the course of negotiating a contract for exporting handmade 'Cupuaçu' products to Germany, Amazonlink encountered obstacles related to intellectual property. The German importers called the deal off because of the existence of a trade mark on the word 'Cupuaçu', registered in the European Union with the Trade Marks and Designs Registration Office of the European Union (OHIM) (Rodrigues 2006, p. 102; Schmidlehner 2003).[54] Amazonlink then carried out a search of the main patent and trade mark office databases and discovered that 'Cupuaçu' had also been registered as a trade mark by Asahi Foods Co. Ltd. with the United States Patent and Trademark Office (USPTO) and the JPO, as well as several patent applications that were related to inventions comprising processes of extracting oils and fats from Cupuaçu seed. As a result, Asahi Foods Co. Ltd. was in a position to prevent other producers from using the term 'Cupuaçu' from the labelling of their products and, if the patents were granted, preventing others from using the claimed methods of extracting the oils and fats.

Amazonlink claimed this had caused harm to producers from local communities and indigenous peoples in the Amazon who felt unable to use the word 'Cupuaçu' to describe their exports of jams, sweets and other Cupuaçu products. Producers in the Amazon were instead forced to sell their products under a different name. Amazonlink.org also found that Asahi Foods Co. Ltd. had filed for several patents on claimed inventions derived from Cupuaçu.[55]

A campaign 'Cupuaçu é nosso' ('Cupuaçu is ours'), coordinated by the GTA in collaboration with Amazonlink, other NGOs and groups of small producers then began targeting trade marks on Cupuaçu in an attempt to raise public awareness of this and other cases of alleged misappropriation and their impact on the commercial, ethical and cultural activities of the local communities and indigenous peoples of the Amazon. In this sense, the Cupuaçu case became emblematic of the broader campaign against biopiracy in Brazil and helped to mobilize public opinion and attract media attention at both the national and international level and to increase the awareness and engagement of local communities and indigenous peoples themselves in the debate on how to address alleged cases of biopiracy in Brazil.

Widening the debate beyond the narrow legal issue of determining whether the trade marks or patents should be revoked in relation to Cupuaçu, the campaign also used the case to highlight the type of arrangements and ethical standards that should be adopted under Brazilian national law to prevent biopiracy and to ensure that local communities and indigenous peoples receive an equitable share of the benefits resulting from the commercial exploitation of goods, often undertaken by foreign companies, derived from the biodiversity of the Amazon.

The campaign emphasized that the fight against biopiracy and the introduction of measures to ensure a fair and equitable share of benefits for local communities and indigenous peoples were in line with the positions that Brazil had adopted internationally at the CBD-COP, the WTO and other international fora where the relationship between intellectual property and CBD principles were being discussed.

The campaign received support from local communities and indigenous peoples, as well as from national and international NGOs. This put strong pressure on the Brazilian government to take an active interest in addressing the impact of intellectual property rights on local communities and indigenous peoples in the Amazon. The campaigners believed that the Lula government in Brazil, especially via Environment Minister Marina Silva, should play a part in their fight against biopiracy and take the fight to multilateral fora such as the WIPO (Schmidlehner 2003).

Amazonlink and GTA, in partnership with other organizations, worked with the local communities and indigenous peoples of the Amazon that produce Cupuaçu products to initiate a legal challenge with the aim of ensuring annulment of the trade mark at the JPO on grounds that a proper name of a natural species cannot be trade marked.

In 2003 Amazonlink approached IDCID, who assisted in formulating the legal argument.[56] IDCID invested six months of its time, without any additional external funding, to draw up the legal strategy for opposing trade marks and patent applications on 'Cupuaçu'. From a strategic perspective, IDCID considered the case of great symbolic value in terms of creating greater awareness of the issues surrounding biopiracy – and the value of this included raising awareness amongst the Amazonian peoples themselves so that they could have a greater appreciation of the legal tools available to protect their indigenous products and traditional knowledge. From a legal perspective, IDCID considered the intellectual property rights granted to be detrimental to Brazilian cultural, environmental and commercial interests (Rodrigues 2006, p. 103).

Using funding provided by the Amazonian Working Group and USAID,[57] Brazilian law firm Trench, Rossi & Watanabe was approached and instructed to commence legal proceedings and in turn used its association with international law firm Baker & McKenzie to represent the Amazon peoples in legal proceedings before the JPO.[58] The decision to commence the legal proceedings in Japan rather than at OHIM or the USPTO was taken at the beginning of March 2003 because preliminary legal analysis revealed that the deadline for requesting invalidation of the registration of the trade mark 'Cupuaçu' would expire on 20 March 2003, while the wider significance of challenging Asahi Foods Co. Ltd. in its own home territory was also considered an important factor (Rodrigues 2006, p. 103).[59]

Financial resources for instructing Baker & McKenzie were provided by the GTA through its grants from USAID and the World Bank (Rodrigues 2006, p. 102). The INPI also supported the petition to cancel the trade mark granted by the JPO, while the Brazilian Minister of Environment, Marina Silva, a well-known Amazonian activist, and the Brazilian Ministry of Foreign Affairs offered political support (Rodrigues 2006, p. 102). Nonetheless, despite requests for financial support from the Brazilian government, none was forthcoming.

On 20 March 2003 Amazonlink, GTA, APA Flora, IDCID (under its former name CIITED) and others filed an administrative procedure order to cancel trade mark registration 4126269 before the JPO. The subsequent decision of the JPO,[60] handed down on 18 February 2004, to cancel the trade mark on Cupuaçu was based on grounds that there was an absence of an alternative term to Cupuaçu for competitors, and that it is not possible to register a word trade mark that indicates, in a common way, the name of raw materials, or in the alternative the possibility of misleading consumers who buy products produced with fat and oils extracted from sources other than 'Cupuaçu' (Rodrigues 2006, p. 103).

The legal significance of the decision lies in the fact that it clarified that a term of indigenous origin, known within Brazil as a generic denomination of a raw material, should be kept in the public domain (Rodrigues 2006, p. 103). Strategically, for NGOs cancellation of the trade mark became, in the words of the President of Amazonlink, Michael Schmidlehner, 'a landmark in the formation of Amazonian and Brazilian civil society's self-assertion and capacity to act', adding that '[a]nother important aspect is that this lawsuit and the campaign has given us the opportunity to alert communities and broadcast information and clarifications about biopiracy in general'.[61]

Furthermore, the JPO refused Asahi Food Co. Ltd.'s application for a patent on the processing of Cupuaçu seeds into a chocolate-like product, Cupulate. The decision was based on the fact that the Brazilian Agricultural Research Corporation, EMBRAPA, had previously disclosed the process in an earlier patent application.

Ultimately, although the term 'biopiracy' does not apply to the registration of trade marks as this does not involve any genetic resources, the Cupuaçu trade mark case was perceived as a victory against biopiracy in Brazil (Rodrigues 2006, p. 103). On 8 March 2004 more than two thousand people participated in a public event against biopiracy, organized by Amazonlink, in commemoration of the cancellation of the name Cupuaçu as a trade mark in Japan, with a giant banner reading 'Cupuaçu é nosso' exposed in the city centre park in Rio Branco, the capital of the state of Acre, Brazil.[62]

ANALYSIS OF THE 'CUPUAÇU IS OURS' CAMPAIGN

Amazonlink worked extremely efficiently on a small budget and scarce resources. A tiny NGO with only eight staff, Amazonlink undertook all its activities during the Cupuaçu campaign with an anonymous private donation of £8000, made through Greenpeace, from a UK citizen.

In addition to involving legal experts with the technical knowledge and professional status necessary to bring proceedings before the JPO, Amazonlink played an important role in awareness-building and advocacy activities, and organizing Cupuaçu campaign workshops at grassroots level. In terms of maintaining the momentum of the campaign and ensuring that its implications were felt more widely by the Brazilian government, these inputs by Amazonlink were crucial so that local communities and indigenous peoples could engage in public debates and demonstrations about the intellectual property issues related to Cupuaçu in an informed way.

It is also notable that, prior to the 'Cupuaçu is ours' campaign, the indigenous and local communities involved had had negative experiences of working with large international NGOs in relation to conservation issues and are consequently still highly sceptical when international NGOs offer to assist communities with intellectual property-related issues concerning biopiracy. International NGOs are seen as foreigners coming to exploit rather than help indigenous and local communities and there is a perception that they are funded by industry.

One example of an interaction on conservation issues that exacerbated this negative perception of international NGOs was the implementation of UNESCO's Man and Biosphere (MAB) programme in the state of Acre, Brazil.[63] A group of six international NGOs (including the Nature Conservancy[64] and the World Wildlife Fund[65]) presented local communities in the state of Acre with a fully developed project. Claiming that they had learnt about the project only through newspaper articles, local communities rejected the project on grounds that it lacked prior consultation and transparency. Meeting with the NGOs in an attempt to broker an agreement on the project, local community leaders are reported to have responded angrily, telling NGOs 'we will not be your slaves' and demanding the creation of a participatory council to further discuss implementation of the MAB project and how it could be implemented in the state of Acre.[66]

By working locally and borne out of a small NGO's work aimed at providing rural producers in the Amazon with buyers of sustainable products abroad, Amazonlink established a relationship of trust and collaboration with local communities and indigenous peoples that had been absent in these groups' previous relations with international NGOs working on land rights and deforestation issues.

The 'Cupuaçu is ours' campaign grew out of the efforts of a local NGO to openly challenge the existence of patents and trade marks on Cupuaçu and products derived from it. More widely, the campaign also served as an example to highlight concerns associated with biopiracy and to mobilize public opinion in Brazil and the federal government to take action.

The existence of coalitions, networks and linkages between NGOs, indigenous peoples and local communities, academic experts and legal practitioners was a significant factor in the outcome in terms of the cancellation of the trade mark on Cupuaçu in Japan. This was not in itself a case of biopiracy but a direct consequence was the mobilizing of support for and awareness of the broader biopiracy campaign in Brazil. The case was a symbolic triumph in what local communities and indigenous peoples consider a battle to reclaim national sovereignty over the biological and cultural legacy of these groups in Brazil.

The 'Cupuaçu is ours' campaign was significant because local communities and indigenous peoples played a direct role as stakeholders articulating and highlighting the issues involved. The NGOs involved in the 'Cupuaçu is ours' campaign also played an important role in supporting local communities and indigenous peoples, helping them to build their campaigning skills in terms of asserting their rights in a wider sense. It also helped local communities and indigenous peoples to reassert and preserve the traditional management systems for the cultivation of Cupuaçu, highlighting the importance of traditional knowledge held by local communities and indigenous peoples.

The campaign was also important in helping different stakeholders to provide inputs into Brazilian policy positions related to international intellectual property and the conservation and sustainable use of bio-diversity, in particular with regard to on-going discussions at the CBD, WTO and the WIPO. In the words of Michael Schmidlehner, President of Amazonlink, '[f]iling requests for the revoking of patents and trade-marks can only be a small part of the strategy to realise the autonomy of indigenous peoples. Even efforts to create legal mechanisms to protect tra-ditional knowledge will not resolve the problem in the long run. If we are interested in sustainable development and fair relations with traditional cultures, the discussion must go to the roots of the problem. Patents on life forms must be rejected and the concept of intellectual property itself needs to be reassessed' (Schmidlehner 2003).

NGOs representing indigenous peoples and local communities have also had complex relationships with the Brazilian federal government. At times the relationship has been a fruitful one. In the recent past, for instance, there was greater access to the Ministry of Environment than the Ministry of Agriculture by virtue of Minister of Environment, former rubber tapper and environmentalist, Marina Silva's close connections with NGOs and wider social movements in the Amazon rainforest of Brazil. However, following Marina Silva's resignation, it is once again the economic policy-making ministries including trade and agriculture that hold the real power and traditional criticisms that the federal government is not adequately representing the interests of indigenous peoples and local communities have once more come to the fore.

The Cupuaçu campaign also highlighted disconnection that exists between Brazilian intellectual property-related policies internationally and domestically that have also been observed in relation to HIV/AIDS activists. The evidence-based arguments of local communities and indig-enous peoples offer great potential for development-orientated intellectual property norm-setting and policy-making activities at multilateral institu-tions but this knowledge resource has been significantly under-utilized thus far in the multinational context.

Delegates representing developing country governments at multilateral institutions are often unaware of the high quality specialized knowl-edge and the potential for evidence-based arguments on the impact of intellectual property law and policy that could be derived from local communities and indigenous peoples. Reasons for this include tensions that emerged within national coordination of intellectual property policy-making mechanisms. Local communities and indigenous peoples are also excluded from engagement with multilateral norm-setting and policy-making processes by the fact that they often have little or no access to the internet. They also face a barrier to participation given that English is the language of the internet and global advocacy networks but is not widely spoken by the general population in Brazil. This excludes activists from, and prevents their participation in, internet-based information exchange activities.

Indigenous peoples and local communities in Brazil also find it difficult to attract funding to allow them to travel and participate in intellectual property-related norm-setting and policy-making activities at multilateral institutions. This effectively excludes them from participation and leads to their reliance on representation by national delegations, even though these groups often have an antagonistic or, at best, ambivalent relationship with government at local and national level in Brazil.

In conclusion, motivated by the belief that indigenous groups and local communities in the Amazon have an inalienable human right to protect the biodiversity over which they are the custodians, Amazonlink worked effectively in coalition with other NGOs such as GTA, with academics and with legal experts who brought the technical knowledge and professional status necessary to bring proceedings before the JPO, proceedings which were ultimately successful in terms of having the Cupuaçu trade mark revoked.

The 'Cupuaçu is ours' campaign also worked well because it involved wider social movements at grassroots level. This was crucial for maintaining the momentum necessary so that local communities and indigenous peoples could engage in public debates and demonstrations about the intellectual property issues related to Cupuaçu in an informed and articulate way. Not for the first time, coalition building and the interface between human rights and intellectual property rights had proved crucial to the outcome of the case.

NOTES

1. Public health service delivery is shared equally by the different levels of government: federal, state, municipal and the national health system (Sistema Único da Saúde – SUS). In practice, the delivery and management of health services is increasingly being decentralized to the state and municipal levels, reflecting the government's sensitivity to the population's preference for more local governance. The federal level of government defines the policies and regulations, grants technical and financial support for the states

and municipal governments and provides some service delivery. State and municipal governments in turn contribute the remainder of the health budget and share responsibility for health service delivery (Cohen and Lybecker 2005, p. 214).

2. A study conducted by Fabiola Sulpino Vieira (2007), Evolução dos Gastos do Ministério da Saúde com Medicamentos, found that, while total health expenditure by the Brazilian Ministry of Health increased by 9.6 per cent between 2002 and 2006, drug expenditure alone increased by 123.9 per cent over the same period. http://portal.saude.gov.br/portal/arquivos/pdf/estsudo_gasto_medicamentos.pdf.

3. Data provided by the National STD and AIDS Programme website. Available at: http://www.aids.gov.br/data/Pages/LUMIS9DDD0E43ENIE.htm.

4. INPI is a federal institution created in 1970, and linked to the Ministry of Development, Industry and Foreign Trade. Supported by Industrial Property Law number 9.279/96, the INPI has as its main purpose to execute in Brazil the rules that regulate industrial property and to register contracts concerning transfer of technology, industrial property licensing, and franchising, taking into account its social, economical, juridical and technical function. It is also the responsibility of the INPI to evaluate conventions, treaties, and agreements on industrial property which Brazil is party to.

5. Article 230(3) of Law 9.279/96 provides that 'once the provisions established in this Article have been satisfied and the granting of the patent in the country where the first application was filed has been proven, the patent shall be granted in Brazil, just as it was granted in its country of origin'.

6. Including in particular Zidovudine (AZT), Didanosine (ddI), Lamivudine (3TC), Stavudine (d4T), Indinavir (IDV), Ritonavir (RTV) and Nevirapine (NVP) (Love 2006, p. 1).

7. A study conducted by the Federal University of Rio de Janeiro shows that, had pipeline patents not been granted to some of the drugs purchased by the Ministry of Health between 2001 and 2005, the country would have saved US$420 million.

8. Lei 9.279/96 da Propriedade Industrial, translated in *British Industrial Property Law* 23 (1998), reproduced in de Mello e Souza (2005, p. 201, n. 92).

9. In 2003 an additional Presidential Decree 4.830/03 clarified the scope of these situations under Article 71 further. These revisions provided clearer definitions of national emergency and public interest and simplified the mechanism for issuing compulsory licences by giving the Ministry of Health greater authority to act. According the Shadlen (2009, p. 48), Presidential Decree 4.830/03 crucially stipulates that private firms supplying the government constitutes 'public use' and is thus acceptable under Article 71, and also requires patent owners to transfer technological knowledge in the case of compulsory licences, thus increasing the Ministry of Health's capacity to leverage price reductions from patent-holding pharmaceutical firms.

10. A notable exception was the statement made by the then Minister of Health the previous year *Statement of José Serra, Minister of Health, to the 2001 USTR Special 301 Report*, 3 May 2001. Available at: http://www.cptech.org/ip/health/c/brazil/serra05032001.html.

11. The Ministry of Health's budget for purchasing antiretroviral drugs in 2007 was R$984 million. Authoritative estimates demonstrate that 80 per cent of this money is used to acquire patented medicines and 20 per cent is spent on generic drugs that are manufactured domestically by Brazilian companies. The fact that such a huge portion of the budget is being spent on patented medicines has put the sustainability and universality of this healthcare policy in jeopardy.

12. *Brazil – Measures Affecting Patent Protection. Request for the Establishment of a Panel by the United States.* WTO Document WT/DS199/3, 9 January 2001. Available at: http://www.wtocenter.org.tw/SmartKMS/fileviewer?id=73103. See also *Press Communique by the Government of Brazil*, 25 June 2001, in which Brazil maintained its conviction that Article 68 is fully consistent with the TRIPS Agreement and an important instrument available to the Government, in particular in its efforts to increase access of the population to medicines and to combat diseases such as AIDS. Available

at: http://www.cptech.org/ip/health/c/brazil/brazilstatement06252001.html (visited 23 February 2009).

13. WTO Reporter, 'United States Drops WTO Case against Brazil Over HIV/AIDS Patent Law' (26 June, 2001). Copyright 2001 by The Bureau of National Affairs, available at: http://www.cptech.org/ip/health/c/brazil/bna06262001.html.

14. Jorge Beloqui, GIV, interview with the author, 19 March 2006.

15. One more recent example of the extent to which non-English speaking activists could be excluded from debates on access to medicines taking place in multilateral forums was the fact that HIV/AIDS NGOs in Brazil were completely unaware of the joint Brazil-Kenya proposal to the WHO for a Global R&D Framework.

16. Section 204 U.S.C. *Preference for United States industry.*

'Notwithstanding any other provision of this chapter, no small business firm or nonprofit organization which receives title to any subject invention and no assignee of any such small business firm or nonprofit organization shall grant to any person the exclusive right to use or sell any subject invention in the United States unless such person agrees that any products embodying the subject invention or produced through the use of the subject invention will be manufactured substantially in the United States. However, in individual cases, the requirement for such an agreement may be waived by the Federal agency under whose funding agreement the invention was made upon a showing by the small business firm, nonprofit organization, or assignee that reasonable but unsuccessful efforts have been made to grant licenses on similar terms to potential licensees that would be likely to manufacture substantially in the United States or that under the circumstances domestic manufacture is not commercially feasible.'

USPTO Manual of Patent Examining Procedure (MPEP): http://www.uspto.gov/web/offices/pac/mpep/documents/appxl_35_U_S_C_204.htm.

17. *Brazil – Measures Affecting Patent Protection.* Notification of Mutually Agreed Solution WT/DS199/4, G/L/454, IP/D/23/Add.1, 19 July 2001. See also Joint US-Brazil Statement, 25 June 2001, available at: http://www.cptech.org/ip/health/c/brazil/statement06252001.html.

18. Ultimately, however, Oxfam retained its distance from the core group. ActionAid, meanwhile, subsequently withdrew from access to medicines issues in Brazil altogether in a move described by some Brazilian HIV/AIDS activists interviewed for this book as 'pitiful'.

19. C. Raghavan (2001), *US to withdraw TRIPS dispute against Brazil, South-North Development Monitor* (SUNS). Available at: http://www.twnside.org.sg/title/withdraw.htm.

20. United Nations Commission on Human Rights (2001) at para 56.

21. On 4 May 2007, Brazil finally issued a compulsory licence for the ARV Efavirenz after failing to reach agreement with the patent owner, Merck, to lower prices of the drug. Announcing the compulsory licence, the Ministry of Health said that the action would reduce the cost of purchasing Efavirenz, currently used by 75000 of the 180000 people living with HIV/AIDS in Brazil, by up to US$240 million between 2007 and 2012, when Merck's patent expires. Meanwhile President Luiz Inácio Lula da Silva, signing the decree granting the compulsory licence, said 'between our business and our health, we are going to take care of our health'. *Brazil Issues Compulsory Licence for AIDS Drug*, Bridges Weekly Trade Digest, Vol. 11, Number 16, 9 May 2007. In other instances, the Brazilian government has opted for voluntary agreements with multinational pharmaceutical companies. On 9 May 2006, for instance, Minister of Health Agenor Álvares and the Vice-President of Gilead Science, Joseph Steele, signed an agreement that resulted in a 51 per cent price reduction of the ARV drug tenofovir. The price of each capsule consequently reduced from US$7.68 to US$3.80, representing an immediate saving to the Brazilian National STD and AIDS Programme of US$31.4 million per annum. *Brazilian deal on tenofovir – translation of Ministry of Health Press Release of 9th May*, posting on IP-Health list server by Michel Lotrowska, MSF, 16 May 2006.

22. United Nations Commission on Human Rights (2001) at para 58.

23. In 2006, GTPI/REBRIP member organizations also attempted to exploit administrative channels to prevent the INPI from granting undue patents for essential medicines. The group submitted inputs for the examination of two patents: the first referred to an application by Abbott for a second patent for the Lopinavir/Ritonavir combination (Kaletra) and the second was for a patent application made by Gilead for its Tenofovir Disoproxil Fumarate medication (Viread). Third party inputs to patent examination are a provision contained in Brazilian Industrial Property Law that permits any interested parties to submit documents and information to assist in the examination of patent applications being analysed by the INPI (Article 31, Industrial Property Law 9.279/96). The purpose of the two submissions to the INPI was to present the technical grounds for not granting patents for these two antiretroviral drugs. The inputs called into question the patent claims of each medicine using different arguments. In the case of Tenofovir Disoproxil Fumarate, each of the substances described were known in the state of art before the application's filing date. The active ingredient that combats HIV/AIDS is Tenofovir, which has been known since 1989, and the other compounds developed have no new technical effect for a specialist in the subject, since they are standard practices used in organic synthesis. This application for an invention patent, therefore, does not present any inventiveness.

24. In November 2007, FENAFAR, on behalf of GTPI/REBRIP, filed a formal complaint to the General Attorney's Office, claiming that pipeline provisions of the 1996 Industrial Property Law violate constitutional rights. The filing relies on constitutional texts asserting: (i) the supremacy of society's interests and the pursuit of the country's technological and economic development over intellectual property protection; and (ii) society's vested right to the content of certain patents, as the objects of pipeline patents were already in the public domain before the Industrial Property Law was passed. As of late 2008, the complaint was still under analysis (Rosina et al. 2008, p. 185).

25. Rebrip Intellectual Property Working Group: http://www.rebrip.org.br/_rebrip/pagina.php?id=655.

26. Conectas is a Brazilian NGO that seeks to strengthen the experience exchange between human rights practitioners of the southern hemisphere. Conectas: Who we are: http://www.conectas.org/historico.php?idioma=en.

27. The Ministry of Health's National STD and AIDS Programme is the national authority on combating the epidemic. Its principal mission is to reduce the incidence of HIV/AIDS, to control other STDs and to improve the quality of life of people living with HIV/AIDS (Brazilian Ministry of Health, Health Surveillance Secretariat and National Programme on STD and AIDS 2008, p. 9).

28. *Non Governmental Organizations-NGOs and Federal State Prosecutors Will Move Civil Action for Compulsory Licensing of Kaletra*, ABIA press release, 1 December 2005, available at: http://www.cptech.org/ip/health/c/brazil/abia11302005.html.

29. Pedro Chequer left his post as Director of the Brazilian National STD and AIDS Programme on 3 April 2006. His replacement was paediatrician and public health specialist Mariângela Simão.

30. It contrasts with the decision of the federal government to issue a compulsory licence for the ARV Efavirenz, the patent for which is owned by Merck, less than two years later. At the beginning of 2007, the Ministry of Health engaged in negotiations with Merck with regard to the price of Efavirenz, a highly effective drug used by 38 per cent of HIV/AIDS patients in Brazil. After several months of unsuccessful negotiations, on 24 April 2007, Ordinance no. 886 declared Efavirenz a drug of national public interest. This was followed, on 4 May 2007, by Presidential Decree no. 6.108 which granted a compulsory licence for the manufacture of Efavirenz for non-commercial use by Brazil's public laboratories (Rosina et al. 2008, p. 191). Within months, the Brazilian government had reported a reduction of 72.2 per cent in the cost of supplying this drug, demonstrating the effectiveness of the threat of compulsory licensing as a negotiating tool when dealing with patent-owning multinational pharmaceutical companies (National STD and AIDS Programme 2008, p. 87).

31. *Sign on by the Brazilian Network for the Integration of Peoples (REBRIP)*, post on IP-Health list server by Pedro de Paranaguá Moniz, Fundação Getúlio Vargas (FGV – Getúlio Vargas Foundation), 2 March 2006.
32. *Release (inglês e português) – Organisations Contest the Constitutionality of the Brazilian IP Law (Organizações contestam a constitucionalidade da Lei de Propriedade Industrial)*, post on IP-Health list server, Renata Reis, ABIA, 20 November 2007.
33. According to FENAFAR, in total, 1182 patent applications were filed under the pipeline mechanism in Brazil, many of them relating to the treatment of HIV/AIDS and cancer, including the ARV drug Efavirenz and the cancer medicine Glivec.
34. The INPI drafted guidelines for examining patent applications in the areas of biotechnology and pharmacy filed after 31 December 1994 and this document is designed to help examiners interpret the Brazilian patent law and so determine what does and what does not qualify for patent protection. However, these guidelines are much broader than the rules contained in Brazil's intellectual property legislation and they are also inconsistent with the objectives of the Brazilian Constitution for protecting intellectual property (Article 5, item XXIX of the Constitution), causing countless patents to be granted in breach of the prevailing rules in the country. GTPI/REBRIP argue that the INPI guidelines allow the possibility of protecting new uses of known products, facilitating the practice known as ever-greening to the detriment of protection for legitimate pharmaceutical innovations. In addition, the guidelines permit the patenting of Deoxyribonucleic acid (DNA) sequences, under the justification that they are merely chemical compounds and not a part of living beings, the latter not considered patentable under Brazilian law.
35. *Brazilian Local Groups Launch Campaign against Patent Abuse*, posting on IP-Health list server, Renata Reis, 3 December 2008. The prior informed consent mechanism originates from the creation of the National Health Surveillance Agency (ANVISA) under Provisional Measure 2.006/99, subsequently converted into Law 10.196/01 (Murphy and Rodrigues 2005, p. 3). Under the prior informed consent mechanism, any pharmaceutical patent application that is approved by the INPI is then sent to the Ministry of Health for review and the patent is issued only after officials in ANVISA issue 'prior consent' (Shadlen 2009, p. 47). This means that, once the INPI has completed its examination of the patent application, it is forwarded to ANVISA which in turn analyses the patent applications, verifies whether the patentability requirements have been met, and conducts a material analysis based on whether the granting of the patent has implications for access to medicines (Basso 2006, p. 55). ANVISA has legal supremacy over the INPI (Murphy and Rodrigues 2005, p. 4) and, in theory, can deny the granting of a pharmaceutical patent or processes against INPI's recommendation (Rosina et al. 2008, p. 193). In practice, this rarely happens. The most recent report (2008) published by ANVISA shows that out of the 1083 patent requests sent to it for analysis, 709 (65 per cent) were accepted, 44 (4 per cent) were not, and 330 processes (30 per cent) are still ongoing. In the rare cases where a patent application is not accepted by ANVISA, the applicants have a right of appeal. In the event of a conflict between ANVISA and INPI, meetings are held in an attempt to reach a consensus; in the event of an impasse, the patent will not be granted. In theory, the prior consent mechanism is important, as it could prevent the granting of pharmaceutical patents that work against public health interests. In practice, however, it is unclear that any patent application has ever been denied due to ANVISA's efforts (Rosina et al. 2008, p. 193) and ANVISA has failed to publish its own guidelines of examination (Murphy and Rodrigues 2005, p. 4). In 2009 in the National Trade Estimates Report, the United States raised concerns regarding Brazil's Law 10.196 of 2001, which includes a requirement that ANVISA approval be obtained prior to the issuance of a pharmaceutical patent. On 23 June 2008 ANVISA issued Resolution RDC 45, standardizing, to some extent, the procedures for review of pharmaceutical patent applications. Nonetheless, ANVISA's role in reviewing such patent applications remains non-transparent and has contributed to an increasing backlog in the issuance of patents (United States Trade Representative 2009, p. 44).

36. Presidential Decree 3.201 of 6 October 1999, available at: http://www.cptech.org/ip/health/c/brazil/PresDecree.html.

37. In May 2005 HIV/AIDS activists welcomed a decision by Brazil to turn down US funds because of a clause in the agreement condemning prostitution. The US development agency, USAID, had offered Brazil around $40m (£21m). But Brazil's Pedro Chequer, head of the Brazilian National STD and AIDS Programme, said the US's conservative approach to treating the disease would not help. *Brazil turns down US Aids funds*, BBC News, 4 May 2005. Available at: http://news.bbc.co.uk/1/hi/world/americas/4513805.stm.

38. *Background Document for 3rd Commission Meeting, Brazil, 31 January–4 February 2005*, Commission on Intellectual Property Rights, Innovation and Public Health (CIPIH), available at: http://www.who.int/intellectualproperty/events/meeting3/en/.

39. Rather than engaging in campaigning and mass activism, IDCID is composed of four academic working groups on: services; poverty and development; WTO dispute settlement; and intellectual property. The aim of IDCID is to provide technical inputs to add greater sophistication to policy debates. The intellectual property working group of IDCID was set up in 2002 under the coordination of Professor Maristela Basso and, on 11 and 12 March 2004, hosted a conference entitled '10 Years of TRIPS – Democratization of Access to Health' organized jointly with MSF and the GTPI/REBRIP. Amongst speakers at the event were Pascale Boulet and Michel Lotrowska of MSF, and James Love of CPTech and Brazilian parliamentary representatives Deputy Jandira Feghali and Deputy Roberto Gouveia Nascimento.

40. *Biopiracy in the Amazon – Introduction*, available at: http://www.amazonlink.org/biopiracy/index.htm.

41. See, for example, IP-Watch, 'Brazil Fights to Make Case for International Biodiversity Protection', 31 May 2006.

42. In Brazil there is currently a provisional law on genetic resources and traditional knowledge, 'Medida Provisória No. 2186-16/01', partially regulated by the Decree No. 3.945 of 28 September 2001.

43. The CBD under Article 15 recognizes 'the sovereign rights of States over their natural resources, the authority to determine access to genetic resources rests with the national governments and is subject to national legislation'.

44. Marina Silva resigned her post as Brazilian Environment Minister on 14 May 2008, citing difficulties she had faced 'for some time' in implementing the government's environmental agenda. BBC News: *Brazil's Amazon minister resigns*, available at: http://news.bbc.co.uk/1/hi/world/americas/7399715.stm.

45. The 'Growing Diversity' workshop was part of the 'Growing Diversity' project launched in January 2000 by four NGOs: GRAIN (Barcelona, Spain), Centro Internazionale Crocevia (Rome, Italy), Bread for the World (Stuttgart, Germany) and the Swedish Society for Nature Conservation (Stockholm, Sweden). The main objective of the project was to help empower and strengthen groups involved in local management of biodiversity in Africa, Asia and Latin America. GRAIN, 2002, Growing Diversity, *Seedling*, July 2002, GRAIN Publications, available at: http://www.grain.org/seedling/?id=198. The final report of the 'Growing Diversity' project is available at: http://www.grain.org/gd/en/gd-final-en.pdf.

46. The Amazonian Working Group (GTA) is a network of over 600 NGOs and other grassroots organizations working in the Brazilian Amazon Region. See: http://www.gta.org.br/gta.php. Profile of GTA available at: http://www.amazonia.org.br/english/guia/detalhes.cfm?id=13604&tipo=6&cat_id=84&subcat_id=410.

47. Rio Branco Commitment of 19 May 2002. See GRAIN (2003) *The Growing Diversity Project: Process and Results*, page 24, available at: http://www.grain.org/gd/en/gd-final-en.pdf.

48. *Amazonlink: who we are*, available at: http://www.amazonlink.org/amazonengl.htm.

49. *Biopiracy in the Amazon – Cupuaçu*, available at: http://www.amazonlink.org/biopiracy/cupuacu.htm.

50. JPO trade mark no. 4126269.
51. JP2001348593. Abstract: Oil and fat derived from Cupuaçu, method of producing the same and its use.
52. Requested patent: EP1219698. Abstract: fat originating in Cupuaçu seed, process for producing the same and use thereof.
53. Requested patent: WO0125377. Abstract: fat originating in Cupuaçu seed, process for producing the same and use thereof.
54. Community trade mark 000923151.
55. *The Cupuaçu case*, available at: http://www.amazonlink.org/biopiracy/cupuacu.htm.
56. See http://idcid.org.br/.
57. Maristela Basso, IDCID, interview with the author, 20 March 2006.
58. Brazilian law firm Trench, Rossi & Watanabe has access to an international network through its association with international law firm Baker & McKenzie, see: http://www.trenchrossiewatanabe.com.br/ing/index.html.
59. On 11 December 2003 the Brazilian diplomatic representation in Brussels filed a cancellation request (number 764) to cancel Community trade mark 000923151 while the USPTO published a cancellation decision on the US 'Cupuaçu' trade mark on 23 February 2005.
60. Decision of the Japanese Patent Office in *amazonlink.org et al v. Asahi Foods*, 18 February 2004.
61. *Trademark 'Cupuaçu' cancelled in Japan*, available at: http://www.amazonlink.org/biopiracy/2004_03_01.htm.
62. Rio Branco – Acre – Brazil: Amazonlink.org celebrates first 'Cupuaçu victory' with Capoeira and Rock, available at: http://www.amazonlink.org/biopiracy/2004_03_08.htm.
63. The UNESCO Man and the Biosphere Programme (MAB), proposes an interdisciplinary research agenda and capacity building aiming to improve the relationship of people with their environment globally.
64. *About Us: learn more about the Nature Conservancy*, available at: http://www.nature.org/aboutus/?src=t5.
65. *Welcome to WWF*, available at: http://www.wwf.org/.
66. Michael F. Schmidlehner, Amazonlink, interview with the author, 23 March 2006.

6. India

INTRODUCTION

On 31 December 1600, Queen Elizabeth I granted a Royal Charter to the 'Governor and Company of Merchants of London trading with the East Indies' and began a process leading to British colonial rule of the Indian subcontinent, administered initially by the East India Company and, from 1858, by the British Crown until independence was secured in 1947. This history is significant because India's struggle against colonial rule has had profound implications for the culture of social activism that informs Indian NGOs today and, in particular, how human rights principles are used to frame debates on the impact of intellectual property rights on Indian society.

The origins of the Indian patent system lie in the Patents Act of 1856, which closely followed the British Patents Act of 1852 (Ragavan 2006, p. 278). Then, following the transfer of rule from the East India Company to the British Crown, subsequent legislative instruments were introduced in the form of the Patents Act 1859, the Patents and Designs Act of 1872 and the Inventions and Designs Act of 1888. These were later consolidated into the Patents and Designs Act of 1911, which was the legislation in force at the time that India became independent.

After gaining independence from Britain in 1947, the Indian government set up two committees of enquiry to recommend patent law reforms. The first, the Patents Enquiry Committee (1948–1950), also known as the Tek Chand Committee, concluded that India's patent provisions enabled foreign companies to obtain patent rights beyond the scope of their inventions and recommended incorporating compulsory licensing provisions to minimize the potential for abuse of monopolies (Mueller 2007, p. 511; Rangnekar 2005, p. 3; Ragavan 2006, p. 279).[1]

The second, the Committee on the Revision of the Patents Laws (1957–1959), known as the Ayyangar Committee, looked more specifically at poverty issues and noted the high mortality rates in India.[2] The Ayyangar Committee then recommended that granting patents in critical areas such as food and medicines be curtailed since the high price of patented products could deny Indian citizens access to resources and violate the right to life, enshrined in Article 21 of the Constitution of India (Ragavan 2006, p. 285).[3]

ARTICLE 21 OF THE CONSTITUTION OF INDIA: PROTECTION OF LIFE AND PERSONAL LIBERTY

No person shall be deprived of his life or personal liberty except according to procedure established by law.

Of particular concern to the Ayyangar Committee was the fact that, at that time, foreign pharmaceutical companies supplied almost 85 per cent of medicines in India and, according to the United States Senate Subcommittee on Anti-Trust and Monopoly (the Kefauver Subcommittee), by 1961, prices for pharmaceutical products in India were amongst the highest in the world (Keayla 2005, p. 2).

So, in order to protect the constitutional right to life and promote industrial development in India, the Ayyangar Committee recommended that product patents should not be granted in critical areas such as food and pharmaceutical products.[4] Instead, patent protection should be limited to the method of making food, pharmaceuticals and chemicals, leaving the final products free from patent protection and consequently allowing local generic drug companies to manufacture without infringing patent rights (Ragavan 2006, p. 286).

The Ayyangar Committee also recommended that India ensure that patented inventions were worked locally to facilitate industrial development, with the government giving powers to revoke patents or issue compulsory licences in order to redress instances where foreign patent owners were not working the invention locally (Ragavan 2006, p. 287).

As a result of the Ayyangar Committee's recommendations, the Patents Act of 1970, which came into force on 20 April 1972, was designed as a response to growing concerns in India about how best to strike a balance between patents rights as incentives to innovate on the one hand and how best to protect the public interest and promote industrial development in India on the other. In line with the Ayyangar Committee's recommendations, Section 5 of the Act introduced differential treatment of food, pharmaceutical and chemical inventions by making available patent rights only for the processes of manufacture (Chaudhuri 2005, p. 37). By excluding protection of the end product, several manufacturers could each own patents for different processes of manufacturing the same pharmaceutical products (Rangnekar 2005, p. 4; Ragavan 2006, p. 289).

SECTION 5 OF THE INDIAN PATENTS ACT OF 1970

(1) In the case of inventions–

- (a) claiming substances intended for use, or capable of being used, as a food or as medicine or drug, or
- (b) relating to substances prepared or produced by chemical processes (including alloys, optical glass, semiconductors and inter-metallic compounds)

no patent shall be granted in respect of claims for the substance themselves, but claims for the methods or processes of manufacture shall be patentable.

The Indian Patents Act of 1970 also limited the term of protection for process patents on food, pharmaceutical and chemical inventions to five years,[5] with a licence of right authorizing any person to manufacture a patented product,[6] notwithstanding the patentee's approval, available for food, pharmaceutical or chemical inventions after three years.[7] With the objective of encouraging local manufacturing of inventions, the Indian Patents Act of 1970 also introduced powers for the Comptroller of Patents to issue compulsory licences based on the patent owner's ability to work the invention in India to the public's advantage.[8]

PATENTS AND ACCESS TO MEDICINES

This system of not granting patents for inventions that related to food, pharmaceutical or chemical products prevailed until the coming into force of the TRIPS Agreement and allowed the Indian pharmaceutical industry to develop considerable expertise in reverse engineering and developing new methods of manufacture in order to become highly efficient producers of generic medicines.

The Indian government did not seek the views of NGOs or other stakeholders before undertaking initial negotiations on the TRIPS Agreement in the late 1980s (Daz 2003, p. 38). In part this was because at that time, in contrast to many other countries, where there has been a significant level of engagement with intellectual property-related issues on the part of NGOs and wider social movements, in India, only a few groups had worked effectively on these issues in a sustained and coherent way (see also Daz 2003, p. 38). Furthermore, the groups that were following intellectual property-related issues had generally been fragmented, with little evidence of the type of coalition building between NGOs so evident internationally or in countries such as South Africa and Brazil that we have observed elsewhere in this book.[9]

Nevertheless, a number of well-informed individuals came forward to articulate concern about the increased cost of pharmaceutical products that would result from new international norms requiring patent protection regardless of the products in question (Matthews 2002, p. 31). In particular, the National Working Group on Patent Laws provided the focal point for informed debate in India (Rangnekar 2005, p. 7).

National Working Group on Patent Laws

Although the National Working Group on Patent Laws is not formally constituted as an NGO, it has considerable influence on patent policy in India given its composition as an informal expert group of former government officials, senior members of the judiciary and academic experts. The National Working Group on Patent Laws uses the expertise of its members to prepare briefing papers for government and stakeholders, host workshops and produce information to raise public awareness about the impact of patents on Indian society (see also Daz 2003, p. 38).[10] Under the stewardship of its convenor B.K. Keayla (a former Patent Office official and an influential figure, having retired from his post as Commissioner of Payments in the Government of India), the National Working Group on Patent Laws has taken significant steps to raise awareness about the complex issues involved in achieving compliance with the TRIPS Agreement (see also Daz 2003, p. 39).

The National Working Group on Patent Laws was formed in 1988 as a response to India's involvement in the Uruguay Round of the GATT. At that time there was little understanding about the impact of intellectual property rights on public health in India,[11] so the National Working Group on Patent Laws focused in particular on the implications of the TRIPS Agreement for the affordability and availability of medicines.

When India subsequently became a founding member of the WTO, it was obliged to introduce a series of amendments to the Patents Act of 1970 that were designed to ensure compatibility with obligations set out in the TRIPS Agreement. These amendments included measures designed to meet the obligation contained in Article 27.1 of the TRIPS Agreement to extend patent protection to all fields of technology, including food, pharmaceutical and chemical products. In order to articulate concerns about the adverse impact of compliance with the TRIPS Agreement in India, the National Working Group on Patent Laws then set up the first of four People's Commissions to examine the scope and nature of obligations and the likely implications of new international standards of intellectual property protection and enforcement.

The First People's Commission

The first People's Commission was convened in 1993 and consisted of three former judges of the Supreme Court, together with a retired chief justice of the Delhi High Court.[12] The Commission conducted two sets of hearings. The first hearings were held on 26 November 1993 and 10–11 December 1994, with the second hearings taking place on 20–22 April 1994 and 15–16 July 1994.

At the hearings, academics, economists, scientists, journalists, lawyers, politicians and grassroots activists were invited to make written and oral submissions. Subsequently, when its final report was published in 1996, the first People's Commission painted a picture of TRIPS implementation as post-colonial foreign intervention in India. The Commission's report used combative language, describing India's obligations under the TRIPS Agreement as a form of 'conquest by patent' and identifying the United States as the chief protagonist of the 'patent folly' that TRIPS contained (see Krishna Iyer et al. 1996, p. 2). In particular, the Commission's report expressed concern about the impact on India's sovereignty, democracy and the Constitution. It criticized the Indian government for failing to formulate a comprehensive analysis of the likely effects on the WTO Agreements on the economy and the country's democratic institutions.

Crucially, the Commission's report also made explicit reference to the fact that the impact of the TRIPS Agreement on drug prices and access to medicines in India could conflict with the right to life enshrined in Article 21 of the Constitution of India (see Krishna Iyer et al. 1996, p. 61). Pointing out that the Supreme Court of India had concluded that the right to health, including access to medical treatment, is a fundamental right,[13] the report argued that the Indian Patents Act 1970 could not be rewritten to allow the grant of patents for pharmaceutical products since this would constitute a violation of Article 21 of the Constitution (see Krishna Iyer et al. 1996, p. 62). So, from the outset, the National Working Group on Patent Laws was adept at framing concerns about the impact of the TRIPS Agreement on access to medicines as a human rights issue.

Then, on 27 July 1996, the implications of patents for pharmaceutical products were brought centre stage by the decision of the United States to request that the WTO Dispute Settlement Body (DSB) establish a panel to resolve its complaint against India in relation to Articles 63, 70.8 and 70.9 of the TRIPS Agreement.

The US Complaint to the WTO Dispute Settlement Body

As a developing country Member of the WTO, under Article 64.2 of the TRIPS Agreement, India was entitled to delay until 1 January 2000 bringing their laws, regulations and practices into conformity with the new obligations.[14] In addition, under Article 65.4 of the TRIPS Agreement, India was entitled to delay for an additional five years (until 1 January 2005) patent protection in areas of technology, such as pharmaceutical products, not protected within its territory prior to the entry into force of the TRIPS Agreement.

In order to take advantage of the extended transitional period before India was required to provide for pharmaceutical patent protection, under Article 70.8 of the TRIPS Agreement, the country was obliged to set up a 'mailbox' system for filing of pharmaceutical product applications which would then be reviewed when patent protection was made available by the end of the transitional period.[15]

ARTICLE 70.8 OF THE TRIPS AGREEMENT: PROTECTION OF EXISTING SUBJECT MATTER

Where a Member does not make available as of the date of entry into force of the WTO Agreement patent protection for pharmaceutical and agricultural chemical products commensurate with its obligations under Article 27, that Member shall:

(a) Notwithstanding the provisions of Part VI, provide as from the date of entry into force of the WTO Agreement a means by which applications for patents for such inventions can be filed;

(b) Apply to these applications, as of the date of application of this Agreement as if those criteria were being applied on the date of filing in that Member or, where priority is available and claimed, the priority date of the application; and

(c) Provide patent protection in accordance with this Agreement as from the grant of the patent and for the remainder of the patent term, counted from the filing date in accordance with

Article 33 of this Agreement, for those of these applications that meet the criteria for protection referred to in subparagraph (b).

In addition, under Article 70.9 of the TRIPS Agreement, India was required to set up a system for granting exclusive marketing rights (EMRs) for a period of five years following the completion of regulatory approval procedures for a pharmaceutical product by India's medicines evaluation agency, the Central Drugs Standard Control Organization (CDSCO). If a decision on the granting or rejection of a product patent application is made before the five-year EMRs period came to an end, the exclusive marketing right would cease straight away. These provisions were to apply provided that a patent had been granted for the same product in another WTO Member and marketing approval had also been obtained in another Member.

ARTICLE 70.9 OF THE TRIPS AGREEMENT: PROTECTION OF EXISTING SUBJECT MATTER

Where a product is the subject of a patent application in a Member in accordance with paragraph 8(a), exclusive marketing rights shall be granted, notwithstanding the provisions of Part VI, for a period of five years after obtaining marketing approval in that Member or until a product patent is granted or rejected in that Member, whichever period is shorter, provided that, subsequent to the entry into force of the WTO Agreement, a patent application has been filed and a patent granted for that product in another Member and marketing approval obtained in such other Member.

In fact, in December 1994 and March 1995, the Indian government had made two attempts to implement legislation to bring India's laws into compliance with Articles 70.8 and 70.9 of the TRIPS Agreement.[16] Both, however, lapsed due to the failure of either proposal to obtain the support of a parliamentary majority (Macdonald-Brown and Ferera 1998, p. 69). As a result, on 2 July 1996, the US submitted a request to the WTO DSB for consultations regarding India's failure to establish a suitable mailbox system in accordance with Article 70.8 or establish a system for EMRs by 1 January 1995. The US also argued that India had failed to comply with the transparency requirements under Article 63 of the TRIPS Agreement that required WTO Members to notify the Council for TRIPS any laws, regulations, judicial decisions and administrative rulings made effective which pertain to the TRIPS Agreement (Macdonald-Brown and Ferera 1998, p. 70).

ARTICLE 63 OF THE TRIPS AGREEMENT: TRANSITIONAL ARRANGEMENTS

1.   Laws and regulations, and final judicial decisions and administrative rulings of general application, made effective by a Member pertaining to the subject matter of this Agreement (the availability, scope, acquisition, enforcement and prevention of the abuse of intellectual property rights) shall be published, or where such publication is not practicable made publicly available, in a national language, in such a manner as to enable governments and right holders to become acquainted with them. Agreements concerning the subject matter of this Agreement which are in force between the government or a governmental agency of a Member and the government or a governmental agency of another Member shall also be published.

2.   Members shall notify the laws and regulations referred to in paragraph 1 to the Council for TRIPS in order to assist that Council in its review of the operation of this Agreement. The Council shall attempt to minimize the burden on Members in carrying out this obligation and may decide to waive the obligation to notify such laws and regulations directly to the Council if consultations with WIPO on the establishment of a common register containing these laws and regulations are successful. The Council shall also consider in this connection any action required regarding notifications pursuant to the obligations under this Agreement stemming from the provisions of Article 6*ter* of the Paris Convention (1967).

3.   Each Member shall be prepared to supply, in response to a written request from another Member, information of the sort referred to in paragraph 1. A Member, having reason to believe that a specific judicial decision or administrative ruling or bilateral agreement in the area of intellectual property rights affects its rights under this Agreement, may also request in writing to be given access to or be informed in sufficient detail of such specific judicial decisions or administrative rulings or bilateral agreements.

> 4. Nothing in paragraphs 1, 2 and 3 shall require Members to disclose confidential information which would impede law enforcement or otherwise be contrary to the public interest or would prejudice the legitimate commercial interests of particular enterprises, public or private.

In the absence of transparency, the concern was that there would be an insufficient degree of security and predictability to protect the legitimate expectations of WTO Members regarding trading conditions and would therefore contravene a fundamental principle of the WTO and its agreements.

India did not dispute that its executive authorities did not have the legal authority to grant EMRs in accordance with the TRIPS Agreement. However, it argued that no such applications had been received and that in any case it would take many years before anyone would be in a position to apply for the grant of EMRs. India also argued that it was not obliged to provide for EMRs until 1 January 2000, at the end of the transitional period provided for in Article 65.2 of the TRIPS Agreement rather than 1 January 1995 when the TRIPS Agreement came into force. On the same grounds, India also argued that it was not required to meet its obligations to notify the Council for TRIPS of the laws and regulations in force until 1 January 2000.

Following the failure to reach a mutually satisfactory solution, on 27 July 1996 the US then requested that the DSB establish a panel to adjudicate on the complaint. When the panel reported its findings on 5 September 1997, it found that even if the practice of the Indian Patent Office was to continue to receive applications and store them separately for future action, the absence of legislation to this effect resulted in a lack of legal certainty in the operation of the mailbox system that rendered it inadequate to serve its purpose (see also Macdonald-Brown and Ferera 1998, p. 71) and that failure to notify the Council on TRIPS did not meet India's obligations under Article 63 of the TRIPS Agreement (see also Garde 2008, p. 248; Mueller 2007, p. 519).[17]

A comparison between the effects of legal challenges relating to implementation of the TRIPS Agreement in South Africa, Brazil and India is instructive at this point. We have seen previously in this book that in South Africa the High Court action brought by global pharmaceutical companies, complaining about the compulsory licensing provisions of the South African Medicines and Related Substances Control Amendment Act 1997, acted as a stimulus for NGOs to engage with the problems that patents could cause for public health and access to medicines in a way that had not previously been apparent. We have seen also that in Brazil the US complaint to the WTO DSB concerning the compulsory licensing and local working provisions of Industrial Property Law 9.279/96 acted as a catalyst for NGOs to focus for the first time on the fact that patents can act as a barrier to access to medicines, particularly for people living with HIV/AIDS.

However, the US complaint to the WTO DSB had no such impact in India. It did not act as a defining moment for NGO engagement with patents and access to medicines issues in anything like the way legal disputes concerning implementation of the TRIPS Agreement stimulated NGO engagement with patents and access to medicines issues in South Africa and Brazil. The reasons for this appear to be two-fold.

First, the largely technical nature of the mailbox, EMRs and transparency provisions of the TRIPS Agreement did not reach out with the same level of immediacy to grassroots activists in India when compared with the legal challenges to compulsory licensing provisions which had received so much attention in South Africa and Brazil.

Second, the impact of the TRIPS Agreement on access to medicines was already well known in India within a relatively small group of highly technocratic individuals operating under the auspices of the National Working Group on Patent Laws, many of whom had engaged with patents and access to medicines issues for over two decades prior to the US complaint to the WTO. These experts had been involved in patent law issues since the drafting of the Patents Act of 1970 and continued to be so after the US complaint had been concluded. The issues in India were consequently not new to the National Working Group on Patent Laws. Meanwhile, for the wider NGO community representing people living with HIV/AIDS, in July 1996 the transitional arrangements for implementation of the TRIPS Agreement simply did not carry the same resonance as the compulsory licensing provisions did in South Africa and Brazil.

The Second People's Commission

Instead of stimulating widespread mobilization of NGO activism in protest about the implications of the TRIPS Agreement for access to medicines in India, the response to the US complaint to the WTO DSB was relatively muted. For its part, the National Working Group on Patent Laws continued to address the technical detail of India's legislative provisions and began to adopt a strategy of bringing on board a wider group of interests to support its recommendations.

When the second People's Commission was set up in 1999, its membership comprised not only senior judges (as had the first People's Commission) but also eminent scientists and economists. This broadened the legitimacy of what the Commission had to say. In terms of its focus, the remit of the second Commission was specifically to analyse the transitional period obligations under the TRIPS Agreement that had been subject to the US complaint to the WTO DSB.[18] As a result, when it was published, the Commission's report reiterated the right of the Indian government to utilize the full range of flexibilities available in the TRIPS Agreement when amending national legislation to implement the Agreement.

The National Working Group on Patent Laws then played a significant role in the drafting of legislation designed to ensure that transitional obligations required by the TRIPS Agreement were put in place and the Patents (Second Amendment) Act was subsequently enacted to introduce a system for the granting of EMRs to ensure that India meet its obligations under Article 70.9 of the TRIPS Agreement on 26 March 1999.[19]

The New Delhi International Symposium on the TRIPS Agreement and Public Health

The National Working Group on Patent Laws continued to expand its network of supporters. It began to work collaboratively with international NGOs and, in the run-up to the Doha Declaration on the TRIPS Agreement and Public Health, on 4 June 2001, hosted an international symposium on TRIPS and access to medicines jointly with MSF. The meeting took place in New Delhi and brought together Indian activists, former trade negotiators including S.P. Shukla, formerly India's chief negotiator at GATT, and representatives of international NGOs including Ellen 't Hoen and James Orbinski of MSF and James Love of CPTech.[20] The meeting was to prove an important landmark event. It highlighted to the international NGO community the extent of the problems that implementation of the TRIPS Agreement could cause for public health and access to medicines in a developing country like India which had previously been reliant on access to relatively cheap generic medicines. In this respect, Indian activists began to provide important evidence-based arguments to underpin the rhetoric of the international access to medicines campaign which in turn benefited from concrete examples of how patents could have adverse implications for the availability of life-saving pharmaceutical products.

The 4 June symposium also fed into the work of the joint Parliamentary Committee that was scrutinizing the draft Patents Bill. In December 2001, the Parliamentary Committee reported to both Houses of Parliament that the flexibilities and freedoms emphasized in the WTO Doha Declaration on the TRIPS Agreement and Public Health of November 2001 had not been fully implemented in the Revised Patents Bill, which was subsequently passed by Parliament with few amendments in May 2002.

The Third People's Commission

In the meantime, in order to maintain the momentum of its campaign to ensure that TRIPS flexibilities were fully utilized in India, in January 2002 the National Working Group on Patent Laws, together with the Public Interest Legal Support and Research Centre, set up a third People's Commission, chaired by former Prime Minister of India I.K. Gujral. Members of the third Commission included Professors Yashpal and Dubey, Shri B.L. Das, Dr Yusuf Hamied and Dr Rajeeve Dhavan. The third Commission focused specifically on the link between access to medicines and human rights, reviewed the WTO Doha Declaration on the TRIPS Agreement and Public Health of November 2001 and made explicit reference to the relationship between the fundamental rights to life guaranteed to the citizens of India by virtue of Article 21 of the Constitution that should be safeguarded in terms of ensuring access to medicines.

In particular, after reviewing the range of flexibilities available in the TRIPS Agreement, the Commission's report noted that the right to health is part of the right to life enshrined in Article 21 of the Constitution, as confirmed by the Supreme Court. The Commission's report also reiterated that the Indian Constitution should be fully respected and that there should be no compromise in terms of amending India's patent laws where they conflict with human rights principles.

The Fourth People's Commission

A fourth People's Commission was then convened, again chaired by former Prime Minister of India I.K. Gujral, to scrutinize the draft of the Patents (Amendment) Bill of December 2003 which was intended to ensure full compliance with the TRIPS Agreement by the Indian Patents Act. When the fourth Commission published its report in October 2004, it called for a fundamental review of the TRIPS Agreement and urged the Indian government to push for this in co-ordination with other developing countries. Reiterating that the Indian Constitution guarantees the fundamental rights of its citizens, particularly with regard to the right to life in Article 21, the Commission's report then criticized the draft Patents (Amendment) Bill of December 2003.

For the Commission, the draft Bill failed to uphold the principles enshrined in the Ayyangar Committee's recommendations and the Patents Act of 1970. In addition, in drafting the Bill, the government was criticized for failing to make creative use of the flexibility provided in Articles 7 and 8 of the TRIPS Agreement and in the Doha Declaration on the TRIPS Agreement and Public Health. By using its report to make explicit the link between the right to health and flexibilities inherent in the TRIPS Agreement, the Commission had once again framed implementation of the TRIPS Agreement as a human rights issue, capable of conflicting with fundamental principles enshrined in the Indian Constitution.

In terms of utilizing TRIPS Agreement flexibilities to uphold the human right to life, the report of the fourth Commission recommended in particular, that for the purposes of obtaining a product patent for a pharmaceutical invention, the grant of a patent should be restricted to a 'new chemical entity'. This restriction on the grant of patents for pharmaceutical products was considered fully compliant with the TRIPS Agreement in view of an apparent flexibility contained in Article 27.1. This flexibility exists because the TRIPS Agreement does not define what constitutes an invention, only specifying in Article 27.1 what requirements must be met in order that an invention should be considered patentable – including the requirement that the invention be 'new'. As a result, a patent claim relating to a pharmaceutical product may relate to an active ingredient as such independently of or jointly with formulations, salts, prodrugs, isomers, and so on, or cover any of these subject matters separately (Correa 2000, p. 25). This provided India with considerable flexibility to determine for itself what constitutes an invention for the purposes of granting a patent.

The fourth Commission's report also called for the retention of the existing provision on pre-grant opposition contained in the Patents Act 1970, noting that similar provisions existed in the patents acts of other countries. Pre-grant opposition was first introduced into Section 9 of the Patents Act 1911 and carried forward in Section 25(1) of the Patents Act 1970 (Mueller 2007, p. 567). The People's Commission report pointed out that the new Bill contained a proposal to dilute the existing provision in the Patents Act 1970 as amended by the Patents (Second Amendment) Act 2002 and also pointed out that there was no requirement in the TRIPS Agreement to do so, and that such dilution would be against India's national interest. The concern was that, in the absence of pre-grant opposition, third parties such as patient groups, NGOs, or generic drug companies could not challenge the grant of a patent but would instead be required to rely on post-grant proceedings in India to bring an action claiming, for instance, that the patent granted is invalid on grounds of lack of patentability.

Jan Swasthya Abhiyan

Working alongside the National Working Group on Patent Laws, Jan Swasthya Abhiyan (JSA) adopted a different strategy. It used the language of human rights principles to mobilize its network of activists and raise public awareness about the implications of patenting pharmaceutical products for access to medicines. Founded in 2000 following the first People's Health Assembly in Savar,[21] JSA is an informal coalition of 22 public health-related networks, comprising groups such as the Delhi Science Forum, women's groups, trade unionists and patients' groups. It has a remit to work on how science and technology impacts on people's lives. Using its networks to link up with grassroots activists, JSA was able to mobilize large numbers of people and start a mass campaign to argue that the scope of patents for pharmaceutical products should be limited.[22] Using the strategy of arguing that the right to healthcare is a fundamental right under the Indian Constitution, JSA then lobbied Members of Parliament and policy makers extensively in the run-up to the Patents (Third Amendment) Act of 2005.

Patents (Third Amendment) Act of 2005

Following the expiry of the transitional periods permitted under Article 65.4 of the TRIPS Agreement, the Patents (Third Amendment) Act of 2005 extended product patents to all patentable subject matter including inventions related to food, pharmaceuticals and chemical products. It also set the term of protection afforded by a patent to 20 years.[23] Crucially, however, with the relationship between patents and access to medicines now high on the political agenda following the awareness raising work of JSA, the National Working Group on Patent Laws, international NGOs including MSF, Oxfam and CPTech also ensured that the issues at stake received global coverage.[24] As a result, a coalition of NGOs was able to propose provisions to ensure that the Act limited granting of patents for pharmaceutical products in a way that was consistent with recommendations originally contained in the fourth People's Commission report a year earlier (see also Arup and Plahe 2010, p. 28).

In an attempt to draw a distinction between genuinely patentable inventions and the practice of 'evergreening' spurious inventions (see also Garde 2008, p. 250),[25] Section 3(d) of the Act sets out that the mere discovery of a new form of a known substance is not to be considered an invention but that this could be regarded as such if it enhances the efficiency of a known invention. An explanation is then added to Section 3(d) to clarify that salts, polymers and other new versions are to be treated as

> ## SECTION 3(d) OF THE INDIAN PATENTS ACT (1970), AS AMENDED BY THE PATENTS (AMENDMENT) ACT 2005
>
> The following are not inventions within the meaning of this Act, –
> . . .
> the mere discovery of a new form of a known substance which does not result in the enhancement of the known efficacy of that substance or the mere discovery of any new property or new use for a known substance or the mere use of a known process, machine or apparatus unless such known process results in a new product or employs at least one new reactant.
>
> *Explanation.*–For the purposes of this clause, salts, esters, ethers, polymorphs, metabolites, pure form, particle size, isomers, mixtures of isomers, complexes, combinations and other derivatives of known substance shall be considered to be the same substance, unless they differ significantly in properties with regard to efficacy.

the same substance and not as new, patentable, forms unless they differ in their properties significantly in terms of being more efficient (see also Arup and Plahe 2010, p. 28). The provision has been described by MSF as an essential tool for keeping open the door for generic manufacture of medicines (MSF 2009, p. 5). However, for patentees the concern is that Section 3(d) excludes some applications that, on the usual criteria of patentability, would qualify as inventions.

Furthermore, in line with the recommendation of the fourth People's Commission, the Patents (Third Amendment) Act 2005 retained in the Patents Act pre-grant opposition that allows third parties to oppose patent applications prior to its grant. This procedure is set out in Section 25.

Section 25 of the Patents (Amendment) Act of 2005 allows 'any person' standing to bring pre-grant oppositions proceedings and, as a result, generic producers initiate oppositions, as have NGOs (Arup and Plahe 2010, p. 33; Mueller 2007, p. 570). In fact, NGOs have increasingly seen pre-grant opposition as an opportunity to use statutory flexibilities to oppose pharmaceutical patent applications (Mueller 2007, p. 640) and, as we shall see below, the retention of pre-grant opposition proceedings has had a profound impact as NGOs increasingly challenge the validity of patent applications for pharmaceutical products.

SECTION 25 OF THE INDIAN PATENTS ACT OF 1970 (AS AMENDED BY THE PATENTS (AMENDMENT) ACT, 2005): OPPOSITION TO GRANT OF PATENT

(1) At any time within four months from the date of advertisement of the acceptance of a complete specification under this Act (or within such further period not exceeding one month in the aggregate as the Controller may allow on application made to him in the prescribed manner before the expiry of the four months aforesaid) any person interested may give notice to the Controller of opposition to the grant of the patent on any of the following grounds, namely: –

a. that the applicant for the patent or the person under or through whom he claims, wrongfully obtained the invention or any part thereof from him or from a person under or through whom he claims;

b. that the invention so far as claimed in any claim of the complete specification has been published before the priority date of the claim –

i. in any specification filed in pursuance of an application for a patent made in India on or after the 1st day of January, 1912; or

ii. in India or elsewhere, in any other document:

   Provided that the ground specified in sub-clause (ii) shall not be available where such publication does not constitute an anticipation of the invention by virtue of sub-section (2) or sub-section (3) of section 29;

   a. that the invention so far as claimed in any claim of the complete specification is claimed in a claim of a complete specification published on or after the priority date of the applicant's claim and filed in pursuance of an application for a patent in India, being a claim of which the priority date is earlier than that of the applicant's claim;

   b. that the invention so far as claimed in any claim of the complete specification was publicly known or publicly used in India before the priority date of that claim.

Explanation – For the purposes of this clause, an invention relating to a process for which a patent is claimed shall be deemed to have been publicly known or publicly used in India before the priority date of the claim if a product made by that process had already been imported into India before that date except where such importation has been for the purpose of reasonable trial or experiment only;

c. that the invention so far as claimed in any claim of the complete specification is obvious and clearly does not involve any inventive step, having regard to the matter published as mentioned in clause (b) or having regard to what was used in India before the priority date of the applicant's claim;
d. that the subject of any claim of the complete specification is not an invention within the meaning of this Act, or is not patentable under this Act;
e. that the complete specification does not sufficiently and clearly describe the invention or the method by which it is to be performed;
f. that the applicant has failed to disclose to the Controller the information required by section 8 or has furnished the information which in any material particular was false to his knowledge;
g. that in the case of a convention application, the application was not made within twelve months from the date of the first application for protection for the invention made in a convention country by the applicant or a person from whom he derives title;
but on no other ground.
(2) Where any such notice of opposition is duly given, the Controller shall notify the applicant and shall give to the applicant and the opponent an opportunity to be heard before deciding the case.
(3) The grant of a patent shall not be refused on the ground stated in clause (c) of sub-section (1) if no patent has been granted in pursuance of the application mentioned in that clause; and for the purpose of any inquiry under clause (d) or clause (e) of that sub-section, no account shall be taken of any secret use.

In addition, although not explicitly proposed in the fourth People's Commission report, the Patents (Amendment) Act of 2005 also added an entirely new feature to the Patents Act in the form of post-grant opposition. This can only be filed by a person able to demonstrate an interest in the patent, for instance because that person is engaged in or is promoting research in the same field as that to which the invention relates (Mueller 2007, p. 573).

Furthermore, the Patents (Amendment) Act of 2005 also amended the Patents Act of 1970 by adding a new Section 92A which provides that a compulsory licence shall be available for manufacture and export of patented pharmaceutical products to any country having insufficient or no manufacturing capacity in the pharmaceutical sector for the concerned product to address public health problems, provided a compulsory licence

---

SECTION 92A OF THE INDIAN PATENTS ACT OF 1970 (AS AMENDED BY THE PATENTS (AMENDMENT) ACT, 2005): COMPULSORY LICENCE FOR EXPORT OF PATENTED PHARMACEUTICAL PRODUCTS IN CERTAIN EXCEPTIONAL CIRCUMSTANCES

(1) Compulsory licence shall be available for manufacture and export of patented pharmaceutical products to any country having insufficient or no manufacturing capacity in the pharmaceutical sector for the concerned product to address public health problems, provided compulsory licence has been granted by such country or such country has, by notification or otherwise, allowed importation of the patented pharmaceutical products from India.

(2) The Controller shall, on receipt of an application in the prescribed manner, grant a compulsory licence solely for manufacture and export of the concerned pharmaceutical product to such country under such terms and conditions as may be specified and published by him.

(3) The provisions of sub-sections (1) and (2) shall be without prejudice to the extent to which pharmaceutical products produced under a compulsory licence can be exported under any other provision of this Act.

Explanation. – For the purposes of this section, 'pharmaceutical products' means any patented product, or product manufactured through a patented process, of the pharmaceutical sector needed to address public health problems and shall be inclusive of ingredients necessary for their manufacture and diagnostic kits required for their use.

has been granted by the importing country *or* that it has, by notification or otherwise, allowed importation of the patented pharmaceutical products from India.

The insertion of a new Section 92A into the Indian Patents Act of 1970 followed intense lobbying by NGOs, particularly the National Working Group on Patent Laws, which argued that India should utilize to the full flexibilities available in the TRIPS Agreement, and in particular the WTO Decision of 30 August 2003, in order to facilitate access to medicines.

Since the coming into force of the Patents (Amendment) Act of 2005, a Mumbai-based NGO called the Lawyers Collective HIV/AIDS Unit has been at the forefront of attempts to use the opposition procedures available under Section 25 to challenge the validity of patent applications for pharmaceutical products. Often acting in coalition with patients' groups or other NGOs acting on behalf of people living with HIV/AIDS, it has done so on grounds that these patents do not constitute inventions within the meaning of Section 3(d) and are therefore not patentable subject matter. It has also campaigned vociferously to assert that implementation of the obligation contained in Article 27.1 of the TRIPS Agreement to extend the availability of product patents to all patentable subject matter (including inventions related to food, pharmaceuticals and chemical products) should be done in a manner which does not conflict with the right to health as set out in Article 21 of the Indian Constitution and international human rights agreements that India is a party to.

The Lawyers Collective HIV/AIDS Unit

The Lawyers Collective was founded by Anand Grover and Indira Jaising in 1980 with the aim of giving free legal advice, representing clients in legal aid cases and, most importantly, intervening in public interest cases on a range of legal issues.[26] The Lawyers Collective then established a separate HIV/AIDS Unit in 1998,[27] as a result of Anand Grover's involvement in the case of Dominic D'Souza.

D'Souza, a well known theatre artist and celebrity, was being held under the Goa Public Health (Amendment) Act, 1986. Under the Goa Public Health (Amendment) Act, if the authorities suspected that any person was HIV positive, that person could be tested without their consent and, if found to be HIV positive, could be quarantined in an institution (Grover 2005, p. 205). When it transpired that the reason that D'Souza was being detained was that he had given a blood donation that had subsequently been tested and that identified him as being HIV positive, the case raised for the first time in activists' consciousness the fact that a human rights-based approach was needed if the interests of people living with HIV/AIDS in India were to be represented effectively.

Framing the rights of people living with HIV/AIDS in terms of the human rights accorded to them under the Constitution, the Lawyers Collective HIV/AIDS Unit then took the debate about HIV/AIDS beyond the realm of technical issues that could be left to specialists in clinical medicine and raised the prospect of the rights of the individual being threatened, particularly if access to medicine in India was not being ensured (Ramasubban and Rishyasringa 2005, p. 191).

Dr Ishwar Gilada, a medical practitioner in Mumbai, asked Anand Grover to appear before the Goa Bench of the Bombay High Court on behalf of D'Souza given his background in biochemistry and as a human rights activist. Before the Court, Grover argued that the isolationist strategy of the Goa Public Health (Amendment) Act had no rational basis and that there was no opportunity for the person who had tested HIV positive to challenge what had been said about him (Grover 2005, p. 207). In response, the Court rejected the argument against the isolationist aspect of the law on the basis that a single WHO document stated that isolation of an HIV positive person may be resorted to in certain circumstances. However, the Court held that principles of natural justice have to be read into the statute and that the person has to be given the opportunity to rebut any finding declaring him HIV positive (Grover 2005, p. 207).

D'Souza subsequently became the first Indian HIV positive activist and his case left an indelible impression on Anand Grover and the Lawyers Collective, which reached the conclusion that it was ready to commit to expanding its work on the human rights of people living with HIV/AIDS on a full-time basis. This attracted the attention of international donor agencies, including the United Nations Development Programme (UNDP), the European Commission, the Swedish International Development Agency (SIDA) and the Ford Foundation.[28]

The Lawyers Collective HIV/AIDS Unit then started to organize workshops and began to engage in HIV/AIDS advocacy work. Workshops were organized not only for people living with HIV/AIDS but also for the judiciary. Recognizing that there was a need to sensitize legal professionals and judges to HIV/AIDS if human rights-related issues were to be promoted through the courts, the Lawyers Collective HIV/AIDS Unit brought on board Justice Kirby, a senior judge of the High Court in Australia, and Justice Cameron of the South African Court of Appeal, the latter closely associated with the AIDS Law Project there. Bringing in these senior members of the judiciary proved crucial in terms of sensitizing Indian judges about the rights of people living with HIV/AIDS. A number of workshops were held in Mumbai, Ahmedabad, Delhi, Kochi,

Bangalore and Kolkata for High Court judges, the subordinate judiciary and members of the Indian Bar Associations.

The Lawyers Collective HIV/AIDS Unit also began a programme representing those who are vulnerable to HIV/AIDS including sex workers, injecting drug users, gays, lesbians, trans-gendered communities and other sexual minorities whose vulnerability is exacerbated due to non-recognition of their rights.[29] It began educating the Indian public about the rights of people living with HIV/AIDS, publishing a series of information leaflets for different stakeholders detailing the issues in simple and direct ways. It also began to link with the wider HIV/AIDS NGO community through the Indian Network of Positive Persons (INP+), which operates regionally throughout India.

The Affordable Medicines and Treatment Campaign

When global pharmaceutical companies brought a High Court challenge relating to the South African Medicines and Related Substances Control Amendment Act 1997,[30] greater attention in India began to be paid to the fact that affordability and accessibility to ARVs was a major issue for people living with HIV/AIDS. In response, in May 2001 the Lawyers Collective HIV/AIDS Unit launched the Affordable Medicines and Treatment Campaign (AMTC).[31]

AMTC, a coalition of NGOs, patient groups, healthcare providers and activists that aims to improve accessibility and affordability of medicines and treatment for every individual in India, including people living with HIV/AIDS, emphasized that the right to life and health is a fundamental right guaranteed to every person living in India and is non-negotiable.

Framing the patents and access to medicines issue in terms of human rights, on 11 October 2004 Anand Grover then wrote to the Chair of the National Human Rights Commission (NHRC) on behalf of AMTC, asserting that implementation of product patent protection should not result in the denial of the right to health guaranteed under Article 21 of the Constitution of India and the International Covenant on Economic, Social and Cultural Rights (ICESCR).[32] The letter called on the NHRC, using its mandate under Section 2 (d) and (f) of the Indian Protection of Human Rights Act of 1993 rights, to intervene urgently to ensure peoples' right to health.

In particular, the AMTC called on the NHRC to: seek information from the Government of India regarding the steps which are already taken or under consideration to safeguard the right to health under the product patent regime; recommend to the Government of India the steps to be taken to ensure the enjoyment of benefits of scientific progress and its application, an obligation under the ICESCR; make recommendations to the Government of India on the options available within the TRIPS Agreement to safeguard the right to health; and to hold consultations with concerned individuals and groups on the implications of intellectual property rights on peoples' right to health.

Global Coalition Against the Indian Patent Amendment

Having pushed human rights issues to the fore, in 2004 AMTC then convened the Global Coalition against the Indian Patent Amendment (GCAIPA). This informal network of developing country NGOs included representatives of Brazilian NGOs such as Alexandra Nino (GESTOS) and Veriano Tero (ABIA), together with members of the National Working Group on Patent Laws, AMTC and JSA. TAC and the AIDS Law Project in South Africa also lent their support and provided legal, strategic and campaign advice.

GCAIPA then used the same tactics that had worked to such good effect in South Africa when NGOs demonstrated against global pharmaceutical companies, forcing them to abandon their High Court challenge to the South African Medicines and Related Substances Control Amendment Act. It also reflected the NGO strategy of mass demonstrations to raise public awareness that had been used previously in Brazil, where NGOs had opposed the US complaint to the WTO DSB against Brazil regarding Article 68 of Industrial Property Law 9.279/96.

Building on NGO experiences in South Africa and Brazil, GCAIPA organized a Global Day of Action on 26 February 2005. Mass protests were held in Andhra Pradesh, Bangalore, Chennai, Dharwad, Goa, Hyderabad, Kerala, Kolkata and Pune demanding that the right to life and the right to health enshrined in the Indian Constitution to be kept sacrosanct and calling for the Indian Patent (Amendment) Bill to make maximum use of the flexibilities available in the TRIPS Agreement to ensure access to medicines.[33]

By the time the Third Patents (Amendment) Act became law on 5 April 2005, the NGOs involved in GCAIPA had played a crucial role in increasing public awareness both within India and internationally, contributing to a favourable political environment in which the legal expertise of the National Working Group on Patent Laws could convert campaigning demands into concrete proposals that were ultimately incorporated into the Act. This was particularly significant when the Act followed the campaign's calls to limit the grant of a patent for a pharmaceutical product invention under Section 3(d) and retain the pre-grant opposition mechanism under Section 25 of the Act.

Patent Opposition

By 2006 the global coalition that had mobilized prior to the Third Patents (Amendment) Act began to shift away from its earlier emphasis on human rights and had started instead working in earnest on the more technically detailed issue of pre-grant opposition. Since then, with support from MSF and NGO colleagues in Brazil and South Africa, Indian NGOs have filed numerous pre-grant opposition proceedings against the patent applications of global pharmaceutical manufacturers.

When the mailbox was 'opened' in 2005, one of the first patent applications for a pharmaceutical product was the Novartis drug Gleevec, a drug used to treat leukemia that was already controversial in India because it had been the first to be accorded EMRs status in 2003 (see also Garde 2008, p. 251). In January 2006, Novartis requested that its patent application be examined and the application was then opposed by the Indian pharmaceutical manufacturers Natco Pharma, Ranbaxy and Cipla, together with the Cancer Patients Aid Association (CPAA) (see also Basheer and Reddy 2008, p. 134; Arup and Plahe 2010, p. 35). The Assistant Comptroller of the Patent Office in Chennai then upheld the arguments presented in the pre-grant opposition and refused to grant Novartis a patent for Gleevec on several grounds, including the fact it was only a new polymorphic form of a known compound and that the properties did not differ significantly with regard to efficacy and therefore did not constitute an invention within the meaning of Article 3(d). This allowed the Indian pharmaceutical companies to continue manufacturing their versions of the drug, priced at a cost 8–12 times cheaper than the Novartis brand name version.

In response, Novartis challenged the ruling of the Patent Office, arguing that the patent was valid under Section 3(d) and also presenting alternative arguments to claims that Section 3(d) was not valid under Article 14 of the Constitution of India and was not consistent with the TRIPS Agreement (Basheer and Reddy 2008, p. 134; Garde 2008, p. 252).

ARTICLE 14 OF THE CONSTITUTION OF INDIA: RIGHT OF EQUALITY

The State shall not deny to any person equality before the law or the equal protection of the laws within the territory of India.

The High Court of Madras, however, held that the language of Section 3(d) of the Patents Act was not arbitrary or vague and therefore was not in violation of Article 14 of the Constitution.[34] The Court refused jurisdiction on the question of whether Section 3(d) was consistent with the TRIPS Agreement, noting that this question could only be settled through the dispute settlement mechanism of the WTO (see also Basheer and Reddy 2008, p. 138; Garde 2008, p. 253).

In addition to the Gleevec case, numerous other oppositions have specifically targeted patent applications relating to ARV therapy for people living with HIV/AIDS (see also Arup and Plahe 2010, p. 33). On 30 March 2006, for instance, the Indian Network of People Living with HIV/AIDS (INP+), the Manipur Network of Positive People (MNP+) with legal support provided by AMTC and the Lawyers Collective HIV/AIDS Unit jointly submitted their opposition to a patent application filed in the Kolkata patent office by GSK for Combivir, a fixed-dose combination of zidovudine and lamivudine (or AZT and 3TC). MSF ensured that the opposition received press coverage globally[35] and, in August 2006, GSK announced that it was withdrawing the Combivir patent application.

The Lawyers Collective HIV/AIDS Unit has also shown itself to be tenacious and persistent in the pursuit of patent revocation even when pre-grant opposition proceedings have proved unsuccessful. It has worked closely in coalition with a range of domestic and international NGOs to follow through this strategy.

In December 2008, in the first ever instance of a patent being revoked after being granted, the Madras High Court set aside a patent that had been granted to Hoffman-La Roche in June 2007 for Valganciclovir. The drug is an important treatment of active cytomegalovirus retinitis (CMV) infection that causes blindness in people living with HIV/AIDS.[36]

The case arose because the Chennai Patent Office had granted the patent without first hearing the pre-grant opposition that the Lawyers Collective HIV/AIDS Unit had previously filed together with two NGOs representing people living with HIV/AIDS, the Indian Network for People Living with HIV/AIDS (INP+) and the Tamil Nadu Network of Positive People (TNNP+). The pre-grant opposition proceeding had been launched on the grounds that the Valganciclovir patent application of Roche in 2006 was for a pre-1995 molecule. Under the Indian Patents Act 1970 (as amended in 2005), pharmaceutical product patented elsewhere ten years before the Indian Patents Act of 2005 were not eligible for patent protection in India.[37]

Valganciclovir was invented by Roche in 1994 and first patented in the US the same year. The application to revoke the patent was therefore based on the fact that the patent claims 'valganciclovir hydrochloride' which is a hydrochloride salt of ganciclovir and, since ganciclovir and its salts were known (disclosed in US patent US4355032, published on 19 October 1982) they failed the novelty test as set out in Section 3(d) of the Indian Patents Act, namely that new forms of an old drug including salts are not patentable.

The Chennai Patent Office had argued that it was not required to listen to pre-grant oppositions before granting a patent. However, following grant of the patent, in June 2008 an NGO representing people living with HIV/AIDS, the Delhi Network of Positive People (DNP+), filed a post-grant opposition against the patent Valganciclovir at the Chennai Patent Office on the grounds that the drug was a known compound and, at most, a 'new form' of an already known substance with no improvement in efficacy.[38]

The validity of the patent was in question because, as we saw above, Section 3(d) of the Patents Act 1970 (as amended in 2005) does not allow patents on new forms of old drugs. Seeking to revoke the patent, the Delhi Network of Positive People (DNP+) was joined in its post-grant opposition by three generic drug companies based in India (Matrix, Ranbaxy and Cipla). The commercial significance of the case was particularly crucial for Cipla which, in May 2008, had launched a generic version of Valganciclovir on the domestic market in India at a price of Rs. 980.00 for four tablets. This price was extremely low when compared with Rs. 4160 for the equivalent number of pills that Roche charged in India. Roche had filed an infringement suit against Cipla in the Mumbai High Court and sought a permanent injunction, restraining Cipla from manufacturing, offering for sale and exporting Valganciclovir.[39] The Delhi High Court had held that the mere grant of a patent is no indication of its validity and that the standards employed by the patent office in scrutinizing the patent application may have been wanting. This, the Court held, was to be determined during the post-grant opposition proceedings.

Then, on 30 April 2010, the Indian Patent Office in Chennai concluded that on the basis of the post-grant opposition proceeding brought before it the patent granted to Roche for Valganciclovir should be set aside on grounds that it did not constitute a patentable invention within the meaning of Section 3(d) of the Patents Act. The Indian Patent Office stated that only one of the process claims made by Roche is valid and, in line with the arguments presented in both the pre- and post-grant oppositions, has determined the company's claims for a product patent on Valganciclovir to be invalid.[40]

The value of post-grant, as well as pre-grant, opposition proceedings has therefore been clearly demonstrated by the actions of Indian NGOs.

Yet, with approximately 11 000 pharmaceutical patent applications still in the mailbox system, there seems little prospect of opposition proceedings being brought in any except the most contentious cases, particularly given the resource limits of the Indian NGOs involved.

EVALUATION OF THE ACHIEVEMENTS OF INDIAN NGOS ON PATENTS AND ACCESS TO MEDICINES

During the period since the TRIPS Agreement came into force, Indian NGOs including the National Working Group on Patent Laws and the Lawyers Collective HIV/AIDS Unit have played a significant role in raising awareness about the impact of patent law on access to medicines in India. They have used human rights to good effect to frame their arguments. In turn, this has contributed to a policy-making climate in which, since 2006, the Indian government has been markedly more receptive to concerns raised by NGOs about intellectual property-related access to medicines issues. The NGOs themselves feel that their viewpoints are now taken more seriously by the Indian government. However, the overall picture of NGO relationships with government departments is patchy and the Indian government can perhaps be best described as pragmatic about how it uses the information and inputs it receives from NGOs. What is more, the relationship between NGOs and the Indian government is often affected by the need for officials to take into account other factors alongside the arguments presented by NGOs. These other factors include, perhaps not surprisingly, bilateral pressure from the US in particular and the concerns of multinational companies seeking to invest in India and looking for reassurance that their patent portfolio is likely to be protected and enforced there.[41]

It is certainly the case that NGOs achieved a number of significant concessions in the Patents Act (Amendment) Act of 2005, particularly on patentability and pre-grant opposition. However, in practice, it is the extent to which these concessions are utilized that will ultimately determine whether pre-grant opposition procedure is an effective and practical mechanism to improve access to medicines in India. In a broader sense, since it will be impossible for Indian NGOs to oppose pharmaceutical product applications in every instance, perhaps the greatest long-term impact of NGO engagement with patent oppositions will actually be the extent that the awareness of the implications of patents for access to medicines has been raised in the public consciousness both in India and throughout the globe.

The Lawyers Collective HIV/AIDS Unit also hopes that the patent oppositions will improve the quality of scrutiny of pharmaceutical product applications by examiners and encourage the Indian Patent Office to undertake more searching examinations based on Section 3(d) of the Patents Act. If this transpires to be the case, it will ultimately be deemed to be the important scrutiny mechanism that NGOs envisaged when they originally worked so hard to see its inclusion in the Patents (Amendment) Act of 2005 (see also Arup and Plahe 2010, p. 33).[42]

It is also worth noting that, in part due to the fact that Indian NGOs have moved on from legislative drafting to focus more on dealing with the practicalities of pre-grant oppositions, the human rights perspective is now less prominent in India than it has been in South Africa and Brazil. In part this may be because the Indian population has yet to feel the impact of price changes on new pharmaceutical products, and ARVs in particular, to the same extent as in other countries. There is also the paradox in India that, although about 2.5 million people are living with HIV/AIDS, this corresponds to a national adult prevalence of approximately 0.36 per cent,[43] so even though less than 10 per cent of people needing ARV treatment are receiving it,[44] the overall impact of patents on access to ARVs is often considered to be relatively small.

In fact, for millions of the people living in rural India, it is the threat that the international regime of intellectual property rights has posed for the livelihoods of farmers rather than the relationship between patents and access to medicines that has been of particular concern and it is to this issue that we now turn.

FARMERS' RIGHTS IN INDIA

Over 200 million people, approximately 33 per cent, of the Indian population depend upon agriculture for their livelihoods.[45] This agrarian population has experienced great changes since the early 1990s, with the emphasis of Indian agricultural policy shifting away from producing food for subsistence living to the commercialization of agriculture. A central tenet of this market-driven approach to increasing productivity and competitiveness in Indian agriculture has been to focus more on research and applied technology, particularly biotechnology. NGOs in India have responded to these changes in agricultural production by pressing the government to offer alternative approaches to industry-led agricultural development and emphasizing the important role that Indian farmers have to play in ensuring food security through crop diversity.

One of the main concerns of NGOs advocating farmers' rights in India is that intellectual property rights on plants, particularly patents on plant genes and the protection of plant varieties, also known as plant breeders' rights (PBRs), can increase the cost of seeds that farmers need to buy, thus consequently reducing the access they have to new varieties. Traditionally, farmers have been able to freely plant, exchange and sell seeds. However, patents and PBRs restrict farmers' ability to sell seeds from crops that they grow and in some cases even their ability to reuse those seeds themselves (Commission on Intellectual Property Rights 2002, p. 3).

NGOs in India have highlighted the extent to which, historically, farmers have themselves selected, produced and improved plant varieties over the centuries through traditional means of seed exchange. They have thus argued that the role of farmers in conservation and development of plant genetic resources should be recognized, rewarded and balanced against the rights of commercial plant breeders. NGOs in India have also expressed concern that PBRs grant monopolies to commercial firms, displacing small-scale farmers and driving up the cost of agricultural production.

These issues were first identified by NGOs when, on 20 December 1991, the Director General of the GATT, Arthur Dunkel, put forward a compromise package of texts during the Uruguay Round of multilateral negotiations that included the draft TRIPS Agreement (the Dunkel draft). This led NGOs in India to raise concerns about the impact of global intellectual property rights of rural farmers and the wider implications for biodiversity and conservation. Initially, the concern was that the TRIPS Agreement would be incorporated into Indian law in such a way as to allow the patenting of plant genes, with profound and adverse implications for farmers' rights in India.[46]

Foremost amongst the NGOs working on these issues in India have been Navdanya, Gene Campaign and the Forum on Biotechnology and Food Security. Each has campaigned for the Indian government to abstain from introducing patent protection for plant varieties in India and has called for the introduction of legislation to protect farmers' rights. Close working relationships between NGO activists and wider social movements at grassroots level in rural communities have been a key factor in this process.

The Research Foundation for Science, Technology and Ecology and Navdanya

One of the first NGOs to become involved with farmers' rights in India was Navdanya, founded by Dr Vandana Shiva as a social movement for biodiversity, conservation and farmers' rights. In 1981 Shiva set up the Research Foundation for Science, Technology and Ecology (RFSTE) to connect to communities and gather evidence of the need for ecological conservation. Then, in 1984, following the great drought in the Indian state of Karnataka, RFSTE set up Navdanya with the aim of achieving a paradigm shift in terms of how the interests of ordinary Indians was represented, particularly in relation to building new models of campaigning for the conservation of agricultural diversity in the country.

Working with the aim of promoting justice and sustainability by putting farmers at the centre of the conservation agenda, Navdanya's belief is that multinational companies' appropriation of agriculture should be resisted, and that biodiversity and traditional knowledge should be kept in the hands of ordinary people. For Navdanya, this has also become the key to fighting poverty in India. As a result, it has worked consistently to promote agricultural diversity through seed saving, sustainable farming alternatives and by challenging patents on natural resources such as Neem and Basmati.[47]

Using emotive language to evoke the image of patents as instruments of post-colonial conquest (Shiva 2001, p. 18), Navdanya framed implementation of the TRIPS Agreement as being a threat to people's fundamental right to food and health (Shiva 2001, p. 78). At a technical level, it worked closely with the National Working Group on Patent Laws and provided inputs into the drafting of legislation to amend the Patents Act of 1970. Navdanya also provided important inputs into new legislation on plant variety protection and farmers' rights.

Navdanya worked in coalition with other organizations, particularly farmers' groups in local communities and wider social movements at grassroots level, to raise awareness about the impact of intellectual property rights on agricultural diversity. In addition, it collaborated internationally with farmers' groups in other developing countries, building a South-South dialogue between activists within the NGO community.[48]

Gene Campaign

Gene Campaign was set up in 1993 by Suman Sahai as a national grassroots level organization to promote wider understanding of the likely impact of patents on new seeds and plant varieties on food security in India and on the livelihood of small farmers in particular. To achieve these aims, Gene Campaign works to empower local communities so that they can retain control over their genetic resources in order to ensure food and livelihood security.[49]

Gene Campaign has raised the profile of concerns about the impact of the intellectual property rights for agriculture, farmers' rights and food security by engaging with farmers and villagers in rural communities, working on the rationale that unless people at the grassroots level are aware of problems associated with patents, campaign efforts were not likely to be successful. Gene Campaign visited farmers' organizations and gradually built up the grassroots movement against patents on seeds.

Gene Campaign argued that a *sui generis* system of plant breeders' rights could not exist without being balanced with explicit farmers' rights. As a result, Gene Campaign began a national farmers' rights campaign, protesting against the TRIPS Agreement and the granting of patents on seeds and life forms.[50] The campaign began with a rally in New Delhi on 3 March 1993, involving three major farmers' organizations, which did much to raise awareness in the farming community and exert political pressure about the need to recognize formally the existence of farmers' rights in intellectual property law.

Forum on Biotechnology and Food Security

The Forum on Biotechnology and Food Security, chaired by the influential writer Dervinder Sharma, also played an important role in mobilizing support of farmers' rights. As an independent group that included some of the best-known and distinguished agricultural scientists, biotechnologists, economists, and farmers in India, the Forum on Biotechnology and Food Security was listened to by the Indian government because of the expertise it could offer.

A Charter of Farmers' Rights

On 6 March 1993, RFSTE and Navdanya co-organized a consultation workshop on Biodiversity, Farmers' Rights and Intellectual Property Rights in New Delhi at which a Charter of Farmers' Rights was drawn up by leaders of different farmers' organizations, together with representatives of NGOs with environmental, health and consumer interests participating in a consultation workshop.[51] In particular, the Charter emphasized that farmers have a fundamental right to conserve, reproduce, and modify seed and plant material. Patent systems and *sui generis* systems of plant variety rights were criticized as creating production, distribution and import monopolies. Instead, the Charter made explicit reference to Article 19 of the Indian Constitution, which gives every citizen the freedom to practise his or her occupation. This freedom entails the right to shape one's means of production and, since seeds are the primary tool of agricultural production, the rights of farmers to produce, reproduce, modify and sell seed must be safeguarded under Article 19. According to the Charter, any changes to the intellectual property regime as a result of the Dunkel draft must not deny farmers their right to freedom of occupation as protected in Article 19.1(g) of the Indian Constitution.

ARTICLE 19.1 OF THE CONSTITUTION OF INDIA: RIGHT TO FREEDOM

(1) All citizens shall have the right–
(*a*) to freedom of speech and expression;
(*b*) to assemble peaceably and without arms;
(*c*) to form associations or unions;
(*d*) to move freely throughout the territory of India;
(*e*) to reside and settle in any part of the territory of India; [and]
. . .
(*g*) to practise any profession, or to carry on any occupation, trade or business.

The Charter of Farmers' Rights also reaffirmed faith in the Indian Patents Act of 1970, which exempts horticulture and agriculture from patentability and upheld farmers' right to protect biodiversity on their farms and to reproduce and modify seed freely as being non-negotiable.

The Charter was followed by the largest rally of farmers and NGO activists, which took place on 2 October 1993, organized by the Karnataka Rajya Raitha Sangha (KRRS – Karnataka State Farmers' Association) at which over half a million Indian farmers protested against the TRIPS Agreement provisions of the Dunkel draft, focusing on a clear and simple message encompassed by the slogan 'no patents on seeds'.[52]

Meeting India's Obligations under the TRIPS Agreement

By 1995, when the TRIPS Agreement came into force, NGOs had used the right of farmers to practise their profession, as set out in Article 19.1(g) of the Indian Constitution, to frame their argument that the Indian government should utilize the flexibility contained in Article 27.3(b) of the TRIPS Agreement to exclude from patentability plants and animals. Attention then focused more specifically on the technically complex matter of what type of *sui generis* legislation India should introduce while still demonstrating compatibility with the TRIPS Agreement.

As we saw in Chapter 3, although Article 27.3(b) of the TRIPS Agreement does not specify how WTO Members should comply with the obligation to provide for the protection of plant varieties, one possible *sui generis* system of protection is the UPOV Convention. It will be recalled that the 1978 text of UPOV allowed farmers to reuse the seed they had purchased from breeders for the following year's sowing under certain conditions. However, the 1991 version does not contain the so-called 'farmers' privilege' to use freely seeds gathered from their harvest as further planting material. India is not a member of UPOV and the government has been made well aware of the differences between the 1978 and 1991 versions of the Convention by Indian NGOs including Navdanya and Gene Campaign, working in coalition with international NGOs including IATP, ETC, ITDG and the UK Food Group Network.

This coalition of NGOs argued that, while meeting its obligations under Article 27.3(b) of the TRIPS Agreement to introduce legislation to ensure the protection of PBRs, provision should be also made to allow farmers to retain control over seed production and distribution. To achieve this, the NGOs argued that, rather than becoming a signatory to the 1991 version of UPOV, the rights of farmers should be incorporated alongside the rights of breeders in *sui generis* legislation in India. Gene Campaign played a particularly important role in this NGO-led effort.

The Convention of Farmers and Breeders

In December 1998 Gene Campaign took the initiative by publishing a draft treaty, presented as an alternative to UPOV and a forum for implementing farmers' and breeders' rights in developing countries. Called the Convention of Farmers and Breeders (CoFaB), the draft treaty set out detailed legislative provisions designed to work to the advantage of farmers in developing countries. In presenting this document to the Indian government, Gene Campaign argued that the CoFaB was a better model for India than UPOV.

Specifically, Article 2(1) of CoFaB recognized the rights of farmers by arranging for the collection of a farmers' rights fee from the breeders of new plant varieties. The fee was to be levied for the privilege of using traditional plant varieties either directly or through the use of those varieties in plant breeding programmes. Article 2(2) of CoFaB then provided that farmers' rights would be granted to communities of farmers and, where applicable, to individual farmers as well. Article 2(3) of CoFaB then set out a system of revenue collection from farmers' rights fees that would flow into a National Gene Fund (NGF). Distribution of the funds would be decided by a multi-stakeholder body set up for the purpose. Finally, Article 2(4) of CoFaB provided for the recognition of the right of the breeder of a new variety by the grant of a special title called the Plant Breeders' Right.[53]

In support of the CoFaB approach, Gene Campaign stressed that there was nothing in Article 27.3(b) of the TRIPS Agreement that prevents a WTO Member from granting farmers' rights and that this provision in

Article 27.3(b) explicitly mandates a *sui generis* system that can be different from simply transposing the UPOV Convention into national law. Initially, however, the Indian government did not accept arguments in favour of adopting CoFaB wholesale as the Indian legislative approach to meeting its obligations under the *sui generis* provision of Article 27.3(b) of the TRIPS Agreement. Nonetheless, the intervention of NGOs had by this point significantly raised the level of public awareness to the point that there was widespread recognition of the fact that alternatives to the UPOV Convention could be adopted. This in turn led to more critical thinking about the appropriateness of the UPOV Convention in the Indian context.

Protection of Plant Varieties and Farmers' Rights Act of 2001

Following these initiatives and the sustained intervention of NGOs over a number of years, farmers' rights were eventually incorporated into Section 39(1) of the Indian Protection of Plant Varieties and Farmers' Rights Act of 2001 (see also Sahai 2001, p. 11).

SECTION 39(1) OF THE PROTECTION OF PLANT VARIETIES AND FARMERS' RIGHTS ACT OF 2001: FARMERS' RIGHTS

Notwithstanding anything contained in this Act,–

(i) a farmer who has bred or developed a new variety shall be entitled for registration and other protection in like manner as a breeder of a variety under this Act;

(ii) the farmers' variety shall be entitled to registration if the application contains declaration as specified in clause (h) of sub-section (1) of section 18;

(iii) a farmer who is engaged in the conservation of genetic resources . . . shall be entitled in the prescribed manner for recognition and reward from the Gene Fund . . . [con't]

Provided that material so selected and preserved has been used as donors of genes in varieties registrable under this Act;

(iv) a farmer shall be deemed to be entitled to save, use, sow, resow, exchange, share or sell his farm produce including seed of a variety protected under this Act in the same manner as he was entitled before the coming into force of this Act;

> Provided that the farmer shall not be entitled to sell branded seed of a variety protected under this Act.
>
> *Explanation:* For the purposes of clause (iv), 'branded seed' means any seed put in a package or any other container and labelled in a manner indicating that such seed is a variety protected under this Act.

Section 39(1)(i) of the Act puts farmers' rights on a par with plant breeders' rights by giving farmers the entitlement to apply for registration of a plant variety as well as for registration of a farmer's variety. Furthermore, the definition of a farmer's variety, set out in Section 2(k) of the Act, includes a variety that has been traditionally cultivated and evolved by the farmers in their fields, and a wild relative or 'landrace' of a variety about which the farmers possess common knowledge (see also Bultrini 2009, p. 232). The Act also provides for reward and recognition, and establishes a benefit sharing mechanism. Plant breeders, however, expressed their concern about the Act.

The International Seed Federation (ISF) announced that it was unhappy because the legislation did not constitute an effective system for protecting plant breeders' rights consistent with the 1978 Act of the UPOV Convention. ISF also complained that it was not acceptable that farmers have the right to sell seeds in the same Act as breeders' rights since this created confusion.[54] Navdanya, on the other hand, complained that there was more that could be done to improve farmers' rights in the Act and emphasized that this was just the first step (Shiva and Jafri 2001).

Renewed Attempts to Join UPOV

Following adoption of the Indian Protection of Plant Varieties and Farmers' Rights Act of 2001, it was anticipated that India would not become a signatory to the UPOV Convention since it had demonstrated compliance with the TRIPS Agreement through *sui generis* legislation. Despite this, on 30 May 2002, the Indian Cabinet announced that it had approved a government decision to join UPOV. NGOs reacted angrily, arguing that the Act of 2001 could not be compatible with the 1991 version of the UPOV Convention and pointing out that there had been no parliamentary debate prior to the government taking this decision (see, for example Sahai 2002).

Gene Campaign then filed a Writ Petition at the Delhi High Court on

1 October 2002, claiming that joining UPOV would be contrary to the Protection of Plant Varieties and Farmers' Rights Act of 2001 and would also be a violation of the Indian Constitution. The provisions of the Constitution cited in the Gene Campaign Writ Petition were as follows: first, Article 14 (the State shall not deny to any person equality before the law or the equal protection of the laws within the territory of India); second, Article 21 (no person shall be deprived of his life or personal liberty except according to procedure established by law); third, Article 38 (the State shall strive to promote the welfare of the people by securing and protecting as effectively as it may a social order in which justice, social, economic and political, shall inform all the institutions of the national life); fourth, Article 47 (the State shall regard the raising of the level of nutrition and the standard of living of its people and the improvement of public health as among its primary duties); and, fifth, Article 48-A (the State shall endeavour to organize agriculture and animal husbandry on modern and scientific lines and shall, in particular, take steps for preserving and improving breeds). Gene Campaign asked that the Court direct the government not to take action which was not in the interests of the Act and make clear that those rights should be neither impaired nor diluted by any future act of the government (Kumar and Sahai 2003, p. 78).

Following the issuance of the Writ Petition, Gene Campaign continued to argue against India's accession to UPOV. Its publications have pointed out that Article 8(j) of the CBD calls for the international community to respect, preserve, maintain knowledge, innovations and practices of indigenous and local communities embodying traditional lifestyles relevant for the conservation and sustainable use of biological diversity (Bala Ravi 2003, p. 71). To date, India has not joined UPOV nor has it become a signatory to the UPOV Convention.

EVALUATION OF NGOS' ACHIEVEMENTS IN THEIR CAMPAIGN TO GAIN RECOGNITION FOR FARMERS' RIGHTS IN INDIA

The recognition of farmers' rights in the Protection of Plant Varieties and Farmers' Rights Act of 2001 took nearly eight years to achieve. At critical points in the process leading to its adoption, NGOs utilized a rights-based approach to frame its arguments for achieving a balance between PBRs and farmers' rights. RFSTE and Navdanya began this process in 1993 by making explicit reference to Article 19.1(g) of the Indian Constitution, which gives every citizen the freedom to practise his or her occupation. Gene Campaign then also used a rights-based approach strategically in

2002 when it issued a Writ Petition claiming that the Indian government's decision to join UPOV would not only be contrary to the Protection of Plant Varieties and Farmers' Rights Act of 2001 but would also be a violation of numerous provisions of the Indian Constitution.

The achievements have been remarkable given that the entire debate about farmers' rights in India was generated by such a small number of NGOs working with relatively scarce resources compared to their larger international NGO counterparts. However, the current situation is far from perfect. There is a relative absence of links between NGOs and grassroots activism in India; the sporadic meetings with farmers' groups, for instance, that are not an adequate substitute for sustained engagement with these issues in Indian rural society. There is also a need for enhanced technical expertise within the NGO community working on intellectual property-related agriculture issues in India. This is particularly important because, especially when dealing with government officials, NGOs risk a loss of credibility if they do not demonstrate the high levels of technical competence that NGOs have demonstrated elsewhere in other contexts when making explicit the link between intellectual property, human rights and development.[55]

NOTES

1. The Indian Patents and Designs Act 1911 was subsequently amended in 1950 to incorporate this recommendation by introducing compulsory licensing provisions.
2. High mortality rates had been identified in India's First Five Year Plan in 1950.
3. The Supreme Court has held subsequently in *Bandhua Mukti Morcha v. Union of India* (AIR 1984 SC 802) that the right to life in Article 21 includes the right to health. The Supreme Court has also made clear in *State of Punjab v. Mohinder Singh Chawla* (1997 2 SCC 83) that the Indian government has a constitutional obligation to provide health facilities. It stated in *Paschim Banga Khet Mazdoor Samity v. State of West Bengal* (AIR 1996 SC 2426 at 2429 para 9) that failure to provide a patient timely medical treatment is a violation of the patient's right to life, and in *State of Punjab v. Ram Lubhaya Bagga* (1998 4 SCC 117) that there is an obligation on the State to maintain health services (Mathiharan 2003).
4. N. Rajagolala Ayyangar, Report on the Revision of the Patents Law (1959), paragraph 101.
5. Section 53(1)(a) of the Indian Patents Act 1970.
6. Section 88 of the Indian Patents Act 1970.
7. Section 87(1) of the Indian Patents Act 1970.
8. Section 84 of the Indian Patents Act 1970.
9. Biswajit Dhar, Centre for WTO Studies, Indian Institute of Foreign Trade, interview with the author, 7 April 2006.
10. Anand Grover, Lawyers Collective HIV/AIDS Unit, interview with the author, 3 April 2006.
11. Amit Sen Gupta, Delhi Science Forum, interview with the author, 5 April 2006.
12 Justice V.R. Krishna Iyer, Justice O. Chinnappa Reddy, Justice D.A. Desai and Justice Rajinder Sachar.
13. *Vincent v. Union of India* (AIR 1987 SC 990).

14. Except in respect of the principles of national treatment under Article 3 of the TRIPS Agreement and most-favoured-nation status under Article 4 of the TRIPS Agreement.
15. Under Article 70.8 of the TRIPS Agreement, the patent applicant was able to claim the original filing or priority date and thus substantiate the novelty of the product for which the patent was being sought (Macdonald-Brown and Ferera 1998, p. 69).
16. The Patents (Amendment) Ordinance of 1994 and the Patents (Amendment) Bill of 1995.
17 *India – Patent Protection for Pharmaceutical and Agricultural Products.* WTO Document WT/DS50/R, 5 September 1997 and the subsequent Appellate Body Report WT/DS50/AB/R of 19 December 1997.
18. As a developing country Member of the WTO, under Article 65.2 of the TRIPS Agreement India was entitled to delay applying the TRIPS Agreement until 1 January 2000. Furthermore, under Article 65.4 of the TRIPS Agreement, for areas of technology not protected at the date that the TRIPS Agreement came into force, India could delay until 1 January 2005. This meant that India could delay making available patents for food, pharmaceutical and chemical products until that date. However, in order to take advantage of the longer transitional period, India was obliged under Article 70.8 of the TRIPS Agreement to set up by 1 January 1995 a means by which patent applications for pharmaceutical and agricultural chemical products could be filed so that the applicants could then claim the filing date as the priority date when the transitional arrangements permitted by the TRIPS Agreement came to an end (the so-called 'mail-box' provision). Furthermore, during the period that patent applications for pharmaceutical and agricultural chemical products could be filed under the mail-box provision, Article 70.9 of the TRIPS Agreement contained an additional requirement that exclusive marketing rights be granted for a period of five years after obtaining marketing approval in India or until a product patent was granted or rejected there. This requirement for the granting of exclusive marketing rights only applied when, after 1 January 1995, a patent application had been filed and a patent granted in another WTO Member and marketing approval was also obtained there. The term 'exclusive marketing rights' means that if the patent applicant is in a position to supply the market with a product, whether through local manufacturing or importation, an exclusive right to sell may have the effect of curtailing potentially competing local producers just as effectively as the grant of a patent, although it would not preclude such manufacturer from exporting and selling the products in foreign countries where patent protection was not in force (UNCTAD-ICTSD 2005, p. 774).
19. Patents (Amendment) Act 1999. Available at: http://www.patentoffice.nic.in/ipr/patent/patact_99.PDF.
20. Source: http://www.delhiscienceforum.net/index.php?option=com_content&task=view&id=93&Itemid=2.
21. 'You can't blame liberalisation for all our woes', Archna Devraj, *Infochange Agenda*, June 2005. Available at: http://infochangeindia.org/20050602392/Agenda/Access-Denied/-You-can-t-blame-liberalisation-for-all-our-woes.html.
22. Amit Sengupta, Delhi Science Forum, interview with the author, 5 April 2006.
23. Patents (Amendment) Act 2005. Available at: http://www.patentoffice.nic.in/ipr/patent/patent_2005.pdf.
24. Ellen 't Hoen, MSF, interview with the author, 22 November 2005.
25. 'Evergreening' is the term used to describe the process whereby pharmaceutical companies seek to reformulate, recombine and repackage the active ingredients and change the methods of administration such as the dosages and the administration routes in order to obtain a new patent for pharmaceutical products soon to reach patent expiry (Arup and Plahe 2010, p. 28).
26. Anand Grover trained as a biochemist and lawyer. In addition to founding the Lawyers Collective HIV/AIDS Unit he is a member of the UNAIDS Reference Group on HIV/AIDS and Human Rights and in 2008 was appointed as the Special Rapporteur on the

right of everyone to the enjoyment of the highest attainable standard of physical and mental health by the UN Human Rights Council.

27. Anand Grover, Lawyers Collective HIV/AIDS Unit, interview with the author, 3 April 2006.
28. Anand Grover, Lawyers Collective HIV/AIDS Unit, interview with the author, 3 April 2006.
29. Lawyers Collective HIV/AIDS Unit website. Available at: http://www.lawyerscollective.org/hiv-aids.
30. Events in South Africa have been credited with providing a 'shot in the arm' to the AMTC. See *Health-India: Group Helps Keep up Fight vs. Expensive Drugs*, T.V. Padma, Inter Press Service, 7 May 2001. Available at: http://www.inhousepharmacy.com/generics/generic-info-2.html?PHPSESSID=b8569ff48f415027c17d84939c2d411b.
31. Anand Grover, Lawyers Collective HIV/AIDS Unit, interview with the author, 3 April 2006.
32. Letter from the Affordable Medicines Treatment Campaign to India's National Human Rights Commission, 11 October 2004. Available at: http://www.hrw.org/english/docs/2004/10/22/india9556.htm.
33. '26 February is the Global Day of Action against Indian Patent Ordinance', GCAIPA Press Release, 8 February 2005. Available at: http://www.mumbai.indymedia.org/en/2005/02/210107.shtml.
34. *Novartis AG v. Union of India*, (2007) 4 MLJ 1153 (High Court of Madras, 6 August 2007).
35. 'Patent application for AIDS drug opposed for first time in India', MSF Press Release, 30 March 2006. Available at: http://www.doctorswithoutborders.org/press/release.cfm?id=1776. 'Valganciclovir Patent Set Aside in India', MSF Statement, 4 December 2008. Available at: http://www.msfaccess.org/main/access-patents/valganciclovir-patent-set-aside-in-india/.
36. 'Invalid Patent on Valganciclovir Affects Access to Treatment – Leads to Patent Dispute in Bombay High Court', posted on the IP-Health list by Kajal Bhardwaj, 20 October 2008.
37. 'Cipla, NGO to contest patent grant to Roche', Unnikrishnan, C.H., 3 December 2007. Available at: http://www.livemint.com/Articles/PrintArticle.aspx.
38. 'Delhi NGO opposes patent for Roche's HIV drug', The Economic Times. Available at: http://economictimes.indiatimes.com/News/News_By_Industry/Delhi_NGO_opposes_patent_for_Roches_HIV_drug/articleshow/3173583.cms.
39. *F. Hoffman-La Roche Ltd. and Another v. Cipla Ltd.* I.A. 642/2008 IN CS (OS) 89/2008.
40. 'India revokes patent granted to Roche's Valcyte (valganciclovir): Reports – Cipla launched a generic version of valganciclovir in 2008 while the anti-viral was under patent in India', *Dance with Shadows*. Available at: http://www.dancewithshadows.com/pillscribe/india-revokes-patent-granted-to-roches-valcyte-valganciclovir-reports/. 'Victory for Access to Medicine as Valganciclovir Patent Rejected in India', MSF Press Release 6 May 2010.
41. Suman Sahai, Gene Campaign, interview with the author, 7 April 2006.
42. Anand Grover, Lawyers Collective HIV/AIDS Unit, interview with the author, 3 April 2006.
43. *2.5 million people living with HIV in India: Revised estimates show lower HIV prevalence in India*, UNAIDS, 6 July 2007. Available at: http://www.unaids.org/en/KnowledgeCentre/Resources/FeatureStories/archive/2007/20070704_India_new_data.asp.
44. 'India has most AIDS infections', James Sturcke, *The Guardian*, 30 May 2006. Available at: http://www.guardian.co.uk/print/0,,329492736-106925,00.html.
45. 'World Bank Supports Agriculture Development and Innovation in India with US$200 Million', *World Bank News Release*, 18 April 2006.
46. 'India not Isolated at GATT Talks', *The Pioneer*, 10 October 1992.
47. Navdanya website. Available at: http://www.navdanya.org/.

48. Vandana Shiva, Navdanya, interview with the author, 5 April 2006.
49. Suman Sahai, Gene Campaign, interview with the author, 7 April 2006.
50. See, for example, 'Protest Against Patenting Organisms', *The Times of India*, 1 July 1992; and 'Seeds of Satyagraha', *The Hindustan*, 14 April 1993.
51. *A Charter of Farmers' Rights 1993*. Available at: http://www.agobservatory.org/library. cfm?refID=29551.
52. 'Indian Farmers Rally against GATT, Bio-Patents', *SUNS Online*, 4 October 1994. Available at: http://www.sunsonline.org/trade/areas/intellec/10040093.htm.
53. Full text of CoFaB is available at: http://lists.essential.org/upd-discuss/msg00001. html; see also 'India's Plant Variety Protection and Farmers' Rights Act,' Suman Sahai, *Bridges Comment,* October 2001, pp. 11–12. Available at: http://www.iprsonline. org/ictsd/docs/SahaiBridgesYear5N8Oct2001.pdf; 'COFAB, A Developing Country Alternative to UPOV', Suman Sahai. Available at: http://www.genecampaign.org/ Publication/Article/Farmers%20Right/cofab_a_developing_country_alternative.pdf.
54. Minutes of *WIPO-UPOV Symposium on Intellectual Property Rights in Plant Biotechnology*, 24 October 2003, Geneva, page 8, available at: http://www.upov.int/en/ documents/Symposium2003/panel_discussion.pdf.
55. Suman Sahai, Gene Campaign, interview with the author, 7 April 2006.

7. Emphasizing the link between intellectual property, human rights and development: the role of NGOs and social movements

INTRODUCTION

The link between intellectual property rights and human rights has been an important factor in the impact that NGOs have achieved in drawing attention to the potentially adverse effects of intellectual property rights on marginalized, poor, disadvantaged and vulnerable sectors of society in developing countries.

This human rights-based approach first came to prominence when international NGOs began to frame intellectual property-related issues by using the emotive language of human rights to underpin substantive arguments that public health, access to medicines, the right to health and the right to life were at risk due to the patent provisions of the TRIPS Agreement. International NGOs began to campaign for access to medicines through the full utilization of flexibilities contained in the TRIPS Agreement and framed the issue in terms of human rights. By so doing, the human rights frame ultimately added moral authority to the access to medicines campaign, which in turn contributed to a greater emphasis on the importance of using in-built flexibilities in the TRIPS Agreement and the need to permanently amend the TRIPS Agreement provisions on compulsory licensing.

Emphasizing framing strategies has become increasingly common in narratives of NGO engagement with intellectual property rights and development. In fact, the relationship between intellectual property rights, human rights and development is in some respects of narrower application. In other respects it goes much deeper than has been previously acknowledged.

Framing the impact of intellectual property rights in terms of human rights is a strategy of relatively narrow application because attempts to frame the impact of intellectual property rights on farmers, indigenous peoples and local communities in developing countries as human rights issues have been nowhere near as pronounced as they were for public health and the access to medicines campaign. The reason is that the human rights implications of intellectual property rights as they relate to agriculture, genetic resources and traditional knowledge do not carry the same moral resonance, nor have they received the same level of attention or profile, as the human rights implications of the TRIPS Agreement have done for public health and access to medicines.

In other respects, NGOs in a number of prominent developing countries have done much more than framing the discourse on intellectual property rights in terms of the language of human rights. Instead, in South Africa, Brazil and India, NGOs have used human rights law in substantive terms hitherto not considered by those emphasizing framing strategies. NGOs in these countries have used rights enshrined in national constitutions before national courts as tools with which to challenge the scope and application of intellectual property law in a very real and concrete way.

NGOs representing people living with HIV/AIDS in South Africa, for instance, have used strategies that had worked previously to such good effect during the anti-apartheid struggle and highlighted primacy of human rights principles under the country's constitution. In *Minister of Health & Others v. Treatment Action Campaign & Others*, human rights principles enshrined in the South African Constitution were used to overturn the decision of the South African government's refusal to make Nevirapine available in the public health sector and to set out a timeframe for a national programme to prevent MTCT of HIV.

However, NGOs in South Africa also demonstrated that recourse to human rights law is not a magic bullet that can resolve all issues pertaining to patents, public health and access to medicines. Rather, NGOs showed remarkable flexibility in their strategy, using human rights principles where appropriate but also treating this as part of a larger armoury of legal instruments that could be utilized as appropriate. Other approaches were based, in particular, on competition law and the constitutional right of access to information.

In the realm of genetic resources and traditional knowledge in South Africa, it is also instructive to note that it has been NGO activists in South Africa whose backgrounds were in the use of human rights to fight the worst abuses of the apartheid regime that emerged as legal representatives of the indigenous San people when they negotiated a benefit sharing agreement for commercialization of the patent relating to the appetite suppressant properties of the succulent *Hoodia gordonii*.

Following a traumatic period of military rule in Brazil, NGOs also used the knowledge of human rights that they acquired during the struggle for democracy to campaign successfully for universal access to ARVs for people living with HIV/AIDS. This belief in the primacy of human rights, particularly the right to health enshrined in the Brazilian Constitution, impacted subsequently on the decision of NGOs to mobilize in support of the Brazilian government in its attempts to achieve a balance between the patents for pharmaceutical products and the right to health through the compulsory licensing provisions of federal law. Those provisions were subject to a US complaint to the WTO and in turn led to sustained and detailed engagement with issues relating to patents, public health and access to medicines on the part of the Brazilian NGO community.

To a lesser extent, the work of NGOs on behalf of indigenous peoples and local communities in Brazil has also been underpinned by the belief that those people have an inalienable human right to protect the biodiversity over which they are custodians, even when those community rights come into conflict with the individual, private, rights associated with intellectual property.

Human rights have also played an important role in defining the way that Indian NGOs have engaged with the impact of intellectual property rights on the poor, the disadvantaged and vulnerable sectors of society. When India's struggle for independence from British colonial rule ended in 1947, human rights and in particular the right to life enshrined in the Indian Constitution formed the basis of the Ayyangar Committee's recommendation that granting patents in critical areas such as food and medicines be curtailed. The Committee's reasoning for this recommendation was that the prohibitively high price of patented products could violate the right to life. This human rights approach in turn informed the subsequent approach of NGOs working to ensure that amendments to India's patents legislation utilized to the full extent flexibilities contained in the TRIPS Agreement. In the post-TRIPS implementation period, as other NGOs become involved with patents and access to medicines issues, it was once again an underlying concern that the human rights of people living with HIV/AIDS were being abused which informed their approach. This led in turn to NGOs originally versed in human rights law to engage to a greater extent with the technical aspects of patent law. They began initiating pre-grant patent oppositions against pharmaceutical product patent applications in a way that they could not have foreseen when they originally began campaigning on human rights issues associated with HIV/AIDS some years earlier.

NGOs in India also made explicit reference to human rights guaranteed by the Indian Constitution in relation to farmers' rights, particularly the constitutional right of every Indian citizen to practise his or her occupation. After successfully campaigning for the introduction of legislation to protect farmers' rights, NGOs in India then returned to a human rights-based approach in the battle to prevent India becoming a signatory to UPOV, with all that would have entailed for the perceived erosion of newly-acquired farmers' rights. On this occasion, they referred explicitly to the constitutional right that no person shall be deprived of his or her life or personal liberty and the obligation of the Indian government to uphold those rights by refraining from becoming a signatory to the UPOV Convention.

The extent that human rights have been used by NGOs seeking to alleviate the adverse impacts of intellectual property rights on development are therefore far greater than was previously thought. In the light of this, how might the relationship between intellectual property rights, human rights and development be utilized more widely by NGOs to inform debate in the future?

INTELLECTUAL PROPERTY RIGHTS AND HUMAN RIGHTS[1]

At the heart of the debate on intellectual property rights and human rights lies a distinction between individual rights and community rights. Three possible interpretations are available: the first is that intellectual property rights have no human rights dimension and are purely legal rights; the second is that intellectual property rights are human rights, with the emphasis on property rights and individual concerns; the third interpretation is that some aspects of intellectual property rights have potentially adverse implications for human rights (see also 3D: Trade - Human Rights - Equitable Economy 2005).

The first interpretation, namely that intellectual property rights have no human rights dimension and are purely legal rights appears incorrect because it has been undermined as an approach by the solemn declaration by the States members of the Assembly of the Berne Union for the Protection of Literary and Artistic Works, 1986. The solemn declaration asserted clearly and unambiguously that 'copyright is based on human rights and justice and that authors, as creators of beauty, entertainment and learning, deserve that their rights in their creations be recognized and effectively protected both in their country and in all other countries of the world'. If patents are viewed in the same way, the arguments that intellectual property rights have no human rights dimension are further undermined.

With regard to the second interpretation, namely that intellectual property is essentially the same as property in tangible assets and must therefore be secured by the same legal guarantees, industry lobbyists assert that the protection of intellectual property rights has long been recognized as a basic human right and those concerned about human rights made a conscious and concerted effort to ensure that intellectual property rights were protected (Giovanetti and Matthews 2005). In support of this claim, they draw on the Constitution of the United States and the American Declaration on the Rights and Duties of Man.

ARTICLE 1, SECTION 8, CLAUSE 8 OF THE U.S. CONSTITUTION

To promote the progress of science and useful arts, by securing for limited times to authors and inventors the exclusive rights to their respective writings and discoveries.

AMERICAN DECLARATION OF THE RIGHTS AND DUTIES OF MAN, ARTICLE 13

He likewise has the right to the protection of his moral and material interests as regards his inventions or any literary, scientific or artistic works of which he is the author.

This is the rationale for arguing that provisions made by international human rights documents with regard to property cover intellectual property, with the latter elevated to the status of fundamental rights. It is also asserted that intellectual property rights have been accorded the status of fundamental rights by international human rights instruments of the UN. Foremost amongst the international human rights instruments that are often claimed to regard the right to own property as including the right to own intellectual property are Articles 17 and 27 of the Universal Declaration of Human Rights.

Article 15(1) of the UN International Covenant on Economic, Social and Cultural Rights (ICESCR) of 1966 contains a similarly worded provision to the Universal Declaration (United Nations 1966).

Chapman, in a discussion paper submitted to the United Nations Economic and Social Committee (2000b), intellectual property rights should be viewed as human rights because the three provisions of Article 15(1) ICESCR were viewed by drafters as intrinsically interrelated; the rights of authors and creators were not just good in themselves but were

ARTICLE 17 OF THE UNIVERSAL DECLARATION OF HUMAN RIGHTS

(1) Everyone has the right to own property alone as well as in association with others.
(2) No one shall be arbitrarily deprived of his property.

ARTICLE 27 OF THE UNIVERSAL DECLARATION OF HUMAN RIGHTS

(1) Everyone has the right freely to participate in the cultural life of the community, to enjoy the arts and to share in scientific advancement and its benefits.
(2) Everyone has the right to the protection of the moral and material interests resulting from any scientific, literary or artistic production of which he is the author.

ARTICLE 15(1) OF THE ICESCR

The States Parties to the present Covenant recognize the right of everyone:

(a) to take part in cultural life;
(b) to enjoy the benefits of scientific progress and its applications;
(c) to benefit from the protection of the moral and material interests resulting from any scientific, literary or artistic production of which he or she is the author.

understood as essential preconditions for cultural freedom and participation and scientific progress. However, Chapman goes on to point out that, conversely, human rights considerations impose conditions on the manner in which authors' rights are protected in intellectual property regimes. For Chapman, to be consistent with the provisions of Article 15, intellectual property law must assure that intellectual property protections complement, fully respect, and promote other components of Article 15, so that the rights of authors and creators facilitate rather than constrain cultural participation on the one side and scientific progress and access on the other. The language of the ICESCR underscores the importance of the obligation to respect the moral and material interests of the author, artist, inventor and creator but, in contrast with the individualism of intellectual property law, Chapman argues that a human rights approach also recognizes that an author, artist, or creator can be a group or a community as well as an individual.

Chapman also points out that intellectual property rights have an intrinsic value as an expression of human dignity and creativity and that, put another way, artistic and scientific works are not first and foremost economic commodities whose value is determined by their utility and economic price tag. A human rights approach takes what is often an implicit balance between the rights of inventors and creators and the interests of the wider society within intellectual property paradigms and it makes it far more explicit and exacting.

For Chapman, from a human rights perspective, the rights of the creator are not absolute but conditional on contributing to the common good and welfare of society. Chapman concludes that, because a human rights approach also establishes a different and often more exacting standard for evaluating the appropriateness of granting intellectual property protection, in order for intellectual property to fulfil the conditions necessary to be recognized as a universal human right, intellectual property regimes and the manner in which they are implemented must be consistent with the realization of the other human rights, particularly those in the ICESCR.

This leads us to the third interpretation of intellectual property rights and human rights, namely that some aspects of intellectual property rights have potentially adverse implications for human rights. The report of the High Commissioner on Human Rights on the impact of the TRIPS Agreement on human rights of 27 June 2001, acknowledged that Article 15 ICESCR identifies a need to balance the protection of both public and private interests (United Nations Commission on Human Rights 2001, p. 5).

On the one hand, Article 15 recognizes the right of everyone to take part in cultural life and to enjoy the benefits of scientific progress and its applications. On the other hand, the same article recognizes the right of everyone to benefit from the protection of the moral and material interests resulting from any scientific, literary or artistic production of which he or she is the author.

Taking these two aspects of Article 15 together, the ICESCR could be said to bind States to design intellectual property systems that strike a balance between promoting general public interests in accessing new knowledge as easily as possible and in protecting the interests of authors and inventors in such knowledge. Of course, as the report of the High Commissioner on Human Rights points out, the balance between public and private interests found under Article 15 ICESCR (and under Article 27 of the Universal Declaration) is one familiar in intellectual property law. For the report of the High Commissioner on Human Rights, there is consequently a degree of compatibility between Article 15 and traditional intellectual property systems, but the question is essentially where to strike the right balance, namely whether greater emphasis should be given to protecting interests of inventors and authors or to promoting public access to new knowledge.

On 21 November 2005, the UNCHR Committee on Economic, Social and Cultural Rights adopted General Comment 17 elaborating on the right of everyone to benefit from the protection of the moral and material interests resulting from any scientific, literary or artistic production of which he is the author, as set out in Article 15, paragraph 1(c), of the Covenant.[2] General Comment 17 noted that the right of everyone to benefit from the protection of the moral and material interests resulting from any scientific, literary or artistic production of which he or she is the author is a human right, which derives from the inherent dignity and worth of all persons. General Comment 17 notes that this fact distinguishes Article 15, paragraph 1(c) and other human rights from most legal entitlements recognizable in intellectual property systems.

It stated that human rights are fundamental, inalienable and universal entitlements belonging to individuals and, under certain circumstances, groups of individuals and communities. General Comment 17 also noted that human rights are fundamental as they are inherent in the human person as such, whereas intellectual property rights are first and foremost means by which States seek to provide incentives for inventiveness and creativity, encourage the dissemination of creative and innovative productions, as well as the development of cultural identities, and preserve the integrity of scientific, literary and artistic productions for the benefit of society as a whole.

General Comment 17 goes on to suggest that, in contrast with human rights, intellectual property rights are generally of a temporary nature, and can be revoked, licensed or assigned to someone else. While under most intellectual property systems, intellectual property rights, with the exception of moral rights, may be allocated, limited in time and scope, traded, amended and even forfeited, human rights are timeless expressions of fundamental entitlements of the human person.

Whereas the human right to benefit from the protection of the moral and material interests resulting from one's scientific, literary and artistic productions safeguards the personal link between authors and their creations, and between peoples, communities, or other groups and their collective cultural heritage, as well as their basic material interests which are necessary to enable authors to enjoy an adequate standard of living, intellectual property regimes primarily protect business and corporate interests and investments. Moreover, the General Comment stated that the scope of protection of the moral and material interests of the author provided for by Article 15(1)(c) does not necessarily coincide with what is referred to as intellectual property rights under national legislation or international agreements.

INTELLECTUAL PROPERTY RIGHTS, PUBLIC HEALTH AND ACCESS TO MEDICINES

In terms of the relationship between intellectual property rights and the right to health, it will be recalled that under Article 27.1 of the TRIPS Agreement, patents must be available for all fields of technology. This scope of coverage includes the availability of patents for pharmaceutical products. However, when considering the availability of patents for pharmaceutical products, we have also seen on numerous occasions in this book the link made explicit between intellectual property and human rights in terms of the importance of taking into account the right to life, the right to health and the entitlements to be accorded during motherhood and childhood. In international human rights law, the relevant provisions in this respect are contained in Article 25 of the Universal Declaration of Human Rights of 1948.

ARTICLE 25 OF THE UNIVERSAL DECLARATION OF HUMAN RIGHTS

(1) Everyone has the right to a standard of living adequate for the health and well-being of himself and of his family, including food, clothing, housing and medical care and necessary social services, and the right to security in the event of unemployment, sickness, disability, widowhood, old age or other lack of livelihood in circumstances beyond his control.
(2) Motherhood and childhood are entitled to special care and assistance. All children, whether born in or out of wedlock, shall enjoy the same social protection.

This principle of the right to health is underpinned by Article 12 of the ICESCR.

ARTICLE 12 OF THE ICESCR

1. The States Parties to the present Covenant recognize the right of everyone to the enjoyment of the highest attainable standard of physical and mental health.
2. The steps to be taken by the States Parties to the present Covenant to achieve the full realization of this right shall include those necessary for:

(a) The provision for the reduction of the stillbirth-rate and of infant mortality and for the healthy development of the child;
(b) The improvement of all aspects of environmental and industrial hygiene;
(c) The prevention, treatment and control of epidemic, endemic, occupational and other diseases;
(d) The creation of conditions which would assure to all medical service and medical attention in the event of sickness.

The UN Committee on Economic, Social and Cultural Rights has elaborated, in General Comment 14 of 11 May 2000, on the concept of the highest attainable standard of health, as set out in Article 12 of the ICESCR (United Nations Economic and Social Committee 2000a). General Comment 14 sets out the content of the right, obligations on States to respect, and fulfil the right, the elements of international cooperation relevant to implement the right, as well as acts constituting violations of the right. In particular, General Comment 14 states that health is a fundamental human right indispensable for the exercise of other human rights. General Comment 14 also makes clear that the reference to Article 12(1) of the Covenant to 'the highest attainable standard of physical and mental health' is not confined to the right to health care and that, on the contrary, the wording of Article 12(1) acknowledges that the right to health embraces a wide range of socio-economic factors that promote conditions in which people can lead a healthy life and extends to the underlying determinants of health, such as food and nutrition, housing, access to safe and potable water and adequate sanitation, safe and healthy working conditions, and a healthy environment.

General Comment 14 makes specific reference to the promotion of research; access to affordable treatments, in particular essential drugs; HIV/AIDS; national measures for the promotion of the right to health; clarification of international obligations; and acts that constitute violations of the right to health. Furthermore, General Comment 14 notes that, while the notion of 'the highest attainable standard of health' in Article 12(1) of the Covenant must be understood as taking into account both the individual's biological and socio-economic preconditions and a State's available resources, the right to health must be understood as a right to the enjoyment of a variety of facilities, goods, services and conditions necessary for the realization of the highest attainable standard of health.

According to the report of the High Commissioner on the impact of TRIPS on human rights, States are bound to promote the right to health through the ensuring of access to affordable treatments. The right to health contains certain essential elements to be applied by States according to the prevailing national conditions. These elements include ensuring the availability, accessibility, and quality of health facilities, goods and services. The report of the High Commissioner goes on to state that accessibility also includes the notion of affordability, namely that health facilities, goods and services must be affordable to all, whether privately or publicly owned.

General Comment 14 also examines the specific steps that States should undertake in fulfilment of their obligations, particularly in the context of Article 12(2)(c) ICESCR, which indicates that States that are parties to the ICESCR must undertake steps necessary for 'the prevention, treatment and control of epidemic, endemic, occupational and other diseases'. The control of diseases refers to States' individual and joint efforts to make available relevant technologies and the promotion of strategies of infectious disease control.

Furthermore, the right to health includes a right to facilities, goods and services, under Article 12(2)(d). This obliges States to provide equal and timely access to basic preventive, curative and rehabilitative health services and appropriate treatment of prevalent diseases, injuries and disabilities, preferably at the community level. The right to facilities, goods and services also includes the provision of essential drugs.

The right to health obliges States to take into account HIV/AIDS in respecting, protecting and fulfilling the right to health. General Comment 14 notes that formerly unknown diseases, such as HIV/AIDS and others, as well as the rapid growth of the world population have created new obstacles to the realization of the right to health which need to be taken into account when interpreting Article 12.

General Comment 14 goes on to set out some of the national measures that States must take to implement the right. It notes that, as with other rights, States are obliged to respect, protect and fulfil the right to health. It states that '(t)he obligation to respect requires States to refrain from interfering directly or indirectly with the enjoyment of the right to health. The obligation to *protect* requires States to take measures that prevent third parties from interfering with Article 12 guarantees. Finally the obligation to *fulfil* requires States to adopt appropriate legislative, administrative, budgetary, judicial, promotional and other measures towards the full realization of the right to health'.

General Comment 14 sets out international obligations under the right to health. Specifically, States that are parties to the ICESCR should recognize the essential role of international cooperation and comply with their commitment to take joint and separate action to achieve the full realization of the right to health, taking into account the gross inequality in the health status of people, particularly between developed and developing countries. States parties should ensure that the right to health is given due attention in international agreements and States parties should take steps to ensure that these instruments do not adversely impact upon the right to health. Similarly, States parties have an obligation to ensure that their actions as members of international organizations take due account of the right to health. General Comment 14 recognizes that while States are ultimately responsible for compliance with the ICESCR, all members of society, including the private business sector, have responsibilities regarding the realization of the right to health. States that are parties to the ICESCR also have international obligations to 'provide essential drugs, as from time to time defined under the WHO Action Programme on Essential Drugs' and to 'take measures to prevent, treat and control epidemic and endemic diseases'. Further, international organizations, including WHO and WTO, should cooperate effectively with States to build on their respective expertise in relation to the right to health.

Finally, General Comment 14 notes certain acts that constitute violations of the right to health. Violations of the right to health can be the result of the actions of States, or the actions of other entities insufficiently regulated by the State. Violations of the obligation to protect the right to health include the failure to regulate individuals, groups or corporations so as to prevent them from violating the right to health of others. Violations of the obligation to fulfil the right to health include, amongst others, the failure to adopt or implement a national health policy designed to ensure the right to health of all; insufficient expenditure which results in non-enjoyment of the right; and the failure to take measures to reduce the inequitable distribution of health facilities, goods and services.

The United Nations High Commissioner for Human Rights,

Sub-Commission on the Promotion of Human Rights has also affirmed, in Resolution 2000/7, that the right to protection of the moral and material interests resulting from any scientific, literary or artistic production of which one is the author is, in accordance with Article 27(2) of the Universal Declaration of Human Rights and Article 15 of the ICESCR a human right, subject to limitations in the public interest (United Nations High Commissioner for Human Rights, Sub-Commission on Human Rights 2000).

The Sub-Commission also declared in Resolution 2000/7 that since the implementation of the TRIPS Agreement does not adequately reflect the fundamental nature and indivisibility of all human rights, including the right of everyone to enjoy the benefits of scientific progress and its applications, the right to health, the right to food and the right to self-determination, there are apparent conflicts between the intellectual property rights regime embodied in the TRIPS Agreement and international human rights law.

The Sub-Commission, in Resolution 2000/7, encouraged the UN Committee on Economic Social and Cultural Rights (CESCR) to clarify the relationship between intellectual property rights and human rights, including through the drafting of a general comment on this subject. It recommended to the WIPO, the WHO, the United Nations Development Programme (UNDP) and other relevant United Nations agencies that they continue and deepen their analysis of the impacts of the TRIPS Agreement, including a consideration of its human rights implications.

In addition, the Sub-Commission, in Resolution 2000/7, commended the Conference of Parties to the CBD for its decision to assess the relationship between biodiversity concerns and intellectual property rights in general, and between the Convention on Biodiversity and TRIPS, in particular, and urged it also to consider human rights principles and instruments in undertaking this assessment. It also encouraged the NGOs to promote with their respective governments the need for economic policy processes fully to integrate and respect existing human rights obligations, and to continue to monitor and publicize the effects of economic policies that fail to take such obligations into account.

The starting point for a consideration of the operational aspects of intellectual property systems with regard to access to drugs is that access to essential drugs is a human right. While the protection and enforcement of intellectual property rights can provide a more secure environment for the transfer of technology to developing countries, it can also provide a basis for charging higher prices for drugs and for technology transfer which can restrict access for the poor.

The precise nature of concerns about the impact of intellectual property rights on fundamental human rights can in fact be seen most clearly in the Statement of CESCR of 2001, which addressed explicitly this link between human rights and the right to health. The Statement presents a substantial argument that is worthy of particular note.

STATEMENT OF THE UN COMMITTEE ON ECONOMIC, SOCIAL AND CULTURAL RIGHTS OF 2001

5. Human rights derive from the inherent dignity and worth of all persons, with the human person as the central subject and primary beneficiary of human rights. The moral and legal guarantees of fundamental freedoms, protections and entitlements both derive from and support people's self-respect and dignity . . . To be consistent with obligations in respect of international human rights, intellectual property regimes must promote and protect all human rights, including the full range of rights guaranteed in the Covenant.

6. The fact that the human person is the central subject and primary beneficiary of human rights distinguishes human rights, including the right of authors to the moral and material interests in their works, from legal rights recognized in intellectual property systems . . . Human rights are fundamental, inalienable and universal entitlements belonging to individuals, and in some situations groups of individuals and communities . . . Human rights are fundamental as they derive from the human person as such, whereas intellectual property rights derived from intellectual property systems are instrumental, in that they are a means by which States seek to provide incentives for inventiveness and creativity from which society benefits . . . In contrast with human rights, intellectual property rights are generally of a temporary nature and can be revoked, licensed or assigned to someone else. While intellectual property rights may be allocated, limited in time and scope, traded, amended and even forfeited, human rights are timeless expressions of fundamental entitlements of the human person . . .

Whereas human rights are dedicated to assuring satisfactory standards of human welfare and well-being, intellectual property regimes, although they traditionally provide protection for individual authors and creators, are increasingly focused on protecting business and corporate interests and investments . . .

> Moreover, the scope of protection and the moral and material interests of the author provided under Article 15 of the Covenant does not necessarily coincide with what is termed intellectual property rights under national legislation or international agreements . . .
>
> 8. A human rights-based approach focuses particularly on the needs of the most disadvantaged and marginalized individuals and communities. Because a human right is a universal entitlement, its implementation is evaluated particularly by the degree to which it benefits those who hitherto have been the most disadvantaged and marginalized and brings them up to the mainstream level of protection . . . Thus, in adopting intellectual property regimes, States and other actors must give particular attention at the national and international levels to the adequate protection of human rights of disadvantaged and marginalized individuals and groups, such as indigenous peoples.

So, did the CESCR Statement resolve once and for all the tensions between human rights and intellectual property rights? Well, it certainly set out a manifesto for NGOs that seek to promote the balance between the rights of the disadvantaged and marginalized in society on the one hand and the rights of intellectual property owners on the other, over intellectual property rights.

So how is this discourse on intellectual property rights, human rights and the right to health likely to develop in the future? One indication of the shape of the debate to come can be found in the World Health Assembly (2006), *Public Health, Innovation, Essential Health Research and Intellectual Property Rights*. In this resolution, the World Health Assembly appears to have reignited the debate on the relationship between human rights and the right to health, asserting the significance of intellectual property rights as human rights by: 'Stressing that the Universal Declaration of Human Rights provides that "everyone has the right freely to participate in the cultural life of the community, to enjoy the arts and to share in scientific advancement and its benefits" and that "everyone has the right to the protection of the moral and material interests resulting from any scientific, literary or artistic production of which he is the author."' At the same time, the resolution noted that the World Health Assembly is concerned about the impact of high prices on access to medicines. The tensions between the right to own intellectual property rights and the implications this could have on high prices for pharmaceutical products and on access to medicines were clearly set out in the resolution.

Subsequently, at the Sixty-First World Health Assembly on 24 May 2008, the *WHO Global Strategy and Plan of Action on Public Health, Innovation and Intellectual Property* attempts to balance the right to health with the right to own intellectual property (World Health Assembly 2008). Accordingly, the *WHO Global Strategy* sought to achieve this balance by, first, calling for more efforts to be made to implement States' obligations arising under applicable international human rights instruments with provisions relevant to health, while at the same time acknowledging the Universal Declaration on Human Rights.

In many respects, therefore, the debate encapsulated by deliberations at the World Health Assembly appears to have run full circle. Tensions remain between, on the one hand, the interpretation of intellectual property as a human right in terms of property and ownership and, on the other hand, the right to health as a human right, with all this implies for intellectual property rights and access to medicines.

How this tension is resolved and the extent to which intellectual property rights, human rights and the right to health can be best interpreted in developing countries where problems of access to medicines are most acute will depend largely on the capacity of those developing country governments to utilize the language of human rights to their advantage. In this respect, as the General Comment 14 on the right to health confirmed, it is the duty of all those in a position to assist, including NGOs, to provide 'international assistance and cooperation, especially economic and technical' in order to enable developing countries to meet their obligations under the Convention. Accordingly, it is 'incumbent upon developed States and other actors in a position to assist, to develop international intellectual property regimes that enable developing States to fulfil at least their core obligations to individuals and groups within their jurisdictions'.

On 1 August 2008, the new UNHCR Special Rapporteur on the right of everyone to the enjoyment of the highest attainable standard to physical and mental health was appointed. That Special Rapporteur was Anand Grover of the Lawyers Collective HIV/AIDS Unit in India. A powerful advocate for developing country NGOs had therefore come to the heart of the UN, tasked with monitoring the impact of intellectual property rights on health in developing countries. On 31 March 2009, Grover submitted a report dealing specifically with access to medicines and intellectual property rights, TRIPS Agreement, and the effect of TRIPS-plus free trade agreements (FTAs) on developing and least-developed countries (United Nations 2009). The report concluded that the TRIPS Agreement and FTAs have had an adverse impact on prices and availability of medicines, making it difficult for countries to comply with their obligations to respect, protect and fulfil the right to health. The report recommended that developing and least-developed countries should review their laws and policies and to consider whether they have made full use of flexibilities contained in the TRIPS Agreement or included TRIPS-plus measures and, if necessary, to consider amending their laws and policies to make full use of the flexibilities available to them.

In the light of the UNHCR Special Rapporteur's report, the link between the right to health and the utilization of flexibilities contained in the TRIPS Agreement, and the review of national implementing legislation, look set to remain central to NGOs' campaigns to promote access to medicines in developing and least-developed countries in the future.

INTELLECTUAL PROPERTY RIGHTS AND AGRICULTURE, GENETIC RESOURCES AND TRADITIONAL KNOWLEDGE

NGOs acting for and on behalf of farmers, indigenous peoples and local communities in developing countries have also raised concerns about the privatization of genetic resources and traditional knowledge and the unfair exploitation of these resources without permission or respect of customary laws (see also Swiderska 2006, p. 1). Questions then arise about the extent that human rights can assist NGOs in their attempts to secure the maintenance of traditional farming practices, or protect traditional knowledge and biodiversity in the face of privatization of genetic resources and the introduction of intellectual property rights regimes.

With regard to the rights of farmers, recognition of the human right to food and the right to be free of hunger set out in Article 11 of the ICESCR may hold the greatest potential.

Article 11 of the ICESCR provides, in particular, for the right of everyone to an adequate standard of living for himself and his family, including adequate food and the fundamental right of everyone to be free from hunger. This right was emphasized, in 1999, by General Comment 12 of the CESCR on the right to adequate food under Article 11 of the ICESCR which proclaimed that the realization of the right requires the availability of food in a quantity and quality that is sufficient to satisfy the dietary needs of individuals and that is free from adverse substances (United Nations Economic and Social Committee 1999; see also Cullet 2003, p. 13).

Subsequently, Resolution 2000/7 of the UN Sub-Commission on the Promotion of Human Rights acknowledged that there are a number

ARTICLE 11 OF THE ICESCR

1. The States Parties to the present Covenant recognize the right of everyone to an adequate standard of living for himself and his family, including adequate food, clothing and housing, and to the continuous improvement of living conditions. The States Parties will take appropriate steps to ensure the realization of this right, recognizing to this effect the essential importance of international co-operation based on free consent.

2. The States Parties to the present Covenant, recognizing the fundamental right of everyone to be free from hunger, shall take, individually and through international co-operation, the measures, including specific programmes, which are needed:

(a) To improve methods of production, conservation and distribution of food by making full use of technical and scientific knowledge, by disseminating knowledge of the principles of nutrition and by developing or reforming agrarian systems in such a way as to achieve the most efficient development and utilization of natural resources;

(b) Taking into account the problems of both food-importing and food-exporting countries, to ensure an equitable distribution of world food supplies in relation to need.

of actual or potential conflicts between intellectual property rights and human rights that included the consequences of plant breeders' rights and the patenting of genetically modified organisms for the enjoyment of the basic right to food and the reduction of control by communities (especially indigenous communities) over their own genetic and natural resources and cultural values, leading to accusations of biopiracy (see also Dutfield 2003b, p. 17). Accordingly, the Resolution called on the WTO to take fully into account the obligations of Members under the international human rights conventions to which they are parties during its ongoing review of Article 27.3(b) of the TRIPS Agreement.

The link between traditional knowledge and human rights is more difficult to establish in an intellectual property rights context. The drafters of the Universal Declaration of Human Rights and the ICESCR did not primarily have the rights of indigenous groups in mind (see also Yu 2007, p. 18) and emphasized individual authorship and scientific achievement over collective intellectual contribution and customary traditions. Article

15(c) of the ICESCR, setting out the right of everyone to benefit from the protection of moral and material interests for instance, appears intended to apply primarily to individual authors only rather than communities (see also Haugen 2005, p. 674).

As the report of the High Commissioner on Human Rights on the impact of the TRIPS Agreement on human rights acknowledged, there are tensions between intellectual property rights and the protection of the knowledge of local and indigenous communities that may require amendments, adaptations and additions to the intellectual property system (see also Correa 2001, p. 23). Yet as Sub-Commission Resolution 2001/21 made clear, the CBD may still offer the best possibilities in terms of providing the moral authority to safeguard biological diversity and indigenous knowledge (United Nations High Commissioner for Human Rights, Sub-Commission on Human Rights 2001).

In practice what is lacking is adequate legislation in order to ensure the realization of the human rights of indigenous peoples and local communities, including those relating to misappropriation of community-held traditional knowledge over genetic resources, at the national, regional and local level in developing countries and least-developed countries. Framed as a human rights issue, it is therefore with the implementation of national legislation to ensure the rights of indigenous peoples and local communities are protected, including obligations to respect, preserve and maintain knowledge, innovations and practices in accordance with Article 8(j) of the CBD, that NGOs are most likely, and can most usefully, focus attention in the future.

NOTES

1. Some of the analysis in subsequent sections of this chapter is adapted from Matthews (2010, pp. 118–139).
2. The earlier title of the draft document that was eventually adopted as General Comment 17 was General Comment No. 18. This draft document, for which Eibe Riedel (CESCR member, Germany) was Rapporteur, was ultimately adopted by the CESCR on 21 November 2005 and re-numbered as General Comment No. 17 (confusingly, a separate General Comment No. 18 now relates to the right to work (Article 6 of the Covenant)).

8. Reappraising intellectual property rights and development: the role of NGOs and social movements

INTRODUCTION

Since the TRIPS Agreement came into force there has been a rapid growth in the number of NGOs reappraising the relationship between intellectual property rights and development. International NGOs have been highlighting concerns about the impact of intellectual property rights on developing countries and engaging with intellectual property-related policy-making and norm-setting activities in multilateral institutions to an extent not seen previously.

The issues covered by NGOs include a vast array of inter-related topics. In relation to public health and access to medicines, for instance, concerns have ranged from how best developing countries can utilize flexibilities contained in the TRIPS Agreement, to deliberations in the WHO about how best to improve R&D into neglected diseases. Similarly, NGOs have played an important role by contributing to the debate on policy-making and norm-setting activities of the TRIPS Council, UPOV, the FAO, the CBD-COP and the WIPO on access and ownership to plant varieties, genetic resources and traditional knowledge. The contribution of NGOs to the Development Agenda process of the WIPO is also worthy of particular note.

This chapter explains how and why NGOs have been able to play such an important role in supporting the work of developing delegates to multilateral institutions. It then highlights the important role played by developing country NGOs. It also assesses current arrangements that multilateral institutions have for NGO engagement and explains the limits on what NGOs can hope to achieve. The chapter concludes by evaluating the role played by NGOs in the WIPO Development Agenda and outlines the new and emerging issues that NGOs will need to respond to in the future.[1]

ENHANCING THE CAPACITY OF DEVELOPING COUNTRY DELEGATES TO NEGOTIATE

A key factor in understanding how international NGOs have been able to inform intellectual property-related policy-making and norm-setting activities is the relationship that activists have with developing country delegates to multilateral institutions. The processes by which international NGOs give advice to delegates are often so informal that it is difficult to evaluate the impact. The situation is also made more complex by the fact that there are multiple sources of information available to delegates, and different diplomatic and political processes happening simultaneously. In reality, delegates (and their counterparts in national government departments in national capitals) collect different inputs and then decide on their response. There is careful thinking on the part of developing country governments and they are pragmatic about the way they use information and advice provided by international NGOs.

In terms of the advice and technical expertise they provide to developing country delegates, international NGOs have been described as 'resource enhancers' (Dunoff 1998, p. 433). Yet given the intergovernmental nature of the Member-driven multilateral institutions in which intellectual property-related issues are discussed and negotiated, international NGOs are not the primary actors and do not see themselves as such. International NGOs readily acknowledge that they lack the legitimacy to speak on behalf of particular constituencies and did not claim to do so. Consequently, international NGOs tend not to engage in conventional forms of advocacy and lobbying of developing country delegates to multilateral institutions. Yet real, genuine intergovernmental negotiations on intellectual property policy-making and norm-setting activities require a balance between the parties.

In this respect, an important distinction can be drawn between, first, those larger middle-income developing countries whose delegations are supported by intellectual property experts from national government ministries at capital level and, second, lower-income developing and least-developed countries that do not receive detailed advice, support or feedback from national government at capital level. For this second group, it is unlikely that delegates will be intellectual property experts and, in practice, it is impossible for them to cover all the issues within their portfolio. These developing country delegates often come to multilateral institutions with an impossible job but are nonetheless under pressure to understand and engage with intellectual property issues. They are frequently overwhelmed with work and have serious time and resource constraints so there is a constant need for reliable, up-to-date and easy to digest sources of information.

There is also a need for continuing and on-going support for negotiators as delegates are replaced and new people join national missions all the time who may well know nothing about intellectual property rights.

International NGOs help to meet this need, enhancing the capacity of developing countries to negotiate, by raising awareness of the significance of intellectual property issues when delegates first arrive and, after that, by providing advice and technical expertise to keep delegates informed. The intergovernmental organization South Centre also plays an important role in this respect, supporting the capacity of developing country delegates to negotiate.

RAISING DEVELOPING COUNTRY DELEGATES' AWARENESS

Since delegations to multilateral institutions change regularly, there is a constant need for international NGOs to renew their links with delegates and keep awareness of intellectual property issues to the fore. The constantly changing delegations have an impact on the relationships that international NGOs have with delegates in the sense that when the delegate changes there is no guarantee that the new incumbent will retain that delegation's interests in intellectual property because a delegate's personal interest can drive a particular delegation's engagement with intellectual property issues.

For their part, developing countries are receptive to awareness raising, advice and technical expertise provided by NGOs but this varies according to how much a particular developing country delegation feels that it needs to rely on the advice and expertise of international NGOs. Developing countries are also well aware that they can work with NGOs in order to harness public opinion in developed countries, and to use it to their advantage. NGOs can often say things that, in diplomatic terms, developing country governments cannot. This is a useful strategic approach on the part of developing countries so, even where delegations do not depend on NGOs in terms of advice or technical expertise, the work of NGOs can be helpful to their interests because of the influence they can exert on the media and public opinion and, indirectly, on governments in the developed world.

ACHIEVING COHERENCE IN MULTILATERAL INSTITUTIONS

Some coherence is sought by international NGOs that organize meetings to orientate new delegates. In Geneva, where the WTO, the WIPO and the WHO are based, seminars organized by international NGOs and the intergovernmental organization South Centre are actually the main orientation mechanisms on intellectual property issues when they first arrive at their national missions. Delegates appreciate this support but the reality is that international NGOs are providing this support, and find delegates receptive to it, because other intergovernmental organizations are not perceived by delegates to be fulfilling this need in a systematic way.

Difficulties in achieving coherence on policy positions are exacerbated by the differing relationships between the multilateral institutions themselves. This fragmentation does not help when seeking to achieve policy coherence. On disclosure of origin of genetic resources, for instance, the outcomes of deliberations in different multilateral institutions are made more uncertain by the fact that the CBD Secretariat has not been granted observer status to the TRIPS Council.

INTERNATIONAL NGOS AS FACILITATORS

Typically, international NGOs are facilitators. They try to increase coordination and interaction between NGOs and developing countries because they believe that dialogue is useful and worth promoting and, because developing countries' negotiating positions are often not being articulated fully at capital level and delegates are determining the positions taken without adequate support from their governments, international NGOs have sought to facilitate equitable outcomes to negotiations on intellectual property issues in multilateral forums. They do so by addressing information asymmetries between developed and developing country negotiators, providing delegates with information and technical expertise. In this process, two factors are crucial: timing and trust.

Timing is crucial because representatives of international NGOs need to be on hand and ready to be responsive to the information needs of delegates. This means that in relation to the WTO, the WIPO and the WHO, for example, it is often not sufficient for representatives of NGOs to travel to Geneva for key meetings. Effective engagement on a day-to-day basis ultimately requires a permanent presence in Geneva that allows representatives of international NGOs to establish and maintain working relationships with delegates.

In relation to the CBD-COP and FAO, the absence of a permanent fixed location for the delegate community creates a different dynamic, with international NGOs holding seminars and meetings before negotiations take place at periodic intergovernmental meetings and maintaining a

dialogue with delegates based at capital level through regular correspondence and briefing papers.

Trust is important because delegates are more likely to respond to an
individual from an international NGO with whom they have an established and positive relationship. This type of relationship of trust must
exist before delegates feel sufficiently comfortable with international
NGOs to ask for advice and technical expertise. Particularly in Geneva,
delegates and representatives of international NGOs often interact in
formal and informal settings and exchange information, share ideas and
expertise. Within this process of interaction, a great deal depends on
personal relationships and building trust over relatively long periods
of time so, as with timing, permanent NGO representation in Geneva – or
at least maintaining dialogue and establishing long-term relationships – is
extremely important.

If developing country delegations are able to carry out their own independent analysis, and their national policy process is strong enough to
feed relevant information to the delegation, then there would be less need
for NGO inputs into the norm-setting and policy-making activities of
multilateral institutions. If this was the case, institutional processes would
be healthier.

When good relationships are formed, a two-way process of information
exchange and discussion between delegates and international NGOs can
occur, but the main role of NGOs remains that of providing information and supporting delegates. Some larger, middle-income developing
countries also have a great deal of experience of dealing with intellectual
property issues that can help NGOs to find balance in their views. NGOs
are receptive to information from delegates and interacting with developing country delegations helps NGOs to enhance their understanding
of the issues, learn, adapt and evolve their positions depending on the
information needs of delegates and officials based in national capitals.

International NGOs listen to what they hear from delegates and
national government officials and respond accordingly. However, some
delegates interviewed for this book were concerned that it is difficult for
NGOs to evolve because they are driven by the demands (or what they
perceive to be the demands) of their donors. So it is important that NGOs
are aware that developing country delegates and national government
officials harbour these concerns. Nevertheless, NGOs have worked hard to
build a reputation for trustworthiness and, in general, developing country
delegates to multilateral institutions have good working relationships with
them on intellectual property issues.

In Geneva, for instance, delegates to the WTO or the WIPO often have
the confidence to approach international NGOs in the knowledge that

they will receive advice and support that is generally useful to them. These relationships, however, tend not to be institutionalized and are based mainly on contacts at the personal level. This can mean that the continuity of on-going relationships between NGOs and developing country delegations can be undermined, for instance, when an individual working for an NGO leaves their post and is replaced by a new incumbent not known to, or trusted by, delegates.

RELATIONSHIPS BETWEEN INTERNATIONAL NGOS AND DEVELOPING COUNTRY DELEGATES

The extent to which international NGOs provide advice and technical expertise to support developing country delegates, enhancing their capacity to negotiate, will change depending on the issues involved. In part this is because some developing countries have strong views on a particular issue, so the degree of interaction between international NGOs and delegates from developing countries tends to be temporary and issue-based. Other delegates, for instance those from large, middle-income developing countries, follow a broader range of intellectual property-related issues and, in these cases, the relationship between international NGOs and delegates may be of longer duration and cut across issues to a greater extent.

Whether linkages between international NGOs and delegates are short-term and issue specific or of longer duration and cut across issues depends on the particular focus of the international NGO involved, with some international NGOs dealing with a range of issues while others deal with specific topics such as access to medicines, farmers' rights, genetic resources and traditional knowledge. It is also the case that some international NGOs have engaged with intellectual property issues for a relatively short and defined period of time and then ceased to follow the debate once a decision has been taken in a multilateral institution. As we saw in Chapter 2, the Doha Declaration on the TRIPS Agreement and Public Health is a case in point, with many international NGOs involved in the broader coalition of the access to medicines campaign moving on to other issues and not maintaining their relationships with delegates once attention began to focus on the technical detail of what an amendment to the TRIPS Agreement should look like.

Relationships between international NGOs and delegates also change depending on the intellectual property issues involved, with different NGOs following different issues in different multilateral institutions, for example in policy-making and norm-setting activities relating to the CBD-COP, the FAO ITPGRFA and the WIPO IGC. Institutional arrangements are also significant with the WIPO, for example, operating with country groupings that are not present in the WTO context and with international NGOs unable to participate to the same extent in the latter institution because the WTO does not accord NGOs observer status to the TRIPS Council while the WIPO does allow NGO accreditation.

In many instances, the relationship between international NGOs and developing country delegations is further complicated by the fact that there are also different delegates acting as negotiators in different multilateral institutions. A developing country, for instance, may well have one negotiator for the TRIPS Council and another for the WIPO. There is a danger that this results in contradictory positions from the same country in different multilateral institutions. The risks associated with this are particularly salient in relation to disclosure of origin issues, where the WTO, the WIPO, and the CBD-COP all play a role and this itself emphasizes the coordinating role that NGOs play in bringing coherence within developing country delegations. International NGOs perform a useful role in facilitating improved policy coherence by bringing together what is happening in various institutions and also drawing into discussions the relevant government officials based in national capitals. In the latter respect, delegates frequently send briefing papers prepared by international NGOs back to government officials in national capitals, where they inform the policy debate at national level.

DONORS AND INTERNATIONAL NGOS

The activities that international NGOs agree with donors can also have an impact on relationships with delegates to multilateral institutions. Some international NGOs are funded on the basis that their primary function is to support developing countries and, as such they are more inclined to be responsive to what developing countries say they want to work on. Other international NGOs are more independent and are much less reliant on agendas being driven by developing countries. The degree of influence that developing countries have over the work being undertaken by international NGOs depends therefore on the focus of a particular organization, what their core activity is, and if they perceive themselves as primarily providing support to developing country delegates.

Relative to the resources available, international NGOs have achieved a great deal and have had a considerable impact, enriching the debate on intellectual property rights and development. However, there is a very real risk of donor fatigue, with international NGOs constantly under pressure to demonstrate progress, successes and achievements while at the same time making the case that more funding is required for future activities.

International NGOs are also acutely aware of the implications of accepting donations from institutional donors that require that funding is contingent on an input by donors into how the NGO prioritizes its activities. In the final instance, however, international NGOs tend to be pragmatic – if the agenda of donors fits with their own priorities, they will work with donors. If not, they will look elsewhere for funding. So, international NGOs are aware that they must remain vigilant to ensure that they do not become donor driven, either explicitly or implicitly. Donor dependence can lead to pressures for NGOs to champion particular issues or to switch attention away from intellectual property rights and towards more tangible issues of immediate concern.

Improved coordination between the different donors funding international NGOs to undertake work on intellectual property-related issues would also be desirable. This is not a new suggestion but nonetheless warrants further consideration. In April 2001, for instance, a QUNO report raised the possibility of improved coordination by proposing a number of initiatives, including establishing an informal donor group, establishing joint initiatives between donors and developing better information sharing about projects (Quaker United Nations Office 2001, section 1.5).

LEGITIMACY AND ACCOUNTABILITY

There are also important issues to be addressed in relation to the legitimacy of NGOs. Unlike governments, NGOs are neither representative nor electorally accountable. They also typically address a relatively narrow set of interests in comparison to national governments, which typically make policy after balancing of interests (see also Blagescu and Lloyd 2006, p. 11; Dinwoodie 2007, p. 92; Dunoff 1998, p. 433).

Concerns about NGO legitimacy can also be seen in the report of the Commission on Intellectual Property Rights, which identified the phenomena of certain NGOs acting as 'proxy representatives' for the governments of developing countries in international dialogue (Commission on Intellectual Property Rights 2002, p. 166). With such a wide diversity within the NGO community in terms of the interests they represent, the balance of activities between advocacy and research, and how vocal they are in representing their interests, questions remain about whom exactly NGOs represent and to whom they are accountable. The Commission on Intellectual Property Rights called for a more reflective approach to some of the issues (Commission on Intellectual Property Rights 2002, p. 166).

For this reason, it is often argued that the proper forum for NGOs seeking engagement with intellectual property-related issues is at the domestic level. In the same vein, the WTO has urged governments to engage in close consultation with NGOs in domestic policy process.

One initiative that may gain wider appeal in the future and warrants further note here with regard to underscoring the legitimacy of NGOs through greater accountability came in June 2006, when 11 of the world's leading human rights, environmental and social development international NGOs endorsed the first global accountability charter for the non-profit sector.[2]

Although NGOs are subject to national regulations within the countries that they operate in, the Accountability Charter was the first such initiative to set out international, cross-sector standards for international NGOs. It set out core values and operating principles covering issues such as good governance and management, fundraising and multi-stakeholder engagement. It also made specific reference to respect for universal principles (such as the Universal Declaration of Human Rights), independence, responsible advocacy, effective programmes, non-discrimination, transparency and ethical fundraising.[3] The Charter acknowledged that the legitimacy of international NGOs is derived from the quality of their work and the recognition and support of the people with and for whom they work and their members, donors, the wider public, and the governmental and other organizations around the world. It also emphasized that international NGOs can help to demonstrate their legitimacy by responding to inter-generational considerations, public and scientific concerns, and through accountability for their work and achievements.

THE ROLE OF EXPERTS

The role of international NGOs in providing advice and technical assistance to support developing country delegates is not a new trend, but it has become more marked during the past ten years or so in Geneva. Many developing country delegations do not receive instructions or guidance from government departments in their national capitals. As a result, some sub-Saharan African countries, Central American countries and least-developed countries lack an effective connection between capitals and delegations. This is not the case, however, for middle-income developing countries such as South Africa, Brazil or India that do not need the advice or technical expertise of international NGOs because they have sufficient expertise within government.

It is impossible for international NGOs to have all the expertise that developing country delegates require in-house. A mixture of in-house and external expertise tends to be the norm. External experts, usually from academia, are often invited by international NGOs to provide policy advice by participating in workshops with delegates, prepare briefing papers, or be on hand to offer advice on an *ad hoc* basis and at specific events such as a WTO Ministerial Conference or the CBD-COP. These external experts are seen as adding value because NGOs often lack specialist expertise, or because what expertise international NGOs do possess is not of sufficient depth on particular issues. In this respect, experts are used by international NGOs because they provide technical advice and facilitate the process of information exchange and a greater understanding of intellectual property issues.

In terms of allocating resources, it is efficient for international NGOs to use the expertise of academics to provide in depth studies that can inform discussions on intellectual property issues. Experts, normally from academia, provide a constant informal exchange of ideas and are perceived as acting in a similar way to government experts at national capital level who delegates might contact to ask a very specific question in order to be better prepared for a particular negotiation, the expert then responding with advice. Experts are frequently brought in by international NGOs but are not owned by any particular NGO or even by the NGO community more widely. In fact, experts are also consulted directly by delegates and the secretariats of multilateral institutions.

RECEPTIVENESS OF DEVELOPING COUNTRY DELEGATES TO INTERNATIONAL NGOS

The degree to which developing country delegates are receptive to international NGOs varies depending on the extent that a particular developing country feels that it needs additional inputs. However, even large, middle-income developing countries that receive substantial backup from capital are well aware that international NGOs can be useful because they are able to articulate viewpoints that it would be politically or diplomatically unacceptable for governments themselves to make. In this respect, even developing countries that do not depend on international NGOs can find these groups helpful to their interests, particularly because of the influence that can be exerted in the developed world in terms of public opinion and political agendas.

Overall, although the relationship between international NGOs and delegates varies from case to case, with the informal nature of these linkages making it extremely difficult to accurately evaluate their impact, international NGOs have undoubtedly helped developing countries to think about the issues involved and to allow delegates to utilize the expertise that international NGOs can provide. Delegates readily acknowledge the assistance they have received in this respect, particularly in relation to the Doha Declaration on the TRIPS Agreement and Public Health, the TRIPS Council deliberations on disclosure of origin, the WIPO IGC process on genetic resources, traditional knowledge and folklore, and the FAO ITPGRFA.

On these issues, international NGOs working on intellectual property-related issues have established close links with developing country delegates in a way that has not been seen in other policy areas. On the environment or human rights, for example, historically international NGOs have been much more critical of developing country policies than in relation to intellectual property rights. In this sense, the work on intellectual property-related issues has led to a warming of relations and a greater recognition on the part of developing country governments that international NGOs can be useful to them.

Typically, international NGOs help developing country delegates with strategic planning and analysis. This support helps delegates to make informed decisions and improves the quality of negotiations by showing that credible policy alternatives are available. The substantive inputs of international NGOs can also make developing country delegates feel more assertive in their views. As a result, developing country delegates to multilateral institutions have come to view international NGOs as important sources of information on intellectual property-related issues. However, delegates are also pragmatic and tend to view international NGOs as only one element in the group of stakeholders that are listened to and whose views are taken into account (see also Gervais 2007, p. 57).

In view of the fact that developing country delegates to multilateral institutions tend to consult a range of stakeholders and collect different inputs from different sources, in many respects international NGOs have been able to provide a counterweight to industry associations and rights holder groups that have had a traditionally stronger voice, for example, in the WIPO context. In this respect, the more recent engagement of international NGOs with intellectual property-related issues has played a significant role by helping delegates to achieve a more balanced view of the world in the complex environment of multilateral negotiations.

So, developing country delegates use inputs from different stakeholders and are pragmatic about what they find useful at particular moments in time. If the work of international NGOs is useful to delegates, they will use whatever advice and technical expertise is made available to them. However, if there are differences between the policy positions being advocated by international NGOs and those preferred by developing country delegates, there will be limits on the ability of NGOs to influence policy outcomes. This is best illustrated by the fact that, despite the close relationship that existed between international NGOs and developing country delegates on negotiations leading to the Doha Declaration on the TRIPS Agreement and Public Health, developing countries did not follow the advice and expertise offered by international NGOs during negotiations leading to the 30 August 2003 WTO Decision and, subsequently, the 6 December 2005 agreement to amend the TRIPS Agreement's compulsory licensing provisions.

One particular issue of concern is that international NGOs tend to focus on a limited range of issues, whereas developing country governments must address and balance a range of interests and policy perspectives. But the relationship between international NGOs and delegates is still at an early stage and will evolve in the longer term. In particular, it will be important that intellectual property-related issues that international NGOs have not focused on previously in any substantive sense, such as reform of the Patent Cooperation Treaty (PCT), receive greater attention in the future.

INTERNATIONAL NGOS AND DEVELOPING COUNTRY GOVERNMENTS IN NATIONAL CAPITALS

Within developing countries, it is often more difficult for international NGOs to work constructively with national government officials than it is for them to work with delegates to multilateral institutions. When international NGOs engage with national government officials, they often find some ministries more receptive than others to advice and technical expertise. In national capitals the ministry of trade, for example, may have different policy priorities than the ministry of health and there may even be more than one point of view within the same ministry. In this context, it is instructive to note that negotiations that take place at the CBD-COP or the FAO are limited to specific environmental or agricultural policy issues, with officials sent from national ministries rather than being part of permanent missions, and this may account for the fact that some international NGOs perceive it to be easier to liaise with developing country delegates to these multilateral institutions. When negotiations take place at the WTO, wider trade issues (and hence government ministries driven by wider trade agendas) tend to predominate. Of course, national governments also change, so the relationship that developing countries have with international NGOs is itself always in a state of flux.

Developing country governments are constantly under bilateral pressure and are working to accommodate competing domestic interests in a coherent policy approach. This limits the extent to which the advice and expertise of international NGOs will be taken into account. Instead, it will be considered alongside other factors. Developing country governments are attempting to make informed decisions on intellectual property-related issues and it is important for international NGOs to recognize the pressures that developing countries are under when they provide substantive inputs into multilateral processes.

In some developing countries there is a disconnection between what is happening in multilateral institutions and what is happening in national capitals. Thus far, international NGOs have had greater impact in terms of providing advice and technical inputs to developing country delegates based permanently in national missions to multilateral institutions than in terms of engaging with capital-based officials. An important step towards remedying this dislocation between delegates and government officials working in national capitals could be taken if international NGOs that have engaged so successfully with delegates could begin to organize meetings and workshops in national capitals. This would sensitize government ministries to the implications of intellectual property rights for development. Furthermore, rather than organizing these events on a piecemeal basis, the prospects for international NGOs enhancing their engagement with developing country governments by establishing a greater number of national or regional offices should be given serious consideration as a way to link up delegates to multilateral institutions in a more sustained way.

A related problem is how to translate agreements reached in multilateral institutions into action at the national level. The much under-used WTO Decision of 30 August 2003 on the issuance of compulsory licensing is a case in point. Government officials in developing country capitals may well have been exposed already to traditional technical assistance providers from developed country governments, industry associations and rights holder groups, but international NGOs are well placed to provide with different policy options and facilitate further the extent that informed decision-making can underpin intellectual property policy.

In recent years a number of international NGOs have begun to play this type of technical assistance-based role, advising developing country governments on how best to utilize flexibilities contained in the TRIPS Agreement or by organizing regional dialogues to disseminate policy-orientated research and promote dialogue (see also Plaisier and Wijmenga 2004, p. 99). However, the technical assistance work of international NGOs remains less pronounced than the extent that industry and rights holder groups have carried out capacity building initiatives focusing on implementation and enforcement of intellectual property rights in the developing world (Matthews and Munoz-Tellez 2007, p. 638).

RAISING PUBLIC AWARENESS

International NGOs have also played an important role in raising public awareness of intellectual property-related issues. In order to get their message across, they have often used human rights as a frame to simplify, filter and translate the technical complexity of the issues involved so as to make its demands intelligible and morally relevant to the general public (see also de Mello e Souza 2005, p. 286).

This has helped the public to understand that intellectual property rights are important for health, food, indigenous peoples and local communities. International NGOs have proved adept at harnessing the mass mobilization power of the internet to set up numerous campaigning websites, on-line newsletters, email alerts and sign-on declarations, as well as more traditional methods of campaigning such as public demonstrations.

In developed countries, international NGOs have helped ensure that the public, politicians and government officials are now much more aware than they were previously of the actual and potential impact of intellectual property rights on marginalized, poor, disadvantaged and vulnerable sectors of society in developing countries. This is an important addition to the debate and acts as a counterbalance to the interests of producers and rights holders. However, although valuable work to raise public awareness has already been undertaken, there is a constant need for renewal in the public consciousness to help ensure that the relationship between intellectual property rights and development, often framed in terms of human rights, remains high on the political agenda. There is limited capacity for the media and public opinion in the developed world to remain focused on a particular issue and the task of maintaining the public's interest will remain a difficult one for international NGOs.

COALITION-BUILDING

Strategically, the most effective way that international NGOs have been able to raise public awareness is by building coalitions, often supported by broader social movements to mobilize mass support at grassroots level, NGOs have highlighted the actual and potential negative impacts of intellectual property rights in a number of important contexts. Often framed as a human rights issue, awareness has been raised about the implications of intellectual property rights for development in a way that was simply not evident when the TRIPS Agreement was being negotiated. In particular, the potential for intellectual property protection and enforcement to undermine the rights of people living with HIV/AIDS, of farmers, of indigenous peoples and of local communities have been highlighted in new, sophisticated and often profound ways (see also Yu 2008, p. 3).

The benefits of building a coalition are to demonstrate that it is not just one or two NGOs that are interested in the issues, but a whole constituency of interests. It is about trying to generate a critical mass of interests, involving a wide range of people from NGOs, broader social movements, academia and the media, with the ultimate goal of influencing intellectual property policy-making and norm-setting activities.

Coalitions also allow a mix of complementary skills to be brought to bear upon an issue. Some NGOs specialize in bringing people together, some do advocacy work, others work on media campaigns and mobilizing public opinion, while others do technical work on legal issues. In this way, different NGOs bring different expertise and talents to a coalition.

However, coalitions of NGOs are not permanent fixtures. By their very nature they are temporary and issue specific, the membership changing depending on the intellectual property issues and institutions involved. Coalitions also tend to be temporary because of the nature of the processes in multilateral institutions, with delegates typically changing every three years and national policy positions also changing too as new governments come to power with new priorities and agendas. So coalitions tend to reflect changes in the external environment and the personalities involved and are by their very nature temporary and issue specific.

In deciding to build coalitions, NGOs are pragmatic – when there is an issue that brings NGOs together, they come together. Loose coalitions between international and developing country NGOs tend to be the most successful in putting issues on the policy agenda and the relationship between them is symbiotic: international NGOs tend to be well-placed to influence global policy through their work at the level of multilateral institutions, while developing country NGOs are more informed about the practical impact. This link between international and developing country NGOs is often crucial and dialogue is a key aspect of a successful outcome.

LEADERSHIP

Although NGOs tend to feel uncomfortable with notions of leadership of coalitions, emphasizing instead that there are equal partnerships between NGOs, it is often important to have a particular NGO to act as a champion for an issue, keeping the momentum going and facilitating coherence of the NGO position. A broad coalition does not get far and, once the push has been made for a specific policy proposal, the time comes to do the hard, technical work. However, this can also have the drawback that there can be a perceived lack of ownership on the part of those who are not part of the core leadership group.

There also needs to be leadership among developing countries. A concentric circle model describes what is happening best. There is an inner circle of core developing countries that take the lead and have ownership of an issue, with the support of others that are playing a less prominent role in articulating particular policy proposals, and still other developing countries on the periphery but also providing support for the coalition. How national interests on a particular issue are perceived will also be a factor on which developing countries demonstrate leadership. On public health access to medicines, for instance, it was politically and morally expedient to allow the African Group to demonstrate that it had leadership of the issue in the TRIPS Council, given the scale of the HIV/AIDS crisis in sub-Saharan Africa and the decision of Brazil and India, as large-scale producers of generic medicines, to play a less prominent role.

THE ROLE OF NGOS IN DEVELOPING COUNTRIES

While international NGOs have enjoyed a high profile through their inputs into intellectual property-related policy-making and norm-setting activities in multilateral institutions, groups in developing countries have also undertaken good and effective work at the national, sub-national or regional level. However, their activities have not been widely acknowledged because they do not have an international profile.

In fact, as we have seen in this book, an important catalyst for international NGOs to engage with intellectual property rights and development came as a result of a relatively small number of under-resourced but highly committed developing country NGOs. In particular it was activists in South Africa, Brazil and India that first made explicit the actual and potential adverse impacts of intellectual property rights for developing countries that would come to the fore so profoundly in the post-TRIPS era.

The stimulus that was provided by NGO action in these countries was itself driven largely by the discourse and legal principles of fundamental human rights enshrined in national constitutions. These human rights principles were used to articulate concerns that new standards of intellectual property protection and enforcement could have adverse and unintended consequences for marginalized, poor, disadvantaged and vulnerable people in the developing world. Significantly, in each of these countries, the protection of human rights held a special place in the national psyche and this influenced how the public, legislatures and courts viewed the relationship between intellectual property rights and fundamental human rights from a developing country perspective.

In South Africa, this emphasis on the primacy of human rights emanated from the anti-apartheid struggle that came to an end in 1994. In Brazil, the central role accorded to human rights principles in the country's constitution reflected a similar desire to right the wrongs experienced during the military dictatorship that came to an end in 1985. In India, the struggle against colonial rule that ended in 1947 also ensured that human rights played a key role in the nation's constitution, post-independence.

For international NGOs, the catalyst for engagement with intellectual property issues came at a critical moment in March 2001 when, in South Africa global pharmaceutical companies brought a High Court action, complaining about the compulsory licensing provisions of the South African Medicines and Related Substances Control Amendment Act 1997. Almost simultaneously in Brazil, the US complaint to the WTO DSB on the compulsory licensing and local working provisions of Brazilian law acted as a further trigger for international NGOs to focus for the first time on the fact that patents can act as a barrier to access to medicines, particularly for people living with HIV/AIDS. In India, where by 2001 NGOs were already working on reform of the Patents Act of 1970, the controversies surrounding the need to ensure compatibility of national law with the TRIPS Agreement brought the significance of the issues even more sharply into focus.

Yet today many developing country NGOs feel excluded from direct participation in the intellectual property-related policy-making and norm-setting activities of multilateral institutions. Many of them would also prefer direct participation to relying on international NGOs raising issues on their behalf. In some instances, developing country NGOs and broader social movements could even be said to be distrustful of international NGOs. The perception is that some international NGOs are seeking to attract funding from donors by professing to represent the interests of people in developing countries when they have no mandate to do so. Instead, many developing country NGOs, social movements, indigenous peoples and local communities would prefer capacity building initiatives to enable them to represent their own interests, with funding them provided by donors to allow them to travel and participate directly in meetings organized by multilateral institutions.

Networks and coalitions can partially alleviate the exclusion of groups in the Global South from direct participation in intellectual property-related policy-making and norm-setting activities of multilateral institutions. Dialogue and coordination between international NGOs and developing country NGOs, social movements, indigenous peoples and local communities can be achieved through information and dialogue transmitted via the internet.

However, deficiencies in basic infrastructure can be a barrier to participation. In Brazil, for example, social movements, indigenous people and local communities often have a great deal of awareness of issues related to genetic resources and traditional knowledge, but lack access to basic communication resources. The absence of telephones, postal services, the internet and even electricity is a huge barrier to the ability of these groups to engage with the debate on intellectual property rights and development, despite their often profound grassroots knowledge and practical experience of the issues involved. Furthermore, with much of the discourse on the impact of intellectual property rights conducted in English, language is an additional barrier to participation to many NGO activists in countries such as Brazil.

That said, where access to the internet is available and language is not a barrier, the degree of dialogue and coordination has increased substantially in recent years as different groups have become adept at networking and using the internet effectively. To this extent, while lack of resources and language barriers continue to be issues that hinder the ability of developing country NGOs, social movements, indigenous peoples and local communities to engage with debates on intellectual property-related issues, if coordination can be established and barriers overcome, these groups have the potential to be very effective allies alongside their counterparts in the international NGO community, bringing evidence-based arguments that will ultimately enhance the inputs of international NGOs that are able to attend meetings on intellectual property-related issues in multilateral institutions (see also Dinwoodie 2007, p. 90).

Even where developing country NGOs, social movements, indigenous peoples and local communities are knowledgeable and active at the national, sub-national and regional level, these groups rarely have the resources to attend meetings in multilateral institutions. Donors seldom make provision to allow participation, although there are some notable exceptions to this. The CBD-COP, for instance, provides observer status accreditation to numerous representatives of NGOs, social movements, indigenous peoples and local communities while the WIPO IGC process funds participation by over 130 accredited organizations, over half of which are indigenous groups or local communities.

While these initiatives are laudable, the lack of financial resources to enable developing country NGOs, social movements, indigenous peoples and local communities to engage directly with intellectual property-related issues being discussed and debated more widely in the plethora of meetings organized by multilateral institutions remains a major issue for many of these groups. Some developing country NGOs, social movements, indigenous peoples and local communities are not interested in playing a role at the international level, seeing their main focus as being at the national, sub-national and regional level because this is the most efficient use of their resources. Other groups have a real desire to be consulted more fully and to participate directly in the policy-making and norm-setting activities taking place in multilateral institutions.

One option that could alleviate demands for increased funding to bring more groups to meetings organized by multilateral institutions would be for those institutions to make greater use of outreach activities such as regional consultations and public hearings. This would also have the effect of utilizing more fully the expertise and knowledge of groups in developing countries and would bring more evidence-based arguments to the debate.

Examples of previous regional consultations and public hearings include hearings held in various developing country locations by the WHO Commission on Intellectual Property Rights, Innovation and Public Health (CIPIH), during which interested parties were asked to submit documents and to participate in stakeholder meetings in South Africa, Brazil and India.[4] The CIPIH regional meetings were important because they increased understanding of the issues and informed the debate about intellectual property and public health at the WHO. In some countries the CIPIH met with NGOs in separate meetings to those with government representatives, particularly when governments were not enthusiastic about the CIPIH meeting with particular NGOs. The CIPIH met with TAC, for instance, separately to its consultations with the South African government. By enabling developing country NGOs, social movements, indigenous peoples and local communities to participate in consultations and hearings in this way, this type of outreach activity has considerable potential to enhance further the participatory nature of the consultation processes of multilateral institutions.

However, while the WHO CIPIH provides a useful model in this respect, it must be acknowledged that developing country governments are at times sensitive about enhancing participation by some stakeholders due to the perceived implications for claims about land rights or because some of these groups may have been critical of government policy in the past, for example in relation to policies on the provision of ARVs to people living with HIV/AIDS. Multilateral institutions would need to be mindful of these sensitivities and adopt strategies to ensure engagement is as open, transparent and participatory as is practicably possible. Finally, it should be stressed that where regional consultations and public hearings do take place, these should not exceed the remit set out by the multilateral institution concerned.[5]

To some extent, however, the issue is not simply one of whether or not developing country NGOs, social movements, indigenous peoples and local communities should be physically present in multilateral institutions or in regional consultations and public hearings. A physical presence is not enough, nor is it sufficient to encourage these groups to make declaratory statements at meetings. Empowering developing country NGOs, social movements, indigenous peoples and local communities with technical knowledge and the capacity to engage with debates in a meaningful way is also important.

As well as empowering these groups to participate themselves, delegates to multilateral institutions and government officials in national capitals who are working on intellectual property-related issues on a day-to-day basis also need support from people and organizations that are knowledgeable on the technical issues and who can give hands-on advice and can engage with the substance of the debate. Few developing country NGOs, social movements, indigenous peoples or local communities possess this depth of knowledge or the training to articulate their arguments in a policy-oriented way and a great deal more could be done in terms of capacity building to improve the stock of technical knowledge on intellectual property-related issues and assist them in contributing to the policy debate in a constructive way.

While relatively few developing country NGOs, social movements, indigenous peoples and local communities have engaged with debates and negotiations on intellectual property-related issues at meetings organized by multilateral institutions, many have focused on issues at the national, sub-national or regional level. Here, these groups have played an important role interfacing with government officials. This has been important in terms of matching the work that international NGOs have been undertaking with delegates by establishing and maintaining links with government officials in national capitals. There is often a need for additional work to be done by liaising with government officials at the national level, where there may be a lack of information and expertise on intellectual property-related issues. This further work is not only in terms of raising awareness of the issues, but also in terms of the provision of technical information on the policy options available so that governmental officials in national capitals can then respond to these issues in the most appropriate way.

However, it is not always easy for developing country NGOs, social movements, indigenous peoples and local communities to have access to officials dealing with intellectual property-related issues since governments are not always structured in a way that is open to new information sources. The impact of developing country NGOs, social movements, indigenous peoples and local communities may also differ from that of international NGOs because the former are more likely to have an uneasy relationship with policy-makers in government and can be perceived to be critical of developing country governments in a way that international NGOs interfacing with delegates on intellectual property-related issues in multilateral institutions are frequently not.

Yet there is great potential for developing country NGOs, social movements, indigenous peoples and local communities in large, middle-income developing countries such as South Africa, Brazil and India that are knowledgeable and experienced on issues such as access to ARVs for people living with HIV/AIDS, farmers' rights, genetic resources and the traditional knowledge of indigenous peoples to engage in South-South technical assistance to assist their counterparts in other developing countries to address issues relating to intellectual property rights (see also Musungu et al. 2004, p. xiv). Where NGOs exist at all in other developing countries, these groups tend not yet to be knowledgeable about intellectual property rights and have still to acquire the specialist knowledge on intellectual property policy that would enable them to engage with these issues effectively (see also de Paranaguá Moniz 2005, p. 47).

At government-to-government level, there is already some evidence of South-South regional cooperation. In November 2008, for example, Brazilian President Luiz Inácio Lula da Silva and Health Minister José Gomes Temporão and the President of the Fundaçáco Oswaldo Cruz (FIOCRUZ), Paulo Buss, inaugurated a FIOCRUZ office in Maputo, Mozambique. FIOCRUZ intended to establish a pharmaceutical plant in Maputo to produce ARVs. Stavudine and Nevirapine were to be the first ARVs under production.[6] To date, however, so much manufacturing facility has been set up and no practical benefits have been seen.

In Brazil the NGO network GPTI/REBRIP also has as an explicit objective, building links with developing country NGOs working on intellectual property issues outside Brazil on the basis that the sharing of information will help each country achieve tangible results. A good example of this collaboration between developing country NGOs is their coordinated inputs into the patent examination process in different countries. Since the same patent applications are filed in different countries, the same questions are likely to arise about whether to grant a specific patent.

On 20 August 2007, for instance, the Brazilian NGO network GTPI/ REBRIP issued a statement expressing its satisfaction with the decision of the High Court of Chennai in the Novartis case, and congratulating

Indian civil society groups involved in the case.[7] For Brazilian NGOs, a significant factor in the case was the fact that the High Court of Chennai's restrictive interpretation of Indian legislative provisions on the novelty of pharmaceutical patent applications could be useful information for a parallel debate in Brazil. The INPI used guidelines of examination for the novelty of pharmaceutical patent applications in Brazil that were considered by GTPI/REBRIP to be very broad and the outcome of the Novartis case consequently added legitimacy to the GTPI/REBRIP's arguments domestically.

Evidence of substantive collaboration between Brazilian and Indian NGOs then came on 26 June 2008, when the Brazilian NGO ABIA filed pre-grant opposition proceedings in India against the granting of a patent for Tenofovir, one of the most expensive medicines used by Brazil's National AIDS Programme.[8] ABIA's interest was derived from the fact that, if a patent were granted in India, Brazil would not be able to import generic versions of the drug produced by Indian generic drug manufacturers. The pre-grant opposition was filed jointly by ABIA and the Indian NGO Sahara Centre for Residential Care and Rehabilitation.[9]

ARRANGEMENTS FOR NGO ENGAGEMENT WITH MULTILATERAL INSTITUTIONS

Having highlighted the important role played by developing country NGOs, the remainder of this chapter will assess the arrangements for NGO engagement currently in place in the WTO, the WHO, the CBD-COP, the FAO and the WIPO. It will also address the debates currently underway in these institutions about how best to engage further with NGOs, social movements, indigenous peoples and local communities in the future.

WTO

When the WTO was created in 1994, Article V.2 of the Agreement Establishing the WTO stated simply that the General Council may make appropriate arrangements for consultation and cooperation with NGOs concerned with matters related to those of the WTO. Subsequently, on 18 July 1996, the General Council of the WTO adopted a Decision that clarified the framework of relations with NGOs and sought to improve transparency and develop communication (see also Sutherland et al. 2004, p. 42). While recognizing the role NGOs can play to increase the awareness of the public in respect of WTO activities, the WTO Decision of 1996 concluded that 'Members have pointed to the special character of the WTO, which is both a legally binding intergovernmental treaty of rights and obligations among its Members and a forum for negotiations. As a result of extensive discussions, there is currently a broadly held view that it would not be possible for NGOs to be directly involved in the work of the WTO or its meetings. Closer consultation and cooperation with NGOs can also be met constructively through appropriate processes at the national level where lies primary responsibility for taking into account the different elements of public interest which are brought to bear on trade policy-making.'[10]

The WTO Decision of 1996 went on to recognize the role that NGOs can play in increasing the awareness of the public in respect of WTO activities, called on the WTO Secretariat to play a more active role in its direct contacts with NGOs through various means such as the organization of symposia, informal arrangements to receive information NGOs may wish to make available, and by responding to requests for general information and briefings about the WTO. The only further substantive change to arrangements for NGO engagement at the WTO came in 2002, when the General Council decided to expedite the de-restriction of documents, this move alone generating an explosion of easily accessible documentation, much of it available almost simultaneously with its delivery to Members (Sutherland et al. 2004, p. 42).

In general, however, the WTO guidelines on relations with NGOs have remained unchanged since 1996. Given the paradigm shift that has occurred in terms of public awareness of intellectual property-related issues in the intervening period, these formal arrangements may well now not sit well with the current situation. Nonetheless, the guidelines do have the advantage of leaving flexibility for the WTO Secretariat to carry out activities with NGOs that are not specified explicitly, such as the hosting of an annual Public Symposium for NGOs. Furthermore, the fact that NGOs do not have any permanent, statutory relationship with the WTO also means that they can visit the WTO building in Geneva with relative ease, participate in seminars and meet with delegates in the WTO without being inhibited by formal accreditation or procedural issues.

If, in the future, WTO arrangements for engagement with NGOs on intellectual property-related issues were to be enhanced, this could include measures to facilitate NGO accreditation to have observer status at TRIPS Council meetings. However, there is little demand for formal accreditation on the part of public interest NGOs and even some concern that opening up the TRIPS negotiating process to NGOs would simply have the effect of allowing even greater access to NGOs representing industry and rights-holder interests. There is also a fear that, if the WTO is opened up to NGOs then the policy-making and norm-setting process, this would actually become less transparent because the real businesses of intergovernmental negotiations would then be restricted to informal consultations, with Members less willing to discuss substantive issues openly in formal settings where NGOs were present. The WTO is, and will remain, an intergovernmental institution driven by its Members (Sutherland et al. 2004, p. 47).

WHO

Compared to the WTO, the WHO is relatively advanced in its relationships with NGOs and the system for NGO accreditation and engagement is well established. Accredited NGOs can attend meetings and make a statement provided that the main area of competence of the NGO falls within the purview of the WHO, with aims and activities in conformity with the spirit, purposes and principles of the Constitution of the WHO and which centre on development work in health or health-related fields, and shall be free from concerns which are primarily of a commercial or profit-making nature.[11]

To be accredited by the WHO, an NGO will normally be required to have an international structure or scope, and represent a substantial proportion of the persons globally organized for the purpose of participating in the particular field of interest in which it operates. In addition, the endeavours of the CIPIH to engage with NGOs and other stakeholders in developing countries may provide a useful model for outreach, consultation and engagement with non-governmental interests in developing countries in the future.

CBD-COP

The CBD-COP has been relatively open to participation by NGOs in its activities. NGOs have good access to the plenary meetings, are able to hold side-events and to make statements during the meetings. Furthermore, NGO representatives are able to get access to the restricted access government delegation area at CBD-COP meetings, provided they accompany a government delegate, where they can interact with and lobby delegates directly. In the Ad Hoc Working Group on ABS, for instance, NGOs can present documents and are allowed to participate in meetings. They can also engage informally with the CBD Secretariat. At a formal level, however, there is a need to align the CBD processes for NGO engagement with existing ad hoc practices. The accreditation process is particularly unclear and, on 23 March 2006, the CBD Secretariat submitted a proposal to the

CBD-COP 8 meeting, on grounds that NGOs were major stakeholders in the issues addressed by the CBD that generated a great deal of concern amongst the NGO community because the CBD had traditionally been very open and NGOs were concerned that formalization would reduce their ability to participate.[12] NGOs have traditionally been admitted to meetings of the CBD under Article 23.5 of the Convention,[13] but the Secretariat took the view that a proper accreditation procedure was required.

Following statements by the representatives of Argentina, Austria (on behalf of the European Union), Canada, China, Norway and the representative of the activist organization Ecoropa, together with a statement made on behalf of the Tebtebba, the Sammi Council, the Tulalip tribes, the Indigenous Information Network and the Asia Indigenous Peoples' Pact, the Chair of the CBD-COP 8 meeting said that he would prepare a text reflecting the views that had been expressed and submit it to the Working Group for its consideration.[14] To date, however, no follow up activity has been undertaken on the proposal.

In practice, most of the contact between NGOs and delegates to the CBD-COP are informal in any case. The CBD-COP is, and will remain, an intergovernmental process, so member governments will continue to take the lead, while NGOs are permitted to hold side-events at the CBD-COP and make statements after delegates have spoken. However, NGOs are mindful of the need to ensure that opportunities for NGO participation are not eroded in the future and are also aware of the need to demonstrate more sophisticated arguments in the face of industry and rights-holder groups that present articulate, convincing and focused arguments that are difficult for public interest NGOs to counter effectively at present.

FAO

The FAO allows NGOs considerable access to attend and participate in meetings.[15] NGOs are able to send observers to the FAO Conference and Council, circulate their views, speak before the Committee on Relations with International Organizations and before technical committees of the Conference. They are not, however, permitted to participate in discussions unless requested by the chairman. Upon request and with the consent of the General Committee of the Conference, NGOs may also speak before the FAO Conference itself and can be invited by the Director-General to participate in experts meetings, technical conferences or seminars on subjects which fall within their fields of interest. They may also receive non-confidential information and submit written statements.

In addition, the CGRFA includes representatives from NGOs, academia, business and farmers' groups and NGOs such as ETC (formerly

RAFI) and Practical Action (formerly ITDG) have a long record of participating in CGRFA meetings. NGOs have been involved in advocating farmers' rights and, in general, have been supportive of the CGRFA process. However, given that the discussions taking place in the CGRFA context are about agriculture, there is an on-going debate about whether farmers should in fact be the main stakeholder voice, supported by NGOs, rather than NGOs seeking to speak on behalf of farmers. With this in mind, Practical Action has adopted a new model for engagement with farmers in the context of the Forum for Food Sovereignty, established in 2001. This is comprised of farmer organizations and fisher folks from different regions, supported by a number of specialists. The idea behind the Forum for Food Sovereignty is for the international platform to be driven by people and communities at grassroots level, supported by NGOs, rather than vice versa. From the NGO perspective, the Forum should be monitored and observed as a possible model for engagement with grassroots stakeholders in the future.

WIPO

The WIPO was officially created in 1970, replacing the *Bureaux Internationaux Reunis pour la Protection de la Propriete Intellectuelle* (BIPRI – the United International Bureau for the Protection of Intellectual Property), and admitted as a special organization to the United Nations on 17 December 1974 (see also Halbert 2006, p. 9). NGOs observing the creation of the WIPO overwhelmingly represented the interests of intellectual property owners, specifically copyright producers and predominantly from Europe and North America.[16]

From the outset, NGO accreditation was available under the General Rules of Procedure of the WIPO, Rule 8(3). This stated that: 'Observers shall be accredited by the competent authority of their State or the competent representative of their organization, in a letter, note or telegram addressed to the Director General; if they represent a State, such communication shall preferably be effected by the Ministry of Foreign Affairs.' In addition to Rule 8 of the General Rules of Procedure of the WIPO, it is standard practice that the rules of procedure of individual WIPO committees permit NGOs accredited with observer status under Rule 8 to be invited also to attend WIPO bodies such as the Standing Committee on Copyrights and Related Rights (SCCR),[17] the Standing Committee on the Law of Patents (SCP),[18] and the Intergovernmental Committee on Intellectual Property and Genetic Resources, Traditional Knowledge and Folklore (IGC).[19]

Yet until relatively recently, there was little evidence of dissent in the

WIPO concerning the rationale of strengthening intellectual property protection and the positive correlation between intellectual property rights and development (see also Musungu and Dutfield 2003, p. 16). The WIPO publication *Intellectual Property – A Power Tool for Economic Growth*, for instance, written by then Director General Kamil Idris set out to 'demystify intellectual property' and described 'ideas – that patents are not relevant to developing nations, or that they are incompatible with the economic objectives of developing nations' as 'pernicious myths' (WIPO 2003).

Few Members or accredited NGOs openly questioned the role of the WIPO as a UN agency or its activities in relation to intellectual property rights. In many respects, developing countries were still coming to terms with implementation of intellectual property legislation and it took time before the actual impact became fully understood. This is also why until recently developing countries' main concern in the WIPO has been with accessing technical and legal assistance from the Secretariat in order to implement their newly-acquired intellectual property-related obligations, in particular the TRIPS Agreement.[20] In addition, the WIPO had historically been considered something of a backwater by NGOs (James Love interviewed by Nguyen 2005) and few had focused on the activities of the WIPO nor applied for accreditation to it until late 2003.[21]

It was not until international NGOs reflected on their engagement with the TRIPS Agreement, public health and the access to medicines campaign, that a growing feeling emerged that the Doha Declaration on the TRIPS Agreement and Public Health in 2001 had produced scarcely any concrete changes in the day-to-day practice of handling intellectual property rights (Love 2007, p. 360). From an international NGO perspective, despite the considerable power of the WIPO, its power had gone uncontested for a long time, so the objective was to get a better grasp of how the WIPO functioned with a view to effectively modifying its procedures (Love 2007, p. 360).

In the autumn of 2003, an NGO coalition of the Trans-Atlantic Consumer Dialogue (TACD) and Consumers International jointly organized a meeting in Lisbon on the WIPO's work programme. Experts from developing countries attended along with representatives of the European Commission, the US government and the WIPO Secretariat (Love 2007, p. 362). During the meeting, participants began to reflect on the possibility of launching a campaign that was broader than looking at the WIPO's work programme. As a result, in September 2004, public interest NGOs held a conference on 'The Future of WIPO'.

The Future of WIPO Conference was organized by the TACD and took place on 13–14 September 2004, immediately before the WIPO

General Assembly annual session.[22] The conference was attended by government representatives and by multiple stakeholders including representatives from academia, NGOs, industry and representatives of the WIPO Secretariat itself. Discussions focused on the proper mandate of the WIPO and its organizational structure. Crucially, the conference brought attention to the need for a Development Agenda for the WIPO.

The Geneva Declaration framed the debate on the impact of intellectual property rights as a crisis in the field of access to and innovation of knowledge. The Declaration was critical of the WIPO, but also invited the institution to play a positive role, outlined alternative economic models, proposed new ways for inventors to work, new modes of sharing and circulating information – all inscribed in a coherent legal framework (Love 2007, p. 363). It was seen as influential because delegates from developing country governments felt that they had good support from NGOs, while developed country delegates were reputedly impressed by the number of prestigious signatures that the Declaration attracted, including those of prominent Nobel Prize winners (Love 2007, p. 363).

Then, on 27 August 2004, Argentina and Brazil published a proposal for establishment of a Development Agenda for the WIPO to be considered at the thirty-first session of the General Assembly on 27 September to 5 October 2004.[23] The seven-page proposal was based on the idea that a development dimension needed to be considered alongside intellectual property protection (on the Development Agenda more generally see Halbert 2006, p. 24; May 2007, p. 76; Menescal 2005, p. 783; Schultz and Walker 2006, p. 8). It sought changes in a wide range of the WIPO's activities and programmes including with respect to norm-setting; technology transfer; enforcement; technical assistance; and stakeholder participation in the WIPO (see also Musungu 2007a).

To some extent, the Development Agenda proposal mirrored the much earlier draft resolution presented by Brazil and Bolivia to the UN General Assembly in 1961.[24] This had sought to focus discussion on the adverse effects of the patent system on developing countries. However, unlike the 1961 draft resolution, the Development Agenda proposal of 2004 was not limited to patent-related issues (Basso and Rodrigues 2005, p. 7; Menescal 2005, p. 764). Instead it sought changes to a wide range of the WIPO's activities and programmes and was groundbreaking in many ways.[25] It called for a broad range of stakeholders to be included in discussions on intellectual property and proposed the active participation of NGOs in the WIPO to ensure that in intellectual property norm-setting a proper balance is struck between the producers and users of technological knowledge, in a manner that fully services the public interest.

As such, the Development Agenda proposal presented for the first time a comprehensive alternative as a framework in which intellectual property-related issues could be discussed based on developmental criteria. It also called for far-reaching reforms in the WIPO on grounds that the organization had not fully incorporated development concerns into its activities. Importantly, the proposal presented an opportunity for NGOs and other stakeholders concerned with the current deficiencies of the intellectual property regime to come together to reflect on alternatives and devise action-oriented proposals.[26]

After lengthy discussions and somewhat difficult negotiations, at the 2004 General Assembly the Members of the WIPO decided to explore the Development Agenda by establishing a series of three Inter-sessional Intergovernmental Meetings (IIMs). These meetings would provide a forum for Members to discuss the proposals contained in the Development Agenda document, together with other proposals that Members might wish to submit.[27] Three IIMs took place in Geneva: on 13–15 April 2005, 20–22 June 2005 and 20–22 July 2005. The WIPO then invited NGOs to attend a discussion on intellectual property and development on 15 September 2005. Some 47 NGOs responded to the WIPO's invitation. However, although the meeting was open to all accredited NGOs having permanent observer status and also to NGOs granted ad hoc accreditation to attend the IIMs,[28] a number of high profile NGOs complained that the event was organized at short notice, making participation impossible for those without a permanent presence in Geneva.

At the WIPO General Assembly on 26 September to 5 October 2005, closed informal meetings were then held in which delegations disagreed on whether to continue the discussions in IIMs that report directly to the General Assembly or to confine them to the WIPO Permanent Committee on Cooperation for Development Related to Intellectual Property (PCIPD). Members eventually reached a last-minute compromise, agreeing to establish a Provisional Committee on the Development Agenda (PCDA) to continue discussions on proposals to mainstream a development agenda into all of the WIPO's work.[29]

Mandated to report to the WIPO General Assembly on the outcomes of its discussions, the PCDA met twice in 2006 and two further times in 2007. At the first session of the PCDA on 20 February 2006, the question of engagement with NGOs was addressed specifically in Annex 1 of document PCDA/1/6/Prov.2. This set out a proposal to 'formulate and adopt measures designed to improve participation by civil society and other stakeholders in WIPO activities, relevant to their respective domains and interests'. It also contained proposals 'to undertake measures to ensure wider participation of civil society and public interest groups in WIPO's activities'.

Subsequently, at the second session of the PCDA on 22 June 2006, Argentina submitted a further proposal that included arrangements designed to ensure wider participation of NGOs in WIPO discussions, adopting UN criteria regarding NGO's terminology, acceptance and accreditation.[30] The following day, on 23 June 2006, that proposal was incorporated in the annex of document PCDA/2/2, which called for WIPO norm-setting activities to be preceded and effectively guided by debates and public hearings with open participation by all Member countries and all stakeholders. The focus on NGO participation was therefore apparent at various stages of the Development Agenda negotiating process.

After a long and tortuous process of negotiations, the Development Agenda was finally adopted by the General Assembly of the WIPO on 24 September to 3 October 2007. The General Assembly adopted 45 recommendations made by the PCDA but ultimately these did not include the more far-reaching proposals on NGO engagement that had surfaced at the first and second sessions of the PCDA (see also Chon 2010, p. 452). Nonetheless, the 45 recommendations agreed had ensured that development considerations now form an integral part of WIPO's work. Members also agreed to establish a new Committee on Development and Intellectual Property (CDIP) to carry forward a development-orientated work programme for the WIPO in six clusters.[31]

As a result of the Development Agenda process, there is a perception that the WIPO is now more transparent and inclusive, allowing for the participation of a broad range of organizations and elaboration of different views and much richer and more open debate (Ashton-Hart 2006, p. 15). What is more, NGO engagement with the Development Agenda process helped raise awareness of the issues and created a wider social movement focused on intellectual property rights and development (see also Love 2007, p. 363).[32] As a result, NGO participation in the WIPO is much greater today than it was before the Development Agenda process commenced.

Practical implementation of the Development Agenda in the WIPO will be a long-term process. However, despite concerns that it has politicized the policy-making and norm-setting process in the WIPO, it has undoubtedly also succeeded in reshaping the debate on the relationship between intellectual property rights and development. Future participation in the Development Agenda also presents additional challenges to NGOs. They will need to maintain momentum, continue to monitor discussions and pro-actively engage in debate in the WIPO and other multilateral institutions in a sustained and on-going way.

Future Arrangements for Engagement with NGOs in Multilateral Institutions

While formal arrangements for NGO engagement with intellectual property policy-making and norm-setting activities in multilateral institutions are important, the nature of intergovernmental organizations is that Members retain decision-making powers and the role of NGOs will ultimately remain, as it should, that of supporting and informing delegates in these processes. The most significant inputs of NGOs are likely to continue to be those of providing advice and technical expertise rather than in terms of direct participation through attending meetings organized by multilateral institutions and making interventions during these events. NGOs do not, and should not, rely on the panacea of enhanced formal participation in multilateral institutions in the future. Rather, their work is more effective at the informal level, providing advice and technical expertise in order to improve the flow of information and inform the policy-making and norm-setting process.

There is constant, informal, off-the-record dialogue between the various secretariats of multilateral institutions and NGOs but, since the policy-making and norm-setting process ultimately concerns Members, it is with the latter rather than with secretariats that NGOs should continue to focus their efforts. For NGOs, increasing their engagement with government officials at the national level would seem advantageous in the future, particularly since it is in national capitals that governments should ultimately be formulating policies on intellectual property rights.

The secretariats of multilateral institutions can themselves assist with this process by ensuring transparency and the fast and efficient flow of adequate information to stakeholders. In this respect, it should be noted that information is currently often available to international NGOs that have a presence in multilateral forums much faster than it is to developing country NGOs that operate at the national, sub-national or regional level. International NGOs, for instance, often receive hard copies of papers directly from delegates attending meetings in multilateral institutions long before these are made available on official websites. More could also be done by the secretariats of multilateral institutions to ensure an inclusive approach that would encourage wider interest and understanding of their proceedings through greater transparency and greater timeliness in the posting of documents. In this respect, however, it may well be that the constraints on transparency and timeliness are being driven by the concerns of Members rather than by secretariats of multilateral institutions concerned.

NEW AND EMERGING ISSUES

In the past, most of the work of NGOs on intellectual property-related issues has been reactive, that is to say reacting to policy developments and agendas set by other actors. In part this is inevitable given that NGOs are under-resourced and it is difficult for them to plan activities in the longer term. Recent manifestations of this are NGO responses to intellectual property provisions in bilateral and regional trade agreements (FTAs).[33]

Recently, however, a more proactive form of NGO engagement with intellectual property-related issues has been apparent. Proposals for disclosure of origin in the TRIPS Council are one example of this, while there has more recently been an increasing focus on alternative frameworks for promoting innovation, for example through a medical R&D Treaty for neglected diseases, prize funds and through the broader R&D. Copyright, A2K and fair use exemptions are also now increasingly the focus of NGO activities, as are technical assistance (see, for example, Musungu 2007b), patent harmonization, and proposals for a new Anti-Counterfeiting Trade Agreement (ACTA). Another example of proactive work by NGOs is the WIPO Development Agenda (see also Okediji 2009, p. 140), although to some extent this has itself been seen as a defensive move in some quarters given its significance as a counterweight to proposals for a WIPO Substantive Patent Law Treaty (SPLT).

Nevertheless, the prospect of a more proactive form of NGO engagement with intellectual property-related issues has its limits. The fact that NGOs have, in the past, been mainly reacting to policy developments is in part a problem of lack of resources in that NGOs and developing countries try to prioritize, to focus on what seems more important and to select issues where they think their input can be most significant.

In reality, covering all intellectual property policy-making and norm-setting activities across multiple forums remains a huge task for NGOs, not least in the face of perceived forum-shifting on the part of developed countries as manifested in the TRIPS-plus intellectual property provisions of bilateral and regional FTAs and, most recently, in the proposed ACTA (Matthews 2008, pp. 13–19). Faced with severe resource and time constraints, the dynamism of intellectual property-related issues in different multilateral forums and at regional and bilateral levels presents an extremely difficult task for NGOs seeking to cover all relevant policy-making and norm-setting activities. Crucially, in bilateral and regional negotiations the numerical advantage of developing countries and their ability to build alliances are severally reduced (de Mello e Souza 2005, p. 279). In fact, developed country governments may well be deliberately employing a strategy of breaking up developing country coalitions on intellectual property issues by utilizing bilateral and regional negotiations to introduce TRIPS-plus intellectual property standards through the back door (see also Drahos 2002, p. 208; Morin 2008, p. 8).

CONCLUSION

Many factors influence the outcome of intellectual property-related policy-making and norm-setting activities in multilateral institutions. The complexity of negotiating environments makes it extremely difficult to ascertain conclusively what the impact of NGOs has actually been. Nonetheless, by building coalitions and often utilizing human rights to highlight the impact of intellectual property rights on marginalized, poor, disadvantaged and vulnerable sectors of society in developing countries, NGOs have undoubtedly influenced the debate on the interface between intellectual property rights and development in new and far-reaching ways. NGOs, working collaboratively together and with broader social movements that mobilize grassroots support, have contributed to a much deeper understanding of the impact that intellectual property rights can have on public health and access to medicines, food security, traditional knowledge and local communities. As such, they have played a critical role in reappraising the relationship between intellectual property rights and development in ways that will continue to have profound implications for many decades to come.

NOTES

1. Some of the analysis in subsequent sections of this chapter is adapted from Matthews (2007, pp. 1369–87).
2. The 11 international NGOs are: ActionAid International, Amnesty International, CIVICUS World Alliance for Citizen Participation, Consumers International, Greenpeace International, Oxfam International, International Save the Children Alliance, Survival International, International Federation Terre des Homes, Transparency International, World YMCA. Source: Oxfam Press Release, 7 June 2006, *NGOs Lead by Example: World's international NGOs endorse accountability charter*, available at: http://www.oxfam.org/en/news/pressreleases2006/pr060606_ngo_charter.
3. The full text version of the International Non-Governmental Accountability Charter is available at: http://www.ingoaccountabilitycharter.org/
4. The CIPIH terms of reference were to: summarize the existing evidence on the prevalence of diseases of public health importance with an emphasis on those that particularly affect poor people and their social and economic impact; review the volume and distribution of existing research, development and innovation efforts directed at these diseases; and consider the importance and effectiveness of intellectual property regimes and other incentive and funding mechanisms in stimulating research and the creation of new medicines and other products against these diseases; analyse proposals for

improvements to the current incentive and funding regimes, including intellectual property rights, designed to stimulate the creation of new medicines and other products, and facilitate access to them; produce concrete proposals for action by national and international stakeholders.

5. For example, CPTech raised concerns that informal consultations held in Casablanca on 16 February 2005, that resulted in a recommendation that the WIPO IGC address issues of sufficiency of disclosure and genetic resources with a view to progressive development and codification of international intellectual property law, may have exceeded the remit provided by the WIPO General Assembly with respect to matters of substance, specifically SPLT negotiations and the work programme of the SCP and the IGC. *CPTech written submission to the WIPO IGC on Genetic Resources, Traditional Knowledge and Folklore (June 2005)*, Thiru Balasubramaniam, post on IP-Health list server, 9 June 2005.

6. *Brazil, EU Collaborate on Local Production of AIDS Drugs in Mozambique*, Intellectual Property Watch, 10 November 2008.

7. *Nota GTPI em ingles*, post on IP-Health list server by Renata Rais, ABIA, 20 August 2007.

8. *Brazil Introduced an Opposition to a Patent on an AIDS Medicine*, post on IP-Health list server by Michel Lotrowska, MSF, 28 June 2008.

9. Prior to this, in Brazil, the INPI's initial examination had found the patent application failed to meet the patentability criteria on grounds of lack of novelty, given that the active ingredient in Tenofovir had been widely-known since the 1980s.

10. *Guidelines for arrangements on relations with Non-Governmental Organizations, Decision adopted by the WTO General Council on 18 July 1996*, WT/L/162, paragraph VI. Available at: http://www.wto.org/english/forums_e/ngo_e/guide_e.htm.

11. *Principles Governing Relations with Nongovernmental Organizations*, World Health Organization, paragraph 3.1. Available at: http://www.who.int/civilsociety/relations/principles/en/index.html.

12. *Draft Policy for the Accreditation of Non-Governmental Organisations to the Convention on Biological Diversity*. UNEP/CBD/COP/8/30, 28 February 2006.

13. '. . . Any other body or agency, whether governmental or non-governmental, qualified in fields relating to conservation and sustainable use of biological diversity, which has informed the Secretariat of its wish to be represented as an observer at a meeting of the Conference of the Parties, may be admitted unless at least one third of the Parties present object. The admission and participation of observers shall be subject to the rules of procedure adopted by the Conference of the Parties.' Article 23.5 Convention on Biological Diversity. Available at: http://www.cbd.int/convention/convention.shtml.

14. *Report of the Eighth Meeting of the Conference of the Parties to the Convention on Biological Diversity (COP 8)*, 20–31 March 2006 – Curitiba, Brazil, UNEP/CBD/8/31. Available at: http://www.cbd.int/doc/?mtg=cop-08.

15. *FAO Policy Concerning Relations with International Non-Governmental Organizations*, Report of the Conference of FAO, Seventh Session – Rome, 23 November to 11 December 1953. Available at: http://www.fao.org/docrep/x5576e/x5576e0i.htm.

16. Asian Broadcasting Union (ABU); European Broadcasting Union; Inter-American Association of Industrial Property (ASIPI); International Alliance for Diffusion by Wire (AID); International Association for the Protection of Industrial Property (IAPIP); International Bureau for Mechanical Reproduction (BIEM); International Chamber of Commerce (ICC); International Confederation of Societies of Authors and Composers (CISAC); International Federation of Actors (IFA); International Federation of Film Distributors' Associations (FIAPF); International Federation of Journalists (IFJ); International Federation of Musicians (FIM); International Federation of Patent Agents (FICPI); International Federation of the Phonographic Industry (IFPI); International Gesellschaft fur Urheberrecht (INTERGU); International League Against Unfair Competition (LICCD); International Literary and Artistic Association

(ALAI); International Publishers' Association (IPA); International Secretariat of Entertainment Trade Unions; International Union of Cinematograph Exhibitors (UIEC); International Writers' Guild (IWG); Union of European Patent Agents; Union of National Radio and Television Organizations of Africa (URTNA). Source: Bogsch (1992, p. 125) quoted in Halbert (2006, p. 14).

17. *Standing Committee on Copyrights and Related Rights First Session*, 2–10 November 1998, paragraph 8, Geneva: WIPO, SCCR/1/2. Available at: http://www.wipo.int/edocs/mdocs/copyright/en/sccr_1/sccr_1_2.pdf.

18. *Standing Committee on Patents, First Session*, 15–10 June 1998, paragraph 6, Geneva: WIPO, SCP/1/2. Available at: http://www.wipo.int/edocs/mdocs/scp/en/scp_1/scp1_2.pdf.

19. *Intergovernmental Committee on Intellectual Property and Genetic Resources, Traditional Knowledge and Folklore, First Session*, 30 April–3 May 2001, paragraph 8, Geneva: WIPO, GRTKF/IC1/2. Available at: http://www.wipo.int/edocs/mdocs/tk/en/wipo_grtkf_ic_1/wipo_grtkf_ic_1_2.pdf.

20. Under the 1995 agreement between the WIPO and the WTO, the International Bureau of the WIPO is tasked with providing legal-technical assistance and technical cooperation to developing countries. See: Agreement between the World Intellectual Property Organization and the World Trade Organization (1995). Available at: http://www.wipo.int/treaties/en/agreement/pdf/trtdocs_wo030.pdf.

21. NGOs that make a request to the General Assembly for accreditation with observer status may have to wait up to a year before the next Assembly, held at the end of September and beginning of October each year, formally accepts their request.

22. See 'The Future of WIPO Conference Summary Report'. Available at: http://www.tacd.org/cgi-bin/db.cgi?page=view&config=admin/docs.cfg&id=261.

23. *Proposal by Argentina and Brazil for the Establishment of a Development Agenda for WIPO*, 27 August 2004, WO/GA/31/11.

24. UN Document no. A/C.2/L.565/Add.1.

25. The Development Agenda proposal was later co-sponsored by a wider coalition of 14 developing countries: Argentina; Bolivia; Brazil; Cuba; Dominican Republic; Ecuador; Egypt; Iran; Kenya; Peru; Sierra Leone; South Africa; Tanzania; and Venezuela.

26. An example is the proposal for an Access to Knowledge Treaty. The text of the proposal for an Access to Knowledge Treaty, dated 9 May 2005 is available at: http:www.cptech.org/a2k/a2k-debate.html.

27. In addition to the original and elaborated Development Agenda proposal by the Friends of Development group, other proposals for the establishment of a Development Agenda for WIPO include proposals by: the African Group (WIPO document IIM/3/2); a proposal by Chile (WIPO document PCDA/1/2); Colombia (WIPO document PCDA/1/3); and the United States of America (WIPO document IIM/1/2, further elaborated in WIPO document PCDA/1/4).

28. *WIPO Invites NGOs to Discussion on IP and Development*. WIPO Press Release PR/413/2005, 16 September 2005. Available at: http://www.wipo.int/edocs/prdocs/en/2005/wipo_pr_2005_413.html.

29. 'WIPO Members Create New Forum to Discuss Development Agenda', ICTSD Bridges Weekly, 9(33), 5 October 2005. Available at: http://www.ictsd.org/weekly/05-10-05/story2.htm.

30. *Provisional Committee on Proposals Relating to a WIPO Development Agenda: Proposal on the Decision of the PCDA on the Establishment of a WIPO Development Agenda*, 23 June 2006, Geneva: WIPO, PCDA/2/2.

31. Cluster A: Technical Assistance and Capacity Building; Cluster B: Norm-setting, Flexibilities, Public Policy and Public Domain; Cluster C: Technology Transfer, Information and Communication Technologies and Access to Knowledge; Cluster D: Assessment, Evaluation and Impact Studies; Cluster E: Institutional Matters including Mandate and Governance; Cluster F: Other issues (to approach intellectual property enforcement in the context of broader societal interests and especially

development-oriented concerns). Available at: http://www.wipo.int/ip-development/en/agenda/recommendations.html.

32.   Among the NGOs that began to engage more forcefully with intellectual property rights issues as a result of the Development Agenda process were the Electronic Frontier Foundation (EFF), IP Justice, Union for the Public Domain (UPD) and 3D: Trade - Human Rights - Equitable Economy.

33.   See, for example, *Public Health at Risk: A US Free Trade Agreement Could Threaten Access to Medicines in Thailand*, Oxfam International Briefing Paper, April 2006. Available at: http://www.oxfam.org.uk/resources/policy/health/bp86_thailand.html. See also *Free Trade Agreements and Intellectual Property Doom Access to Medicines*, Joint Statement by Health GAP, MSF, Oxfam International, Third World Network, TNP+, EATG, GAT, SGAC, Solidarite Sida, Canadian HIV/AIDS Legal Network, Korean HIV/AIDS Wide Action, MTAG+, posted on IP-Health list server, 16 August 2006.

Appendix

INTERVIEWS CONDUCTED FOR THIS BOOK

The research for this book has been informed by inputs from the individuals listed below, who were interviewed during fieldwork undertaken between November 2005 and June 2006. Any errors remain those of the author.

Switzerland: Geneva/Zurich

Martin Watson (QUNO); Pedro Roffe (ICTSD); Julia Oliva (CIEL); James Love (CPTech); Sisule Musungu (South Centre); Ellen 't Hoen (MSF); Jennifer Brant (Oxfam International); François Meienberg (Berne Declaration); Cecilia Oh (WHO); Davinia Ovett (3D); Carin Smaller (IATP); Elizabeth Türk (UNCTAD); David Vivas (ICTSD); Anna Wang (Medicines for Malaria Venture); Rashid Kaukab (South Centre); Christoph Spennemann (UNCTAD); William New (IP Watch); Sangeeta Shashikant (TWN); Bernard Kuiten (WTO); Jayashree Watal (WTO); Adrian Otten (WTO); Charles Clift (WHO); Anthony Taubman (WIPO); Denis Croze (WIPO); Mathias Daka (Permanent Mission of Zambia); Alejandro Neyra (Permanent Mission of Peru); Ambassador Dr Manzoor Ahmad and Mujeeb Ahmed Khan (Permanent Mission of Pakistan); Maigari Buba (Permanent Mission of Nigeria); Ambassador Alberto L. Dumont (Permanent Mission of Argentina); Guilherme de Aguiar Patriota (Permanent Mission of Brazil); Eric Noehrenberg (IFPMA); Jose Victor V. Chan-Gonzaga (Philippines Mission to the WTO); a representative of the Permanent Mission of Kenya; Bernard Pécoul (Drug for Neglected Diseases Initiative).

South Africa: Johannesburg/Pretoria/Cape Town/Stellenbosch

Tenu Avafia (UNDP); Jonathan Berger (AIDS Law Project); Randall Williams (Department of Trade and Industry); Samu Dube and Louise Hilditch (ActionAid); Rachel Wynberg (Biowatch); Calvin Manduna (TRALAC); Angela Andrews (Legal Resources Centre).

Brazil: São Paulo/Curitiba (Including ad hoc Observer Status at CBD COP 8)

Carlos Passarelli (Brazilian Ministry of Health); Jorge Beloqui (GIV); Maristela Basso (IDCID); David Hathaway (Interpreter, consultant, economist); Luis Eugenio Cifuentes (IMCA and CBCD, Colombia) and Alejandro Montero (CET-SUR and CBCD, Chile); Susan Finston (American BioIndustry Alliance, Washington, DC); David Cooper and Marie Annick Moreau (CBD Secretariat, Canada); Representatives of Brazilian local peoples' groups: Cemen (Cooperativa de mujeres estrativistas)/Estado de Pare, Ilha de Marajó; Edna Marajoara, Directora; Seringal Bon Futuro/Estado de Acre, Island on Rio Libertade; Lorival Montero (Comunidad local de Seringueros (rubber-tappers)) Estado de Acre – Edison Bastista (Local Communities of the Amazon); Michael F. Schmidlehner (Amazonlink).

India: Delhi

Anand Grover (Lawyers Collective HIV/AIDS Unit); B.K. Kealya (National Working Group on Patent Laws); Amit Gupta (Delhi Science Forum); Vandana Shiva (Navdanya); Suman Sahai (Gene Campaign); Devinder Sharma (Forum for Biotechnology and Food Security); Biswajit Dhar (Centre for WTO Studies, Indian Institute of Foreign Trade).

United Kingdom

Geoff Tansey (consultant); Michael Bailey and Ruth Mayne (Oxfam GB); Ruth Okediji (University of Minnesota, USA); Patrick Mulvany (Practical Action/ITDG).

TELEPHONE INTERVIEWS

In addition to face-to-face interviews, telephone interviews were undertaken with the following individuals:

Roger Chennells (SASI, Stellenbosch, South Africa); Andre de Souza (Pontifícia Universidade Católica do Rio de Janeiro, Brazil); Michel Lotrowska (MSF, Rio de Janeiro, Brazil); Chee Yoke Ling (TWN, Malaysia); Pat Mooney (ETC, Canada); Tewolde Berhan Gebre Egziabher (Environmental Protection Authority, Addis Ababa, Ethiopia); Clive Stannard (FAO, Rome, Italy).

WRITTEN RESPONSES

Written responses were also received from the following individuals:

Jean Marc von der Wied (AS-PTA, Rio de Janeiro, Brazil); Renata Reis (ABIA/REBRIP, Rio de Janeiro, Brazil); Carlos Correa (University of Buenos Aires, Argentina); Steven Price (Public Interest Intellectual Property Advisors, Washington, DC, USA).

Bibliography

3D: Trade - Human Rights - Equitable Economy (2005), *Background Note: Intellectual Property, Human Rights and the Drafting of the General Comment on Article 15(1)(c) ICESCR*, Geneva: 3D.

Abbott, Frederick M. (2005), 'The "Rule of Reason" and the Right to Health: Integrating Human Rights and Competition Principles in the Context of TRIPS', in Thomas Cottier, Joost Pauwelyn and Elisabeth Bürgi (eds), *Human Rights and International Trade*, Oxford: Oxford University Press, 279–300.

Abbott, Frederick M. (2008), 'Post-mortem on the Geneva Mini-Ministerial: Where does the TRIPS Agreement go from here?' *ICTSD Information Note No. 7, August 2008*, Geneva: International Centre for Trade and Sustainable Development (ICTSD).

Agência Nacional de Vigilância Sanitária (2008), *Medicamentos genéricos*, http://www.anvisa.gov.br/hotsite/genericos/index.htm.

AIDS Law Project (2007), *18-Month Review: January 2006 to June 2007*, Johannesburg and Cape Town, South Africa: AIDS Law Project, http://www.alp.org.za/pdf/Publications/ALP%20Annual%20Reviews/ALP_2006-2007_Review.pdf.

Arup, Christopher and Plahe, Jagjit (2010), 'Pharmaceutical Patent Networks: Assessing the Influence of India's Paragraph 3(d) Internationally', *Intellectual Property Quarterly*, 1: 15–43.

Ashton-Hart, Nick (2006), 'Public Participation Brings a Fresh Approach to WIPO', *Bridges*, **10**(8), December 2006–January 2007, www.ictsd.org.

Avafia, Tenu, Berger, Jonathan and Hartzenberg, Trudy (2006), *The Ability of Select Sub-Saharan African Countries to Utilise TRIPS Flexibilities and Competition Law to Ensure a Sustainable Supply of Essential Medicines: A Study of Producing and Importing Countries*, TRALAC Working Paper No. 12, Stellenbosch, South Africa: US Printers.

Baker, Brook K. (2004), *Processes and Issues for Improving Access to Utilise TRIPS Flexibilities in Non-Producing Countries*, London: DFID Health Systems Resource Centre.

Bala Ravi, S. (2003), 'Who Benefits and Loses with India's Accession to UPOV?', in Ujjwal Kumar and Suman Sahai (eds), *Status of the Rights of Farmers and Plant Breeders in Asia*, New Delhi: Gene Campaign, 70–75.

Basheer, Shamnad and Reddy, Prashant (2008), '"Ducking" TRIPS in India: A Saga Involving Novartis and the Legality of Section 3(d)', *National Law School of India Review*, **20**(2): 131–55.

Basso, Maristela (2006), 'Intervention of Health Authorities in Patent Examination: The Brazilian Practice of Prior Informed Consent', *International Journal of Intellectual Property Management*, **1**(1–2): 54–73.

Basso, Maristela and Rodrigues, Edson (2005), 'Exploring Options and Modalities to Move the IP Development Agenda Forward', *UNCTAD-ICTSD Dialogue on IPRs and Sustainable Development: Revising the Agenda in a New Context*, 24–28 October, Bellagio, Italy.

Berger, Jonathan (2006), 'Advancing Public Health by Other Means: Using Competition Policy', in Pedro Roffe, Geoff Tansey and David Vivas-Eugui (eds), *Negotiating Health: Intellectual Property and Access to Medicines*, London and Sterling, VA: Earthscan.

Blagescu, Monica and Lloyd, Robert (2006), *2006 Global Accountability Report: Holding power to account*, London: One World Trust.

Bogsch, Arpad (1992), *The First Twenty-Five Years of the World Intellectual Property Organisation from 1967 to 1992*, WIPO Publication No. 881(E), Geneva, Switzerland: International Bureau of Intellectual Property.

Boulle, Jacqui and Avafia, Tenu (2005), *Treatment Action Campaign (TAC) Evaluation*, http://www.tac.org.za/Documents/FinalTACEvaluation-AfaviaAndBoulle-20050701.pdf.

Braithwaite, John and Drahos, Peter (2000), *Global Business Regulation*, Cambridge: Cambridge University Press.

Brazilian Ministry of Health, Surveillance Secretariat and National Programme on STD and AIDS (2008), Targets and Commitments made by the Member States of the United Nations General Assembly Special Session on HIV/AIDS (UNGASS-HIV/AIDS): Brazilian Response 2005–2007. Country Progress Report, http://data.unaids.org/pub/report/2008/brazil_2008_country_progress_report_en.pdf.

Bultrini, Dubravka Bojic (2009), *Guide to Legislating for the Right to Food*, Rome, Italy: Food and Agriculture Organization of the United Nations, http://www.fao.org/righttofood/publi09/guide_on_legislating.pdf.

Cabrera Medaglia, Jorge (2009), *Study on the Relationship between the ABS International Regimen and Other International Instruments which Govern the Use of Genetic Resources: The World Trade Organisation (WTO); the World Intellectual Property Organisation (WIPO); and the International Union for the Protection of New Varieties of Plants (UPOV)*. Comments of UPOV for the Secretariat of the Convention on

Biological Diversity, http://www.cbd.int/doc/programmes/abs/studies/ study-regime-04-en.pdf.

Cameron, Edwin and Berger, Jonathan (2005), 'Patents and Public Health: Principle, politics and paradox', *Proceedings of the British Academy*, 331–69.

Chaudhuri, Sudip (2005), *The WTO and India's Pharmaceuticals Industry: Patent Protection, TRIPS and Developing Countries*, New Delhi: Oxford University Press.

Chennells, Roger (2007), 'Ethics and Practice in Ethnobiology: The Experience of the San Peoples of South Africa', in Charles, R. McManis (ed.), *Biodiversity and the Law: Intellectual Property, Biotechnology and Traditional Knowledge*, London: Earthscan: 413–27.

Chon, Margaret (2010), 'A Rough Guide to Global Intellectual Property Pluralism', in Rochelle Dreyfuss, Harry First and Diane Zimmerman (eds), *Working within the Boundaries of Intellectual Property*, Oxford: Oxford University Press, 445–69.

CIEL (2007), *The Gap between Indigenous People's Demands and WIPO's Framework on Traditional Knowledge*, Geneva: The Center for International Environmental Law, http://www.wipo.int/tk/en/igc/ngo/ ciel_gap.pdf.

Cohen, Jillian Clare and Lybecker, Kristiana M. (2005), 'AIDS Policy and Pharmaceutical Patents: Brazil's Strategy to Safeguard Public Health', *World Economy*, **28**(2): 211–30.

Commission on Intellectual Property Rights (2002), *Integrating Intellectual Property Rights and Development Policy*, London: Commission on Intellectual Property Rights.

Commission on Intellectual Property Rights, Innovation and Public Health (2006), *Public Health, Innovation and Intellectual Property Rights*, Geneva: World Health Organization, http://www.who.int/ intellectualproperty/report/en/.

Correa, Carlos (2000), *Integrating Public Health Concerns into Patent Legislation in Developing Countries*, Geneva: South Centre.

Correa, Carlos (2001), *Traditional Knowledge and Intellectual Property: Issues and Options Surrounding the Protection of Traditional Knowledge*, Quaker United Nations Office, Geneva, Switzerland: Discussion Paper Series.

Costa Chaves, Gabriela, Fogaça Vieria, Marcela and Reis, Renata (2008), 'Access to Medicines and Intellectual Property in Brazil: Reflections and Strategies of Civil Society', *Sur Journal*, **8**, http://www.surjournal.org/ eng/conteudos/getArtigo8.php?,artigo.chaves.htm.

Cullet, Philippe (2003), *Food Security and Intellectual Property Rights in Developing Countries*, IELRC Working paper 2003-3, Geneva,

Switzerland: International Environmental Law Research Centre, http://www.ielrc.org/content/w0303.pdf.

Daz, Keshab (2003), 'The Domestic Politics of TRIPS: Pharmaceutical Interests, Public Health, and NGO Influence in India,' Paper prepared for the Research Project on 'Linking the WTO to the Poverty-Reduction Agenda', Part of the DFID-Funded Globalisation and Poverty Research Programme, Gujarat Institute of Development Research, Ahmedabad, India.

Deere, Carolyn (2008), *The Implementation Game: The TRIPS Agreement and the Global Politics of Intellectual Property Reform in Developing Countries*, Oxford and New York: Oxford University Press.

Dinwoodie, Graeme B. (2007), 'The International Intellectual Property System: Treaties, Norms, National Courts, and Private Ordering', in Daniel Gervais (ed.), *Intellectual Property, Trade and Development. Strategies to Optimize Economic Development in the TRIPS-Plus Era*, Oxford: Oxford University Press, 61–114.

Drahos, Peter (2007), 'Four Lessons for Developing Countries from the Trade Negotiations over Access to Medicines', *Liverpool Law Review*, **28**: 11–39.

Drahos, Peter (2008), 'Does Dialogue Make a Difference? Structural Change and the Limits of Framing', *The Yale Journal Pocket Part*, **117**: 268–73.

Drahos, Peter with Braithwaite, John (2002), *Information Feudalism: Who Owns the Knowledge Economy?*, London: Earthscan.

Drezner, Daniel W. (2005), *Gauging the Power of Global Civil Society: Intellectual Property and Public Health*, mimeo.

Dunoff, Jeffrey L. (1998), 'The Misguided Debate Over NGO Participation at the WTO', *Journal of International Economic Law*, **1**, 3: 433–56.

Dutfield, Graham (2003a), *Intellectual Property Rights and the Life Science Industries: A Twentieth Century History*, Aldershot: Ashgate.

Dutfield, Graham (2003b), *Protecting Traditional Knowledge and Folklore: A Review of Progress in Diplomacy and Policy Formulation*, Geneva, Switzerland: ICTSD/UNCTAD Project on IPRs and Sustainable Development Issue Paper No. 1.

Earth Negotiations Bulletin (2006), *First Session of the Governing Body of the International Treaty on Plant Genetic Resources for Food and Agriculture: 12–16 June 2006*, **9**(364): 12 June 2006, http://www.iisd.ca/vol09/enb09364e.html.

Essential Action (2007), *Pharmaceutical Links of NGOs: Contributing to the World Health Organization's Second Public Hearing on Public Health, Innovation and Intellectual Property*, Washington, DC: Essential Action, 7 November 2007, mimeo.

Fourie, Pieter (2006), *The Political Management of HIV and AIDS in*

South Africa: One Burden Too Many?, Basingstoke and New York: Palgrave Macmillan.

Friedman, Steven and Mottair, Shauna (2004), *A Rewarding Engagement? The Treatment Action Campaign and the Politics of HIV/AIDS*, Working Paper, Durban, South Africa: Centre for Civil Society and School of Development Studies, University of KwaZulu-Natal.

Galvão, Jane (2005), 'Brazil and Access to HIV/AIDS Drugs: A Question of Human Rights and Public Health', *American Journal of Public Health*, **95**(7): 1110–16.

Garde, T.V. (2008), 'Circumventing the Debate over State Policy and Property Rights: Section 3(d) of the Indian Patents Act Law', in Wolrad Prinz zu Waldeck und Pyrmont, Martin J. Adelman, Robert Brauneis, and Josef Drexl (eds), *Patents and Technological Progress in a Globalised World: Liber Amicorum Joseph Straus*, Berlin, Germany: MPI Studies on Intellectual Property, Competition and Tax Law, Springer.

Gervais, Daniel (2007), 'TRIPS and Development', in Daniel Gervais (ed.), *Intellectual Property, Trade and Development. Strategies to Optimize Economic Development in the TRIPS-Plus Era*, Oxford: Oxford University Press.

Giovanetti, Tom and Matthews, Merrill (2005), *Intellectual Property Rights and Human Rights*, Lewisville, Texas: Institute for Policy Innovation.

GRAIN (2001), *'TRIPS-plus' Through the Back Door: How Bilateral Treaties Impose Much Stronger Rules for IPRs on Life than the WTO*, GRAIN Briefing, http://www.grain.org/briefings/?id=6.

GRAIN (2005), *Seedling*, July 2005 issue, http://www.grain.org/seedling/?id=344.

Grover, Anand (2005), 'Meeting the Unmet Legal Needs of Positive People: The Lawyers Collective HIV/AIDS Unit', in Radhika Ramasubban and Bhanwar Rishyasringa (eds), *AIDS and Civil Society: India's Learning Curve*, Jaipur: Rawat Publications, 197–224.

Halbert, Debora J. (2005), *Resisting Intellectual Property*, Abingdon and New York: Routledge.

Halbert, Debora J. (2006), 'The World Intellectual Property Organization: Changing Narratives on Intellectual Property', paper presented at *Frontiers of Regulation: Scholarly Debates and Policy Challenges*, an international conference organized by the European Consortium for Political Research, Standing Group on Regulatory Governance and the Centre for the Study of Regulated Industries, School of Management, University of Bath, 8 September.

Haugen, Hans Morten (2005), 'Traditional Knowledge and Human Rights', *Journal of World Intellectual Property*, **8**(5): 663–77.

Heywood, Mark (2004), *How South Africa's HIV/AIDS National Treatment Plan was Won: Sustaining a Civil Society Campaign for Socio-Economic Rights*, South Africa: Treatment Action Campaign, http://www.tac.org.za/Documents/PriceofDenial.doc.

Hilary, John (2004), *Divide and Rule: The EU and US Response to Developing Country Alliances at the WTO*, South Africa: Action Aid International.

Hoen, Ellen 't (2002), 'TRIPS, Pharmaceutical Patents, and Access to Essential Medicines', *Chicago Journal of International Law*, **3**: 34.

Jawara, Fatoumata and Kwa, Aileen (2003), *Behind the Scenes at the WTO: The Real World of International Trade Negotiations*, London and New York: Zed Books.

Kapczynski, Amy (2008), 'The Access to Knowledge Mobilization and the New Politics of Intellectual Property', *The Yale Law Journal*, **117**: 804–85.

Keayla, B.K. (2005), 'Amended Patents Act: A Critique', *Combat Law*, **4**(2), http://www.indiatogether.org/cgi-bin/tools/pfriend.cgi.

Krishna Iyer, V.R., Chinnappa Reddy, O., Desai, D.A. and Sachar, Rajinder (1996), *People's Commission on the Constitutional Implications of the Final Act Embodying the Results of the Uruguay Round of Multilateral Trade Negotiations*, New Delhi, India: Centre for Study of Global Trade System and Development.

Kumar, Ujjwal and Sahai, Suman (eds) (2003), *Status of the Rights of Farmers and Plant Breeders in Asia*, New Delhi: Gene Campaign.

Lang, Andrew (2007), 'The Role of the Human Rights Movement in Trade Policy-Making: Human Rights as a Trigger for Social Learning', *New Zealand Journal of Public and International Law*, **5**: 147–72.

Law and Treatment Access Unit of the AIDS Law Project and the Treatment Action Campaign (2003), *The Price of Life: Hazel Tau and Others vs GlaxoSmithKline and Boehringer Ingelheim: A Report on the Excessive Pricing Complaint to South Africa's Competition Commission.* Joint publication of the Law and Treatment Access Unit of the AIDS Law Project and the Treatment Action Campaign, http://alp.org.za/modules.php?op=modload&name=News&file=article&sid=222.

Lewis, Jane (2001), *TRIPS on Trial: The Impact of WTO's Patent Regime on the World's Farmers, the Poor and Developing Countries*, Action Aid, Berne Declaration, IATP, Misereor.

Love, James P. (2006), 'TRIPS, TRIPS+, and new paradigms: The role of NGOs in shaping the debate', paper prepared for the Chicago-Kent College of Law conference on *Intellectual Property, Trade and Development: Accommodating and Reconciling Different National Levels of Protection*, Chicago, Illinois, 12–13 October.

Love, James P. (2007), 'Nongovernmental Generation of International

Treaties – An Interview with Gaëlle Krikorian', *Nongovernmental Politics*, New York: Zone Books, 359–67.

Macdonald-Brown, Charters and Ferera, Leon (1998), 'First WTO Decision on TRIPS: India-Patent Protection for Pharmaceutical and Agricultural Chemical Products', *European Intellectual Property Review*, **20**(2): 69–73.

Mathiharan, K. (2003), 'The Fundamental Right to Health Care', *Indian Journal of Medical Ethics*, October–December, **11**(4).

Matthews, Duncan (2002), *Globalising Intellectual Property Rights: The TRIPS Agreement*, London and New York: Routledge.

Matthews, Duncan (2004), 'The WTO Decision on Implementation of Paragraph 6 of the Doha Declaration on the TRIPS Agreement and Public Health: A Solution to the Access to Essential Medicines Problem?', *Journal of International Economic Law*, **7**(1): 73–107.

Matthews, Duncan (2005), 'TRIPS Flexibilities and Access to Medicines in Developing Countries: The Problem with Technical Assistance and Free Trade Agreements', *European Intellectual Property Review*, **28**(11): 420–27.

Matthews, Duncan (2006), 'From the August 30, 2003 WTO Decision to the December 6, 2005 Agreement on an Amendment to TRIPS: Improving Access to Medicines in Developing Countries?', *Intellectual Property Quarterly*, **2**: 91–130.

Matthews, Duncan (2007), 'The Role of International NGOs in the Intellectual Property Policy-Making and Norm-Setting Activities of Multilateral Institutions', *Chicago-Kent Law Review*, **82**(3): 1369–87.

Matthews, Duncan (2008), 'The Fight Against Counterfeiting and Piracy in the Bilateral Trade Agreements of the EU', *Briefing Paper prepared for the European Parliament Committee on International Trade*, Directorate-General for External Policies of the Union, Brussels: European Parliament.

Matthews, Duncan (2010), 'Intellectual Property Rights, Human Rights and the Right to Health', in F.W. Grosheide (ed.), *Intellectual Property and Human Rights: A Paradox*, Cheltenham, UK and Northampton, MA, USA: Edward Elgar, 118–39.

Matthews, Duncan and Munoz-Tellez, Viviana (2006), 'Bilateral Technical Assistance and the TRIPS Agreement: The United States, Japan and the European Communities in Comparative Perspective', *Journal of World Intellectual Property*, **9**(6): 629–53.

Matthews, Duncan and Munoz-Tellez, Viviana (2007) 'Parallel Trade: A User's Guide' in Anatole Krattiger, Richard T. Mahoney, Lita Nelsen, et al. (eds), *Intellectual Property Management in Health and Agriculture*

Innovation: A Handbook of Best Practices, Oxford: MIHR and Davis, USA: PIPRA.

May, Christopher (2006), 'The World Intellectual Property Organisation and the Development Agenda', paper presented at *Frontiers of Regulation: Scholarly Debates and Policy Challenges*, an international conference organized by the European Consortium for Political Research, Standing Group on Regulatory Governance and the Centre for the Study of Regulated Industries, School of Management, University of Bath, 8 September.

May, Christopher (2007), *The World Intellectual Property Organization: Resurgence and the Development Agenda*, London and New York: Routledge.

Mayne, Ruth (2002), 'The Global Campaign on Patents and Access to Medicines: An Oxfam Perspective', in Peter Drahos and Ruth Mayne (eds), *Global Intellectual Property Rights: Knowledge, Access and Development*, Basingstoke and New York: Palgrave Macmillan.

Mbali, Mandisa (2005), *The Treatment Action Campaign and the History of Rights-Based, Patient-Driven HIV/AIDS Activism in South Africa*, Research Report No. 29, University of KwaZulu-Natal Centre for Civil Society, http://www.ukzn.ac.za/ccs/files/RReport_29.pdf.

Mello e Souza, André de (2005), *The Power of the Weak: Advocacy Networks, Ideational Change and the Global Politics of Pharmaceutical Patent Rights*, unpublished doctoral thesis, Stanford University.

Menescal, Andréa K. (2005), 'Changing WIPO's Ways? The 2004 Development Agenda in Historical Perspective', *Journal of World Intellectual Property*, **8**(6): 761–96.

Mercurio, Bryan (2006), 'TRIPS-Plus Provisions in FTAs: Recent Trends', in Lorand Bartels and Federico Ortino (eds), *Regional Trade Agreements and the WTO Legal System*, Oxford and New York: Oxford University Press, 215–37.

Morin, Jean-Frédéric (2008), 'Multilateralising TRIPS-Plus Agreements: Is the US Strategy a Failure?', Working Paper, http://ssrn.com/abstract=1276464.

MSF (2009), *HIV/AIDS Treatment in Developing Countries: The battle for long-term survival has just begun*, Campaign for Access to Essential Medicines, http://www.msfaccess.org/fileadmin/user_upload/diseases/hiv-aids/07_16%20BattleForLongTermSurvival_LowRes_FINAL%203.pdf.

Mueller, Janice M. (2007), 'The Tiger Awakens: The Tumultuous Transformation of India's Patent System and the Rise of Indian Pharmaceutical Innovation', *University of Pittsburgh Law Review*, **68**(3).

Murphy, Bryan D. and Rodrigues, Edson B. (2005), *Brazil's Prior Consent*

Law: A Dialogue between Brazil and the United States over where the TRIPS Agreement Currently Sets the Balance Between the Protection of Pharmaceutical Patents and Access to Medicines, Paper 891, Berkeley, CA: The Berkeley Electronic Press, http://law.bepress.com.expresso/eps/891.

Musungu, Sisule F. (2004), 'A Review of the Outcomes of WIPO Discussions on the Development Agenda Proposal', *Bridges*, **8**(9), October, http://www.iprsonline.org/ictsd/docs/Musungu_Bridges8-9.pdf.

Musungu, Sisule F. (2007a), 'WIPO Development Agenda – as the dust settles, pondering what is the agenda, whether it is a success or hot air', *Thoughts in Colours blog*, Monday 9 July, http://thoughtsincolours. blogspot.com/2007/07/wipo-development-agenda-as-dust.html.

Musungu, Sisule F. (2007b), *A Conceptual Framework for Priority Identification and Delivery of IP Technical Assistance for LDCs during the Extended Transition Period under the TRIPS Agreement*, Geneva: Quaker United Nations Office, http://www.quno.org/geneva/pdf/economic/Issues/Priority-ID-English.pdf.

Musungu, Sisule F. and Dutfield, Graham (2003), *Multilateral Agreements and a TRIPS-plus World: The World Intellectual Property Organisation (WIPO)*, Geneva and Ottawa: Quakers United Nations Office and the Quaker International Affairs Programme.

Musungu, Sisule F., Villanueva, S. and Blasetti, R. (2004), *Utilizing TRIPS Flexibilities for Public Health Protection through South–South Regional Frameworks*, Geneva: South Centre.

Mutter, Karl (2005), 'Traditional Knowledge Related to Genetic Resources and its Intellectual Property Protection in Colombia', *European Intellectual Property Review*, **27**(9): 327–33.

Nguyen, Eric (2005), 'A "Development Agenda" at WIPO: A Shift in IP policy on the International Stage – An Interview with James Love of The Consumer Project on Technology', *U.C. Davis Business Law Journal*, **22**(5), http://blj.ucdavis.edu/article/561/.

Odell, John S. and Sell, Susan K. (2006) 'Reframing the Issue: The WTO Coalition on Intellectual Property and Public Health, 2001', in John S. Odell (ed.), *Negotiating Trade: Developing Countries in the WTO and NAFTA*, Cambridge: Cambridge University Press, 85–114.

Okediji, Ruth L. (2009), 'History Lessons for the WIPO Development Agenda', in Neil Weinstock Netanel (ed.), *The Development Agenda: Global Intellectual Property and Developing Countries*, Oxford: Oxford University Press.

Orbinski, James (2008), *An Imperfect Offering: Dispatches from the Medical Frontline*, London: Rider Books/Ebury Publishing/Random House.

Oxfam (2001a), *Dare to Lead: Public Health and Company Wealth*, Oxfam Briefing Paper on GlaxoSmithKline, Oxford: Oxfam, http://www.oxfam.org.uk/resources/policy/health/downloads/daretolead.pdf.

Oxfam (2001b), *Formula for Fairness: Patient Rights before Patent Rights*, Oxfam Briefing Paper on Pfizer, Oxford: Oxfam, http://www.oxfam.org.uk/resources/policy/health/downloads/cb_pfizer.pdf.

Paranaguá Moniz, Pedro de (2005), *The Development Agenda for WIPO: Another Stillbirth? A Battle Between Access to Knowledge and Enclosure*, mimeo.

Pécoul, Bernard, Chirac, Pierre, Trouiller, Patrice and Pinel, Jacques (1999), 'Access to Essential Drugs in Poor Countries: A Lost Battle?' *Journal of the American Medical Association*, **281**(4): 361–7.

Pérez-Casas, Carmen (2000), *HIV/AIDS Medicines Pricing Report. Setting Objectives: is there a political will?* MSF, http://www.msfaccess.org/fileadmin/user_upload/key-publication/Durban%20report%20update%20dec%202000.pdf.

Petit, Michael, Collins, Wanda, Fowler, Cary, Correa, Carlos and Thornström, Carl-Gustaf (2000), 'Why Governments Can't Make Policy – The Case of Plant Genetic Resources in the International Arena', Background Paper prepared for the *Global Forum on Agricultural Research*, 21–23 May, Dresden, document no. GFAR/00/02-03.

Plaisier, Nora and Wijmenga, Paul (2004), *Evaluation of Trade-Related Technical Assistance. Three Geneva Based Organisations: ACWL, AITC and QUNO*. IOB Working Document, The Netherlands: IOB.

Quaker United Nations Office (2001), 'Development Co-operation, TRIPS, Indigenous Knowledge and Genetic Resources', *Report based on a seminar held by the Quaker United Nations Office at Jongny-sur-Vevey, Switzerland, 6–7 April 2001*.

Ragavan, S. (2006), 'Of the Inequals of the Uruguay Round', *Marquette Intellectual Property Review*, **10**(2): 273–304.

Ramasubban, Radhika and Rishyasringa, Bhanwar (2005), *AIDS and Civil Society: India's Learning Curve*, Jaipur, India: Rawat Publications.

Rangnekar, D. (2005), 'No Pills for Poor People? Understanding the Disembowelment of India's Patent Regime', *CSGR Working Paper No. 176/05*, University of Warwick: Centre for the Study of Globalisation and Regionalisation.

Rodrigues, Edson B. (2006), 'Japan Trade Mark Act, Secs. 3(1)(iii), 4(1)(xvi) – Cupuaçu', *International Review of Intellectual Property and Competition Law*, **37**(1), 98–103.

Rosina, Monica Steffen Guise, Wang, Daniel and de Campos, Than Christina (2008), 'Access to Medicines: Pharmaceutical Patents and the Right to Health', in Lea Shaver (ed.), *Access to Knowledge in Brazil: New*

Research on Intellectual Property, Innovation and Development, New Haven, CT: Information Society Project, Yale Law School, 166–214.

Sahai, Suman (2001), 'India's Plant Variety Protection and Farmers' Rights Act 2001', *Bridges*, **8**(11): http://www.iprsonline.org/ictsd/docs/SahaiBridgesYear5N8Oct2001.pdf.

Sahai, Suman (2002), 'Civil Society Trashes India's Decision to Join UPOV: NGOs Demand Discussion in Parliament', *AgBioIndia*, New Delhi: India.

Scherer, Frederick M. and Watal, J. (2001), 'Post-TRIPS Options for Access to Patented Medicines in Developing Countries', CMH Working Paper Series, World Health Organization, Commission on Macroeconomics and Health, Geneva, Switzerland: World Health Organization, June.

Schmidlehner, Michael (2003), 'Cupuaçu – a case of Amazonian self-assertion', *Seedling*, April, GRAIN, http://www.grain.org/seedling/?id=234.

Schultz, Michael F. and Walker, David B. (2006), 'The New International Intellectual Property Agenda', in *Are Intellectual Property Rights Human Rights?* Washington, DC: The Federalist Society for Law and Public Policy Studies.

Sell, Susan K. (2002), 'TRIPS and the Access to Medicines Campaign', paper prepared for *Access to Medicines for the Developing World: International Facilitation or Hindrance?* Conference sponsored by the University of Wisconsin Law School, Madison, Wisconsin, 9–10 March.

Sell, Susan K. (2003), *Private Power, Public Law: The Globalization of Intellectual Property Rights*, Cambridge and New York: Cambridge University Press.

Sell, Susan K. and May, Christopher (2001), 'Moments in Law: Contestation and Settlement in the History of Intellectual Property', *Review of International Political Economy*, **8**(3): 467–500.

Sell, Susan K. and Prakash, Aseem (2004), 'Using Ideas Strategically: The Context Between Business and NGO Networks in Intellectual Property Rights', *International Studies Quarterly*, **48**: 143–75.

Shadlen, Kenneth (2009), 'The Politics of Patents and Drugs in Brazil and Mexico: The Industrial Bases of Health Policies', *Comparative Politics*, **42**(1): 41-58.

Shiva, Vandana (1996), *Protecting Our Biological and Intellectual Heritage in the Age of Biopiracy*, New Delhi: Research Foundation for Science, Technology and Natural Resource Policy.

Shiva, Vandana (2001), *Protect or Plunder? Protecting Intellectual Property Rights*, London and New York: Zed Books.

Shiva, Vandana and Bhutani, Shalini (2001), *An Activist's Handbook on*

Biodiversity, New Delhi: Research Foundation for Science, Technology and Ecology.

Shiva, Vandana, Bhutani, Shalini, Prasad, Urvashi, Jafri, Afsar H. (1999), *An Activist's Handbook on Biodiversity*, New Delhi: Research Foundation for Science, Technology and Ecology.

Shiva, Vandana and Jafri, Afsar H. (2001), *The Need for a Genuine Sui Generis Law to Defend Farmers' Rights as Traditional Breeders: The Inadequacies of the PVP Act, 2001*, RFSTE/Navdanya.

SIDA (2001), *AIDS: The Challenge of this Century – Prevention, Care and Impact Mitigation*, Swedish International Development Cooperation Agency Report.

Siplon, Patricia D. (2002), *AIDS and the Policy Struggle in the United States*, Washington, DC: Georgetown University Press.

Smallman, Shawn (2007), *The AIDS Pandemic in Latin America*, Chapel Hill: The University of North Carolina Press.

Smolders, Walter (2005), 'Disclosure of Origin and Access and Benefit Sharing: The Special Case of Seeds for Food and Agriculture', Quaker United Nations Office, Geneva, Switzerland: QUNO Occasional Paper 17.

Stannard, Clive, van der Graaff, Niek, Randell, Alan, Lallas, Peter and Kenmore, Peter (2004), 'Agricultural Biological Diversity for Food Security: Shaping International Initiatives to Help Agriculture and the Environment', *Howard Law Journal*, **48**(1): 397–430.

Sullivan, Sian (2001), 'Difference, Identity, and Access to Official Discourses: Hai‖om, "Bushmen", and a Recent Namibian Ethnography', *Anthropos: International Review of Anthropology and Linguistics*, **96**: 179–92.

Sulpino Vieira, F. (2007), 'Right to Health Litigations: A Discussion on the Observance of the Principles of Brazil's Health System', *Revista de Saúde Pública, Scientific Electronic Library Online*, **42**(2), http://www.scielo.br/scielo.php?script=sci_arttext&pid=S0034-89102008000200025&lng=e&nrm=iso&tlng=en.

Sutherland, Peter et al. (2004), *The Future of the WTO: Addressing Institutional Challenges in the New Millennium*, Geneva: World Trade Organization.

Swiderska, Krystyana (2006), *Protecting Traditional Knowledge: A Framework Based on Customary Laws and Bio-cultural Heritage*, paper for the International Conference on Endogenous Development and Bio-Cultural Diversity, 3–5 October.

Tansey, Geoff (1999), *Trade, Intellectual Property and Biodiversity: Key Issues and Options for the 1999 Review of Article 27.3(b) of the TRIPS Agreement*, London: Quaker Peace and Service, and Geneva: Quaker United Nations Office.

Tansey, Geoff (2002), *Food Security, Biotechnology and Intellectual Property: Unpacking Some Issues around TRIPS. A Discussion Paper*, Geneva: Quaker United Nations Office.

Távora dos Santos Filho, Ezio (2000), 'Real Challenges for Real Actors: The Role of Advocacy and Activism in the Fight against AIDS in Brazil', *Sexual Health Exchange*, **4**, http://www.kit.nl/ils/exchange_content/html/ 2000_4_real_challenges_asp?

UNAIDS (2008), *Report on the Global AIDS Epidemic*, Geneva, Switzerland: UNAIDS.

UNCTAD-ICTSD (2005), *UNCTAD-ICTSD Resource Book on TRIPS and Development*, Cambridge: Cambridge University Press.

United Nations (1966), *International Covenant on Economic, Social and Cultural Rights, adopted 16 December 1966*, 993 U.N.T.S. 3 General Assembly Resolution 2200 (XXI), 21 U.N. GAOR Supp. (No. 16) at 49, U.N. Doc.A/6316.

United Nations (2009), *Report of the Special Rapporteur on the Right of Everyone to the Enjoyment of the Highest Attainable Standard of Physical and Mental Health (Anand Grover)*. United Nations General Assembly, Eleventh Session, 31 March, Agenda Item 3, A/HRC/11/ 12.

United Nations Commission on Human Rights (2001), *Economic, Social and Cultural Rights: The Impact of the Agreement on Trade-Related Aspects of Intellectual Property Rights on Human Rights: Report of the High Commissioner*, 27 June, E/CN.4/Sub.2/2001/13/.

United Nations Economic and Social Committee (1999), *General Comment No. 12 on the Right to Adequate Food (Article 11 of the International Covenant on Economic, Social and Cultural Rights)*. Committee on Economic, Social and Cultural Rights, Twentieth session, Geneva, 26 April–14 May, E/C.12/1999/5.

United Nations Economic and Social Committee (2000a), *General Comment No. 14 on the Right to the Highest Attainable Standard of Health (Article 12 of the International Covenant on Economic, Social and Cultural Rights)*. Committee on Economic, Social and Cultural Rights, Twenty-second session, Geneva, 25 April–12 May, E/C.12/2000/4.

United Nations Economic and Social Committee (2000b), *Discussion paper submitted by Dr. Audrey R. Chapman for the American Association for the Advancement of Science (AAAS) on Implementation of the International Covenant on Economic, Social and Cultural Rights*, Committee on Economic, Social and Cultural Rights, E/C.12/2000/12, Geneva: United Nations.

United Nations Economic and Social Committee (2005), *General Comment No. 17 on the Right of Everyone to Benefit from the Protection of the*

Moral and Material Interests Resulting from any Scientific, Literary or Artistic Production of which he is the Author (Article 15(1)(c) of the Covenant), Committee on Economic, Social and Cultural Rights, Thirty-fifth session, 7–25 November, E/C.12/2005/GC/17.

United Nations High Commissioner for Human Rights, Sub-Commission on Human Rights (2000), *Resolution 2000/7: Intellectual Property Rights and Human Rights*.

United Nations High Commissioner for Human Rights, Sub-Commission on Human Rights (2001), *Resolution 2001/21: Intellectual Property Rights and Human Rights*.

United States Trade Representative (2009), *2009 National Trade Estimate Report on Foreign Trade Barriers*, http://ustr.gov/assets/Document_Library/Reports_Publications/2009/2009_National_Trade_Estimate_Report_on_Foreign_Trade_Barriers/asset_upload_file405_15451.pdf.

Waal, Alex de (2006), *AIDS and Power: Why There is no Political Crisis – Yet*, London and New York: Zed Books.

Watal, Jayashree (2001), *Intellectual Property Rights in the WTO and Developing Countries*, The Hague, Netherlands: Kluwer Law International.

WIPO (2001), *Intellectual Property Needs Expectations of Traditional Knowledge Holders: Report on Fact-finding Missions on Intellectual Property and Traditional Knowledge (1998–1999)*, Geneva, Switzerland: WIPO, http://www.wipo.int/tk/en/tk/ffm/report/index.html.

WIPO (2003), *Intellectual Property – A Power Tool for Economic Growth*, Geneva: World Intellectual Property Organization, http://www.wipo.int/about-wipo/en/dgo/wipo_pub_888/index_wipo_pub_888.html.

World Bank (2008), *Global Economic Prospects 2008 – Technology Diffusion in the Developing World*, Washington, DC: The International Bank for Reconstruction and Development/The World Bank, http://siteresources.worldbank.org/INTGEP2008/Resources/complete-report.pdf.

World Health Assembly (2006), *Public Health, Innovation, Essential Health Research and Intellectual Property Rights: Towards a Global Strategy and Plan of Action*, Fifty-ninth World Health Assembly, WHA59.24, 27 May.

World Health Assembly (2008), *Global Strategy and Plan of Action on Public Health, Innovation and Intellectual Property*, Sixty-first World Health Assembly, WHA61.21, 24 May.

Wynberg, Rachel (2004), 'Rhetoric, Realism and Benefit-Sharing: Use of Traditional Knowledge of *Hoodia* Species in the Development of an Appetite Suppressant', *Journal of World Intellectual Property*, **7**(6): 851–76.

Yu, Peter K. (2007), 'Ten Common Questions about Intellectual Property and Human Rights', *Legal Studies Research Paper No. 04-27*, Michigan State University College of Law.

Yu, Peter K. (2008), 'Building Intellectual Property Coalitions for Development', *CIGI Working Paper No. 37*, Waterloo, Ontario, Canada: Centre for International Governance Innovation.

Index